Reports of the Research Committee

of the

Society of Antiquaries of London

No. XIII

The Tombs and Moon Temple of Hureidha (Hadhramaut)

By

G. Caton Thompson, F.S.A.

Oxford

Printed at the University Press by John Johnson for

The Society of Antiquaries

Burlington House, London

1944

PRINTED IN GREAT BRITAIN

586

LIST OF CONTENTS

Part III. THE CAVE-TOMBS

Part IV. TYPOLOGY

Part V. VARIA

Part VI

Part VII. EPIGRAPHY

By PROF. G. RYCKMANS

LIST OF PLATES

b

INTRODUCTION

MY desire to visit south-west Arabia originated in 1929 when I was occupied with the Zimbabwe problem and the interconnected question of Arab influence in south-east Africa. In the following years the desire grew, stimulated anew by advances in palaeolithic research in Africa and the Near East. South Arabia then was archaeologically still *terra incognita*, though burdened by ever-growing loads of futile theory.

The opportunity came in 1936 when Freya Stark planned to return to the Hadhramaut to extend her journeys of an earlier visit and amplify her knowledge of a then little-known land and people, whose peculiar interest she had demonstrated so enchantingly in *The Southern Gates of Arabia*.

The plan slowly took shape; official and financial support were obtained. It was agreed that scientific results would be doubled, the disabilities of possible illness diminished, by the inclusion of a third member of the little expedition. And since, in a land then unused to Europeans, a feminine party was less likely to arouse opposition than a mixed one, Elinor Gardner was invited to join us.

We reached Aden on October 31, 1937; Mukalla, seaport of the Hadhramaut on November 7. Six days later we left for the interior, and a long wasteful prologue to the winter's work, controlled, probably unnecessarily, by the coincidence of Ramadhān, began in the three main towns of the Wadi Hadhramaut, Terim, Seiyun, and Shibam.

Illness of all three members of the party developed at the more than insalubrious Shibam, and on December 20, when at last Elinor Gardner and I, the first back on our legs, set off for the real objective, Hureidha in the Wadi 'Amd, it might be said that nothing had been accomplished scientifically. The great Wadi had been archaeologically unresponsive; its geology far from stimulating.

To our credit nothing had accrued but an abundance of surface palaeoliths; some rock graffiti on boulders near Seiyun and Shibam;[1] notes on aeolian silts and gravels in the Wadi 'Adim near Terim;[2] a small collection of surface oddments—sherds, obsidian microliths, and beads—from the known pre-Islamic site of Sūne in the same lateral wadi;[3] and a similar collection from an unimportant site I found near Shibam.[4] Yet later all these depressingly unrelated items became surprisingly serviceable and could be fitted into a framework of information built up gradually in the excavations at Hureidha.

Arrived at Hureidha serious work could begin. Elinor Gardner and I[5] settled in a small house found for us in the village by the Mansab, Sayyid Ḥasan ibn Ahmed el 'Aṭṭas, whose kindly welcome banished at once all fears of disapproval of our activities; and prospecting for sites began immediately. Within two days my choice fell on a large

---

[1] Cf. pp. 180–184.
[2] Cf. pp. 4–5.
[3] Cf. pp. 101, 134–5.   [4] Cf. pp. 134–5.

[5] Freya Stark rejoined us from Aden Hospital on Dec. 26 after a fortnight's absence, but was confined to her room again, on and off, for weeks.

irregular sandy knoll out on the bare plain of the Wadi 'Amd, about 50 minutes' ride from our quarters, and excavations which exposed the Moon Temple beneath it began on Christmas Eve.

From then till February 3 work proceeded vigorously and the Temple, an adjacent farmstead, and an ossuary cave-tomb were cleared to the limits imposed by over-compressed time. There were still about four weeks left in which to expand the results.[1] Particularly I wanted primary burials. But a fortnight spent underground in the stifling dust and unventilated poisons of the ossuary resulted in the acute bronchitis well known to Egyptian excavators; malaria was added, and I spent three precious weeks in bed and convalescing.

Six days remained. Tomb A6 had already been marked down as worth a test, so to avoid delay I concentrated on it. The gods were not altogether unmindful of their obligations.

Throughout these weeks Elinor Gardner's work on the ancient irrigation and local geology went forward steadily, despite the burden of two invalids nearly a fortnight's journey from chemist or doctor.

Excavations closed down on March 3, and on the 5th she and I started on the return to Mukalla. A night was spent at Meshhed to visit the big ruin-field[2] and compare its surface sherds and beads with those of Hureidha. Thence to Terim and the coast. Aden was regained on March 12, and the cases of antiquities dispatched to England.[3] The first archaeological expedition to the Hadhramaut was over.

On March 15, free at last to relax, we boarded A. Besse and Co.'s little coastal vessel *El Hak* and returned to Egypt in leisurely luxury, visiting Djibuti, Hodeidah, Yenbo, and Jeddah as our ship discharged or collected her cargo.

This record of the work accomplished contains nothing spectacular. Incense routes play no part;[4] there were no rich finds. There is no reason to think that the Hureidha of antiquity—the Madâbum of our inscriptions—was more important, less provincial, than it now is. Yet, since the archaeology of the everyday life of humble people is no less important or interesting, and really far more informative of the general level of indigenous culture of its time and place than the archaeology of the rich, I have no regrets.

It is a most enjoyable task to acknowledge the help given by well-wishers of many categories. The needs of an archaeological venture—money, scientific backing, official sanction, and the expert help of specialists in many branches of research—were assured from the start.

Our special indebtedness to Lord Wakefield, whose name the expedition bore, is well known. The Royal Geographical Society generously supported a party which included two past holders of its geographical awards and a former member of its Council. Mr. Louis Clarke, on behalf of the Fitzwilliam Museum, and the Museum of Archaeology

---

[1] A date of departure early in March had been decided on: Elinor Gardner was due to resume her work at Bethlehem for the Wellcome Expedition; Freya Stark planned a journey to the sea in search of Qana. This she successfully accomplished (cf. *Geographical Journal*, Jan. 1939).

[2] Cf. p. 100.

[3] Antiquity laws had not then been framed for the Aden Protectorate: the return of a representative collection to Aden was agreed with Mr. Ingrams.

[4] Cf. pp. 153-4.

and Anthropology, at Cambridge, gave much-valued help. A comprehensive type collection from the Temple and tombs at Hureidha is at the former; the palaeoliths, *in situ* and surface, at the latter. From the Ashmolean Museum, Oxford, also came encouragement and a contribution, which it has been a pleasure to acknowledge by the donation of a set of type pottery and incense-burners.

Without the consent of H.M. Government at Aden the expedition would have been debarred from entering a land still sensitive to European intrusion. Arrived in the Hadhramaut we came under the care of Mr. W. H. Ingrams, the first Political Officer, Resident at Mukalla, now Chief Secretary at Aden. Preoccupied and overworked as he was at that time with the delicate task of peace-making between turbulent tribes, he might well have hesitated to add us and our experimental mission to his responsibilities. For experimental in every sense it was. No organized excavations had before been attempted; no certainty was possible as to the reactions of the inhabitants to such an unaccustomed thing. Yet, by the winter of our visit, so sure was the Resident's hold that few restraints had to be placed upon the party. Where we might go, where we might not, was quietly intimated, in view of tribal unrest at the time;[1] and we settled at Hureidha where only two white women had before been seen—Mrs. Ingrams and Freya Stark herself—secure in the prestige of the Resident Adviser and his wife.

Not less appreciated was the kindness received from our Arab hosts. At Terim and Seiyun we were welcomed with the princely hospitality of Sayyid Abu Bekr el Kaf; at Hureidha, Sayyid Ḥasan el ʿAṭṭas smoothed out the initial difficulties of the 'chantier' and made us from the moment of arrival feel the warmth of real interest.

The value of the work of the team of experts—Dr. Plenderleith, Mr. Lucas, Mr. Beck, Dr. Frankfort, Dr. Jackson, Dr. Desch, Dr. Morant—whose results form Chapters VIII and XII—needs no emphasis. Professor Ryckmans's section—Chapter XVIII—is a notable contribution to epigraphical learning, which may raise the little Moon Temple to a place of honour to which it would never otherwise have aspired.

Specific questions concerning minerals, ceramics, and glass were referred to Dr. Leonard Hawkes, Dr. Webb, Mr. Philip Game, and Mr. D. B. Harden respectively, and their opinions are incorporated in the text. The services of all these specialists—given in many cases under the abnormal stress of war preparations—are so obvious that thanks would be impertinent.

Save for the air photograph, pl. I, unacknowledged at its owner's request, the photographs were taken by Elinor Gardner, or less frequently by me apart from pls. III, 2; XX, 1, 3; XXV, 1, 2; and LXIII–LXVIII, which are by Freya, Stark. The irrigation plan, pl. LXXII, redrawn by the Royal Geographical Society from Elinor Gardner's sketch-map, and kindly lent by them, is the only professional plan in the book. Our amateur efforts must be forgiven by architects and draftsmen. The colour

---

[1] There was, as a fact, a good deal that winter, and the Shabwa area was closed to us. For a while we were more or less marooned at Hureidha, access to the coast, had it been needed, being hindered by outrages—lootings and murder of inoffensive wayfarers—by the Hamumi tribe. R.A.F. persuasion settled the affair before we left.

plate of beads, pl. xxxviii, is the gift-work of Mrs. Austin Kennett, whose professional help in this task was kindly placed at my disposal by Professor A. B. Cook. Another artist, Miss Dorothy Hawksley, has infused a realism into the ossuary groups on pls. lxxix, lxxx which, while strictly true to the field-plan of their arrangement, adds greatly to their graphic value.

The Oxford Press took the opportunity of this publication of our inscriptions and the lack of a suitable fount to cut an entirely new one here used for the first time. The old south Arabian alphabet consists of twenty-nine letters. The new fount comprises eighty forms, enabling palaeographic variants to be printed correctly. The value of this will be realized on reading the palaeographic section of Professor Ryckmans's chapter.

It had been my hope to include a preface from Dr. Ditlef Nielsen, with whom I have had the benefit of several conversations about our results. But the invasion of Denmark has prevented this. The war has also made it impossible to consult either him or Professor Ryckmans at Louvain on the text as a whole. Consequently any comments I make on the inscriptions in the Temple chapters are my own, unauthorized by expert opinion. My last letter from Professor Ryckmans was dated April 23, 1940, and he approved my suggestion that in the event of German invasion of his country Dr. A. F. L. Beeston should be asked to undertake the epigraphical proof reading. Part VII accordingly has been kindly seen through the Press by him.

I am proud to see my work bearing the *imprimatur* of the Society of Antiquaries of London, whose generosity has made possible such a fully illustrated record. The Oxford Press is famous for soothing the anguish of archaeologists whose work it publishes and meeting their peculiar demands. I can once more endorse that reputation.

In conclusion I wish to express my gratitude to Miss Dorothy Hoare, who, in unselfishly reading through the manuscript, has made many suggestions towards its improvement.

NOTE ON THE ARRANGEMENT

As the material dealt with is not large, I have preferred a treatment which strives not to separate objects, more than necessary, from their excavatory contexts. Specialists' reports are thus treated not as appendices but as integral parts of the work. An exception, however, has been made of Professor Ryckmans's great epigraphic contribution. In this, to facilitate the printing of *separata*, the inscriptions from whatever source, formal and informal, are treated as a whole.

The pottery, however, which, being the first collection from south Arabia, is specially important, together with some other common objects, has been dealt with separately and in detail in classificatory chapters, to satisfy typological needs.

The plates are arranged as far as practicable on the same principle, being grouped at the end of the chapter or section they illustrate. The pottery photographs, pls. xxvii–xxxvi, are thus placed in their positional context to illuminate textual allusions *en passant.* Scale drawings and sections of the same pots, of interest only to those studying the typology, are grouped after the classificatory chapters.

Measurements are metric throughout. Ranging-poles, sometimes used as a scale, are 2 m. long. No scale is shown in the pottery photographs, as I consider that distortion of a straight object against a rounded one reduces its value. The scale drawings supply this need.

G. C. T.

April 1940.

PART I
PHYSICAL SETTING

B

I. THE QUATERNARY PERIOD IN WADI ʿAMD

Synopsis. Systematic work on changes of coastal levels is necessary before a satisfactory grasp of the physiography of the inland drainage system can be obtained. Such work was impracticable on our expedition, but relevant observations were made by E. W. Gardner at disconnected points.

At Mukalla raised beaches at R.L. 19 and 15 m. were examined, and a palaeolithic flake industry noted on fresh-water gravels at ±32 m. A similar industry, widespread in the Hadhramaut, was subsequently discovered *in situ* in Wadi ʿAmd, in terraced stream gravels as well as in the valley's main filling of aeolian silt. These newly established dating points lead to the conclusion that the cutting of the Wadi Hadhramaut and its main tributaries is pre-Quaternary, probably Pliocene. A major erosional phase was succeeded by a major depositional phase. A minor erosional phase, subdivided by gravel depositions into at least three stages, completes the observed sequence, and since palaeolithic times no appreciable alteration has occurred in the inland valleys visited. Climatic sequences are tentatively suggested.

Exposition. The palaeolithic implements which provide the indispensable dating fossils in a consideration of the Pleistocene will be published separately, and given the full illustration and typological description which would be distracting in this volume dedicated to the study of the historic period.

Nevertheless, if only in a physiographic sense, the historic reposes upon the deposits of the prehistoric and is in countless ways influenced by them. In Hureidha the pre-Islamic irrigation system, the ancient cultivation, the sites we excavated, even the tombs, are all the unconscious products of their Quaternary environment and may not, in any complete study, be deprived of it. But here only a sketch is needed.

Already on the doorstep of the Hadhramaut, at Mukalla, became apparent the restless shifts of sea-level along the coast. Raised beaches at ± R.L. 19[1] and 15 m., and an extensive erosional plain to the north-east of the town at about R.L. 32 m.,[2] where palaeoliths of Levallois type were found, though not *in situ*, gave evidence of a wealth of recent geological features in the immediate vicinity. There is reason to suppose that considerably higher marine transgressions of Quaternary age would be found if more prolonged work than E. W. Gardner could manage in our five days' visit had been possible.[3]

It is self-evident that without detailed geological knowledge of the coastal region no amount of work in the great Wadi Hadhramaut itself, which finds the sea 140 miles east of Mukalla under the changed name of the Wadi Maseila, can clear up the many physiographical problems posed by that great 300-mile-long artery of inland drainage.

Such a study was not our province even had the essential freedom to roam at will been possible, which, under the then existing regulations, and in the circumstances of our expedition, it was not. All we attempted was to study the Pleistocene geology piecemeal

---

[1] This level was noted in 1919, and marine fossils of existing species got from it. O. H. Little, *Geology and Geography of Mukalla* (p. 221).

[2] Described, with sketch-plan and section, by us in *Geog. Journ.*, Jan. 1939 (pp. 20–1).

[3] Marine deposits, said to be recent, up to 45 m. were noted at some unspecified locality, not since reidentified, by H. J. Carter in 1853. *Journ. Bombay British Asiatic Soc.* iv (p. 445). Referred to in note 2 above.

at disconnected points whenever and wherever opportunity allowed, with special concern for the evidence of past climatic changes, the geological date of the deeply sunk trenches which form the wadi system of the Hadhramaut hinterland, and, archaeologically, the palaeolithic sequence in that region.

A characteristic view of this remarkable drainage system in a desert land is seen from the air in pl. 1. The main valley in the middle stretch which we traversed between Terim and Henīn—a distance of some 80 km.—is a broad flat-floored trough, widening gradually from 3 or 4 km. at Terim to over three times that distance at the point of entry from the south of the combined Wadis 'Amd and Do'an. The bounding cliffs, the 300-m. height of which seems dwarfed by the breadth of the contained valley, are recessed into succeeding uniform bays by the entry of short lateral wadis eating their ways back by headward erosion into the desert plateaux. Interspaced at long intervals are major tributaries from north and south.

These cliffs consist of Eocene limestones over Cretaceous sandstones, partly of Nubian age, with discontinuous cappings in places of later Tertiary sediments. A thick, brecciated talus-slope at their base, due to erosion of the basal sandstone and consequent fall of overlying strata, appears to plunge beneath the valley floor. Its formation began in the remote past, for not only has it been cut into hillocks detached from the parent cliff, but the breccia itself contains unpatinated, unrolled chert implements and cores of rough Levallois type; and large quantities, richly weathered, may be collected upon its surface. No doubt is possible that the cliff profile has remained substantially unchanged since Quaternary times.

The valley filling is remarkable. From cliff to cliff, save for the skirting scree, it is choked by a deposit of sandy silt forming a level desert plain, along which the modern monsoon flood-channel threads a relatively insignificant narrow, shallow course. No sign of former higher water-levels, witnessed in normal river valleys by bordering terraces, was seen in the length we covered. The filling is, geologically, the most important episode in the wadi's history after its initial cutting. It also chokes the lateral valley floors; and away on the high-plateau watershed at about 1800 m. above sea-level, between the Wadi Hadhramaut and the coast, a similar sandy silt was noted in the shallow water-courses.

What manner of valley floor was roamed by those palaeolithic hunters encamped on the scree slopes, where presumably they gathered to collect from the limestone debris chert nodules for their implements, to flake them perhaps in the cool of the cliffs shadowed from the fierce tropical sun? The answer was worked out bit by bit by E. W. Gardner, not in the Wadi Hadhramaut, where good sections were lacking, but in two of its major laterals, the Wadis 'Adim and 'Amd, both entering from the south, and lying some 80 km. apart as the crow flies.

The banks of the Wadi 'Adim near the pre-Islamic ruins of Sūne provided on a generous scale the necessary sections. They showed 15 m. of the old filling which consists of a 4 to 8 m. capping of the sandy silt overlying coarse gravels. These gravels traced downstream steal gradually beneath the present slope and disappear. They are presumably drowned deep beneath the silt filling and, in all probability, join up with similarly buried gravels in the main valley. The dating evidence for these deposits was, however, found, not here in a hurried visit, but later in the Wadi 'Amd when we were living at Hureidha, 24 km. above the junction of this valley with the Wadi Hadhramaut.

Wadi 'Amd, seen in aerial panorama in pl. 1 taken above Hureidha, is a major tributary, 120 km. long. It shows unchanged all the geological characteristics of the main valley which, thanks to the miracle of long-range aerial photography, is visible in the far distance over the separating plateau. The same monotony of embayed 300-m. cliffs bounds it; its floor, away from laborious irrigation, is a level desert plain of sandy silt. The modern flood-bed threads a narrow channel in it, meandering some 16 km. above Hureidha across the valley floor to skirt the talus border of the northern cliffs (pl. 1, 3). And here, at several points, its banks provide the key to the later geological history of the valley. They show at favoured spots some 10 to 12 perpendicular metres of the valley filling—a fine-grained arenaceous deposit, with the vertical jointing of loess and aeolian deposits generally. But horizontal clay bands and scattered lines of pebbles assert water action as well; and to meet the double claim we propose to use the word 'aeolian silt' to describe it.

Neither the probable depth of this infilling nor the nature of its underlying deposits could anywhere be ascertained, and they must remain speculative until such time—if ever—as public utility works necessitate deep bores, or the curiosity of some geological philanthropist is aroused. The existing wells, though deep (von Wissmann states some to be about 100 m.), lie in the rising sides of the valley. But whatever proportion to the whole their depth may represent, there is little doubt it is relatively small.

In discussing the age of the infilling we can therefore speak only of the top 10 m. or so, but this much at any rate is not in doubt, for embedded in it at different points were an unabraded Levallois-type core and flake. Moreover, whilst the Wadi 'Amd was quietly accumulating its mighty deposits of aeolian silt, the little lateral ravines, more turbulent, were discharging coarse gravels, which shot out on to the silty plain; and these localized outwash fans became engulfed in the main-valley deposits.[1] From these lateral outwash gravels we collected a number of similar but rolled Levallois-type tools, and travertine pebbles derived from deposits in the gorges.[2]

Following upon these events, the next incident recognized was a more active phase in the Wadi 'Amd's history. Gravel-bearing torrents swept down and cut a narrow channel in the aeolian silt—a channel still followed by the monsoon flood (seen in pl. 1, 3). But the Pleistocene date of initiation is certain, for its ancient gravels survive in three terraces at 10, 5, and 3 m. respectively above the present flood-bed. These terraces rest

[1] Illustrations of the major points appeared in our article 'Climate, Irrigation and Early Man in the Hadhramaut', *Geog. Journ.*, Jan. 1939.

[2] For more information about these travertines see above article.

against the aeolian silt and are not carved out of it. All contain rolled flake tools and cores, still of Levallois type.

The bed of the monsoon flood, so disproportionately small in its wide valley, is, nevertheless, the still active link between late Pleistocene times and now. The silt filling, a flat, unending desert, remains a fossil witness to Quaternary events of great magnitude. Potentially fertile, it became to the pre-Islamic civilization of the Wadi 'Amd an invitation to prosperity. They canalized the flood far upstream and diverted it across the barren plain to fertilize by means of secondary channels a wide expanse, and transformed the sandy Quaternary waste into cultivated plots, interspersed with farmsteads (see Chapters II, XV). Here, too, they erected a temple to the worship of their fertility moon-god, raising its platform upon a packing of great boulders from the Quaternary flood-bed. In the brecciated scree, below the cliffs haunted by their palaeolithic fore-runners, they cut the burial chambers of their dead.

SUMMARY AND SOME DEDUCTIONS. The late geological history of the Wadi 'Amd may, we think, judging from observations also in the Wadis 'Adim and Hadhramaut, be safely taken to represent in its main outlines that of the whole drainage complex of the central and western Hadhramaut we traversed.

The *earliest* archaeologically dated deposits in the Wadi 'Amd are the *latest* geological features in it. These, in descending order of age, are:

(1) The upper 10 m. of the aeolian silt filling and its contemporary lateral outwash gravels.
(2) The cutting of a relatively narrow flood-channel and the formation in it of:
(3) A terrace of coarse gravels with travertine pebbles interbedded with aeolian silt at 10 m.
(4) A terrace of coarse gravels with current-bedded sands at 5 m.
(5) A terrace of coarse gravels with current-bedded sands at 3 m.

Coincident with all was the gradual accumulation of brecciated talus below the cliffs (a cumulative process, uninterruptedly at work, though probably at widely different speeds, since the first etching of the valley began).

These episodes, excepting (2), are each individually dated by palaeolithic flakes and cores of Levallois type, which in south-west Arabia evidently covered, unchanged, a very long time-span. Even assuming (as we think probable) the persistence of this culture into the later palaeolithic in these regions, it must, in episode (1) above, stretch back into a different climatic epoch which can hardly be later than middle palaeolithic times.

Such archaeological considerations leave no option but to attribute the unknown basal levels of the valley infilling to a considerably earlier epoch, at latest early Quaternary, and the initial cutting of the great valley system to Pliocene or Plio-Pleistocene times. That it must be post-Miocene we know from the local marine deposits of that epoch. Knowledge of Pliocene events is unfortunately scanty. O. H. Little records conglomerates believed to be of that epoch, up to 1,000 m.[1] (Hureidha lies at 800 m.); but he never mapped far from the coast. He states his belief that during that epoch important earth movements, with resultant folding and faulting, took place, while torrents began to etch out the present drainage lines.[2]

With this view we are in general agreement. Nevertheless the great limestone pene-plain of the interior has been comparatively resistant to the faulting and folding Little indicates for the coastal regions. But the interdependence of the inland valleys, draining via the main artery of the Wadi Hadhramaut to the Arabian Sea, on coastal levels and earth movements, no less than on local physiographic mechanisms such as stream capture, needs no emphasis: and without the needed detailed examination of the seaward end of the Wadi Hadhramaut—the Wadi Maseila—reconstruction of more generalized geological events must be tentative. Nevertheless the following scheme may be justified:

MAJOR EROSIONAL PHASE, when the Wadi Hadhramaut and its main tributaries were cut. This in all probability took place in geological stages. The initial cutting must be at least as early as late Tertiary. It can hardly, as has been held, be synchronous with even the beginning of the Glacial Age in Europe. Oscillations of sea-level. Earth movements. High precipitation.

MAJOR DEPOSITIONAL PHASE (eventually to be sub-divided). The valleys were filled to some unknown depth with deposits. The upper part of these is aeolian silt of palaeo-lithic age. In the Wadi 'Adim this silt overlies coarse gravels of unmeasured depth. Elsewhere the basal constituents are unknown, but are also probably coarse gravels. This phase therefore seems to embrace a climatic shift to drier and perhaps windier conditions.

MINOR EROSIONAL PHASE, represented by the cutting of the aeolian silt and deposition of gravel in place of silt. This can be subdivided into three stages, the 10-, 5-, and 3-m. terraces, all of palaeolithic age. Wetter climate than at present.

---

[1] *Geology and Geography of Mukalla* (pp. 88–92).   [2] Op. cit., pp. 117, 119.

COMPOSITE AIR VIEW OF WADI 'AMD AT HUREIDHA
1. Wadi Hadhramaut 2. Hureidha. 3. Flood Channel. 4. Moon Temple Site. 5. Tombs A5 and A6. 6. Area of mapped irrigation

II. ANCIENT IRRIGATION IN WADI 'AMD

SYNOPSIS. Though the existence of derelict and ruined irrigation works in south-west Arabia has been reported by all travellers there, none seems to have been mapped or studied in detail, and their dates, including even that of the famous Marib dam, are unknown. All is speculative, therefore, as to the period which first saw ordered systems of irrigation in that land, or their origin.

Extreme aridity seems to have succeeded the Pleistocene climatic changes, and if the Hadhramaut wadis of the hinterland were inhabited by settled populations, however small, their existence must have depended on experience of water exploitation, learnt, presumably, in more favoured places. The essential semi-civilization of ancient south-west Arabia sprang, not from her export trade in luxury products, the importance of which (for a limited and late period only in any case) has been unwisely exaggerated in popular estimation, but in the unspectacular development of an effective method of irrigation and dry farming which made large areas habitable on a higher standard than that of bedouins dependent, like animals, on rock pools and springs.[1] The study of that development is probably far the most important task which awaits archaeology in the Aden Protectorate.

At Hureidha an anciently cultivated area, now desert, evidently contemporary with the Moon Temple and the tombs, and therefore datable within limits, was examined and mapped by E. W. Gardner.

GENERAL PRINCIPLES OF IRRIGATION. With the passing of the Pleistocene cycle of climatic oscillations, the existing system of extreme aridity seems to have become early established, and direct rainfall is at present rare. Away from the few valleys favoured with perennial pools or even streams watered by sub-soil drainage,[2] man was dependent upon the periodic and uncertain arrival of spring floods down the inland wadis and lateral ravines, collected sometimes far afield on the high-plateaux watersheds at the season of monsoon rain; upon rock springs, often in inaccessible cliffs; or upon his own skill in digging wells to a water level supplied from the same ultimate source, and often at considerable depth, and in constructing cemented cisterns.

There is fair certainty that when the earlier history of south-west Arabia comes to be pieced together, it will be found that its earliest essays in social organization, its first charter of collective advance from barbarism, sprang from the needs of water conservation and a gradually developed system of wadi irrigation, designed as much to avert destruction by flood[3] as to utilize it to the best advantage. Speculation may still freely play over the question of whether this development took place at a relatively early or late date compared with the great pioneer civilizations of the Near and Farther East.

One may surmise that wadis with perennial water supplies from springs or sub-soil drainage were the first to become centres of permanent settlement, and that these witnessed the earliest experiments in irrigation, which, on gradual mastery, could be transferred to and practised in the dry wadis. That all this arose and evolved under

---

[1] Mr. Bertram Thomas, I fear, might not agree. See *The Arabs*, 1937, p. 30.

[2] Parts of Wadi Maseila and some of its tributaries, including Wadi 'Adim; also Wadi Meifa'a, and Wadi Hajr.

[3] The terrific force of the flood in a tropical desert country needs no emphasis. Mr. Ingrams reports a flood high-watermark in the Wadi Maseila 20 ft. above the channel bed (*Geog. Journ.*, Dec. 1936, p. 543).

foreign inspiration, direct or indirect, is very probable.[1] Arabia's contribution to the world's material progress has presumably always been negligible. That it happened relatively late, though speculative, seems to me, reviewing the inadequate evidence, equally probable.

But the dating of an irrigation system more directly than by archaeological inference is a difficult, sometimes an impossible, and always a lengthy task.[2] In a peaceful community the incessant reparations of dams and dykes, canals and revetments, the incorporation of older work in newer, effaces the evidence generation by generation; whereas in less happy circumstances—a dislocation of population, a cessation of communal responsibility from whatever cause—nature, so carefully curbed and conserved, reverts to elemental power and obliterates in progressive ruin the outlines or detail of her captive story.

The flood-cultivations of ancient south-west Arabia, so noticeable still in their rubble-heaped decay that every traveller breaking new ground adds to their known localities, have been neither dated nor surveyed. Even the approximate dates of the famous Marib dam and its destruction are problematic,[3] despite the help of inscriptions which, among the information, indicate final, post-catastrophic repairs, as late as perhaps the sixth century A.D.[4]

It is unlikely that any rigid principle of construction governed the layout of each local irrigation scheme, though this remains doubtful until numbers have been surveyed in their full extension. But within the elastic limits imposed by the varied demands of terrain, gradient, head, local supply of building stone, population density, and cultivable area, it may be said that the flood-irrigation system[5] applied itself essentially to the threefold task of impounding flood-water by means of barrages across the natural channel; releasing it in more or less controlled quantities through sluices; and finally in distributing it, sometimes directly, sometimes by deflexion, over the desired area of potential cultivation along a master channel, often of considerable length, which fed shorter offsets along its course on one or both sides according to the contours: and these

[1] The Persian *qanat*, for instance, is seen on the coast, and in the Yemen. Whether it was introduced in Achaemenian times, as appears to be the case in the Egyptian oases, remains to be proved. But in view of my inland evidence it need not be necessarily attributed to the later, recognized period of Persian ascendancy, from the 4th to the 6th centuries A.D., in south Arabia. It may be noted that the perennially watered wadis enumerated—the lower reaches of Maseila, Meifaʿa, and Hajr—which fulfil the theoretic requirements of irrigation schools, all flow directly to the sea—a suggestive fact.

[2] An exceptionally neat solution of the dating problem, otherwise presumptive, was provided in 1929 for the early Ptolemaic irrigation system in the Faiyum by Capt. G. A. Gardner's find of a coin of Ptolemy II, year 6 (265 B.C.) in the quarry which had yielded the building stone.

[3] G. F. Hill in *Catalogue of Greek Coins of Arabia, Mesopotamia, and Persia*, 1922, p. lxvi, summarizes opinions which

range from the Achaemenian period to the 6th century A.D. P. K. Hitti in his recent *History of the Arabs*, 1937, p. 55, says: 'The older portions of the dam were constructed in the latter part of the Sabaean period.'

[4] D. G. Hogarth, *Arabia*, p. 5. Hitti, op. cit., p. 64, mentions A.D. 542–3.

[5] Irrigation from perennial sources—springs, wells, and streams—adopts now, and probably formerly, other methods. Amongst these a system of graded terraces along the raised margins of the valley are the most likely, for structural reasons, to survive as a relic of antiquity. I have little doubt that the terrace cultivation of east and south-east Africa, traces of which are widespread and which have been so variously dated by pure conjecture, is related. For further details on perennial irrigation in Hadhramaut see *Report on the Social, Economic and Political Condition of the Hadhramaut*, by W. H. Ingrams, 1937, pp. 57–8.

in turn were often controlled, for relics of small masonry piers, set a metre or two apart in pairs, are numerous, and may have supported little sluice gates, perhaps only informally made of mud and brushwood.

An interesting variant of this generalized arrangement has been recorded by Mr. Philby in Wadi Markha in the Nisiyin country south-east of Marib.[1] There the wadi, after debouching from local hills, narrows to two or three hundred yards before widening out into an arable delta. He postulates a dam with sluices, now vanished, across the narrows; for radiating fanwise over the delta were a number of rough masonry walls which served, he surmised, to divide up the arable into convenient strips, into each of which the water must have been admitted in turn through the sluice gates. A similar method of diverging channels has been independently noted at Marib itself by an Arab explorer, Nazih Mu'aiyid al 'Adhm, who on a visit in 1936 observed twenty-two in the irrigated area below the site of the great dam, of which little but the masonry of the sluices appears now to survive.[2]

Careful surveys are needed of this and all systems, for our experience in Wadi 'Amd showed the difficulty of making sense, without a plan, of these rubble-heaped areas of old irrigation.

To that of Hureidha, mapped by Miss Gardner (pl. LXXII) and now to be described from her notes, we owe our sojourn in that place and the subsequent find there of temple and tombs. For the choice of it, necessarily made in advance, had been primarily decided upon for two main reasons—both wrong as it happened—based on Freya Stark's earlier visit in 1935: one her conviction that the Wadi 'Amd had been the ancient thoroughfare of trade between the Port of Qana and the Shabwa capital, and the other that a very big Sabaean ruin-field existed near Hureidha.[3] Excavation, disrespectful as ever of theory, has shaken the first assumption,[4] and shown the second to be merely the rubble ruins of an irrigation system.

THE ANCIENT SYSTEM AT HUREIDHA.[5] The Wadi 'Amd at and above Hureidha is a level sandy plain of aeolian silt bordered by the dissected talus slopes which mask the toes of the bounding cliffs. The diagram on pl. LXXII is an average cross-section, and the air view on pl. 1 presents the visual scene looking up the valley, of endless cliffs echeloned in perspective by the recesses eaten in their walls by lateral drainage. Skirting their southern base, the monsoon spate still follows the relatively narrow boulder-strewn

---

[1] *Land of Sheba*, 1939, p. 348 and plate.

[2] Quoted by Mr. Philby in *Land of Sheba*, pp. 349, 392–3.

[3] F. Stark, *Geog. Journ.*, Feb. 1936, p. 122: 'There is a very big Sabaean ruin-field south of Hureidha mentioned by van der Meulen, and there seems to be no doubt that the Wadi 'Amd must have been the ancient high road towards the coast, and probably was used into Islamic times.'

[4] F. Stark, op. cit., Jan. 1939, p. 5: 'I have now come to the conclusion that it (i.e. Wadi 'Amd) was a subsidiary way, and that the main route probably ran to the west by Wadi Meifa'a and the great fortress of Naqb al Hajr, to

Beihan and Shabwa by the yet untravelled Wadi Jardan. . . . The smallness of the site at Hureidha, the poverty of objects found there when compared with those in Beihan . . . all point to a small place off the main stream of traffic.' Also *Journ. R. Asiatic Society*, July 1939, p. 482: 'From my point of view, interested as I was chiefly in the tracing of the ancient trade route, the most remarkable point about the temple of Hureidha was its poverty and smallness: it could not have been a station on the great trade route.'

[5] An account will be found also in *Geog. Journ.*, Jan. 1939, 'Climate, Irrigation and Early Man in the Hadhramaut', by G. Caton Thompson and E. W. Gardner.

course of palaeolithic times (cf. p. 5). Given the water there is nothing geographically to prevent the entire plain for hundreds of square miles from becoming light arable land, yielding a return not worse at any rate than the low customary standard of local agriculture. It is, however, desert, and such cultivation as now exists is patched about the outskirts of the little town, itself clustered beneath a snout of cliff at the confluence of a wide lateral valley.

Irrigation is from wells, secondary to flood irrigation, which, however, at the time of our visit had failed to materialize for two or three years. These flood-waters, at that time so eagerly awaited, are partly diverted from the natural torrent-bed several kilometres above Hureidha, and are confined to a 4-m. wide channel of earth and stone alongside and above it till the outskirts of the town are reached. Here it breaks up into a network of runnels and stone-faced conduits, and waters the palm gardens and plots of cereals.

The spate from lateral sources is also curbed, and at the junction with the main valley may be seen well-built stone and earth barrages. Large numbers of fairly modern 'ghost' plots, some of which are visible in the air view, show a recent decline in cultivated area. But this may be attributed to the bellicose tribal conditions in Wadi 'Amd until a few years ago.[1]

But even allowing liberally for doubts as to where the pre-Islamic cultivation ends and the derelict 'modern' begins, since presumably they overlap down the intervening centuries, it may be safely said that within a 5-km. distance from Hureidha north and north-west, between 7 and 10 sq. km. more ground was fertilized than now. The modern population is estimated at 2,000.[2]

It was this area, situated on the now bald plain, which was mapped and studied by E. W. Gardner. It forms, presumably, only a fraction of the whole ancient system; for, in search of the off-take of its main feeder from the torrent-bed, she was led 16 km. upstream. There the latter, which thereafter as far as Hureidha hugs the southern cliffs, swings across the plain to the northern (seen in the far distance in the air view, pl. i, 3); and here, towards the centre of the valley, she found a 30-m. wide canal-bed heading off from it in the required direction. Denudation of the banks and deposition on its floor had levelled its sides to a bare 2 m., and it could be traced for 80 m. only. But given liberal time, doubtless far more could be intermittently made out. The widths—30 m. at its head, 20 m. at Hureidha—are compatible; and the essential point of contact between irrigation system and torrent-bed which supplied it could nowhere be discovered nearer afield. The similar stage of denudation at the extremities, denoting an age in common, is an added reason for postulating a connexion. And finally, and perhaps more cogent, was the discovery, about a kilometre upstream from the off-take, of a ruined barrage (pl. LXXVIII).

[1] In *Journ. R. Central Asian Soc.*, Oct. 1938, p. 514, Mr. Ingrams describes his and Mrs. Ingrams's visit to Hureidha in 1936. 'Hureidha, in the tortured Wadi 'Amd where practically every man's hand was raised against his neighbours', and adds that the Ja'ada in Wadi 'Amd had at least thirty major feuds.

[2] W. H. Ingrams, *Report on the Social, Economic and Political Conditions of the Hadhramaut*, 1937, p. 127.

What remains of this dam is a V-shaped foundation 3.5 m. broad, the point projecting into the flood-channel, with two arms based on the gravel banks. The distance between these arms along the bank is 85 m.: one is 63 m. long, the other, facing down-stream, 40 m. Their extremities burrow into the wadi bank, that of the up-stream arm being the only one preserved (pl. II, 1). Here two stone-pitched slopes diverge from the top of the bank to the wadi floor, revetting a filling of wadi gravel. The slopes consist of eighteen courses of wedge-shaped blocks, averaging 27 × 20 × 45 cm. At the top of the wadi bank the two sides are 3.8 m. apart and converge to a point set 2.60 m. in from the bank (pl. II, 2).

Assuming that a similar structure, for which no evidence now exists, originally projected from the opposite bank, it is likely that sluices and a spill-way controlled the gap between the two piers.[1]

It will be seen from the map and air view, pls. LXXII; 1, that unlike the 'modern' canal which furtively hugs the valley edge of stony talus alongside and above the torrent-bed, which separates it from contact with the silt plain and prohibits any agricultural activities along its course until it gains the wider reaches above Hureidha, the ancient master canal boldly kept to the middle of the valley, along the highest ground, thereby enabling it, where desired, to water the land on both sides.

Except for a break in the centre of the mapped area near Qarif ibn Thabit, where erosion had obliterated a short stretch owing, probably, to a local change in direction and gradient (a fall here of nearly 2 in 250 m. against a 1 in 455 gradient in the long westerly length), the master canal was distinguishable continuously for over 4 km. Much of the western stretch is ill defined, though unmistakable, marked only by a concentration of pebbles in a 20-m. wide band along its course. Minor channels bud off it as shown; but owing to erosion these cannot in most cases be linked up directly with the longer lateral lengths surviving at lower, less vulnerable levels at either side.

In the stretch at lower level, north-east of Qarif ibn Thabit, the main canal, still 20 m. wide, runs along a narrow ridge, possibly partly artificial, enclosed by the 725.5-m. contour, but makes two pronounced right-angle bends. Just beyond one of these the width suddenly narrows to 6 m. on a length of 10 m., and then resumes its usual 20-m. measurement. This narrowing may mark the position of a contrivance to measure the flow, as is found in the Egyptian oases. Finally, the eastern end of this 800-m. length of main canal ends abruptly, and a pair of 8-m. channels branch off north and south at right angles, one at least continuing its course eventually eastwards. The system, however, at this point becomes obscured by drift sand, though it seems to branch into ever-narrowing runnels. Beyond that point no canal was seen, but as an ancient settlement or farmstead swamped in sand lies a kilometre farther on, the probabilities are that the irrigation continues at least as far as that point.

It seems probable that the sections of canals now missing were made, as are their

[1] Circular-nosed piers were used in ancient irrigation canals in northern 'Iraq; not earlier than Parthian date or possibly later. Cf. M. G. Ionides, *Geog. Journ.*, Oct. 1938, pp. 351-4.

modern equivalents, by silt upthrow. Only the important points, such as junctions, deflexions, or contractions seem to have been stone-built; and these survive as innumerable heaps of scattered, or still piled, rubble, leading to the belief that a great Sabaean ruin-field existed.

There seem here to have been three types of channels; the main feeder-canal, 20–30 m. broad, the start of which is believed to be 16 km. up-valley below a stone-built dam; and dependent secondary and tertiary offsets. The secondary channels are those which took off at right angles to a master channel and which distributed the water to the field plots: these are from 4 to 8 m. broad and approximately 2 m. above the general ground-level. The irrigation of the fields themselves was directly controlled by the tertiary runnels, which consist of short, narrow 1-m. ditches budding off at an acute angle either from the main or secondary channels.

Near the southern edge of this system are several small fields or plots edged by high silt banks, shown on pl. LXXII by strong dotted lines. Some may be later in date, or, more probably, ancient plots re-utilized by sedentary bedouins of the locality who practise an opportunist and shifting tillage after direct rainfall. But in nearly all the plots mapped it is noticeable that the levels and positions indicate original contact with the ancient system; and in one instance stone-faced inlet and outlet conduits, with a drop of 50 cm. between them, pointed to ancient construction.

One peculiarity on the map remains to be noted: the horseshoe-shaped depression locally known as Qarif ibn Thabit[1] at the western foot of the island of higher ground on which the Moon Temple A3 and the farmstead A4 were built. It forms, inside the 795-m. contour, a semi-enclosed basin of about 9,800 sq. m. (70 m. wide by 140 m. long), the floor of which touches 792 m. This certainly represents an artificial deepening, for a huge upthrow of silt, rising into a mound some 10 m. high, though now tremendously denuded, bounds the outer extremity (well seen in pl. III, 2, with the 'basin' inside it) and sweeps round in a curve, though on a lesser scale, to abut against the foot of the temple knoll. It clearly represents, both in local tradition and in construction, a 'bund' for water storage, though none of the irrigation channels recognized were in direct contact. Its possible significance in relation to the temple is discussed on p. 59, for the contemporaneity of the two is established beyond doubt by the multitudes of potsherds which lie on and in the silt upthrow banks, or scattered on the basin's floor.

THE DATING EVIDENCE. It remains to consider the dating evidence for the irrigation system as a whole. Elimination comes first.

Modernity—let us say the last 300 years—can be ruled out, for local tradition concerning it is *nil* and even the educated inhabitants of Hureidha seemed unaware of the true nature of the 'Sabaean ruin-field' they have recently become so proud of.[2] The

---

[1] A *Qarif* is an artificial pool; nothing seemed to be known of its origin. F. Stark, *A Winter in Arabia*, p. 69, refers to it as *Karif ath-Thabit*, or The Steadfast Pond.

[2] This was kindly confirmed by Dr. Huzayyin, who visited Hureidha and Meshḥed the year before our arrival, and, as an Egyptian Moslem, probably escaped the careful editing of information which is the lot of Europeans.

existing flood-supply system, itself apparently of some antiquity, follows a completely independent course. From the sixteenth century back to early Islamic times, the amount of foreign wares imported into the Hadhramaut seems to have been large. No abandoned village we visited failed to supply plentiful examples of them;[1] Chinese export porcelain and earthenware (mainly of the 15th century), Persian blue-and-white, besides glazed wares of many sorts, largely undatable because probably local, but including ninth- or tenth-century fragments. On the irrigated plain, amongst the numberless wind-worn sherds examined, not a single example was found.

On the positive side, the area was strewn with those obsidian microliths, cores, and waste which the tombs and Temple so vigorously proclaim to be their contemporaries; and sherds, when recognizable despite sand-blast, belonged mainly to the rough-faced coarse wares of the tomb series.

But paramount as evidence are the relative positions of channels and isolated pre-Islamic 'sites'—probably farm-buildings, some showing good squared masonry—swamped beneath little mounds formed of their own ruin and drift, which banks on that open plain against any hindrance. The larger of them, shown on the map, including the cluster comprising the Temple and farmstead, A3 and A4, hug the banks of the main canal, and have no conceivable reason to be there, exposed and lonely, apart from the dry farming once dependent on it. Their means of normal water-supply is not apparent. Perhaps they were occupied only at the season of spring floods, abandoned when the swift succession of tilling, irrigating, sowing, and harvesting was finished. Perhaps donkeys brought water in skins from wells in the valley side, as to us when we were working there. Perhaps wells tapped a now forgotten underground source, or cisterns held enough for modest needs. The reality of the last is affirmed by one of the Temple inscriptions (no. 4) which refers to a 'well' in lines 6 and 10, and in line 8 to a stepped cistern (see Professor Ryckmans, pp. 158–60). These waterworks we did not find, but too much of the Temple's peripheral area remains undug to deny their presence.

Unfortunately the building yielded no epigraphic reference to the cultivation around it, and it would be speculative to dwell on the probability of tithe land reserved for the deity.

It is happily more explicit as to the place-name of this ancestral Hureidha. It was ⧏⊓H⧏ = MZBM, Maḏâbum; and this includes both Temple and town, for inscription no. 4, line 10, refers to the 'town of Maḏâbum', inscription no. 10, line 2, to the 'anterior façade (of the Temple) of Maḏâbum', and inscription no. 54 to 'Sîn of Maḏâbum', the tutelary divinity.

One would like to be more certain of the locality of this 'town'. In the area surveyed on pl. LXXII there is no possibility of its buried existence anywhere except in the raised patches of 'pre-Islamic sites' shown there. None of these, however, are big enough to cover more than two or three dwellings, except the A3 and A4 area, which forms a bean-shaped sand-swamped island, rising steeply from the 795-m. contour which nearly

---

[1] I hope to publish these, including complete jars bought at Hureidha.

encloses it, to an 'artificial' maximum of 799 m.; 'artificial' in the sense that this altitude is due, probably entirely as far as the upper 2 m. are concerned, to an intermingling of wind-driven sand immobilized by constructional debris. Its dimensions, ± 350 m. by 200 m. or less, are not too small to cover a compact village of about 200 houses, lodging possibly 1,200 souls. Scattered farmstead units in the vicinity might easily increase this total by another 500, bringing it not far short of the present population of Hureidha.

Revetment of dam

Abutment of dam in Wadi bank

PART II
THE MOON TEMPLE

D

THE MOON TEMPLE

SYNOPSIS. The Moon Temple, the first to be excavated in Arabia, stood, visible from afar, on a slight eminence in the then cultivated valley. Its main façade overlooks an artificial depression possibly connected with the Temple service. On the other three sides lies a complex of still buried buildings, which may form part of the 'ḥaram' area. The site was enveloped completely in drift sand, and local tradition knew nothing of it.[1]

The architectural skeleton consists of an oblong stone-paved platform, resting on a deep inner pack of boulders, confined by a retaining wall over 4 m. high. Of the superstructure, hypaethral or enclosed, little remains but the stumps of stone pillars and the plaster and stone skirtings of partition walls, which divide the south-west area into forecourts and passages. Two flights of stone steps gave access to the platform.

The orientation of the building follows the Mesopotamian practice of setting the corners to the four cardinal points. The main façade looks south-west.[2] It had twice been extended, without destruction of its predecessors. The latest building phase is also represented in a complex of small stone shrines and altars at the foot of the main front. Here, in original position, stood a rough baetyl with votive objects, and a semi-iconic stone. Apart from these, the finds included unplentiful sherds; various decorative or symbolic stones; offering tables, and forty-nine formal inscriptions and nine graffiti, used and re-used. All except one, or perhaps two, which are Sabaean, are in the Hadhramautic dialect. In these, Professor Ryckmans traces both palaeographic and phonetic developments, from an archaic group, through a transition, to a more recent series. They provide no absolute dating, but cover the period of time in which the Temple buildings grew to their final form. In twenty-two the dedication to Sîn is preserved. The deities Dât Ḥîmyam, Ḥawl, and Almaqah are also named; and from these inscriptions we learn as well the ancient name of the Temple and town which it served; and that of the local tribe, or perhaps clan or section of it.

DISCOVERY AND WORK. During the first, peripatetic exploration of the pre-Islamic irrigation area on December 22, 1937,[3] the site of buried buildings was located owing to the unnatural banking of drift sand, the condition of which indicated an accumulation of considerable age. This sandy knoll, irregularly raised some 4 m. above the compact aeolian silt floor of the Wadi 'Amd, lies in mid-plain and commands extensive views up and down the valley. It forms an island in the 795-m. contour, about 350 m. long by 200 m. or less wide, and is noteworthy as offering the largest of the scarce areas in the vicinity of Hureidha which could repay excavation.

Nor was the loose sand of this island devoid of antiquities. The usual inexplicable litter of pebbles and small rubbish which marks man's presence, and a powder here and there of disintegrated mud brick clinched the evidence, which was further supported by scarce sherds and masonry fragments, some finely dressed, one of which bore the letters 𐩪𐩬 (𐩪𐩺𐩬 = Sîn).

It was not difficult in the absence of counter-attractions to decide that here must begin the excavations, and here accordingly on December 24 was assembled a perplexed, rather excited, and entirely unskilled group of six men and four urchins from Hureidha village to start work on test trenches and form the nucleus of a gang.[4]

---

[1] If it had, one may suspect that the use of the site as a stone-quarry, which began even before our departure, would have left not one stone standing.

[2] The 'orientation' of Sirwah is NW.–SE., that of Ḥugga, east. The ruin at Shabwa, believed by Mr. Philby to be the temple, faces 'almost exactly north-west' (*Land of Sheba*, p. 91).

[3] E. W. Gardner and I had reached Hureidha on Dec. 20, and spent the 21st getting our things shifted to the little house we occupied the whole time there.

[4] F. Stark's account seems incorrect. Cf. *Winter in Arabia*, p. 67.

The first trench, A1,[1] cut into the western slope, struck a solid foundation of mud brick, 2·30 m. thick, only half a metre below the surface. Two sizes of brick had been used, a smaller on top of a larger.

Smaller size: 26 × 22 × 12 cm.
                23 × 15 × 12 cm.
Larger size: 45 × 32 × 10 cm.
                45 × 32 × 9 cm.
                45 × 32 × 9 cm.

A second test, A2, was then cut higher up the slope and passed through sandy midden with charcoal and sheep bones. Finally on Christmas Day a third test, A3, was made on the south-west crest itself overlooking the Qarif ibn Thabit depression. This struck stone-work which later proved to belong to that part of the Temple platform labelled III. The site became known as A3, and as work progressed the building was subdivided into ten parts, shown in roman numerals on the plan, pl. LXXIV. We were at work on it six days a week until January 15 with fluctuating numbers of workmen, but normally nineteen to twenty-one men and boys. E. W. Gardner generously left her own work of mapping and geology during this time (beginning it only after that date when I moved on to excavate the farmstead and tombs) and helped invaluably: the plans and photographs are hers, and to her is due the deduction of masked façades confirmed by excavations.

We had by that date obtained the plan of the main structure; had proved by deep excavations to its foundations in areas V, VI, and VII that three building periods were represented at the south-west end; had cleared round the four sides of the retaining walls, exposing remains of an extramural pavement at the south-east and north-east sides, with occupational debris below, which was explored to its lowest levels; and had unearthed a complex of stone shrines and altars at the foot of the main south-west façade, of unique character. It was the moment either to stop and gain some insight into the more human aspects of these worshippers of Sīn, by excavations in their secular abodes and tombs, if such could be found; or to extend the Temple excavations to the peripheral buildings which seemed to spread around it, which had produced the brick foundations in trench A1, and which might be important. I decided to risk the former course, since both were not possible in the time remaining.

In the following description it has seemed best to take the three building periods separately, beginning with the oldest. Pl. LXXIII shows the probable sequence of development, and pl. LXXIV the finished building and outbuildings as we found them.

---

[1] These test trenches, A1 and A2, are not marked on the general map, pl. LXXII.

III. THE EARLY TEMPLE. PHASE 'A'

DIMENSIONS. The original building was a compact, unbroken rectangle, measuring 12·50 m. long by 9·80 m. broad.

RETAINING WALLS. Three of these remained untouched by the subsequent additions; the fourth, that of the main façade on the south-west, was covered and buried, undamaged, by the later extensions. These walls, seen in pls. IV, V, are built of freestone[1] rubble blocks set, in fairly regular courses, in gypsum mortar liberally used on both rising and bedding joints (mortar analysis shows 58·1 per cent. gypsum, see p. 61, sample 4). These blocks, unlike those used in the later extensions, which are mainly waterworn boulders,[2] are of quarried material, rough trimmed into oblong or rounded forms. A row of twelve in the north-west wall was measured and showed an average size, on their exposed face, of 38 by 27 cm., with two maxima of 55 by 22 and 53 by 28 cm., and two minima of 25 by 25 and 30 by 32 cm. The average thickness of the wall seemed also to be between 30 and 35 cm.

The quoins, seen in pl. IV, 2, were roughly squared. At the east corner, which was tested down to its foundations, there were seventeen courses, with a total height of 3·86 m.; but the coping is missing at this point, and from its known dimensions another 30 cm. should be added. The wall rested on a single line of stone footings which projected 30 cm.: these in turn were laid, apparently, on natural aeolian silt at a level of 794·26 m. above sea. It suggests that the building site in its origin lay on a peninsula in the 795-m. contour (see map, pl. LXXII) and owed little to nature for its later preeminence.

These retaining walls are built on a batter of 7°, well seen in pl. IV, 1. They were intact except for missing lengths of coping, thanks to the all-enveloping deposits seen to the left of this picture. But an ominous thrust from the interior has forced out the line from the true on the south-east side (see plan, pl. LXXIV); and a wide fissure has developed on the north-west.[3]

COPING. Lengths of this remain on both sides of the northern angle and also at the south corner. Part of the northern coping is seen in pl. V, 1 (and in plan, pl. LXXIII). It shows the massive character of these large oblong stones, that of the northern quoin measuring 1·40 m. long by 0·57 m. high, shaped from a block originally 0·50 m. broad. Their lengths varied, however, considerably, as seen in the plan, those topping the north-east wall being smaller and less well bonded than the pair round the north-west corner, or at the south and south-west angle, where the rising joints are beautifully fitted. It will be noted too, both in plan and on pl. V, 1, that one of the north-east copings is wedge-shaped in thickness, and its neighbour cut on the inner surface into

---

[1] Sandy limestone and soft sandstone were both used; to obviate too close a definition where none is possible, the word freestone is used to cover either or both. [2] Cf. p. 35. [3] Cf. p. 59.

a projecting angle. Moreover, there were examples of re-spacing and bisection, which cannot be original work. It is clear that this length of smaller coping stones was repaired at some later time when stone masonry had deteriorated (as we know it had by building phase 'C'). The levels at the two extremities of the building remain surprisingly constant, viz. north-east coping top R.L. 798·75; south-west coping top R.L. 799·15.

The coping at the southern corner, consisting of five great stones of unequal length, is particularly important because it had been completely masked by the first of the two 'false' façades added later. It disposes abruptly of any attempt to see in these sophisticated drafted borders and 'rustic' panels an embellishment added at one of the later periods. On the contrary they belong here unquestionably to the earliest building.

In pl. VI, 1, the southern corner of this oldest building and its south-west front are seen vanishing behind the masonry of a later stairway;[1] its 'rustic' coping is marked 'A'. In pl. IX, 2 appears this oldest façade after its re-exposure from the inner pack of the 'false' façade which masked it. Not only was it thus hidden vertically, but it had been buried horizontally also beneath later pavements, laid and relaid over it when the two later extensions were added. The relative positions of all three are best seen in the cross-section on pl. LXXV.

It was impracticable to strip this hidden south-west front of the first Temple to its foundations. Work stopped at 2·30 m. below the top of the old coping;[2] but there seems no doubt, in view of the known foundation level of 794·30 m. on the north-east side, and that of the earlier 'false' front of 795 m., that it conformed in total height to ±4·30 m. also. The batter is 7° as on the other three old walls. We exposed it on a length of 4 m. only, or four coping-stone lengths (in area VIII); more would have involved the further destruction of the later pavings and partition walls over it. Its continuation across the south-west front may probably be safely assumed, interrupted centrally perhaps by entrance steps.[3]

The drafted border on these coping stones averages 7 cm. in depth and is roughly tooled diagonally (25–30°). It has an irregularly defined inner edge, merging, at worst, into the central 'rustication'; at best the two meet on a clean line. The drafting and the pecked surface of the centre lie on the same plane, and the term 'rustic' cannot be used *in sensu stricto*.[4]

Unlike the known practice in other pre-Islamic buildings of south-west Arabia, there were no inscriptions let into these main walls; nor was any trace found of the missing coping stones. They had not fallen outside, nor been re-utilized in the later extensions (with dubious exceptions referred to in the account of the second building phase).[5] One suspects that they were filched after the Temple fell into disuse, and before it became completely buried. The extramural shrines were made almost entirely of material thus rifled,[6] and it is possible that the old copings lurk in other, still unexcavated, adjacent buildings.

---

[1] Cf. p. 40.   [2] Cf. p. 30.   [3] Cf. p. 57.   [4] Cf. p. 57.   [5] Cf. pp. 30–1.   [6] Cf. pp. 44–5.

THE INFILLING. These stout retaining walls held up the deep pack of boulders and rubble on which the Temple platform rested. This pack consists of boulders from the torrent-bed, many of great size, with an interstitial infill of small rubble and sand. Pl. V, 1 shows it at the north corner. A test pit was sunk in it for 2·80 m. below the pavement (3·30 m. below the drift surface) but was discontinued as unlikely to add more information, with increasing danger to workmen at depth. No sherds were found and the only intruders were three broken slabs of paving near the top. These might be contemporary mason's rubbish, or bits thrown in with other stones to level up, at a later time, a local subsidence. 'Settling' of this infill must have been a frequent occurrence.

THE PAVEMENT BEDDING, PAVEMENT, AND INSCRIBED STONES. This massive pack was topped by a spread of limestone and sandstone pebbles about 10 to 20 cm. thick, seen in pl. VIII, 1. On this was poured a gypsum plaster (54·5 per cent. gypsum; see analyses, pp. 61–2, sample 1), which bound it, and in turn acted as a smooth bedding for the final pavement slabs. In these pebbles, under the plaster, lay a broken pottery ringstand or pot base, used probably as a mortar, of the type pl. LIV, 8, and with it a small, shapeless, but humanly made, chert core. Chert flakes as well as wood are still used in the Hadhramaut for smoothing plaster walls, but the purpose of a small core is less obvious.

It was not possible to say to what extent this pavement foundation and bedding belong to the original building. The evidence of levels is against, and all one can say is that in all probability the method followed was the same throughout all periods. The cross-section on pl. LXXV suggests that successive resurfacings in areas I, II, and III, necessitated perhaps as much by periodic 'settling' of the boulder core and consequent warping and tilting of the pavement as by direct surface wear, gradually raised the platform level well above that of the coping on the northern walls (Levels: coping-top, north corner, R.L. 798·60; flags of pavement in area II, R.L. 799·20 m.).

On this assumption no paving or superstructure has been admitted on to the plan of the early Temple. Many of the archaic inscriptions belong, presumably, in origin, to this first Temple, but all appear to have been reused at later periods.

The rules followed in judging the primary or later position of an inscription *in situ* are: (*a*) Is it 'unmutilated', i.e. not cut down textually or reshaped to a new place? (*b*) Is the threefold palaeographic and phonetic group to which Professor Ryckmans assigns it[1] in harmony with its architectural position, i.e. a 'late' inscription may be in a primary position in the oldest body of the building, but an 'archaic' one *in situ* in a 'late' architectural area must be in a secondary or even tertiary one. (*c*) Are two or more inscriptions, *in situ* in a connected or interlocking bit of paving, epigraphically contemporary with each other? If not, the latest, either with or without invoking rules (*a*) and (*b*) according to circumstances, gives the dating.

None of the six inscriptions *in situ* in the oldest building pass these tests, and they will

---

[1] Cf. pp. 174–7.

therefore be considered in later sections. The surviving scraps of paving in this quarter are, in any case, meagre and confined to a single patch in area II (shown in the foreground of pl. VIII, 1), and two others in areas IIIa and c.

Inevitably one speculates on the possibility that the earliest of the early inscriptions proposed by Professor Ryckmans—inscriptions nos. 36, 44, 52, and 7, 16, 17a, and 29[1] —might belong to some vanished edifice pre-existing on the same site. But in none of the deepest test pits was any evidence for such a building forthcoming.

The original positions of the archaic inscriptions found in the body of the oldest building remain undetermined. The correlation of the evolving epigraphic material with the enlarging Temple is discussed on pp. 34–5.

OBJECTS. The only architectural object which may confidently be assigned to this first Temple is the offering table (inscription no. 7).[2] Three aspects are shown in pl. XVIII, 3; the fourth (back) edge is uninscribed and lacks a corner; the other back corner had also broken away, but lay near by. The table is in coarse limestone, fashioned from a rectangular slab 9 cm. thick and ± 28 by 25 cm. in length and width. The upper surface is slightly sunk inside a flat plain frame, in the manner illustrated on pl. XVIII, 4 which shows a two-compartment offering dish found later. A guttered projection ends in a rude gargoyle head, which conducts the outflow along the forehead centre. It may seem bold to claim this barbarous piece of sculpture as a bull's head, particularly if compared with the pleasing naturalistic bucranium found in the Temple at Hugga.[3] But an unpublished bull's head from the Yemen, in the Peabody Museum at Harvard, detached from an offering table, exhibits similar treatment of detail, such as the zigzag rendering of wrinkles on the muzzle, the stumps of horizontally set horns, and a vertical bar from forehead downwards, decorated with incised lines in the Peabody specimen, but in our example so unintelligently reproduced that it looks like a long nose. This table is photographed *in situ* in pl. VIII, 1 (marked '7'), and is seen in plan, pl. LXXIII, no. 7. It lay loose beside one of the stone pillars to be discussed later,[4] but there is no evidence except its broken corners that it had ever capped it.[5]

EXTERNAL LEVELS. A complete length of circumambulatory pavement survives outside the north-eastern and half of the south-eastern retaining walls (plan, pl. LXIII). The relative levels of these two are seen in the cross-section, pl. LXXV, 3, level 'C', and it will be noticed that this external paving lies only 1·40 m. below the coping top. This is less than an average man's height, and in pl. IV, 2, a youth standing on this pavement is eye-level with it. There is evidence to assign this paving to the latest phase of Temple usage, phase 'C'.[6]

At the east corner, therefore, at the spot where inscriptions nos. 49 and 50 were embedded in it, a test pit was sunk for 3·95 m. vertically below them to virgin soil. The deposits from the top down and their chief contents were :

---

[1] Cf. pp. 160-1, 165, 169-71, 173, 176.
[2] Fitzwilliam Museum, Cambridge.
[3] Professor Ryckmans on p. 161 gives this and other comparable published references.
[4] Cf. p. 28.
[5] Cf. pp. 160-1.
[6] Cf. p. 38.

Deposit	Absolute levels above sea	Finds
Paving slabs, hard set in 8 cm. of plaster	⎰797·25 m. ⎱797·17 „	Inscriptions 49 and 50 in the paving belong to the third and latest palaeographic group.[1] Both are cut down. Pl. LXVIII, 1 and 4.
Clean sand ±5 cm. passing into	797·12 „	Two sheep or goat bones.
Contaminated sand,[2] with some charcoal specks and occasional stone chips	796·90 „	..
„ „	796·00 „	a. Small frag. black 'stone ware'.[3]
„ „	795·95 „	b. Rim frag., rough brown-red ware (pl. LVI, 10).
„ „	795·40 „	c. Chip of dark gritty ware, not 'stone ware'.
		d. Seven red sherds, including two fine slip-coated; four rim frags.
		e. Red-brown rough rim (pl. LVI, 7).
		f. „ „ (pl. LVI, 9).
„ „	795·25–795·12 m.	g. Fine red-coated rim, horizontally rubbed (pl. LVI, 11).
		h. Sheep or goat bones and teeth.
		i. Side frag., fine red-coated bowl (pl. LVI, 1).
		j. Metal nodule, probably bronze.
„ „	794·95 m.	k. Side frag., fine red-coated bowl (pl. LVI, 3).
(Temple footing)	794·60–·30 m.	l. Discoloured brown-grey rough sherd.
Dark consolidated soil	794·40 m.	m. Specks of white plaster.
Aeolian silt	793·25 „	

No masonry or building chips apart from rough rubble were found at foundation level, though the plaster must be connected with building activities. The test pit, however, about 1·50 × 2 m. large, was not big enough to produce much at any one level, and the sudden relative increase of sherds between 795·25 and 795·12 m. is suggestive of an early 'circumambulatory' level, some 3·45 m. below the coping, at about the height of the fourteenth course in the wall, as against the fifth in the latest phase. This surmise is supported by evidence at the south-west end of the building.[4] The deposit aggradations of the second building, phase 'B', cannot here be identified, apart from the inference that the levels between ±795·25 and 796·90 m. must include them.

Details of the sherds are given in the Pottery Section;[5] here it suffices to note that the diagnostic larger pieces, such as i and k, are similar in ware and closely allied in form to the open, round-bottomed bowls of the tomb series, class VI;[6] that e and g may belong to tomb-class VIIIb;[7] and the small piece of 'stone ware' unmistakably characterizes tomb-classes IX to XIV.[8] They point, limited as they are, to a real typological synchronism between these deposits sealed in by a pavement with Professor Ryckman's latest-phase inscriptions in it[9] and the pari passu accumulation in the ossuary caves.

[1] Cf. Ryckmans, p. 176.
[2] This must throughout have contained a good deal of clay or organic matter, for the section 'cut' clean without fear of caving sides.
[3] Cf. pp. 115–17.   [4] Cf. p. 38.   [5] Cf. pp. 129–31.

[6] Cf. p. 121.   [7] Cf. p. 122.   [8] Cf. pp. 123–8.
[9] The question of a post-'C' building phase, which affects not only the structure of the Temple, but its extramural buildings and levels, is discussed, pp. 59–60.

IV. THE SECOND TEMPLE. PHASE 'B'

GENERAL. Architecturally, three façades at the south-west front were identified. Two inscriptions refer to the 'façade antérieure'. The first, no. 3, already mentioned in connexion with its position in the early Temple, is archaic, but belongs to the fifth or penultimate palaeographic sub-series in the archaic group.[1] It borders, therefore, on the transitional style. It is well cut, on a freestone slab, about 21 by 24 cm. square and about 4 cm. thick (pl. LXIII, 1). Unfortunately, owing to re-utilization in a later pavement, and consequent recutting (perhaps more than once), only two imperfect lines remain, stating 'la façade antérieure du temple . . . et par Dât-Himyam . . .', without more information concerning its purpose.

The other inscription is no. 26 (pl. LXIV, 1). This is a relatively long, three-line text, found in two separate bits on the west steps. Professor Ryckmans assigns it palaeographically to his latest group,[2] and renders:

'Bin'il, fils de 'Ammdamar, le Yarmite, Kabîr de Ramay, a renouvelé la façade antérieure (du temple) de Madâbum, la troisième (année de l'éponymat) 'Adîdum, et avec la participation de (la tribu) Ramay.'

To which of three successive fronts do they refer? Complete certainty there cannot be, but the probabilities seem to favour the second and the last. In the first place, though inscription no. 3 is too mutilated to tell us, we will assume that it refers to renovations or reconstructions, always so meticulously brought to the notice of their tutelary deities by the ancient South Arabians. There are no signs of such on the original south-west façade (pl. IX, 2) in the length we cleared; it is in excellent repair, and mere repointing would hardly merit a dedicatory inscription by the head of the tribe. On the other hand work, sufficiently extensive to merit divine attention, is evident in the second architectural phase, which will now be examined.

DIMENSIONS. While the breadth remained constant, the length is increased by 2·60 m. owing to the addition to the south-west front.

RETAINING WALLS. There is no evidence that any except the new south-west façade, dealt with separately, were touched.

COPINGS. The old set, subject possibly to repairs on the north-east wall at this or a later date, was not apparently altered. But to meet the rise of internal level (cf. Pavement Bedding, below) we have tentatively introduced on the cross-section, pl. LXXV, 2, two additional courses to conform to the interior. This reconstruction has the authority of doubled drafted blocks upon the new 'B' façade at the south-west end.

INFILLING. No recognized change; but a rise in level of the boulder fill in areas II and III of 25–30 cm. above the theoretic line demanded by the single-copings of the old retaining walls, suggests that repacking to stabilize subsidences may have taken place.

[1] Cf. Ryckmans, p. 176.   [2] Cf. p. 176.

PAVEMENT BEDDING, PAVEMENT, AND STONE PILLAR-BASES. Comment has been made upon the rise in platform level. How the pebble-bedding was held in place at the edge is not clear, unless our assumption of raising of the coping is correct.

Granted this premiss, it follows that the five stone pillars which are the only surviving relics of a superstructure in this old body of the Temple were introduced either in the second or third building phase. We have, though with little certainty, shown them in plan already in position in the second.

To facilitate individual reference, these two rows of stumps have in plan been labelled by their compass position. Pl. VIII, 1 shows the northern row. In the foreground, beside the offering table (inscription no. 7) is the square plinth of the north pillar lacking its upper part. Beyond stand the two complete cones of the north-west and west specimens, stripped by us of their pebble and plaster foundation. Three only were undamaged (the north-west, west, and south-east): they had square bases and truncated conical tops which left a slightly projecting angle at the point where one figure passed into the other (see cross-section, pl. LXXV). They were very primitive in appearance, rough-hewn from a single block of limestone, and they varied considerably in measurements. These were approximately:

North. Plinth only; ht. 50 cm. Sides 40 cm. square.

North-west. Total ht. 66 cm. Plinth ht. 41 cm. Sides 41 × 37 cm. square. Conical ht. 25 cm. Diam. at cone apex 22 cm.; at base 40 cm.

West. Total ht. 74 cm. Plinth ht. 49 cm. Sides 35 × 34 cm. square. Conical ht. 25 cm. Diam. at cone apex 30 × 25 cm.; at base 35 cm.

East. No certain trace was found.

South-east. Total ht. 65 cm. Plinth ht. 45 cm. Sides 42 × 35 cm. square. Conical ht. 20 cm. Diam. at cone apex 25 × 20 cm.

South. Broken base of plinth only.

These plinths were well bedded in the pebble and plaster layer beneath the paving. In the north-west plinth 21 cm. was thus sunk below pavement level; in the west plinth 29 cm.; and in the south-east one, 25 cm. These figures, taken in relation to the total heights given above, show above-ground heights of 45, 45, and 40 cm. respectively, and indicate an endeavour to obtain a level summit. The north pillar-base, however, raises other questions. Its foundation level is 25 cm. lower than the others, and this is not equalized by a greater total height of plinth (though the missing cone may have compensated). Moreover, it is difficult to conceive how its conical top, had it been hewn in one piece, could have been broken off. It was as firmly embedded, however, as the others in pebbles and plaster-concrete, and against it on one side lapped the 'crazy pavement' which we assign to the phase C period; but whatever the relative ages of the two, the pavement must have been laid later. A possible explanation of this dropped floor-level in area II will be given in describing a great breach in the north-west retaining wall.[1]

The intercolumnar measurements are unequal:

Longitudinal. North to north-west stump 1·75 m.
North-west to west stump 1·45 m.
South-east to south stump 1·35 m.

[1] Cf. p. 59.

Lateral.   North-east to south-east stump 2·50 m.
                    West to south stump 2·40 m.

The result, as seen on the plan, pl. LXXIII, is that the rows do not truly 'stand to partners'. Nor is exactitude their strong point in their position on the old platform of the Temple, though doubtless they purported to be placed centrally. The longitudinal distances between the outer stumps and the north-east and south-west retaining walls respectively are well spaced (approximately 3·50 m. both ends). But the lateral distances to the outer walls are sadly unequal (3·20 m. on the north-west side, 2·80 m. on the south-east).

Yet their inter-alinement, however rough, does suggest that they represent the bases of pillars, probably of wood, which carried the roof of a small sanctuary in the inexact centre of the old platform. Their spacing must necessarily be close in a region where wood of any length is unobtainable, and where girders and rafters must be short. At Ḥugga near Sanaʻa, which is a sophisticated Sun Temple of probably considerably later date, commanding far greater resources in its construction, and from which, therefore, to draw architectural comparisons would be inept, it may be noted that even there the longitudinal intercolumnar distances were only about 1·25 m., though a large central court, 12 m. wide, around which they stood, separated them laterally.[1]

But if their function as pillar-bases seems a reasonable surmise, though impugned by the absence of any socket or mortise on the smooth flat top of the cone, it might be well to keep in mind the possibility of a baetyllic significance, for the reality of which in this Temple there is ample evidence.[2] If that were so, the position of the bull-headed offering table at the foot of the north pillar would acquire an interest I have denied it.[3] This object, however, judged by its inscription, belongs to the archaic group; and this hypothesis therefore carries with it the presupposition of similar baetyls in the early Temple. In any case, whatever these stumps may finally prove to be as knowledge of Hadhramaut Moon Temples extends, it is possible that they here date from the early building and were merely rebedded in the second.

THE THRESHOLD AREA, III*a*, AND THE PLASTER WALLS. In the nearly exact middle of the old south-west façade considerable alterations were made at this period. On a line with the old coping were erected walls of fine white plaster, thickly facing a now perished core of mud brick: these turned inwards at right angles to define a paved central entrance-passage, 2 m. long by 1·65 m. wide, leading to the 'pillar area' of the main platform (see plan, pl. LXXIII, 2).

These walls, though disintegrated except where supported by stone skirting (as in pl. VII, 2 right), survive recognizably as masses of white powder inside the overburden of drift sand (pl. VII, 1). They must still have been standing, up to half a metre high at least, when the Temple was abandoned to nature's gradual envelopment, and then slowly

---

[1] Rathjens and von Wissmann, *Südarabien Reise*, Band 2, 1932, pp. 33–49, figs. 5, 6, 7. The columns were octagonal with square, decorative capitals. Mr. Philby quotes intercolumnar distances of only 2½ ft. at Shabwa, where he found four square limestone plinths 2½ ft. square, with central circular depressions about 2 ft. in diameter, which indicated the columns must have been round. No wood, of course, could be this diameter. (*Land of Sheba*, p. 88.)

[2] Cf. p. 47.

[3] Cf. p. 24.

pulverized *in situ*. This plaster is technically of low-grade quality, but attractive on account of its pure white colour[1] (gypsum content, 8·6 per cent.; calcium carbonate, 89·8 per cent.; see analyses, pp. 61–2, no. 3).   It must, though pleasing to the eye when polished and probably decorated,[2] have been fragile, and consequently a dado of free-stone slabs, about 8 cm. thick, was embedded on edge to protect the more vulnerable skirtings (as in pl. VII, 2, which, however, actually belongs to the third building phase; cf. p. 40).   In the second phase this skirting is represented by three orthostatic slabs only, in the right-hand entrance wall; but six other squared stone blocks in the other plaster walls seem likely, in view of their shape, to have served as constructional supports. All have been stuccoed on the exposed face to dissemble their different material.   The thin dado slabs did not here exceed 45 cm. in height (60 cm. was the tallest found in the later building): they resembled ordinary pavings tilted on edge, and though chisel-dressed on the exposed face, were hammer-dressed on the reverse, as much probably to increase their purchase in the plaster, horizontal or vertical, as to save labour.[3]

PAVING AND PAVING INSCRIPTIONS. We have, for epigraphic reasons, and with hesitation, assigned the pavement in the passage entrance to the third building phase. It is one of the few cases where the palaeographic and phonetic classification seems at variance with the archaeological probability. This being the case, we have shown the paving on the plans of both 'B' and 'C' phases in order to illustrate the difficulty, which, however, will be discussed with the third building.[4] The flagged area in what we named the South Court, IIIc, as well as the forecourt, area IV, must certainly be considered later work, though re-utilizing much pre-existing material, including an inscribed fragment, no. 6.

The truth probably is that the Temple pavement was subject to fairly frequent repairs; the local sandstone is friable as well as fissile, as we disastrously found when moving inscribed slabs: and this combined with the underlying instability of the boulder core probably necessitated from time to time single replacements as well as more extensive repaving. Only thus, I think, can we account for the introduction of mutilated inscriptions, cut down to fit new positions, and explain the inclusion of examples of all phases of epigraphical development.

And if other justification be needed for lumping all the surviving paving we found *in situ* into the last building period, it should be remembered that the successive extensions of the south-west façade must of themselves have destroyed, directly or indirectly, pre-existing floors, which it would be simpler to relay *de novo* on completion of the work, simultaneously with that of the new area, than to patch.

If there be any temporal connexion between the three stages of epigraphic development and the three architectural phases (which is highly improbable), then inscription

---

[1] A feature greatly admired by our numerous local sight-seers and workmen, who try to achieve it in their own internal decoration schemes.

[2] A tiny piece of ribbed plaster was found later in area VIII loose in the sand. For the probability that decorative or symbolic stone slabs were sometimes also embedded, see p. 50.

[3] Cf. p. 33.

[4] Cf. p. 34.

no. 37 (pl. LXVI, 5), said to show characteristic transitional forms between the archaic and the later groups,[1] should be the contemporary of the second building. But it was found loose in debris near the south-eastern staircase and has no positional value.[2] It has, moreover, unmistakably been cut down on its left edge. One other inscription, no. 8, appears to be contemporary with phase 'B', for later it became covered by the enlargement of the stucco walling. Nevertheless, it also falls into the 'recent' epigraphic group.[3]

THE SOUTH-WEST EXTENSION. The first extension to the south-west façade took the form of a narrow 'false' front, which carried it 2·65 m. forward. The old was left intact; and in area IV, where we sank a test pit, the intermural space was filled with a dry packing of large torrent-worn boulders, with soil to fill the interstices and, in one place, traces of mud brick. This test, on the *inside* of the new façade, was carried down to 2·30 m. only from the overlying pavement; but it exposed, as seen in pl. IX, 2, the seven upper courses and drafted coping of the old south-west front.[4] It would have been difficult to carry it lower on account of the danger of collapse of the 'false' front, bereft of its supporting pack. In the course of this clearance eleven sherds were found in the fill, a piece of slag at 1·33 m., and a sheep or goat molar. The only sherd of diagnostic importance was a piece of black 'stone ware', 1·20 m. below the surface. The others were rough red-brown fragments, the lowest of which came from 1·70 m. The inner face of the 'false' façade consisted of quarried rubble blocks, rough shaped to sub-angular or rounded forms, packed with mud brick, now disintegrated, and smaller rubble. The wall is ±70–80 cm. thick. On its external face, however, we were able to expose it to its foundations by amalgamated test pits in areas V, VI, and VII (see plan of the 'C' building phase, pl. LXXIV). For just as this second front masked the first one, so a third masked the one under discussion.

Details of the masking deposits belong chronologically to the next chapter; but clearance had to be carried down to 4·79 m. below the surface paving (5·15 m. below modern surface level) before the foundation course was reached. The footing lies at an absolute level of just under R.L. 795 m., which is within a few centimetres of that in the old north-east wall.[5] This newer wall consists of nineteen rubble courses, capped by two superposed rows of enormous copings bound together by mortar. Its batter is 7° like the older work, but the quality of workmanship is inferior. Though set in fairly even courses, the vertical face is defective in alinement (due possibly to thrust from behind) and the size of the blocks not so well graded. The footing, unlike the projecting stone foundations of the old Temple walls, is of mud brick. One of these, lying unused and undamaged beside the ground course, measured 25 × 15 × 12 cm., thus resembling the smaller of the two brick sizes noted in A1 (i.e. 26 × 22 × 12 and 23 × 15 × 12 cm.),[6] and 26 × 22 × 12 found in A4.[7]

THE COPING. In the cross-section, pl. LXXV, 2, it will be noticed that the top of the upper coping blocks of this 'false' front projects above the surrounding pavement, and it is

---

[1] Cf. Ryckmans, p. 176.   [2] Cf. p. 55.   [3] Cf. p. 176.   [4] Cf. p. 22.
[5] Cf. p. 21.   [6] Cf. p. 20.   [7] Cf. p. 139.

visible, in pl., III, I, as a raised bench across the platform, then in an early stage or clearance. It is only 4·20 m. long, and consists of two superimposed rows of five great sandstone blocks, the largest measuring 1·10 m. long by 0·60 broad by 0·30 to 0·40 m. thick. Pl. IX, 3 gives details of the tooling, though the lower drafted border is still buried. In style these blocks differ from those in the old Temple. The drafting is similarly diagonal, but does not border the stones on the short edges. The centre, too, is coarsely tooled instead of 'pecked' as in the earlier examples.

PROBLEMATIC RECONSTRUCTION. This narrow but high south-west extension is placed astride the nearly exact centre of the old façade, and taken by itself gives a deceptive appearance of a projecting paved platform in direct relation with the entrance IIIa. But though, without destruction of nearly the whole south-west area from top to bottom,[1] it was impossible, owing to the interference of the third building phase, to find out exactly what part of a larger whole it really did represent, it may confidently be said that some sort of structure continuous with it must have flanked it on both sides. The evidence is partly contained in pl. IX, I, where the southern extremity of the great double coping blocks, marked 'B', are seen to be stepped, i.e. the lower row overlaps the upper; and below both the raw edge of the 4·79-m. rubble 'façade', which they surmount, ends laterally with equal abruptness. The overlap of the copings suggests an unfinished or destroyed bond. Furthermore, completely destructive of the supposition that this rectangle could ever have constituted a self-contained architectural unit, is the fact that the pair of short cross-walls which link the 'false' façade to the old front are not bonded or even mortared at the junction. One of them is seen in the foreground of the same plate (pl. IX, I), and they are so shallow—0·75 m.—that they cannot possibly be regarded as sides to this high, projecting platform. More probably they are merely buttresses. As seen in the photograph they are copiously mortared between their rubble blocks, and are capped by a single line of drafted coping stones, probably filched from the old building, for the dimensions and style are similar.[2] Here, however, they were used not as copings with their main surfaces exposed, but merely as part of the stone paving which covered all this area (a 2-ft. rule lies on the elongated top of one of them; their place in the pavement is best seen in the stone-for-stone plan of the third building, pl. LXXIII, 3. They had been left at that period undisturbed, and the paving was fitted against them and adjusted to their level).

All things considered in these distracting details, we think that in this second building phase the 'false' front extended right across the full width of the old front, possibly in the form of a central structure (which survives as our area IV) and two wings occupying the spaces VIII and X of the plan, one of which carried the staircase;[3] that the

---

[1] The question arises to what extent, in a land where pride in ancestral monuments must be stimulated if they are not to perish, one would be justified, in pioneer excavations, in systematically destroying the structure of one of them. The scientific motives are naturally unintelligible even to the educated inhabitant, who at best can only dimly respond to the historic one. And though doubtless a building such as the Moon Temple has, in fact, been destroyed since we left, one would hesitate, as the first excavator, to give the lead.

[2] Cf. p. 22.

[3] Cf. p. 53. Possible traces at the right level were found beneath the extramural buildings.

third phase builders destroyed these wings in the course of erection of yet another façade and two staircases, both of which lie just where these hypothetical wings would have stood.

THE OBJECTS. Nothing can with certainty be assigned to this second phase except the eleven sherds and slag found in the boulder fill beneath the pavement in area IV. Even these are not all certainly contemporary, for two are wind-worn and were presumably scooped up with the soil thrown in with the boulders. The rest are too small to reconstruct, and the only piece of importance is the scrap of black 'stone ware'. Taken in conjunction with the sherd of similar fabric from the 796-m. level of the external deposits at the east corner which I propose to assign to the aggradation of the second building stage[1] there is some justification for regarding this curious ware, so well represented in the tombs, as being already in vogue at this second phase of the Temple's history.

[1] Cf. p. 25.

V. THE LATEST TEMPLE. PHASE 'C'

GENERAL. The main body of the Temple, enlarged once more to its final dimensions by, we may surmise, Bin'il son of Ammdamar,[1] is seen in the stone-for-stone plan, pl. LXXIII, 3, as we unearthed it. Compared with the old compact rectangle it looks impressive, but closer examination reveals a sad decline in never very high building standards.

DIMENSIONS. The length is increased yet another 2 m. by additions to, and reconstruction of, the south-west front.

RETAINING WALLS. The three old ones remain untouched, except perhaps for a fresh coating of whitewash. Traces of this were found on the new west staircase parapet wall, and on a bit of the old north-east retaining wall: had it been stucco (difficult and costly to apply on such a rough surface), spicules should have been found in the sand.[2] Without much doubt all the external walls were whitened as in a modern mud-brick mosque; and as the internal partitions, too, were of white plaster, we may think of the Temple standing aloft on its white stylobate, visible in that dun landscape for miles.

The new south-west front is described separately.

COPING. Repairs on the north-east wall?[3] None survived on the new façade.

PAVEMENTS. For reasons given we assume that all we found *in situ* were laid at this period.[4] The flags, of whitish sandstone mingled with limestone, were all sizes, but regularly rectangular.[5] The levels on pl. LXXIV show that the paving was reasonably flat, although individual slabs vary greatly in thickness as well as area. It is clear no standard size was attempted; the quarried blocks were worked to their individual capacity and laid in axial conformity with the building. Thicknesses range from 10 to 4 cm. The under faces are roughly hammer-dressed, but the facing surfaces and lateral edges are chiselled to a close-fitting edge. This tooling, as on the drafted borders and dados, is usually diagonal ($\pm$ 25–30°). The inscribed stone, pl. LXVII, 4, is typical, but most pavings were too worn to show tool-marks. The stone-for-stone plan, pl. LXXIII, 3, provides several instances of recessing and interlocking. Some pavings still firmly adhered to their beds; others, where the mortar had perished, lay loose in their sockets.

Pavement in Area II. This is seen in pl. VIII, 1, foreground, and was fragmentary and buckled. Two inscriptions, nos. 1 and 3, are archaic;[6] but though doubtless contemporary with the oldest building in which they lie, both are mutilated and associated *in situ* with no. 2, which is classed in the latest group of 'types archaïques évolués vers un type plus récent'.[7] The paving here must therefore have been relaid with miscellaneous material in the latest phase. No. 7, the bull-spouted offering-table, has been

---

[1] Cf. Ryckmans, pp. 162–3.
[2] Cf. p. 41. [3] Cf. pp. 21–2. [4] Cf. p. 29.
[5] The patchwork paving of Egypt is an interesting

contrast (Engelbach, *Ancient Egyptian Masonry*, p. 130).
[6] Cf. Ryckmans, pp. 157–8.
[7] Cf. Ryckmans, p. 157.

described under phase 'A', where it seems to belong.[1] Inscription No. 45 lay loose in overlying sand.

Pavement in Entrance Passage, Area IIIa.   Discussion was held over from p. 29. A comparison of the plans of phases 'B' and 'C' (pl. LXXIII, 2, 3) discloses the following points. In phase 'B' the paving laps the plaster walls as defined by the dado slabs: in 'C' it runs beneath them. The entrance passage has, therefore, been narrowed (from 1·60 m. in 'B' to 1·25 m. in 'C'). Moreover, it has increased its length 70 cm. by elongation on the south-west side, and added considerably to its thickness. All this is due simply to successive applications of plaster facing to the walls. The un-resolved question lies in the paving. In phase 'B' the row of three well-balanced flags on the north-east side, which includes inscriptions nos. 4 and 5, fits exactly its position. In phase 'C' the last four lines of no. 4 were hidden below the plaster wall (to which it was set at right angles); and thus we found it. It is an eleven-line inscription (pl. LXIII, 3), ±63×30 cm., telling, in Professor Ryckmans's translation, how 'Asamum, fils de Ḥabîsum, Kabir de Ramay, et 'Agnum, aristocrates de la ville de Madâbum, ont dédié à Sīn Dû-Madâbum cette inscription, et s'en sont acquittés au deuxième jour de Dû-Samâw. Et ils ont renouvelé et bâti en construction massive avec leur part (?) le puits Shu'bat, et ils l'ont refait en largeur, et le conduit, et le bassin, et les degrés. Et (ils l'ont bâti) en gros œuvre, et en pierres équarries. Et ils ont ordonné ce (travail) jusqu'au sommet du puits de la ville de Madâbum, et avec la participation de (la tribu) de Ramay, et . . .';[2] the last line (or lines) was already broken (not cut) when the slab was fitted. The surface shows considerable wear. Both its position and condition suggest a slab contemporary with phase 'B', left undisturbed in phase 'C'. But palaeographically and phonetically it falls into the 'recent' group.[3]

Its companion, no. 5, supports it in equivocality. It is ±51×30 cm. in size, inscribed with a mutilated dedication to Sīn, cut on the vertical edge of the slab, 30 cm. high, and consequently hidden if (as one assumes) the pavement formerly continued unbroken north-eastwards. A hand-copy is the basis of Professor Ryckmans's translation,[4] and it cannot therefore be palaeographically grouped; but phonetically it, too, falls into the 'recent' class ('sub-group 8 préformante et suffixe en ḥ').[5]

Inscription no. 8, 26×16 cm., completely buried in phase 'C' by the same stucco wall, must have formed part of the open, paved area IV in phase 'B'. It, too, is phonetically 'recent', and poses an equally perplexing question.

These details are stressed because they illustrate the impossibility of satisfactory synchronism between inscriptions, used and reused, and the building phases. All that is certain is that the active duration of the Temple was long enough to see a threefold palaeographic and grammatical development; but there is no logical reason why these should tally with building developments. Epigraphic evolution is a gradual and probably

---

[1] Cf. p. 24.   [2] Cf. Ryckmans, p. 160.
[3] Cf. Ryckmans, p. 176.
[4] Photographs failed; and the stone being rotten, it broke

up under the unheeding tread of our daily throng of village and bedouin spectators, before a squeeze had been taken.
[5] Cf. Ryckmans, p. 176.

spiral growth; the other a swiftly accomplished action. Our evidence seems best fulfilled if we tentatively assign the archaic and transitional texts to building phase 'A'; and the later group to building phases 'B' and 'C'.

SOUTH-WEST EXTENSION. The final addition to the main front is seen in pl. v, 2, the work, we may suppose, of Bin'il son of 'Ammdamar and the tribe or section of Ramay, whose recording inscription, no. 10+26,[1] does not mention that the work was scamped. Whereas the quarried rubble in the old north-west wall gave a mean size of 38 by 27 cm., the latest builders contented themselves with natural water-worn boulders (used as the infilling in the older period), giving a mean size on a similar measured dozen blocks of only 26 by 18·5 cm., with a maximum of 29 by 25 cm. and a minimum of 18 by 15 cm. The gypsum mortar used, however, does not compare unfavourably with the old sample (gypsum 69·4 per cent.; see analyses, pp. 61–2, sample no. 2) and fairly level courses were achieved. The new work consists of a façade, 6·80 m. long, symmetrically outflanking the five great raised coping blocks of phase 'B' and set on exactly the same bearing as its two predecessors. Narrow steps, however, at the west corner, form a new feature, counterbalanced at the other, south, extremity, by a re-entrant nearly 2 m. deep, which in turn flanks a broad flight of steps ascending the platform at right angles to the other. This re-entrant is not bonded into the main front.

The main wall was cleared to its foundations, and as seen in cross-section, pl. LXXV, 3, consists of only ten courses, six and a half of which were above contemporary ground level and only three and a half below, totalling 2·30 m. only, as against ±4·30 m. in phase 'A' and 4·79 m. in phase 'B'. Its coping, however, had vanished, therefore another 25–30 cm. should be added. The ground course rested on a footing of disintegrated mud brick at R.L. 796·90 m.[2]

THE INTERNAL FILL. In describing the phase 'B' façade, details of the deposits masking it were omitted as they belong to phase 'C'. Three soundings were made in areas V, VI, and VII; these were eventually enlarged into one pit and were carried down from a pavement level of R.L. 799·30 or ·40 to 794·75 m. The pack was predominantly sandy with enough contained clay to bind and give fairly clean sections. At depth it became greasy (with added moisture?). The external face of phase 'B' façade was exposed on one side, and the internal face of the shallow phase 'C' front on the other, which ended little over half-way down. This latest front was of a single thickness only backed by unmortared rubble. The boulders which characterized the inter-pack of façades 'A' and 'B' were absent. In areas V and VII the surface was paved; in area VI unpaved, but a plaster bed ±4 cm. thick witnessed a vanished floor here also. Two shallow cross-walls of rubble, their tops about 4 cm. above the pavements in areas V and VII on their flanks, separated these arbitrary 'areas' and defined them. Their purpose remained obscure and they stopped short of façade 'B' by a few centimetres.[3]

[1] Cf. pp. 162–3.
[2] Cf. mud bricks at R.L. 796·90–·65 m., p. 36.
[3] If regarded as the footings of plaster partition walls, area VI becomes a small, central room about 1·50 m. square.

Arches or doors into it must then be postulated in such walls, with raised sills, plaster-coated, 4 cm. high. It is tempting to envisage a naos or adytum containing a baetyl, particularly in view of the incense-burner.

Sherds in Internal Fill. The objects found in this excavation, which measured ± 3 m. laterally by 1·60 longitudinally, were sixty sherds, mainly in small scraps impossible to reconstruct, rare obsidian, and metal particles. Of no importance in themselves, the wares provide correlations with the tomb potteries, and their levels information concerning deposit aggradation. The following list amalgamates the triple soundings since these were eventually unified.

The first object found, in area VI, was tucked against one of the big coping blocks of the 'false' front of phase 'B'. It is a rectangular limestone incense-burner of a style repeated later in the extramural shrines.[1] It is 5·2 cm. tall (pls. XVI, 3; XVII, 2) with shallow trough and four square legs; the incised surface had been artificially reddened. Its position is important since by no possibility can it be earlier than phase 'C'.

Depth in nearest decimetre below pavement of Areas V, VI, and VII	Absolute levels above sea (R.L. mean of pavements 799·35 m.)	Object	Plates	Comment
cm.			XVI, 3; XVII,	
15–20	799·15–·20	Limestone incense-burner.	2	As above. Cf. also pp. 49–50.
40	798·95	Small sherd, fine red-coated.	..	
		Rim fragment, fine red-coated.	LVI, 4	Part of shallow open bowl with rounded base.
50	798·85	*ditto.	..	See * below.
60	798·75	Rim fragment, coarse brown-red. Sherd ditto.	..	Straight scored line below.
		Rim fragment, fine red-coated.	LVI, 2	Part of shallow open bowl, with marked angular curve to base.
80	798·55	Rim fragment, fine red-coated.	LVI, 6	A plastic band adorns a shallow open bowl.
		*Rim fragment, fine red-coated.	..	Belongs to * above.
		Fragment, short hollow pedestal, coarse red ware.	..	Of the type tomb class III.
1·00	798·35	Two scraps, fine red-coated ware.	..	
		Scrap metal, probably bronze.	..	
1·50	797·85	Three sherds, coarse grey-brown ware.	..	
1·70	797·65	Placage brick of white limestone.	XXI, 3	Length 18·5 cm., breadth 8 cm., max. depth 6·5 cm. The sides are carefully squared for over 1·5 cm., then sharply undercut to a broad keel. Its cross-section denotes probable use as facing to a plaster wall.
2·00	797·35	Rim fragment, coarse red-brown ware.	LVI, 5	A scored line defines a flat expanding rim.
2·45–2·70	796·90–·65	Mud bricks laid flat.	..	No measurements possible, and no regular bedding.
3·35	796·00	Rim fragment, coarse red.	LVI, 8.	Straight scored line below.
3·50	795·85	Metal nodule, probably bronze.	..	
		Rim fragment, coarse brown-red ware.	..	Greyish underside.

[1] Cf. pp. 49–50, 58.

Depth in nearest decimetre below pavement of Areas V, VI, and VII	Absolute levels above sea (R.L. mean of pavements 799·35 m.)	Object	Plates	Comment
3·50	795·85	Five sherds, coarse reddish grey.	..	⎫ Probably similar, but unequally fired.
		Four sherds, coarse red-brown.	..	⎬ None join.
3·70	795·65	Masonry chips.	..	⎭
		Six small sherds, coarse red-brown.	..	
		One sherd, fine red-coated.	..	
4·00	795·35	Masonry chips.	..	
		Obsidian core and chip.	LIX, 2	A small pyramidal core or scraper-core.
		Amorphous chert core?	..	
		Scrap of metal, probably bronze.		
		Ten sherds, coarse red-brown.	..	
		Four sherds, coarse greyer tone.	..	
		Fragment, hollow pedestal, coarse red-brown ware.	..	
		Part of limestone brick with triangular cross-section.	..	Breadth 10 cm., depth 7·2 cm., length incomplete. The section is less accentuated than 1·70 m. specimen.
		Knuckle bone of sheep or goat.	..	Partly burnt.
4·10	795·25	Scrap purplish ochre.	..	The only bit found; but ochre was probably the substance used to redden limestone incense-burners and inscriptions. Cf. p. 50, 157.
		Two small sherds, coarse red.	..	
4·20	795·15	Two small sherds, coarse red.	..	
		Four, ditto, discoloured greyish.	..	
		Two, ditto, coarse brown-red.	..	
4·30	795·05	Obsidian chip.	..	
		Metal scrap, probably bronze.	..	
4·50	794·85	Four discoloured grey sherds.	..	
		One sherd, coarse red-brown.	..	

PROBABLE 'EXTERNAL' LEVELS IN BUILDING PHASES 'A', 'B', AND 'C'. A comparison of this section with that given for the eastern corner on p. 25 provides facts which enable a tentative correlation, and certain deductions, as to the 'circumambulatory' levels of the Temple during the three phases and the proportionate rise in deposits. For phase 'C' we must anticipate some of our evidence, for though the foundation level of its shallow south-west front wall has been stated (R.L. 796·90 m.), its external 'circumambulatory' ground level concerns the next chapter.

The deposits themselves nowhere give helpful stratification, and the incidence of contents alone has been used in support of the deductions. The evidence may best be followed with the cross-sections, pls. LXXV, LXXVI.

Phase 'A'. On p. 25 we deduced from the sudden increase of sherds that the 'circumambulatory' level of the old building at the north-east end was between R.L. 795·12 and 795·25 m., i.e. about 65 cm. above the footing and 3·45 m. below the retaining wall coping above.

At the south-west end the comparable phase 'A' level between the façades 'A' and 'B' was not reached; but we learnt there, from shallow excavations, that the Temple platform rises slightly towards that end and the south-west coping lies 40 cm. higher than its opposite number. Supposing therefore, as seems reasonable, that 'circumambulatory' levels were controlled empirically by the wall height above them and not by devotion to absolute level, we should in the inter-façade 'B' and 'C' deposits have theoretically touched the old 'A' circumambulatory level at ±R.L. 795·55 or ·60 m. Our table above shows how, between R.L. 795·35 m. and 795·65 m., masonry chips and a limestone brick occurred, and below that a comparatively large proportion of the sherds, as well as obsidian. Two and two *may* not prove a phase 'A' level, but they make here something surprisingly like a probable one.

Phase 'B'. This 'circumambulatory' level is far more difficult to deduce. At the north-east end we could do no more than fit it in, by implication, above phase 'A' at R.L. 795·25 m., and below the phase 'C' pavement at R.L. 797·17 m. At the south-west end we have useful evidence in the mud bricks in the inter-façade deposits of phases 'B' and 'C', between R.L. 796·65 and 796·90 m. These levels in the interfill tally suspiciously with the foundation course of façade 'C'; and the conclusion, I think, is suggested that the horizontal bricks in the fill represent the 'circumambulatory' level of phase 'B', which the phase 'C' builders, being lazy creatures, adopted as their nearly ready-made ground-level. In the inter-pack, therefore, of façades 'B' and 'C' I incline to regard everything above that mud-brick level as true, artificial, infilling pack of phase 'C', and anything down to the 'A' 1·35 m. below, as representing a phase 'B' accumulation, possibly of the building period of the 'B' façade, which was finally capped by mud brick, either itself a surface or the foundation for paving slabs. And it seems relevant, moreover, that in both the south-west and the east soundings the scarcity of sherds in the postulated 'B' levels in both stresses their connexion without hope of explanation for their absence.

Phase 'C'. At the east corner we have a welcome datum for the phase 'C' circumambulatory level in the stone pavement, seen in pl. IV, 2, with the 'late' inscriptions nos. 49 and 50 *in situ* at R.L. 797·25 m. At the south-west end this level is confirmed, almost exactly, by the shrines and altars built outside the phase 'C' façade at ±R.L. 797·75 m., the difference being 'compensated' by the tilt of the building.

We may summarize the interrelationships in the table opposite, but stressing its approximate character and disclaiming the rigidity inevitable when fixed figures are invoked.

COMPARISON OF SHERDS IN RELATION TO BUILDING PHASE LEVELS. The immediately striking fact in the table is that in the east corner pit the finer red-coated wares occur, without exception, from 795·20 m. downwards, associated with coarser reddish pottery, in what I have, on deductions drawn solely from the cross-evidence of levels, assigned to phase 'A' deposits. Together these wares include two fragments out of sixteen which can be reconstructed with certainty (pl. LVI, 1, 3), and three other rims which, though small, give a clue as to their form when reinforced by subsequent experience of tomb pottery.

Metres R.L.	Phase	Test pit outside east corner	Phase	Test pit between south-west inter-façades 'B' and 'C'
799·35	Post-'C' ac-cumulation.		'C' inter-façade infilling.	Pavement of 'C' façade.
799·15				(Top of phase 'A' coping on buried façade.)
798·95	" "		" "	Rim fragment, fine red-coated bowl, pl. LVI, 4. Sherd ditto.
798·85	" "		" "	Fine red-coated sherd.
798·75	" "	(Top of phase 'A' coping.)¹	" "	Rim fragment, fine red-coated bowl, pl. LVI, 2 (798·70).
798·55	" "		" "	Rim fragment, fine red-coated bowl, pl. LVI, 6. Pedestal base.
798·35	" "		" "	Two sherds, fine red-coated ware.
797·85	" "		" "	Three sherds, rough brown-grey ware.
797·75	" "		" "	('C' and post-'C' level outside 'C' façade.)
797·65	" "		" "	Limestone placage brick, pl. XXI, 2.
797·35	" "		" "	Rim fragment, coarse red ware, pl. LVI, 5.
797·25	'C'	Paving with 'late' inscriptions 49, 50		
797·17	"	Paving bedding.		
797·12			'B'	Circumambulatory level? Mud bricks 796·90 to 796·65.
796·90	'B'	Circumambulatory level? Top of dirty sand deposit.	"	(Footing of 'C' façade.) Mud bricks.
796·00	"	Black 'stone ware' sherd.	"	
795·95	"	Rim fragment, rough red, pl. LVI, 10.	"	
795·85	"		"	Nine coarse red-brown to grey sherds. One rim fragment.
795·65	"		'A'	Circumambulatory level? Masonry chips. Six coarse red sherds; one fine red sherd.
795·40	"	Dark grey-brown gritty sherd.		
795·35	"			Masonry chips. Limestone brick. Fourteen rough sherds. One pedestal base. Obsidian core and chip.
	"			
795·25	'A'	Circumambulatory level? Two rough red rim fragments, pl. LVI, 7, 9. One fine red-coated rim,		Ochre. Two rough red sherds.
795·20	"	pl. LVI, 11. One fine red-coated		Ten rough red to brown-grey sherds.
795·15		bowl fragment, pl. LVI, 1. Seven red		
795·12		sherds (2 fine), 4 rim fragments.		
795·05				Obsidian chip.
795·00				
794·90		Fine red-coated bowl fragment, pl. LVI, 3.		Temple 'B' façade footing.
794·85				Four discoloured brown-grey sherds.
794·60–·30		Temple 'A' stone footing.		

¹ Items in brackets represent building levels not on the line of vertical section.

The next striking fact is that these red slip-coated wares in the *lowest* levels of the east sounding recur, with one exception only, in the *upper*, post-'B' phase deposits in the south-west inter-façade. They demonstrate neatly what we already knew—that it is, down to a certain level, an artificial fill; but they add the information that the sandy soil which composed it was taken from a source which already contained the broken crockery of phase 'A', as well, very likely, as later ingredients.

To speculate where that deposit lay is more amusing than profitable. But one might venture the guess that the dredgings from the large artificial depression—the Qarif ibn Thabit[1]—at the base of the slope overlooked by the south-west front of the Temple might be a likely source. To this day its upthrow deposits are littered with weathered sherds.

The interrelationship of these reconstructed sherds from the two test pits is seen in pl. LVI, 1–11. The shallow open bowl, pl. LVI, 1, from the east corner, with its smoothly modelled curve, compares with the bowl, in similar fabric, from the south-west fill, pl. LVI, 4. The more angular, almost carinated, basal curve of the open bowl, pl. LVI, 2, from the façade pack, compares as closely as hand-made individuality allows with pl. LVI, 3, from the old 'A' level at the east corner. The bowl, pl. LVI, 6, is unique in its plastic band, but otherwise falls into the same family of bowls in fabric and style.

A brief comparison of this Temple pottery with that in the tombs is given on pp. 129–31.

THE STEPS. (*a*) SOUTH-EASTERN APPROACH. These are seen in pl. VI, 1. Though it is certain that these steps belong to building phase 'C', we have on the plan of phase 'B' (pl. LXXIII, 2) indicated that earlier (and probably longer) steps pre-existed at this point. The ground-level served by this flight, more than its architecture, proclaims its 'C' date: R.L. 798 m., the level of the bottom step, and $\pm 797\cdot70$ m. the ground-level served by it (sandy here and difficult to fix exactly), are the levels of the extramural buildings below the south-west front (i.e. $\pm 797\cdot75$ m.).

The steps, therefore, since a rise of only $1\cdot25$ m. has to be met, are shallow and number only six, the bottom three arranged in an expanding rectangle. We did not destroy the structure, and the view that it is solid overlapping masonry is based on superficial observation. The paving slabs of the visible treads are well graded in size and neatly jointed with gypsum plaster, and it is likely that the patchwork area of the broad third step has lost its surface layer.

In pl. VI, 1, the position of these steps is seen in relation to the south corner of the phase 'A' front (marked 'A'). In the later periods we know for certain that a stone-skirted mud and plaster wall was built upon the same line. Consequently those entering the Temple by the south-east steps were debarred from access to the old main body of the building except by way of the outer forecourt, area VIII, and the inner forecourt, area IV: from thence a right-angle turn through the central passage-entrance III*a* led straight into it.

This paved forecourt, VIII, is seen in pl. VII, 2, with its orthostatic slabs of dado defining the edge of the plaster and mud wall they protected. These slabs are sandstone, tooled on their exposed faces and sides, rough dressed on the back. Their thickness, ± 8 cm., is fairly constant, but other dimensions vary (examples: 25 cm. square; 45×23 cm.) and on the evidence of the set in the photograph it is certain that two slabs were superposed if necessary to give an even height (one of the upper row is seen, fallen

---

[1] Cf. pp. 14, 59.

in the debris behind). The maximum standing height was thus 47–50 cm. The length of this surviving dado was 1·60 m., and it had been coated with fine white stucco and fixed in gypsum mortar.

The layout of partition walling became obscure on the inner (north-west) side of outer forecourt VIII. There were traces of a cross-wall of similar stone-faced plaster through which a square stone drain, centre left in pl. VII, 2, led off (?) water from the higher internal level of forecourt IV (40–50 cm.). Had that cross-wall been continuous, as the line of plaster powder suggested, further entry would have been blocked and the south-east steps useless. There must have been a doorway or open arch here with a raised sill of mud plaster which, in pulverous decay, gave the effect of a continuous line of wall. This and one other to be mentioned are the only places where we have introduced presumptive reconstruction on to the plans.[1]

THE STEPS. (b) WEST APPROACH. These are seen in pl. VI, 2. The flight as it stands[2] must be assigned to phase 'C' for two reasons: (1) its ground-level, R.L. 797·75 m., is that of the south-east steps; (2) it is, as seen in the photograph, a structural part of the 'C' additions to the south-west front, sunk between a re-entrant of the latest façade and a 4-m. prolongation of parapet walling, tacked on, with a vertical joint, and with no attempt to equalize the courses, to the old north-west retaining wall, from its west angle.

This parapet, built apparently either to screen the steps from outside, or, if formerly roofed, to carry a mud and plaster wall, is 2·20 m. (thirteen courses) high and rests on a projecting rubble footing at ±R.L. 797·25 m., i.e. 35 cm. higher than the ground course of the 'C' façade. It ends, for some obscure reason, half a metre short of the façade line. Traces of whitewash on it were unmistakable.

The steps numbered seven, with a possible eighth at the bottom. But the treads are unequally spaced and others may be missing. They were worn smooth and the edges rounded by wear. Two mutilated inscriptions, no. 16 and 16a,[3] both archaic, were built into it. No. 16, on the edge of a slab, had been cut at both ends to fit its position in the ramped end of the staircase wall. No. 16a, also cut down, formed the 'riser' of the fifth step from the top (see pls. VI, 2; LXIV, 4, for both in situ).

Area X on our plans includes both these steps and the narrow, well-paved passageway at the top. This led, as far as could be made out from the exiguous evidence of plaster powder and a solitary dado slab, through an opening between the north-west retaining wall and a partition wall into the old main platform of the building. Alternately our conjectural reconstruction of a continuous partition wall between this area X and the inner forecourt IV is probably susceptible of the explanation proposed for the similar plaster wall across area VIII at the head of the south-east steps; i.e. that a plaster arch or doorway, now impossible to detect, led worshippers from the head of these steps to the right and into the Temple via area IV. This, which seems the more likely, has the added advantage of equilibrium with the opposite side.

[1] Cf. p. 42.
[2] As stated, p. 31, we have no evidence for the 'B' phase building plan at this west corner.
[3] Cf. Ryckmans, p. 165.

In the paving of this passage of doubtful exit was inset inscription no. 9, the only one found which is probably in its original place (pl. VII, 1). Even so the evidence was not quite straightforward, for a stepped arrangement of the paving flags beyond covers its decorative top border and half the top line, giving the impression of the raw edge of a partly dismembered paving superposed on that in which inscription no. 9 was embedded.[1]

The slab is seen *in situ* in pl. VII, 1, with this superposed paving partly over it. The inscription, when fully exposed, measured 1·08 m. long by 0·45 m. wide, and was considerably worn. Its six lines of text (pl. LXIII, 4) tell of its dedication to Sīn by 'Iḫtašam.[2] A heading of four stylized bucrania[3] in low relief (pl. LXIII, 4 detail), inside a sunk panel 14·5 cm. deep, is edged top and bottom by dentils. The inscription is placed in Professor Ryckmans's category of 'caractères évoluant vers un type plus récent'.

PLASTER WALL AND DRAIN BETWEEN AREAS X AND IV–V (pl. XVIII, 2). The probability that this apparently continuous length of wall had, in reality, an arch or other entrance through it has been noted. It prolongs the west re-entrant of the south-west façade, and its width, defined by the single skirting slabs still standing on either side, is exactly similar. Traces of the white plaster of which it was made are seen in the plate, on the right, as well as the stone drain which passed through it and discharged unfeelingly on the third step from the top. This drain is made of a single limestone slab, 84 cm. long by 26 cm. wide (pl. XXII, 3). A square shallow catchment basin, 20 by 17 cm. level with the paving in area V, and like it embedded in plaster, connects with a longitudinal gutter 10 cm. wide. There appears to have been no gargoyle head and the end is simply squared off. It is difficult to believe the contrivance efficacious as a storm-water conduit. More likely it served to lead off the scourings of blood sacrifices in area V.

ROUGH CROSS-WALL ON WEST STEPS. This later blocking of the steps is described on p. 54.

CHARCOAL AND CHARRED WOOD. While clearing the Temple platform of its sand overburden,[4] patches of charcoal or charred wood were found on floor-level at the following points:

Area I. A patch yielding several baskets full from the pavement-stripped area; lying on pebble-and-plaster bedding.

Area III*a*. A charred wooden pole, ±3 cm. in diameter, lay pressed against the base of the 'threshold' slab no. 5. There seems some reason to think from this and the

---

[1] The recurring question of the possible existence of a post-'C' phase in the Temple is dealt with, pp. 59–60.

[2] Cf. Ryckmans, p. 162.

[3] Cf. p. 161. The curious rendering of the bull's horns, with five projections which make them resemble hands (two ears, two horns, and a symbol on the crest), is closely paralleled in a bucranium in *Corpus Inscriptionum Semiticarum*, pars 4,

fasc. i, no. 37. Hands seem to be represented fingers downwards, cf. ibid. 76, 79.

[4] The overburden itself had plentiful charcoal in it, showing that shepherds and bedouin squatted on the ruin-mounds at all periods. Perhaps traditions of its sanctity survived for centuries after the institution of Islam.

position of charcoal under the partitions that wood was used to provide a sort of scaffolding or cradle for better cohesion of the stucco. A considerable quantity of charred wood was found also in the debris of wall III*b*.

Area VIII. North angle of dado (seen in pl. VII, 2). A quantity of charcoal visible in the plate poured out through a ruined joint from the plaster backing.

Area X–V. Under the plaster partition wall lay a quantity of large charcoal. There is no need from these occurrences to assume a conflagration.[1] The charcoal has not been identified.

---

[1] The processes governing the carbonization of vegetable matter are obscure.

VI. THE TEMPLE'S EXTRAMURAL BUILDINGS

GENERAL. On three sides the Temple retaining walls, for want of time, were freed in narrow trenches only.[1] Outside the south-west front alone was a wider and more repaying area examined. From the nature of the debris cleared in these cuttings it is certain that buildings of some kind clustered close to the podium. The pavings shown below the north-east and south-east walls on the plan, pl. LXXIII, 3, indicate how close: for they began along its edges, and in the foreground of pl. IV, 2 (the east corner), raised stone slabs and an open drain below a rubble wall seem to have been surmounted by mud-brick and plaster buildings, the debris of which, mixed with sand, composes everywhere, apparently, the bulk of these peripheral deposits.

Lines of rubble blocks breaking the sand, some way down and parallel to the slope on the north-west side, gave hints also of possible terracing around the outskirts of the Temple area.

In these clearances a number of inscribed slabs, enumerated separately, was found. The wider south-west clearance tells us that Temple masonry, plain and inscribed, was freely used in the extramural buildings; but it is useless to speculate why many of the slabs, lying loose in the fill below the walls, should have been where we found them.[2]

THE APSIDAL SHRINES. A view along these extramural buildings from west to south is seen in pls. X, 2; XI, 1; and their relation to the Temple's 'false' façade 'C' in pl. V, 2. The most striking and undamaged features, in much that remains conjectural, were the shrines.[3]

A linked pair, virtually intact, lay outside the west corner. These may be conveniently designated *Shrines 31 and 29* because of the reused inscriptions of those numbers built into them. Vestigial ruins indicate the probability of three more.

Shrine No. 31 (plan, pl. LXXIV). The apsidal shape which characterizes the pair is best seen in pl. X, 1 and 2. This shrine, differentiated from its twin only by the missing capstone of its 'altar', measured very irregularly ± 2 m. on its longer, apsidal-ended axis and 1·90 m. transversely. It consisted of a bench of mortared freestone slabs, originally three courses high, which edged the shallow earth-sunk pit, in the centre of which stood the 'altar'. The pedestal of this was a rectangle, exactly parallel with the surrounding bench, made of four rubble boulders filled in and supported by interspaced flat slabs. The capstone was not found. These slabs and those which formed the bench are, judged by their chisel-tooled upper faces and sides, and rough hammer-dressed under faces, certainly Temple paving or skirting. They included inscription no. 31

[1] Pl. IV, 1, 2, shows these narrow clearances, with deposits to the left and right respectively.

[2] Fallen from superstructural outer walls of the platform is one of many possibilities, natural or human. But below the south-west façade they seem to have been deliberately brought.

[3] The term is used as a convenience combined with a probability; likewise the term 'altar'. The function of these unique structures is discussed, p. 60.

(centre foreground in pl. x, 2), a slab, 25×40 cm., cut down at the bottom and in worn condition as befits its archaic origin (pl. LXVI, 2).[1] The clearance of the earth inside the structure to a depth of ± 30 cm. produced dark greasy soil containing charcoal and sheep or goat bones in considerable numbers, including two mandibles, unburnt.

Shrine No. 29 (pl. XI, 1, 2). The general character and axial measurements are similar, but the south-south-eastern curve, where formerly it seems to have linked with a third shrine, now almost completely vanished, was less compact. The 'altar' slab, firmly mortared on to its pedestal of boulders, consisted of a large rectangular free-stone block, $\pm 80 \times 50$ cm. in surface area, which had been unequally split along its cleavage plane to about half its former thickness. In pl. XI, 2, under a lens, part of an inscription, no. 29b,[2] bisected by this cleavage, may be seen set upside down. The tooling of this stone is of the coarse pecked variety displayed on the large copings of the 'false' front of phase 'B'.

The levels of the two 'altars' must have been about equal. A difference of 10 cm. between the pedestal top in shrine 31 and the altar slab in shrine 29 is likely to represent the thickness of the missing capstone.

An old inscription, no. 29 ($\pm 46 \times 20.5$ cm.), seen *in situ* in pl. x, 1, was incorporated in the stone bench in the same relative position as no. 31. But whereas no. 31 lay exposed in the top course, no. 29 was in the second and consequently completely hidden until stripped (as seen in the photograph) of its overlying course. The same applies to inscription no. 41 (38×29 cm.) beside it, which lay not only beneath the top layer but in the inner row linking the two shrines. Both belong to the archaic group.[3] It is unlikely that these dedicatory tablets held any meaning for those who reused them.

Dark soil similar to that in shrine no. 31 filled the interior of the structure, but contained nothing but sheep-bone fragments in considerable quantity.

It may be noted in plan, pl. LXXIV, that the apsidal axis of neither shrine is true to the Temple's south-west 'orientation'.

Contiguous Shrine (plan, pl. LXXIV). There seems little doubt that a third linked shrine existed to the south-east, of which only a central stone and four slabs of the north-east arc (one marked 798·2) formed part, as well perhaps as a single stone (beside inscription 27) nearly equidistant on the south-west. All these lay at the level of R.L. 798·20 to ·40 m., and the confusion of masonry beyond, below the Temple stairway, which appears in plan to truncate that segment of this postulated shrine lies a clear metre lower. The awkward position of such a shrine in relation to the Temple steps will be an item to consider in the general survey of relative dating.[4]

Shrine No. 30 (plan, pl. LXXIV). Leaving aside for the moment all structures other than these shrines of curious type, we come, near the middle of the south-west façade wall, to a large 'altar' base, about 65×60 cm. square, set, as was the Temple, on the diagonal to the cardinal points. It lacks its top course and/or capstone, which would raise its existing

---

[1] Cf. Ryckmans, p. 169.
[2] Cf. Ryckmans, p. 169.

[3] Cf. Ryckmans, pp. 169, 171, and pls. LXVI, 1, LXVII, 1.
[4] Cf. pp. 59–60.

level of R.L. 797·80 m. on to a plane with the others. Its surrounding stone bench, including inscription no. 30,[1] is too ruinous to recognize without the aid of shrines 29 and 31; but in their light it seems reasonable to claim it as another. In pl. xi, 1, the circular effect of its ruins is seen beyond the altar table of shrine 29; and in pl. v, 2, inscription no. 30, mutilated and upside down, marks its edge. One stone of the altar base, which differed from those in shrines 29 and 31 in being of squared masonry slabs neatly mortared and jointed into a cube, had the solitary letter ∏ cut on the edge. A dirty, rather sticky, sandy deposit underlay this shrine, containing nothing of note except charcoal particles and sheep or goat remains, unburnt, in considerable quantity distributed throughout.

Shrine No. 20 (plan, pl. LXXIV). This centres upon a large altar, best seen in pl. v, 2, (in relation to the façade and other extramural buildings), and pl. xii, 1, placed outside the re-entrant south corner of the Temple front. The ruinous masonry lying at its base on three sides was impossible to reconstruct into an ordered plan; but it included two well-defined votive offering groups *in situ*, nos. 20 and 23, and perhaps a third, no. 27.

A detailed plan of the complex is given on pl. LXXVII. The altar, in exact alinement with the Temple façade, lies only 70 cm. from it. It measured 1·20 × 0·90 m. The long axis conforms to that of the Temple. There is doubt as to the elevation. On the north-east side, seen in pl. xii, 1, a total height of 85 cm. was certain, but is based on one top slab in position only. The rest is conjectural; and though, on the whole, dubious evidence favours a flat top, it is also possible that it was stepped down the south-west side to a slightly lower level (not exceeding 15 to 20 cm.).

The structure consists of a central core of carelessly assembled masonry, faced on the outside with freestone slabs of different sizes set on edge, and, where visible under a thick layer of white stucco, carefully jointed. These slabs, as elsewhere in the extramural buildings, are pre-existing masonry reused, for the north-west side included an inscription, no. 20, up-ended and partly effaced by plaster coating.[2]

VOTIVE GROUPS AROUND BASE OF ALTAR 20. i. *Group No. 20* (general plan, pl. LXXIV; detailed plan, pl. LXXVII; views, pls. v, 2; xii, 2). In the cross-section, pl. LXXVI, the ground level of the altar, laid without prepared foundations, is seen to be R.L. 797·65 m., or only ± 10 cm. below the pavement and votive groups around it.

Group 20, on the altar's north-east side, filled and overlapped the narrow space separating altar and Temple 'C' façade.[3]

The nucleus of the group was an oblong limestone brick, filched from the Temple and reshaped crudely at one end into a human head (pl. xiv). This object was mortared upright, back to the Temple wall, facing the altar (marked 'A' in pl. xii, 2) inside a neat semicircular kerb of moulded fine white plaster which projected 24 cm. from the wall (gypsum 64·8 per cent.; cf. analyses, pp. 61–2, no. 5). The kerb,

---

[1] Cf. Ryckmans, p. 169.
[2] Cf. Ryckmans, p. 166. Under a lens this may be seen in the altar side, pl. xii, 1.

[3] Which made photography from several angles impossible, and difficult from all.

rounded in section and about 3 cm. high, had been built up in a piece from a thick layer of similar plaster which covered its inside floor and held the image in upright stance. The whole affair stood upon a limestone flag. Within this kerbed floor, vertical before the image, was placed a hollow, splay-based pedestal (C in pl. XII, 2) broken from a long-stemmed pottery goblet of tomb type I, in coarse red-brown porous ware. By the side, on the kerb rim, was a four-legged limestone incense-burner or miniature fire-altar (BI in pl. XII, 2). This overlay a rough pottery saucer (pl. LIV, 9). Two similar incense-burners (B2 and 3 in pl. XII, 2) lay, the one on its side, partly beneath a stucco-covered slab (fallen from the altar top?); the other still upright opposite the image, below the altar wall.[1] The connexion of these three paving slabs with the group is doubtful, as is also that of a fourth lying loose on the far side of the image in pl. XII, 2. Two were still bound together by a coating of plaster, well seen in this plate, which strengthens the theory of altar stones displaced. But a glance at the plan, pl. LXXVII, shows that they cannot have fallen by natural agency on to the place where we found them, and their significance must remain enigmatical. The same doubt besets the arrangement of stones on the other—south-south-east—side of the image. There, a pair of pavings, laid end to end on edge, fenced off as it were the group on that side from contact with things beyond, all but filling the space between the façade wall and the altar. One paving had tipped over on to the plaster kerb. They seemed designed to separate the image group from a flat limestone offering dish in two compartments, and a large pottery saucer with it. These objects are seen *in situ* with the stone 'fender' in pl. XIII, 2.

ii. *Group No. 23* (pl. XIII, 1). This remarkable votive group, seen in the picture vertically from above[2] and from the side in pl. XIII, 3, was backed against the north-west side of the altar. It consisted of a conical baetyl in limestone with flattened base (pl. XV, 1), roughly hammer-dressed all over to shape. This stone stood erect, held in plaster and wedged by two sherds, inside a rectangular 'fender' or edging of six paving slabs laid flat about 20 cm. from the altar side. This 'fender' projected beyond the west angle of the altar and turned the corner partly enclosing a third votive group, no. 27. An unintelligible slab, seen in the plate (pl. XIII, 1) beyond the baetyl, had been placed in the interior space, otherwise empty save for the aniconic stone, on that side.

The whole affair seems originally to have been plastered over, leaving only the upper two-thirds of the baetyl visible. The photograph shows a piece of plaster (left corner), and smears of it are visible on the fender.

Outside the stone edging, symmetrically placed on the north-east side, was an inscribed slab, no. 23, about 27 × 16 × 6·5 cm. in size, thickly covered with plaster (pl. LXXVII). Upon this, firmly embedded, was a rough pottery saucer 14 cm. in diameter, made from a low broken pedestal base. Two deeply cut letters on the slab, ϑℏ, in one corner, coated over by the stucco, had formed a wet-cast upon the plaster-covered base of the saucer when lifted from its bedding. The rest of the slab is covered by graffito scratchings,

[1] Details of these and other votive objects will be found on pp. 48–51.

[2] The picture was taken standing on the altar and looking down.

invisible until the stone was cleaned (pl. LXV, 3).[1] The two formally cut letters are classed as archaic;[2] the graffiti are certainly later work, probably not of one period, and contemporaneity with the votive group is uncertain. The efficacy of a dedicatory graffito may not have been impaired by covering it over with stucco; and the hand which scratched the (supposed) latest of them beside an earlier graffito on the blank space of an archaic stone may have been the one which laid the pottery offering dish upon it in honour of the baetyl (pl. XIII, 1, and inset). On the other hand, either or both graffiti may belong to phase 'C' of Temple development, assuming that to be slightly earlier than the extramural buildings,[3] and the slab here reused simply for convenience. It is one of several of which the upper faces have been artificially reddened.[4]

iii. *Group Nos. 27–8*. On the third, south-west, side of the altar overlooking the west corner lay another group of objects piled on top of each other. The upper layer is shown in plan, pl. LXXVII, and, still imperfectly cleared, in pl. XII, 1. The flat stone edging, or fender, outside the baetyl group on the altar's north-west side returned at the west corner. It included inscription no. 28, 35·5 × 18 cm., bearing a dedication to Sīn (pl. LXV, 5). Though mutilated by a recutting of top and bottom, it belongs to the 'recent' group,[5] and suggests that an even later period is concerned in these altar groups. It is considerably worn. Beside this, standing on a plain flag, was a square, four-legged incense-burner (pls. XVI, 2; XVII, 1); a bronze ear-ring (resembling pl. XLV, 12); and two scraps of corroded bronze. The plain paving slab, 797·99, firmly set like the others in plaster, was bordered by a slab set on edge. Beyond, in the same picture (pl. XII, 1), is seen a massive, curiously reshaped stone, the purpose of which escaped imagination. Two rough pottery saucers formed from low broken pedestals rubbed down (as pl. LIV, 9) completed the upper layers.

The lower was exposed on lifting inscription 28, and the corner-stone 797·86. Beneath these were five very fragmentary inscribed slabs, nos. 27a to 27d and 27f. These acted as a plastered bed for the upper stones. Alongside, beneath the incense-burner slab, lay the interesting decorated piece, no. 27e (pls. XVIII, 1; XXI, 2). The inscribed fragments have no special interest. No. 27a, the largest, 30 × 18 cm., had a red-stained surface; 27d is a Sīn dedication; 27f a rude graffito-covered slab of 24 × 12 cm. (pl. LXV, 4).[6] The pillar-like stone, 27e, lay on its side, placed there, not fallen.

The fourth, south-east side produced nothing. The soil below the groups was greasy and darkened by disintegrated charcoal, it contained nothing but sheep or goat bones in some quantity. The altar and its subsoil were not disturbed.

TYPOLOGY OF THE VOTIVE GROUPS. *Baetyl and Image. Baetyl No. 23* (pl. XV, 1). Greyish hard limestone cone, height 30 cm., base 17 cm. Rough dressed on both sides, no trace of colour or plaster coating.

---

[1] Cf. Ryckmans, p. 167. [2] Ibid., p. 167. [5] Cf. Ryckmans, pp. 169, 176. This slab is seen *in situ*
[3] Cf. pp. 59–60 on the relative dating discussion. in pl. XII, 1.
[4] Cf. p. 157. [6] Cf. Ryckmans, p. 168.

Image No. 20 (pl. xiv). White limestone brick with impurities. Total height 20·5 cm., width 8·4 cm., depth 4 cm. Head and neck 5·5 cm. high. The brick belongs to the class of smooth chiselled slabs abundant in the Temple masonry, such as is shown in pl. xxi, 3 (A3.VI), the dimensions of which are nearly the same. The back of the image, however, though rough to stand hidden against a wall, is not humped for actual engagement. The human features, without ears, are vaguely indicated on a bullet head; and hair, or a hanging head-dress, not infrequent on Yemen statuettes, falls to the shoulders.

Neither of these stones has any near parallel in published material from south Arabia. They are, in their respective ways, more primitive than anything yet found there. The significance of the association of the true baetyl—the aniconic representation of the god— with the semi-anthropomorphic form of image, more probably representative of the votary,[1] in a similar ritual setting, is perhaps impossible to disentangle without additional evidence from comparable groups *in situ*. But whatever their function in the Moon cult at this comparatively late date, they fill typological gaps in the hitherto extant south Arabian baetyl-cum-funerary or votive stele series. No. 23 supplies a late survival of the primeval monolith,[2] which started on its long career towards anthropomorphic development elsewhere, thousands of years earlier, first by the addition of a human mask, incised, without or with the outline of a head;[3] then gradually by the disengagement of the head and a trend towards the rectangular stele form, as in no. 20; passing on to simple representation of limbs, as in the arms and breasts on the otherwise rough stone, pl. xv, 2, which I bought at Hureidha from a local bedouin; and ending in the fully sculptured, grotesque figures in the round, inscribed or not with their owner's names, which, though never yet found *in situ*, come from the Yemen and probably the western Hadhramaut in large numbers.[4]

The fact that all these types crowd together in south Arabia without temporal sequence, and in any case compressed into the space of a few hundred years before and after the Christian era, stresses the backwash of other people's ideas which characterizes the material culture of the ancient kingdoms of the peninsula terminus.

Incense-Burners. Four from the votive groups and one from Temple area VI may be considered together.

A3.20.B1 (pls. xvi, 5; xvii, 4; *in situ* pl. xii, 2, B1). Height ± 11·7 cm. Diam. of trough opening 8·8 × 8·5 cm. Sandy limestone. Rectangular, with four short square legs. Shallow

---

[1] This is Dr. Ditlef Nielsen's view. With great diffidence I suggest it may be a cult image.

[2] Paralleled by the well-known Dushara symbols at Petra, be they the Sun symbol described by G. and A. Horsfield, *The Quarterly of the Department of Antiquities in Palestine*, vols. vii and viii. 3, or the pre-existing Moon symbol advocated by Dr. Nielsen, 'The Site of the Biblical Mount Sinai', *Journ. Palestine Oriental Society*, vol. vii, fasc. 4, 1927, pp. 187–208.

[3] Sir Leonard Woolley has recently unearthed at Atchana, similarly beside a rectangular shrine or altar, a rough conical baetyl, with vaguely indicated features (*c.* 1500–1400 B.C.).

He suggests it marks a transition between the primitive aniconic form and its impending anthropomorphic development. *Illustrated London News*, Dec. 2, 1939, p. 833, figs. 7, 8.

[4] Publications are numerous, and include G. Ryckmans, *Le Muséon*, tomes xl (1927), xlv (1932), xlviii (1935), lii (1939); C. Rathjens and H. von Wissmann, *Südarabien Reise*, Band ii, 1932, pp. 187–98; D. Nielsen, *Handbuch der altarabischen Altertumskunde*, Band i, 1927, pp. 163–5. Artistic detail is discussed by Léon Legrain, *American Journal of Archaeology*, vol. xxxviii. 3, 1934.

trough. The surface is perished, but bears on the rim traces of a red stain. Tool marks indicate a chisel about 6 mm. wide.

A3.20.B2 (pls. xvi, 1; xvii, 3; *in situ* pl. xii, 2, B2). Height ± 14 cm. Diam. of trough opening 9·7× 7·8 cm. Sandy limestone. Rectangular, with four squared legs about 4·7 cm. long, not completely freed in the centre. The sides show zones of freehand cross-hatching, four bands on two sides; three on the other two. Diagonal double cross on each leg. The incisions are thin and shallow and were scratched after the whole surface had been stained with haematite.

A3.20.B3 (pls. xvi, 4; xvii, 5; *in situ* pl. xii, 2, B3). Height ± 9·1 cm. Diam. of trough opening 9·4× 9·1 cm. Sandy limestone. Rectangular, with four square stump legs. The sides bear two bands of cross-hatching, separated by a plain zone. Diagonal double cross on each leg. The surface is haematite-reddened.

A3.27 (pls. xvi, 2; xvii, 1). Height ± 11·2 cm. Diam. of trough opening 9·3× 9·0 cm. Sandy limestone. Rectangular, with four square stump legs. The reddened sides incised as B3.

A3, area VI (pls. xvi, 3; xvii, 2; cf. p. 36). Height 5·2 cm. Diam. of trough opening 6·8× 6·7 cm. Sandy limestone. Rectangular, but unlike the extramural group the breadth is more than the height. Four square legs. Sides decorated, after haematite-staining, with two bands of vertical incisions, probably to imitate ribbing or fluting (cf. crystalline limestone saucers in tomb, p. 133).

The three burners in group 20 contained traces of a greasy, dark-brown substance. Dr. Plenderleith has verified this as resin giving off a fragrant odour on heating; but the amount was insufficient to identify specifically.

Dimensions and general form correspond to the rectangular four-legged limestone series of incense-burners from the Yemen, published[1] and unpublished.[2] But they differ from any I can trace in their zonal decoration of cross-hatchings; and in the reddening, which, as far as I am aware, has not before been reported. They did not appear in the Hureidha tombs (cf. p. 153).

Limestone Offering Dish. A3.20 (pl. xviii, 4; *in situ* pl. xiii, 2). A white slab, 38 × 27 cm., ± 5 to 6·5 cm. thick; chisel-tooled on upper face, rough finished below. In origin a Temple paving or skirting slab. The upper face is divided into two compartments sunk to different depths; a shallow basin, 3·3 cm. deep, 22 × 14 cm.; and a small sunk trough, 5 cm. deep, 13 × 9 cm., transverse in long axis to the other. These are edged and separated by a flat border ± 4·3 cm. wide, with diagonal chisel marks of about 15–20°, which represent the original surface of the slab. The compartments are probably for food and liquid respectively.

Columnar Decorative Stone. A3.27 (pls. xviii, 1; xxi, 2). White limestone. Height ± 27·5 cm. Width 8·3 cm. The back is humped to a maximum depth of ± 8·3 cm. It is probable, therefore, that the object was intended to stand erect as a decorative pilaster—perhaps one of a series—embedded in a stucco-faced altar or other wall. Although the decoration has not been exactly recorded before, its components are well known. The six transverse bars are paralleled in decorative work on the column capitals at Ḥugga,[3] at Gherâs[4]

---

[1] Cf. Ryckmans, *Le Muséon*, tome xlviii, 1935, pls. iii, iv, with inscribed sides. The names of perfumes are sometimes given.

[2] Peabody Museum, Harvard University collection, Kaiky Muncherjee collection, Aden, &c. Mr. Ingrams informed me that a specimen had been found in a grave near Terim.

[3] C. Rathjens and H. von Wissmann, *Südarabien Reise*, Band ii, 1932, p. 48, fig. 14.

[4] Ibid., p. 131, fig. 88.

(associated in both places with dentils; the bars, however, number four), at Haz[1] (six bars). The two narrow vertical sunk panels occur also in the Yemen, though in a more elaborate, double or triple recessed form with the single transverse fillet of our specimen multiplied.[2] But an even nearer parallel is provided by reliefs seen and sketched by Glaser at Medinet el Kuffâr.[3]

Though it may be tempting to see in the central panel in low relief a baetyllic symbol,[4] I am more disposed to think the whole thing may represent a simplified version of the conventionalized façade of a dwelling,[5] apposite if our assumption of its intended position in an altar side is correct. This, however, could be substantiated only if we had the flanking pilasters. In any case there is little doubt that the object still had some sacred significance for those who laid it below the altar.

Other architectural reliefs, not *in situ*, are noticed on p. 56.

Pottery. It is notable that the earthenware in the votive groups is, with one possible exception, broken material re-used. *A3.20 C* (pl. XII, 2 *in situ*). Far the most interesting was the hollow pedestal of a long-stemmed goblet, set upright before the human-headed image. It was in rough red-brown porous ware, 9 cm. high, and in proportions, curve, and material resembled the tall pedestal of the tomb goblet A5.X[1], shown on pl. XLIX, 1. It stood loose (not plastered on to the bedding) on its splayed base. The upper end had been irregularly broken below the join with the goblet bowl, thus producing a hollow cylinder. In such a position its function as a libation vessel cannot be doubted, and goes far to confirm the sanctity of the image. Jars with perforated bases, or hollow cylinders, for earth libations, are usual in the fertility rites of the primary civilizations of antiquity,[6] and here we have doubtless a debased survival.

The remaining specimens are saucers made from broken low pedestal bases inverted. *A3.20D*, *E*. Specimen D, 9·9 cm. in diameter (pl. LIV, 9), when contrasted, upside down, with the pedestals of tomb-classes II and III, is seen to be dissimilar.[7] Specimen E (pl. XIII, 2 *in situ* and pl. LIII, 8) is 22·7 cm. in diameter.[8]

A3.23D (pl. XIII, 1 *in situ*). .Embedded in plaster on inscribed slab no. 23 (cf. p. 47); diameter 14 cm.

A3.27 (plan, pl. LXXVII). Two similar, 13 and 8·8 cm. in diameter respectively.

OTHER FEATURES OF THE EXTRAMURAL BUILDINGS. *The Stone Dado* (plan, pl. LXXIV, 35, pl. XI, 1). Not the least remarkable of the extramural structures was a continuous line of stone skirting or dado which ran parallel to the Temple façade, 2·50 m. from it, delimiting, as it were, some of the shrines and altars described. Over 6 m. of these

---

[1] Ibid., p. 108, fig. 63.

[2] D. Nielsen, *Handbuch der altarabischen Altertumskunde*, Band i, 1927, p. 157, fig. 44, showing a relief in the Ottoman Museum at Istanbul of a conventionalized palace façade.

[3] Ibid., p. 158, fig. 46.

[4] I am so much struck by the resemblance of these transverse-bar motifs, and the much-debated nature of the object found on coins of Bostra, that I have, on pl. XXI. 2´ added a rough sketch of the latter from G. F. Hill's *Catalogue of* *Greek Coins of Arabia, Mesopotamia, and Persia*, pl. IV. 2. In the discussion, p. xxvii, he follows Dussaud in interpreting it as three baetyls, but admits that the transverse bars are obscure.

[5] Cf. p. 151.

[6] M. Schaeffer has recently extended, at Ugarit, the accepted significance, by invoking, very pleasingly, the misunderstood legend of the Danaids. Cf. *Antiquity*, Sept. 1939, pp. 358–9.

[7] Cf. pp. 118–120.   [8] Cf. p. 131.

up-ended freestone slabs still stood erect; their former prolongation past shrine 20 may be inferred from the fact that the votive group 27 stopped short on its line. At the opposite, west, end the skirting finished on a right-angle outward turn of the last slab, planned evidently in relation to the free-standing monolith no. 17 (cf. below) and its attendant masonry. This returned skirting slab is seen in the upper inset, pl. xi, behind the monolith, an inset enlarged from the general view, pl. xi, 1.

Sixteen slabs were used in this length of skirting; all but three were of single height; three were doubled, giving a maximum height of 75 cm. All had been stucco-faced; and though all, with their diagonal, smooth tooling may be attributed to riflings from the older Temple, one (no. 35) at least proclaimed its ancestry more vociferously with the inscription ⟨𝌆⟩ set upside down. This skirting was backed by rubble, and without question represents the facing of a wall. Cross-section, pl. lxxvi, shows that its level corresponds with those of the shrines; but the backing rubble wall goes down an additional metre, and it seems that a pre-existing rubble wall, the footing of which suggests contemporaneity with façade 'B', was refaced by the 'Shrine-builders' at their own higher surface-level. Drift sand had banked behind to a depth and thickness which made it impossible to explore the far side in the time available.

The Monolithic Shrine, No. 17 (plan, pl. lxxiv; pl. xi, upper inset). The plan is confused. A circular monolith, 50 cm. high, with flat top, 22 cm. in diameter, stood erect amid four displaced paving slabs at the south angle of the skirting wall. These pavings include inscriptions nos. 21 and 22. No. 21 (max. 27 × 21 cm., but cut down and subsequently broken, pl. lxv, 1) is archaic.[1] No. 22 (34 × 27 cm., pl. xix, 1) bears the engraving of a right foot, with graffiti on and outside it, which are evidently contemporary work; another graffito with a monogram in the corner may be later.[2] On the other side of the monolith, a pair of large re-used stones inscribed on their edges, nos. 17a and 17b, formed a kind of bench or altar slabs. This pair is seen *in situ* in pl. lxii, 4, with the edge of the monolith to the right. No. 17a (56 × 36 × 8 cm.), an incomplete Sīn invocation, is archaic.[3] No. 17b, inscribed on three sides, two of them hidden (80 × 36 × 9 cm.), is complete, and invokes the Moon God under the Sabaean name Almaqah.[4] This text also is archaic.

Cobble Paving, and Superposed Structures. So far, in describing the extramural buildings no questions of stratigraphy have arisen; their levels have remained constant the whole length, from shrine 31 on the west to shrine 20 on the south; their pavings vary between R.L. 797·90 and 797·70 m.; their raised benches or altar-tops between R.L. 798·50 and 798·10 m.

At the base of the western ascent, the lowest step of which, at R.L. 797·90 m., serves a ground-level of R.L. 797·70 m. (the same as that of the south-east stairs), vertical clearance showed a single buried step of mixed boulders and freestone, 45 cm. vertically below the extramural buildings; and this led to a cobbled pavement, 70 cm. broad, at R.L. 797·10 m., unlike anything found elsewhere.

---

[1] Cf. Ryckmans, p. 166. [2] Ibid., p. 166. [3] Ibid., p. 165. [4] Ibid., p. 165.

This cobbled path and step seem likely to be all that survives of the approach and stairs to the Temple in phase 'B'. The level tallies reasonably with the 'B' circumambulatory, postulated on other considerations.[1] This fragment of evidence failed to develop further. The footing of the rubble wall 35, which appeared to be its contemporary, presumes a former right-angle turn of the cobbled way at the junction of the two.

Vertically above these older remnants lay 1-metre deposits of dirty sand with charcoal, scraps of bronze, comminuted sherds, and sheep bones. Upon this the 'Shrine-builders' had set yet another altar-like structure (plan, pl. LXXIV, 798·4) of two large freestone slabs superimposed and mortared upon each other, 60 × 40 cm. in surface area. In clearing its peripheral deposits the following were found:

Pl. XX, 3. A3.10. A bull-headed libation table in banded sandstone; horns more pronounced, in spite of abrasion, than in no. 7 (pl. XVIII, 3). The shallow trough drains out along a channel between the horns.[2] The table lay, as though placed intentionally, beside the altar.

Pl. LXIV, 3. A3.14*a*. Graffiti on a freestone slab, 23·6 × 17·5 cm.[3]

Pl. XIX, 2. A3.14*b*. Graffiti and engraving of a camel on a freestone slab, 23 × 18 cm.[4]

Pl. XXI, 1. A3.46. An interesting narrow freestone brick, 46·7 × 7·5 cm. by 6·1 deep, cut from a five-line inscription and rendered unintelligible.[5]

None of these three inscriptions is shown in plan as they were loose in the deposit and not *in situ*. But they are probably connected with this 'altar' and may be contemporary work.

Stone Frame (plan LXXIV, no. 32; pls. V, 2; X, 2). This is a puzzle. It consisted of a three-sided limestone frame, cut from a single block, and set upright, like a trilithon, resting on the corner of a great freestone slab. Its vertical members, ± 5 cm. thick, were 38 cm. high; its horizontal span 59 cm. The three facing surfaces and the lateral edges on one side were smoothly tooled: on the other side these edges were raw and suggested a contact-surface. One end of the frame, as seen in pl. V, 2, abutted against masonry, and when disengaged was found to bear an inscription to Ḥawl.[6] The original function of this frame in the Temple edifice must remain conjectural.[7] As re-used by the 'Shrine-makers' it is not less enigmatical.[8]

Drain (plan, pl. LXXIV). A 3-metre length of open stone-kerbed gutter is seen in the plan amongst the south-west extramural buildings. Its average level, ± R.L. 797·86 m., is that of the 'Shrine-builders'' pavement. It consisted of slabs laid on edge, about 8 cm.

---

[1] Cf. p. 38; mud bricks outside 'B' façade at R. L. 796·90 m.

[2] Dimensions were overlooked; the photographic scale gives an approximation. The table was left in the care of the Mansab at Hureidha.

[3] Cf. Ryckmans, pp. 163, 164.

[4] Ibid., p. 164.

[5] Ibid., p. 172.

[6] Ibid., p. 170.

[7] A window frame, or light opening in a roof, are possible.

The fragment of a stone grille at Petra is perhaps the nearest parallel (Horsfield, *Quarterly of the Department of Antiquities in Palestine*, vol. vii, pl. LVII). See also C. Rathjens and H. von Wissmann, *Südarabien Reise*, Band ii, fig. 26.

[8] A pseudo-trilithic cult is very possible in a land of stone-cults. Bertram Thomas has noted 'trilith-monuments' in Dhufar (*Geog. Journ.*, Jan. 1931, pl. 4) and Mr. Ingrams something similar in the Sei'ar country (*Journ. Royal Central Asian Soc.*, July 1936, p. 400) and at Al 'Abr (*Geog. Journ.*, Oct. 1938, p. 306).

apart, after the manner of the drain in pl. LXII, 2. Disintegrated mud brick was recognized in a section vertically below the gutter and formed presumably its bed. The drain was incomplete at both ends, and its purpose is obscure. The slope was northwards.

Inscribed Slabs in South-West Extramural Deposits. Six inscriptions, additional to those reused in the extramural structures, were found in clearance of the south-west front. Though not recognizably *in situ* there seems little doubt they were brought there by the 'Shrine-builders'.

A3.11 (pl. LXIV, 2). 23 × 16 cm. Archaic. Mutilated. A Hawl dedication.
A3.12 (pl. LXIV, 5). 22 × 21 cm. Archaic. Mutilated. A Sīn dedication.
A3.13 (facsimile). 17 × 17 cm. — Mutilated. A Sīn dedication.
A3.15 and 18 (facsimiles). Both very worn and fragmentary.
A3.33 (pl. LXVI, 4). 23 × 19 cm. Recent but mutilated and worn. A Sīn dedication. Reddened surface.

The series seems to confirm the evidence of the inscriptions re-used in the altars and shrines—namely that the 'Shrine-builders' cut no monumental inscriptions but collected and perhaps reshaped older ones ranging from archaic to recent. At most some graffiti might be attributed to them.

Test Pits below South-West Extramural Buildings. Three soundings were made below the shrine building level without results. The deepest went down to R.L. 796·10 m. and should, consequently, have exposed traces of external structures of the 'B' phase had others besides the cobbled pavement at R.L. 797·10 m. existed. The soil was contaminated sand, containing some charcoal, sheep bones in number, and a handful of uninformative small sherds. Just below the 'Shrine-builders'' level a broken schist 'pencil' (pl. LXI, 3) was found; and 90 cm. lower a bronze nail of the type pl. XLV, 17, but with a 1-cm. shank.

Rough Cross-Wall on the West Steps (pl. VI, 2, foreground). On the sixth step from the top had been carelessly piled a loose breastwork, 29 cm. high, of Temple flagstones set uniformly upside down. This improvization, attributable to a period (that of the 'Shrine-builders'?) when access to the Temple, on this side at any rate, was no longer needed, included inscriptions nos. 24, 25, 26.

No. 24 (pl. LXV, 2), 29 × 21 cm., is archaic;[1] no. 25 (facsimile) on the lateral edge of a stone, indeterminate;[2] no. 26 (pl. LXIV, 1), 48 × 31 cm., which forms part of no. 10 found separately below, 'recent'.[3] It is Bin'il's building record. The face is reddened.

INSCRIPTIONS FROM PERIPHERAL TRENCHES BESIDE THE STYLOBATE. (*a*) *North-West Wall.* This side was without pavement to act as a level check: it was singularly devoid, too, of objects compared with the others. Trenching, however, went down to little over R.L. 797 m., and the levels of the objects indicate they reached their positions in 'C' or post-'C' times. No. 38 (pl. LXVII, 3), at R.L. 798·90 m., is an interesting slab reshaped to a narrow brick, 28·8 × 9·8 × 7·20 cm., which has the unusual feature of an informal inscription on its edge as well as a formally inscribed surface.[4] No. 53 (pl. LXVIII, 3),

[1] Cf. Ryckmans, p. 167.　　[2] Ibid., p. 168.　　[3] Ibid., p. 162.　　[4] Ibid., p. 171.

$39 \times 16 \times 7 \cdot 5$ cm., from the extreme north end, is archaic. No. 39 (pl. XXII, 2), at R.L. $797 \cdot 79$ m., is a heavy offering table in limestone, $40 \times 20 \times 10$ cm. The catchment basin is very small and the outlet channel short.

(b) *North-East Wall.* Pl. IV, 2, shows the circumambulatory pavement at R.L. $797 \cdot 25$ m. with the workman standing on it. The superimposed deposits in section to the right are therefore post 'C'. Four inscriptions came from above this pavement, not *in situ.*

No. 34 (pl. LXVI, 3), cut on the edge of a slab, $54 \times 24 \times 10$ cm., is archaic.
No. 36 (pl. LXV, 6), also archaic and worn, is mutilated and measures 31×17 cm.
No. 47 (pl. LXVII, 6), 42×20 cm., in bad condition and mutilated, is also archaic.
No. 48 (facsimile) was a mutilated, small fragment.[1]

(c) *South-East Wall and East Corner.* These slabs fall into four groups: (1) From the south re-entrant, between altar 20 and the south-east steps. (2) From above the un-paved circumambulatory beside the south-east wall. (3) From the lower pavement beside the south-east wall at the eastern end. (4) From the upper pavement, above 3.

1. No. 37 (pl. LXVI, 5). Mutilated, 28×19 cm. It is classed palaeographically by itself in the transitional group linking the latest archaic type to the more recent series.[2] Its level, R.L. $797 \cdot 52$ m., is about 20 cm. below the 'Shrine-makers'' structures. It was not *in situ.*

2. No. 51 (pl. LXVIII, 2). Loose in fill at about R.L. 798 m. Mutilated left margin, 31×20 cm., a Sīn dedication of the latest group.[3]

No. 52 (pl. LXVIII, 5). Loose in fill at about R.L. 798 m. Size $28 \times 16 \times 7 \cdot 5$ cm. Archaic.[4]

3. The pavement shown on pl. IV, 2, gives important evidence concerning the later occupation sequence. It lies at a constant level of R.L. $797 \cdot 25$ cm. and was still firmly set in its plaster bedding 8 cm. thick: in places surface plaster covered its stones. At the east end its flags included inscriptions 49 and 50; the underlying deposits have been described.[5]

No. 49 (pls. LXVIII, 1; LXII, 3 *in situ*). An ornate slab, 44 cm. square along its rectangular margin, but drastically recut the other two sides into steps, anterior to its use as a paving. The surrounding flags were neatly patchworked to fit close (see plan, pl. LXXIII, 3). The inscription is reddened. A panel of six stylized bucrania, in low relief, are under-edged with a worn border of dentils (compare no. 9, pl. LXIII, 4). A stellar cult object forms the panel centre.[6] The inscription is classed amongst the latest of the series.[7] The slab was thickly coated with plaster, seen in an early stage of removal in pl. LXII, 3.

No. 50 (pl. LXVIII, 4). Beside no. 49, separated by a plaster-filled crack, 9 cm. wide; the slab, 48×14 cm., was mutilated; covered by the same plaster spread as 49. Also a 'late' inscription.[8]

4. On p. 44 were mentioned raised masonry and a drain (seen in the foreground of pl. IV, 2; detail, pl. LXII, 2) connected with peripheral buildings at the east corner, uncleared. This drain, a stone-edged but uncovered gutter, 55 cm. long, similar in its construction of slabs laid in mortar end to end on edge to that in the south-west extra-

---

[1] Ibid., pp. 170, 172.
[2] Ibid., pp. 170, 176.
[3] Ibid., p. 173.
[4] Ibid., p. 173.
[5] Cf. pp. 24–25.
[6] Crescent and star are a frequent motif on altars. Cf., *inter alia, Handbuch der altarabischen Altertumskunde,* figs. 64, 65; Dr. Nielsen tells me that the significance of the connecting pillar is not understood.
[7] Cf. Ryckmans, p. 172.
[8] Ibid., p. 173.

mural buildings, discharged on to a patch of paving, superposed on that described in (3), and 10 cm. vertically above it. Dirty soil with charcoal and broken plaster separated the two. This upper paving at R.L. 797·35 m. included three re-used inscriptions.

No. 42 (pl. LXVII, 2). 21·5 × 15 cm., mutilated, is archaic.[1]

No. 43 (facsimile), very fragmentary and worn; phonetically archaic.[2]

No. 44 (pl. LXVII, 4), 30 × 15 cm., a worn boustrophedon, probably mutilated, and classed as one of the oldest inscriptions found.[3]

Loose, *on* this upper pavement level, lay inscription

no. 54 (pl. LXVIII, 6). A broken disk about 38 cm. in diameter and 5 cm. thick. About a third broken off. The purpose of this form is not apparent.[4]

ARCHITECTURAL FEATURES AND RELIEFS NOT FOUND *in situ*. Apart from the decorative pilaster from the votive group 27 (pl. XVIII, 1), the only other reliefs found are shown on pl. XX, 2 and 3. The first three are typical of seven others. Eight lay on the sandy knoll which covered the Temple and its adjacent buildings; consequently they were wind-worn and the detail impossible to recognize (as in pl. XX, 2, third example). The central stone, however, equally of no positional value, established the scale design of the vertical bar in low relief. The tenth specimen, wind-worn, was found in the infilling above the floor of room B in farmstead A4, purloined presumably from elsewhere.

Pl. XX, 3, shows a different form of the same design cut on square panels.[5] The slabs vary from 3 to 6 cm. in thickness and the under sides are flat, not gibbous.

Pl. XXII, 1, shows a solitary length of cornice found in the superficial drift at the south corner. To which phase it belongs must be in doubt, but assuming it lay where it fell, phase 'C' seems indicated. It is only 49 cm. long by 25 cm. wide; the metopic band, irregularly spaced, is truncated horizontally, and the slab must have been the upper member of a double row.

---

[1] Cf. Ryckmans, p. 171.
[3] Ibid., p. 171.
[5] Were it not for this last, the scaled bars might be inter-

[2] Ibid., p. 171.
[4] Ibid., p. 173.

preted as stylized and symbolic palm trunks. A complete representation of a date palm in *Corpus Inscriptionum Semiticarum*, pars 4, fasc. i, no. 72, has a scaled trunk.

VII. DISCUSSION AND CONCLUSIONS

PHASE 'A'. There is no evidence for a Temple earlier than the phase 'A' building. Consequently we assume that the twenty-one archaic inscriptions were contemporary with that earliest building, though none, owing to later reconditioning, was *in situ* primarily in it. The mode of their employment, as paving or as wall tablets, remains unknown in this as in later periods.

Dedication to the Moon God dates back to this earliest Temple; but the place-name, Maḏâbum, does not appear until phase 'C'. The south-west orientation, dissimilar to other recorded temples in south-west Arabia, conforms to the Babylonian ancestral practice of an axis diagonal to the cardinal points. The raised platform style of the building seems derived, probably indirectly, from the same area.[1] Its walls were topped with stones crudely imitating drafted and rustic copings (also not before recorded in this cultural area), an idea inspired by the architectural fashion of one or other of Arabia's northern neighbours, Persia, Phoenicia, and Greece.[2] Neither steps nor internal layout of this building have survived. The sherds, found in the lowest extra-mural levels, include two wares, a fine red slip-coated and a rough red, both present, in fabric and form, in the tombs.

PHASE 'B'. To this rather elusive phase, or to the next, may be assigned the five tapered stones on the old platform. Their function as plinths for wooden posts and brackets supporting the lath and daub roof of a small, free-standing edifice on the stylobate seems probable. Nevertheless, had chance preserved a single specimen only, a *maṣṣebah* would probably have been deduced. Deterioration in building standards marks the new façade, which has a mud-brick instead of a stone footing, and more irregular masonry, the mortar of which had perished. None the less the visible plan becomes more elaborate, owing to the subdivision of the south-west extension into little courts and forecourts. The extramural deposits believed to cover this phase contain singularly few sherds. These, which are rough, lack the red slip-coated finer ware,[3] but include a piece of black 'stone ware' so prominent in the tombs and found also in the Temple infilling.

PHASE 'C'. Though the layout of the south-west platform is further elaborated at this stage, the deterioration in building, instanced by the shallow façade, the absence of bond to the older structure, and the rougher, smaller masonry has increased still more. On the other hand, a certain skill in adapting the last additions to incorporate advantageously

---

[1] Let us say in a diffused sense 'west Asiatic', without instancing Babylonian, Assyrian, or Persian models.

[2] Dating back in Iran to early Achaemenian times, i.e. at Pasargadae, if built by Cyrus about 559–550 B.C. (cf. A. U. Pope, *Survey of Persian Art*, p. 349, pl. 81). In Greece the earliest Attic example appears in a Periclean wall at Eleusis of the 4th century. I am indebted to Prof. D. Robertson for the reference to W. Wrede's *Attische Mauern*, 1933, pp. 23 ff. and 53 ff.

[3] On so few specimens I am not at all disposed to think the ware dies out. The tombs give no such impression.

the 'B' extension stands to the architect's credit. Whereas in the oldest building the 'pillar area' seems to focus interest, in 'C' this centres in the chambers or courts approached by the two stairways; and in area VI we may perhaps discern a shrine, backed by the raised line of great ashlar blocks of the 'B' phase, which forms a low bench or table. It may not be accidental that the only incense-burner found in the building itself came from this place.

GENERAL. An hypothetical elevation of the Temple would be unprofitable at the present stage of imperfect evidence. But the surmised pillar bases and white stucco partitions imply roofing, at least over the central and south-west areas. The only place where posts supported this roof seems to have been the 'pillar area';[1] and if the southwest front also was covered in, as I think was certainly the case, the roof, lightly made probably of plastered twigs, was carried on the mud-cored stucco walls. In this connexion the short length of dentilled cornice (belonging probably to phase 'C'),[2] and the postulated window frame,[3] should be remembered.

The plan of our building could not readily be related to the primitive mosque type.

Whatever the length of time covered by the three buildings, there is no discontinuity. Additions were made as acts of piety and not to repair destruction or decay. We have no rule as yet to measure either the active duration of the edifice as a whole or its individual phases. The study of Hadhramautic inscriptions is still too little advanced for the epigraphic evolution of the Temple tablets to help us in an absolute chronology.

The accumulation of extramural deposits, amounting to about 3 m., which we have tentatively subdivided into their respective phases, is not more informative. At the east corner, undisturbed by façade rebuildings, these accumulating deposits amount, on our proposed scheme, to:

Phase 'A'. $\pm$0·95 m.
Phase 'B'. $\pm$1·65 m.
Phase 'C'. $\pm$0·63 m.

On this evidence 'B' would be the longest phase. But immeasurable factors governing soil accumulation discredit the reliability of such a reckoning, even were the premiss certain. For instance, should the external buildings at the northern end of the Temple be of 'B' date, which is unknown, the rate of extramural accumulation would inevitably increase.

We have been tempted to equate the archaic, including the archaic-transitional inscriptions, with phase 'A'; the later epigraphic series with phases 'B' and 'C'. This scheme assigns twenty-one archaic slabs and the single fully transitional inscription (no. 37) to 'A', thereby allotting a high proportion of the thirty-two which are classified palaeographically to the earliest Temple. If this is reasonably near the truth, then the

---

[1] Very little of the theoretic reconstruction proposed for the Temple of Ḥugga would be applicable, apart from the small flat-roofed open shrine shown in the centre which corresponds in a general way with what I visualize as the roofed edifice in our 'pillar area'. (Cf. Rathjens and Wissmann, *Südarabien Reise*, fig. 31.)

[2] Cf. p. 56.

[3] Cf. p. 53.

decline of tablet cutting kept retrogressive pace with the decline in building standards, culminating in the extramural 'Shrine-builders' who appear to have contributed nothing at all to lapidary craftsmanship, except perhaps some graffito scrawls on older stones.

The attribution of the 'evolved' series to both phases 'B' and 'C' rests on inscriptions nos. 4, 5, 8, and 9 *in situ* on the platform,[1] and to the two stones 49 and 50 *in situ* in the high-level 'circumambulatory' pavement.[2] Both these, though 'late' inscriptions, were re-utilized slabs, which, we suggest, were made in phase 'B', and cut down and re-used, as obsolete, for paving in phase 'C'.

No sherds can confidently be attributed to phase 'C'.

The reservoir and wells of Shu'bat, referred to in inscription no. 4, were not identified. The former is probably situated at the base of the Temple's north-eastern slopes, where the contours quickly touch the main irrigation levels of the master-channel (see cross-section, pl. LXXII). The Qarif ibn Thabit basin, though artificial, can hardly be the spot in the absence of masonry and cement. None the less it seems likely that the basin was made in relation to the Temple requirements or ritual; for at Gheibun near Meshḥed a similar depression was noticed at the south-west foot of ruins which seemed to be those of the temple. The wells of Shu'bat are unlikely to be in the valley plain.

The circumstances which ended the Temple buildings' active service are conjectural: the invocation of a convenient earthquake a commonplace. Yet there is some evidence for such an occurrence. Pl. VIII, 2, shows a breach in the north-west retaining wall, on a level with the northern pillar-base—a breach which has not only tilted the masonry from this point north-eastwards, but has also riven the interior boulder infilling, buckled the pavement in area II, and tilted the northern pillar-base. That the superstructures on the platform collapsed and were not renewed, and the Temple as such abandoned, is an attractive theory (more it is not) when viewed in the light of the extramural buildings.

THE EXTRAMURAL 'SHRINE-BUILDERS'. The question is, Were these shrines contemporary with the 'C' phase or later? That they are earlier than 'C' is ruled out by a glance at a cross-section. Their ground-level is that of the two flights of 'C'-phase steps. If, therefore, they are not contemporary with the 'C' façade, they were built soon enough after for the level not to have risen perceptibly by natural accumulation or drift sand.

For the following reasons we adopt the view of their immediately post-'C' date, without any appreciable break in continuity:

(*a*) The ruined circle of shrine 798·2, if reconstructed, partly blocks the bottom of the west steps.[3]

(*b*) That these west steps subsequently were unused is proved by the cross-wall roughly made of Temple masonry, which included, along with older stones, inscription no. 10 (26), one of the latest of the 'recent' group.[4]

[1] Cf. pp. 34, 42.   [2] Cf. pp. 24, 55.

[3] Cf. p. 45.

[4] Cf. p. 54. The site appears to have become buried in sand soon after its final abandonment. There is no ceramic evidence for early Arab occupation. Consequently it is difficult to attribute this cross-wall to people later than the 'Shrine-builders'.

(c) Inscription no. 28, also 'recent', was re-utilized in the votive group 27–8: it is both worn and recut top and bottom.

(d) The pair of 'late' inscriptions, 49 and 50, *in situ* in a pavement believed to be of 'C' phase, were themselves overlaid by an upper paving, 10 cm. higher, which included three archaic inscriptions. Inscription no. 54, loose at this level, is also 'recent'; its mutilation to discoidal shape is therefore still more recent and is probably the work of the 'Shrine-builders'.

These reasons combined weigh the evidence in favour of the post-'C' date of the extramural shrines. We conclude that the Temple building had been abandoned, perhaps as a result of earthquake damage, but that worship was maintained in shrines below the main façade, built with Temple masonry, including inscriptions ranging from archaic to recent. The culture seems finally degenerate. No inscriptions, apart perhaps from graffiti, can be attributed to the 'Shrine-makers'. Their votive pottery is second-hand rubbish consisting of pedestal and ring bases from the broken pots of their ancestors. Their images are of the most primitive possible type. Nevertheless, the shrines are no mere improvised heaps of stones. They conform to definite functional patterns, and the traditional building methods are maintained in them, at least to the extent of mortaring the re-used masonry with gypsum mortar, and applying white plaster liberally to the surfaces of altars and pavings.

The apsidal shrines seem to have no parallel. Their curious low surrounding benches suggest places of ceremonial feasting—sacrificial or funerary—which a dozen celebrants could share in each shrine round the central altar-table. But the triclinium, in the form in which we know it at Petra, bears no resemblance to them. They remain for the moment unique. That the 'altars' were the centres of animal sacrifices or feasts seems proved by the quantities of sheep or goat bones in the soil around them. None, however, bore drainage channels or hollows.

There is no dating evidence except the indirect guidance given by such sherds as can be confidently related to the tomb pottery, itself dependent in turn upon the dating of foreign imports found with it. The building style, obviously influenced as it is in a broad sense by foreign models, is insufficient in itself to provide a clue more exact than a vague post-sixth century B.C. date. The evidence of the building phases suggests a total duration of considerable length, prolonged further by the extramural shrine-building episode. That same span of time witnessed also an epigraphic development which it is difficult reasonably to compress into a very short period.

More precise estimates may be ventured on the tomb material; and to that rather more fruitful examination must be committed the interrelated question of the Temple chronology.

VIII. REPORT ON MORTARS AND PLASTERS FROM THE TEMPLE

FIVE samples, representative of the mortars and stuccos used in the Temple at different periods, were submitted for analysis to Dr. Plenderleith of the Research Laboratory, British Museum. A sample of the 'cement' from the Aden tanks, secured through the good offices of Miss Vivian Jameson, was added for comparison.

	Area II, Paving bedding NO. 1	*Bedding joint, SW. façade 'C'* NO. 2	*Plaster partition wall IIIb, phase 'B' or 'C'* NO. 3	*Rising joint, SE. retaining wall, phase 'A'* NO. 4	*Plaster kerb before image, A3.20* NO. 5	*Aden tanks* NO. 7
	%	%	%	%	%	%
Moisture . .	3·8	1·5	0·3	4·8	5·6	1·7
Gypsum (hydrated calcium sulphate) .	54·5[1]	69·4	8·6	58·1	64·8	1·3
Calcium carbonate .	12·7	7·0	89·8	9·3	19·1	85·5
Silica (sand, &c.) .	26·0	19·5	1·3	24·8	5·9	8·0
Oxides of iron and aluminium . .	3·0	1·5	trace	2·6	1·1	2·3
Organic matter .	nil	nil	nil	nil	nil	nil
Magnesium salts[2] .	trace	present	trace	trace	present	trace
Undetermined .	. .	1·1	. .	0·4	3·5	1·2
	100·0	100·0	100·0	100·0	100·0	100·0

Contents of Three Incense-Burners by Plaster Kerb, Sample 6. This appears to be mainly plaster covered with a thin layer of resin yielding a fragrant odour on heating. (Signed A. A. Moss.)

Research Laboratory,
British Museum, London, W.C.1.
16th June, 1939.

Dear Miss Caton Thompson,

Dr. Moss has now completed a very careful analysis of all specimens of plaster which you sent for examination, and has calculated the results to gypsum and calcium carbonate. As you will see, the samples vary in type very considerably.

You are no doubt aware of the problem presented in the case of calcium carbonate plasters dating to a period before there is any evidence of the practice of burning limestone. Plaster No. 7 might fall within this category; i.e. if the calcium carbonate in this case is not derived from the action of carbonic acid on what was originally a lime aggregate, then it is not clear what the binding medium actually was. A mixture of the

[1] The figure recorded here indicates the percentage of anhydrous calcium sulphate. This sample (no. 1) appears to consist very largely of a burnt or dehydrated gypsum, and in this respect differs from each of the other samples which contain gypsum in the hydrated form.

[2] Magnesium is present in all the samples, and, from a qualitative analysis, it appears that those portions of nos. 2 and 5 which are returned as 'undetermined', consist largely, if not entirely, of a magnesium salt, presumably magnesium carbonate.

ingredients in quantities given in the analysis would not afford a very effective plaster, because there does not appear to be enough binding medium present either in the form of gypsum or organic matter. A similar observation applies to no. 1, where the gypsum was found to be present in the form of anhydrous calcium sulphate, without binding properties.

The other samples, nos. 2, 3, 4 and 5 would give reasonably good plaster mixes on compounding from the analytical results obtained.

As regards Sample 6, there is not nearly enough resin present for purposes of identification, but it is clear, as you suggest, that a fragrant resin was used as incense.

Yours sincerely

H. J. PLENDERLEITH.

I asked Mr. A. Lucas, F.I.C., to comment upon these analyses in the light of his unrivalled knowledge of ancient Egyptian materials.

MEMORANDUM by MR. A. LUCAS

1. You ask which of the specimens are technically mortars and which plasters. The name depends upon the use to which the material is put and not upon its composition. In my opinion no. 1 is a mortar used as bedding; nos. 2 and 4 are mortars, and nos. 3, 5, and 7 are plasters.

2. No. 1 is very similar in composition to nos. 2 and 4, but in view of Dr. Moss's note it seems probable that the limestone slabs with which it was used were not soaked in water (as should have been done) before use, and so absorbed water and left insufficient for the full hydration of the gypsum.

3. Nos. 2 and 4, although poor qualities of gypsum mortar, are probably natural material, the high proportions of calcium carbonate and sand, in my opinion, being natural impurities and not artificial additions. Similar material is well known in Egypt, where it was employed anciently and where it is still used.

4. No. 3 is a very poor quality of gypsum plaster, containing, as it does, more than 90 per cent. of inert matter, but it may have been specially chosen on account of its white colour, a gypsum with a large proportion of calcium carbonate being more likely to be of a better (i.e. whiter) colour than the usual (natural) gypsum available.

5. No. 5 is of similar composition to the mortars nos. 2 and 4, both the calcium carbonate and the sand, in my opinion, being natural impurities.

6. Dr. Plenderleith's comment on no. 7 puts the matter very clearly. On this question see the notes by Professors Briscoe and Brammall, with Mr. Myers's comments, in *Cemeteries of Armant*, Mond and Myers, 1937, pp. 122–3. Also the remarks of Dr. Thomas, p. 142, and Dr. Janet Matthews, p. 126. Whether 1·3 per cent. of gypsum, with possibly a very small proportion of clay (the aluminium oxide might have been partly present as clay), would be sufficient to act as a binder, I am unable to say. Is it possible that gypsum has been dissolved out during the time it was in use as lining to a water tank?

General view from Temple platform looking NE. down Wadi ʿAmd

General view from Temple platform looking SW. up Wadi ʿAmd. Ponded depression and upthrow
of Qarif ibn Thabit in middle distance

South-east wall, phase 'A', looking towards SE. steps, phase 'C'

East corner of platform, phase 'A', looking north. Workman stands on phase 'C' pavement

Coping at north corner of phase 'A' platform, with boulder fill

South-west façade, phase 'C', looking south, with extramural buildings below. A. Stone frame. B. Inscription No. 30. C. Altar No. 20

South-east steps, phase 'C', masking façade and coping of phase 'A'

South-west steps, phase 'C'. Inscriptions Nos. 16 in parapet and 16a in step. Later
blocking wall at base

Inscription No. 9 *in situ*, stripped of later paving. In rear remains of white plaster partition wall

Forecourt area VIII at head of south-east steps with stone dado and (left) drain. All phase 'C'. Bedouin spectators to rear

Buckled paving in area II, with archaic offering table No. 7 and inscription No. 1.
To rear, conical plinths set in pebble and mortar bed

Breach in north-west wall

Pavement Phase C

FAÇADE C
FAÇADE B

Old Coping as pavement

The two 'false' façades of phases 'B' and 'C'. Foreground: shallow cross-wall with old copings re-used as pavings

South-west façade, phase 'A', stripped of 'false' façades and superposed pavings

Detail of stone dressing on coping of phase 'B'

Linked apsidal shrines 29 and 31 with inscriptions Nos. 29 and 41 *in situ* in bench

The same, looking along south-west façade, with other extramural buildings. Inscription
No. 31 in foreground

Extramural buildings looking south. 1. Altar stone of shrine 29. 2. Stone dado.
3. Monolithic shrine 17. 4. Base of altar 31

Apsidal shrine 29 showing mutilated inscription on altar slab

Above: Monolithic shrine 17
with inscribed bench

Below: Detail of mutilated
altar stone in shrine 29

Altar 20. Inscription No. 28 marked X

Votive group No. 20 *in situ*. A. Image. B. Incense-burners. C. Libation funnel

Baetyl group No. 23 *in situ* seen from above. Inset bottom right, the same seen from the side

Stone offering tray and pottery dish *in situ* in votive group No. 20

Votive group No. 20. Limestone image

Image, bought near Temple
(Height ± 25 cm.)

Baetyl No. 23
(Height 30 cm.)

Limestone incense-burners, with reddened sides
(Scale, No. 1, 14 cm. high)

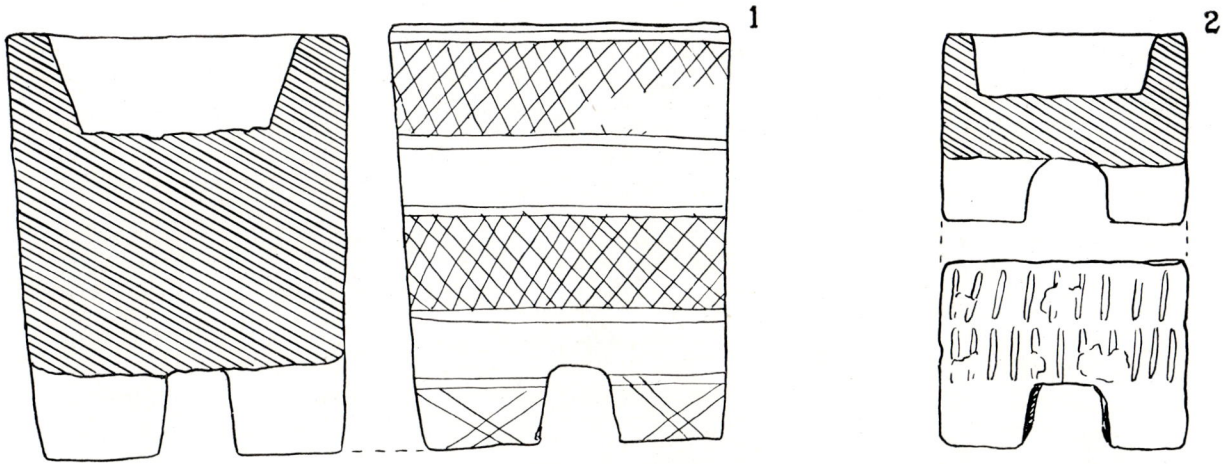

1

A3 27

2

A3.

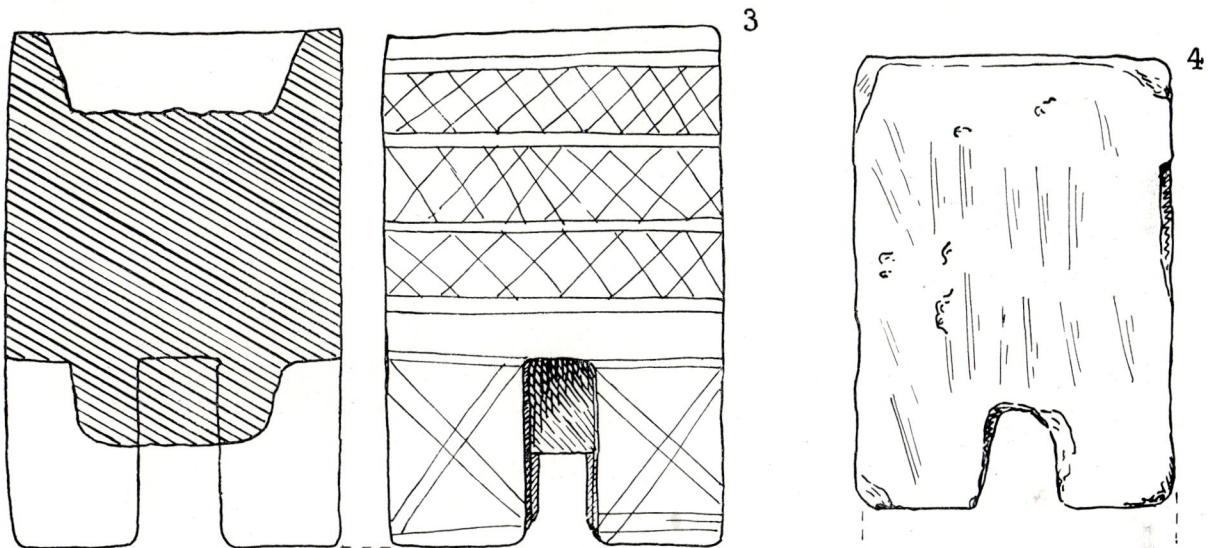

3

A3.20

4

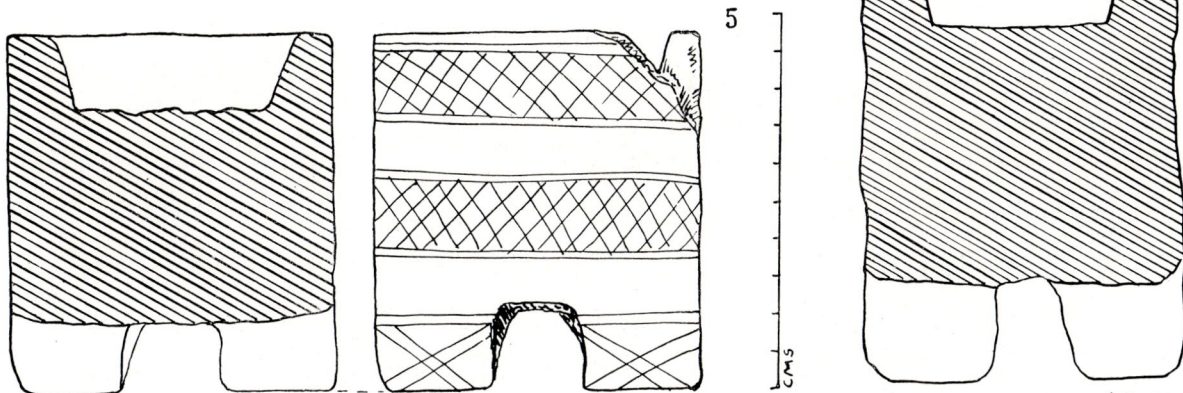

5

A3.20

A3.20

Limestone incense-burners
(Scale half natural size)

1. Columnar stone, possibly baetyllic
2. Drainage or offering stone in parapet wall of SW. steps
3. Bull-headed offering table, with archaic inscription No. 7 on three sides
4. Limestone offering tray, from votive group No. 20

Engraved slab No. 14*b*

Engraved slab No. 22

Channelled slab, probably part of a drain

Relief decoration on limestone bricks

Bull-headed offering table in banded sandstone, No. 10a   Decorated limestone fragment

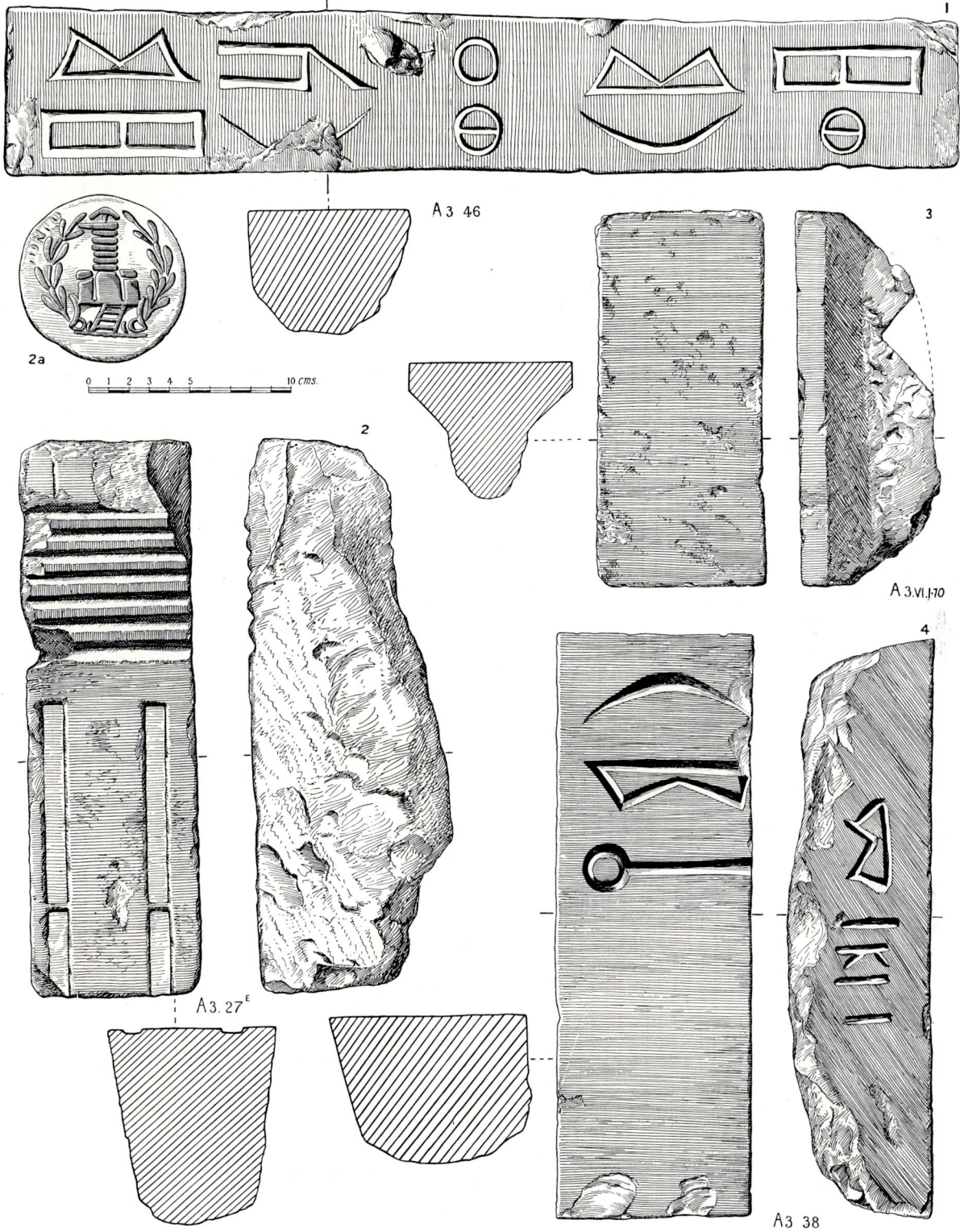

1. Inscription no. 46, showing refashioning. 2. Columnar stone, possibly baetyllic. 2a. Coin from Bostra.
3. Placage stone. 4. Inscription No. 38, showing refashioning

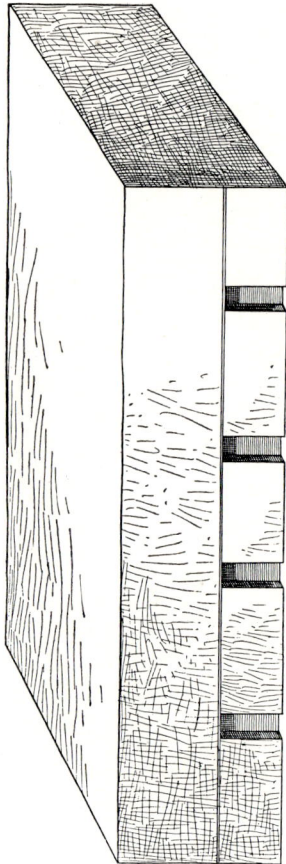

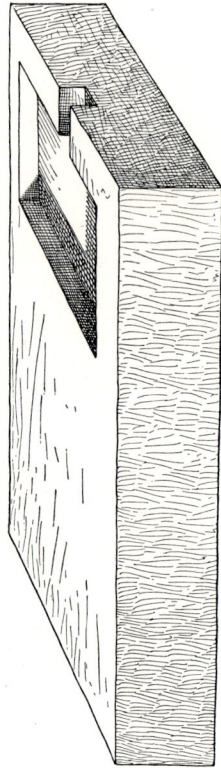

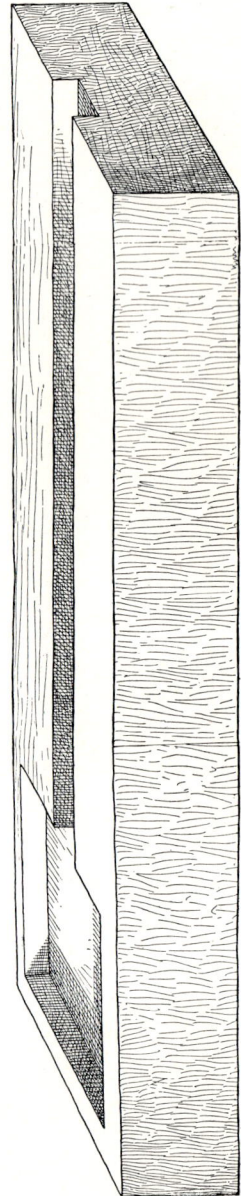

1. Cornice fragment. 2. Offering stone A3. 39. 3. Drainage or offering stone A3. 40

PART III

THE CAVE-TOMBS

IX. THE TOMBS. A5

SYNOPSIS. A number of tombs lie in the scree-slopes of the valley cliffs. Two on the northern side near the Temple were excavated. They are artificial caves cut back in the slope, gained by short inclined approaches carefully repacked with rubble. Tomb A5, unplundered, at least since the last interment, proved to be an ossuary containing fragmentary parts of forty-two hyper-dolichocephalic individuals, thirteen of which are reported upon by Dr. G. M. Morant. These remains and the attendant grave-goods were mainly gathered together in loose groups on the floor or a few centimetres above, with the exception of one more formal arrangement on a rock-cut bench.

The pottery, numbering eighty-seven more or less intact vessels, provides us with the long-awaited nucleus for a south Arabian *Corpus*, without which the archaeology of this region must be at a standstill. Its quality and that of the miscellaneous beads and other objects is not high and denotes a provincial community, though one drawing its ideas and its ornaments from more advanced civilizations.

Tomb A6, near by, similar in construction, but furnished with empty wall-niches, had been plundered anciently. It was not wholly excavated, but yielded the remains of three individuals only, reported on by Dr. Morant. Pots and beads are essentially similar to A5, but denote a more prosperous ownership. This impression is increased by a pair of seals, one of agate with a silver mount, a silver plaque-amulet, inscribed, and a variegated glass vase. In both tombs the beads, as a whole, show marked affinities with the eastern Mediterranean of about the sixth century B.C. (see Beck, p. 96). The seals witness contact with peripheral Achaemenian sources (see Frankfort, p. 103). The Hureidha sepulchres may, therefore, be dated to a somewhat later period, and in themselves probably cover a considerable length of time.

DISCOVERY AND POSITION. On January 18, 1938, when excavations in the Temple and the farmstead had run their abbreviated courses, I moved to the northern cliffs with twenty or more men and boys to test a cave-like opening in the lower scree-slope, reported by E. W. Gardner as a possible burial-place, and any other likely spot marked by old talus displacement, or the clue of sherd or bone (pl. 1, 5).

The rocky slopes of the lower scree, best seen in pl. XXIII, 1, consist of angular and sub-angular limestone and sandstone detritus, accumulated along the foot of the great rock wall of the valley sides. It is of no great thickness (see cross-section of the Wadi 'Amd, pl. LXXII), and the rather abrupt inclination from the valley floor is due to denuded beds of soft Cretaceous sandstone which project from beneath the limestone cliffs; upon these the talus rests. Below the loose rubble surface it has acquired the rock-like consistency of breccia, and dates back in age to palaeolithic times and probably before (see p. 4). A horizontal section, then, into the slope, meets first a varying thickness of hard, cemented scree; and next, beds of buff to red or purple current-bedded sandstone which require little effort to remove.

The ancient south Arabians took advantage of this geological provision. Through the resistant breccia they hacked a downward sloping passage, and in the yielding sandstone carved out sepulchral chambers for their dead. Pl. XXIII, 3, the entrance to tomb A6, shows the workman standing on the sandstone level behind the rough *dromos* through the overlying breccia. The extreme care with which the entrance and approach had been eventually repacked will be apparent from pl. XXIII, 2; this repeats the same view as pl. XXIII, 3, but was taken before our reopening of the tomb—a reopening some two thousand years or more after its last closure. It was of interest to find that re-cementation of the loosened talus-fill had in that period hardly begun.

TOMB TYPES. Here then is the general principle of these tombs in this particular geological setting; the floor and walls will be of soft sandstone, the roof of rough brecciated scree, supported on an 8-metre span by nothing but its own rock-like cohesion.

Variations of this arrangement, however, occur even in the same locality. In places bluffs and small cliffs of sandstone outcrop through the talus (such a bluff cuts the middle sky-line in pl. XXIII, 1); and frequently in these may be seen the now fully exposed openings of former chambers with raised recesses. Weathering of the soft rock, or human depredation, have reduced these to mere cross-sections of their former selves, recalling the gaping holes of façades at Petra in sandstone of similar geological (Nubian) age. In such a bluff, to the immediate west of A6, we noted many such exposed and wrecked chambers opening north with niches similar to those in pl. XXVI, 2, cut in the crumbling rock. The possibility that these had been dwellings rather than tombs should be borne in mind, for they are analogous, in a more primitive way, to the Petra dwellings,[1] and if such be the case would dispose of the difficulty of accounting for a concurrent practice of burial in sunk and carefully hidden chambers, such as A5 and A6, and of interment in exposed rock faces, the entrances to which could never have been successfully disguised. But though on insufficient evidence I am inclined to think the *primary* purpose as dwellings of some of these shelters very possible, many of those seen at Hureidha had been unquestionably sepulchral, for human bones lay on the ground outside.

The less derelict of these shelters, as well as the breccia-roofed hypogeia, are still used as dwellings by the valley-settled bedouins in the Wadi 'Amd, or as goat and sheep-folds, or storerooms for millet-straw and fodder. The interior of one, occupied by the family of our tent-guard, a sedentary bedouin of the Nahd tribe,[2] is shown in pl. XXVI, 2. Like A5 and A6 it is a circular chamber cut in soft sandstone below ground-level, and in the walls are seven niches, about 1·80 m. long by 0·50 m. high, on which the household pots were kept. Near by, in the face of a low sandstone ridge, are the openings of other chambers, emptied of their former contents and used by the same bedouin as outhouses. Probably the small antiquities we got from him, such as the limestone statuette, pl. XV, 2, and the limestone tripod saucer, pl. LVII, 5, came from these rifled tombs, or from the spoil-heaps of older plunderings. Our clearance of tomb A5 has now doubtless added another dwelling to this local housing-estate.

But though many of the more obvious and accessible tombs have in this way been destroyed, quantities of others must exist intact, well hidden beneath their carefully restored overload of scree; and the southern cliffs in the Hureidha district give evidence of being as well provided in this respect as the northern.

[1] So admirably examined and published by G. and A. Horsfield in *The Quarterly of the Department of Antiquities in Palestine*, vols. vii, viii, no. 3.

[2] Travellers in the Hadhramaut have reported several valleys where tribesmen still permanently dwell in caves. But whether these are natural or artificial, tombs or dwellings of an earlier era, has not been stated.

Apart from the excavation of the two Hureidha sepulchres, there appears to be no published record of ancient tomb types in the Aden Protectorate, though unhappily a certain amount of unsystematic, unrecorded digging by visitors has occurred in the past year or two.[1] To Mr. L. P. Kirwan, archaeologist to the Sudan Government, I am indebted for the information that at Baihan his observations, without excavation, suggested that the ancient cemetery, extensively plundered of recent years, consists of slab-covered pits lined with plastered masonry leading to stone-blocked end chambers.[2] Some of these, said local report, had contained multiple burials, and offerings had been found in the entrance pits.

So far as I know, the circular stone cairn-tombs (Arabic 'rudum')—if tombs they be, they furnished no conclusive proof—found by Mr. Philby at Ruwaik and 'Alam Abayadh,[3] 120 km. or so north-west of Shabwa, have not been recorded in the Hadhramaut. The occurrence of such structures is not to be expected in the valleys for topographical reasons; but examples may possibly be found eventually on the remoter plateaux. Until plans and sections of these stripped chambered cairns are published, a comparison with the gravel-covered tumuli of Bahrein,[4] though inviting, must be superficial, however possible a connexion may appear to be. It is, therefore, premature to speculate that the underground circular sepulchres of Wadi 'Amd with their inclined approach may be the valley equivalent or prototype[5] of the circular, above-ground, stone-chambered tumulus with entrance shaft (as at Bahrein),[6] or the circular stone-chambered cairn with entrance passage, but without tumulus (as at Ruwaik, etc.), both of which may be variant forms resulting from geological terrain. Cave tombs of our type are of course abundant in Palestine.

APPEARANCE OF TOMB A5. It was evident that the beginnings of an attempt to open out tomb A5 had been made not long before our arrival. Dislodged rubble lay in heaps outside the still almost entirely blocked entrance; and it was from this that the bifacial chert knife (pl. LXI, 8) had been ostensibly picked up by the neighbouring bedouin cave-dweller on the occasion of E. W. Gardner's exploratory visit (see p. 144). Whether he had put it there in anticipation of the visit (having found it elsewhere) or whether it was an unpremeditated find (in which case it belongs probably to the tomb period, lost perhaps in the replacement of the scree over the entrance) can never now be certain. It has no parallel in our other chert tools from the Hadhramaut, but seems typologically at home with the polished jade axes.

The tomb entrance was still blocked, fortunately, by rubble to within 40–60 cm. of its roof. Through this slit, at the level of one's feet, one could peer down into the interior,

---

[1] Notably at Shabwa and Baihan.

[2] See also F. Stark, *Journ. Royal Asiatic Society*, July 1939, p. 185.

[3] *The Land of Sheba*, pp. 371, 373–5.

[4] *Bahrein*, by Ernest Mackay, 1929.

[5] I am not suggesting that the Hureidha cave tombs themselves are the older: on the contrary they are, archaeologically, of no great antiquity. The age of the Ruwaik structures is completely unknown: that of the Bahrein tumuli still speculative (Dr. Mackay tentatively proposes 1500–1000 B.C. This dating I suspect to be too high; be that as it may, the Bahrein pottery resembles nothing found in the Hureidha tombs).

[6] This, however, is by no means a constant feature in those tombs.

which in its penumbral darkness looked mysterious and large, and see that the deposits, carpeted with goat droppings, filled it to within 70 cm., or less in places, of the unevenly vaulted natural roof.

The entrance, seen after clearance in pl. xxiv, 1, was irregularly oval, and had a maximum width of 2·90 m. and a south-east outlook (132°). No attempt had been, or could have been, made to cut a shapely opening in the intractable breccia, nor were the rugged walls faced in any way with masonry or plaster. In puzzling relationship to the entrance was an alinement of boulders, 9·30 m. long, set horizontally across the scree slope well back behind it, outspanning the cave below by about 1·50 m. at both sides (seen in the cross-section, pl. lxxx). It seemed suggestive of an attempt to demarcate the entrance, but the purpose remains speculative. A foreman's indication of the eventual space of the cavity to be hollowed below? A guide line to mark the position of the sepulchre in perpetuity, when weathering had obscured the repacked entrance?

The first task was to free the approach and entrance. The result is shown in the section, pl. lxxx. From the talus slope the tomb-diggers had cut a steeply declined gang-way, dropping some 2·60 m. on a length of about 3·60 m. This had given them about a metre of breccia to cut through before the sandstone was reached in which the chamber was cut. No steps in this steep descent were identified until the bottom: here a narrow ledge or step, about 30 cm. high, crossed the threshold on a width of 1·50 m. At its foot, practically at floor-level, lay two burial groups.

The sepulchral chamber, driven into the hill-side to a depth of about 7·75 to 8 m., was horseshoe in shape, 8 m. wide at its maximum, and narrowing to the opening. The maximum height was 3·25 m., but the inner part, owing to a lowering of the breccia roof, was only 2·50 m. high. This sudden change in roof-level may have been inten-tional to reduce the strain on the relatively thin crust of unsupported span. In any case an unpleasant fissure, which caused me perpetual misgivings as clearance took us farther and farther in, split the centre (without exposure to the sky). The great deposit pillar left standing by us in the middle of the floor, unnecessarily large for a 'butte témoin', was designed to break a fall should it occur and gave us fictitious but moral support.

The walls were incurved, reducing the floor area, and had been left rough-hewn. The sandstone was bedded in varying hardness; some strata had crumbled more than others, leaving corrugations and projections: some bands were so soft that definition of where wall and infilling met was uncertain. In pl. xxv, 2, the rear wall appears to contain a recess; this was not artificial, but caused by a fall of a soft patch. In such material the ancient tool-marks were unrecognizable. To the same cause may be perhaps attributed the fact that no trace of the excavated rock could be found near any of the cave mouths examined.

Unlike tomb A6 the walls were devoid of niches. Instead, a solitary bench, levelled out from the inward curvature of the sandstone wall to the floor, had been cut just inside the entrance on the eastern side (pl. lxxix). This bench is described in detail under tomb-group VI.

EXCAVATIONS. THE DEPOSITS. The deposits were 2·40 m. thick in the fore part and tailed down to the rear wall. After digging ourselves elbow-room by clearing part of the entrance of its repack of boulders, small rubble, and dust to ground-level, and admitting light and air, the interior deposits were stripped in horizontal sections. The top metre, too near the roof for men to tackle, was cleared by enterprising small boys whose perseverance while doubled up in a suffocating atmosphere of acrid dust cannot be over-praised. They worked in 10-minute shifts. Fortunately the upper layers were archaeo-logically, if not bacteriologically, sterile. At the 1·50-m. level the men could take over; and as the deposits remained sterile almost to floor-level, clearance could proceed apace. Filled baskets were tossed out from hand to hand, the entrance being too steep and narrow to allow of carrying. Sieving had to be done outside, for the dust within was blinding even had there been light enough to see beads and smaller objects. Photography was possible only when the sun shone directly in. These difficulties were regrettable as they prevented in many cases exact record of position of the smaller objects: nevertheless a considerable proportion were spotted *in situ*; it depended on the time of day and their situation in relation to the light. Pottery and larger objects were planned on squared paper in their assumed 'tomb-groups' (pl. LXXIX).

The deposits were as follows:

(3) Desiccated goat droppings and black dust. ± 50 cm.

(2) Dry reddish sand with streaks of whiter dust. ± 75 cm.

(1) Sandy cave earth, becoming moist towards the base. $\pm 1·20$ m.

(3) There was nothing to indicate the age of the droppings; the maximum height of the aperture as we found it—± 60 cm.—would evidently be sufficient to admit goats, and once inside the slightly vaulted roof gave more height.

(2) The red sand, also undatable for lack of contents, represents undoubtedly the accumulation of crumbling walls and infiltered dust. It appears not to have been occupied by man or beast at this stage.

(1) The cave earth seems to be the same as (2), but was more plastic owing to its added moisture.

These deposits are shown diagrammatically in pl. LXXX, and in photograph in pl. XXVI, 1 (with the deposit section to the left); in pl. XXIV, 1, looking into the cave at an early stage of clearance (the upper basket lies on the surface; the lower on the top of layer 3; and the 2-m. levelling pole stands on floor-level); and in pl. XXIV, 2, background.

The age relation between the entrance infilling and the interior deposits is of interest and poses questions more difficult to answer with certainty than in the case of the other-wise comparable tomb A6. The vertical height of the entrance from roof-overhang to floor was close on 3 m.; the width about the same, giving in fact an unusually large aperture to block unless a carefully built masonry or mud-brick wall were erected to hold back the rubble and dust repacking on the up-slope behind it from sliding down into the sepulchre itself, empty, we must suppose, at the time of closure except at burial level. Of such a wall there was no trace. The entrance infilling merged gradually into the cave deposits, as though 'creep' from without had kept pace with accumulation within.

The explanation which seems to me likely is suggested in the reconstructed cross-section on pl. LXXX. In this reconstruction it is presumed that the breccia roof originally projected another metre and a half. That being so, the vertical aperture to be closed would be diminished to little over a metre by the erection of a low cross-wall just outside the line of the supposed overhang. The pack behind would thus, too, be negligible. A ledge, which in fact exists in the slope of the approach at the breccia-sandstone junction, would thus have been the base of such a wall. The skylight still remaining between the wall top and the roof could have been easily blocked by a boulder or slab, and the whole operation finally disguised by a scatter of scree. Entry for fresh interments could thus have been easily effected without the displacement of a great mass of infilling, which has to be assumed on any other supposition. The course of events after the tomb finally fell into disuse was one, we must suppose on this hypothesis, of gradual collapse of the entrance and slow accumulation, *pari passu*, of the interior deposits. The thin overhang of the breccia roof weathered and broke away by stages, scattering its constituent boulders and finer rubble and dust upon the slowly rising level of the threshold below it. The rubble masonry of the cross-wall fell in too, adding its quota to the debris.[1] By the time the red sand deposit of the second interior stratum had reached its present height of nearly 2 m. above floor-level, the roof (still pursuing our hypothesis) had receded to its present position; and now shepherds led their flocks over the rough entrance boulders into the cool half-light of a cave floored with soft sandy earth, giving a head clearance still of some $1\frac{1}{4}$ m. And thus they pattered in and out perhaps for centuries: until the rising level of their droppings and the dust brought in by trotting hooves blocked further ingress.

Nothing was found in the rubble entrance pack; but six small garnet spheroidal beads (pl. XLII, 16) were sieved from near the surface outside and to the right of the entrance. There is no check on their age, nor was garnet found amongst the burial beads; on the other hand, some of the carnelian beads from burials are not less well made (see Beck report, p. 98, no. 9).

BURIAL LEVEL. At about 2·25 m. below the top of the cave infilling it became clear at last that our so far unrewarded labours were not to be in vain. The curves of pots and skulls appeared through the sandy soil, and proved to be practically at floor-level.[2] From the first it was apparent that these lay in great disorder (see pl. XXV, 1) and must represent communal burials which had been either very thoroughly disturbed by robbers or had else been disposed of summarily at the time of interment. Robbery after

---

[1] Remains of such a wall were not at the time recognized as such; but a quantity of large rubble blocks which, reconsidering the matter, I now think may have been its constituents, were scattered through the fill as far as the outlying burial-groups. In Bahrein the entrances were blocked by a dry wall (see E. Mackay, *Bahrein*, p. 12).

[2] Up to 30 cm. above sandstone bottom is termed 'floor-level'. It is unlikely that an absolutely naked rock floor ever existed, for no one entering the cave fails to drag down a shower of dust with him. The cave workmen themselves doubtless left a carpet of sand.

the superposed deposits had formed could be ruled out; they were intact. More or less contemporary robbery cannot, however, be disproved and is not unlikely; but it does not explain the fragmentary condition of the bones nor the incompleteness of the skeletal parts. Not a single body, hardly a single bone, lay in articulation (pl. xxiv, 2, shows a typical group); it was impossible to sort out which belonged to which, or to make up even a complete set of limb bones from any one heap. The skulls alone tell us that parts of forty-two individuals had been committed to the sepulchre, and of this number all but seven lacked lower jaws: even these were not in articulation, or obviously connected with any one skull. One cranium was wedged tightly in a jar to which it was welded by salt formation: it must have been placed there by man, deliberately, after the flesh had disappeared.

The crania lay in all postures and without fixed orientation,[1] though some groups faced consistently north or north-west (see plan, pl. lxxix). Mainly they occurred in twos or threes; but to the rear of the cave a double alinement of fifteen had been arranged (group XI). In one line were eight crania, five of which rested on their bases facing south, and the other three on their sides. The second row of seven nearly touched the first and consisted of six crania resting on their bases and one on its left side. A sixteenth skull cap, no. 39, lay isolated some $\frac{1}{2}$ m. away; and three others, nos. 40–2, were separate and unaccompanied by other parts or objects in the vicinity.

The condition of these human remains was deplorable. Many of the crania had been crushed by earth pressure; the bone was extremely fragile and damp. Hours were spent preparing the best *in situ* for treatment with shellac; but all too often a skull, treated on one side, broke up on being turned or emptied of its weight of contained earth. Thus only thirteen were fit for removal, and even these are incomplete (see Dr. Morant's report, pp. 107–11).

Of these, eleven are adult. Four are certainly, and four probably, male; two are children of eight to fourteen, and twelve to sixteen years respectively, and of the rest one is certainly, and two are probably, female. Four of the above crania came from the big group XI, and these are stated by Dr. Morant to include the two children and two adults, probably a male and female. I am not, unfortunately, competent to determine the sex of skulls, and the proportions of each in the total of forty-two is therefore unknown. But eight immature crania were noted in all (including the two saved), and one of these belonged also to group XI.

Burial Groups. The human remains and burial equipment, particularly the pottery and crania, lay in irregular groups, and it seemed convenient to make these the basis of record. That the line between some of them is ill-defined will be apparent from the tomb plan, pl. lxxix. In the case of groups X and XII, which are dispersed scatters rather than groups, it might admittedly have been better not to subdivide them had the layout been realized in time. To avoid doubt as to group limits a dotted line has in plan been run round each. It must, moreover, be stressed that, apart from these groupings,

---

[1] See Chart, p. 81.

real or imaginary, there was a thin scatter of beads, microliths, sherds, and smaller objects throughout the deposit at the same level in between them.[1] Apart from all this the grouping served both to label the material,[2] and, to a considerable extent at least, indicates the probable interconnexion and order of arrival of the remains which composed them. Typological details of the objects are given in separate sections; but here a group record is desirable.

GROUP I. This was a compact group of sixteen objects and small miscellanea, with a skull cap in bad condition facing west, half a dissociated mandible, and a single tibia. These lay at the entrance, practically touching the threshold step referred to on p. 68. Their position reinforces, I think, the argument advanced earlier in favour of the cave-roof having formerly projected farther; its existing lip directly overlies groups I and II and would discharge storm-water on to them. Such a position is unlikely.

This big group lay in cave-soil about 30 cm. above floor-level, thus confirming by its vertical position the inference of its position in plan—namely that it and group II were the remains last deposited in this sepulchre.

The accompanying pottery and other objects,[3] which lay in confusion, consisted of:

Pottery. A5.I.1.[4] One goblet on tall stem, type I[5] (pls. xxvii, 3; xlix, 2).
   One fragment ditto in grey ware (pl. lvi, 17).
   A5.I.2, 3, 4, 10. Four pedestal bowls and cups, type III (pls. xxx, 3, 6, 8; lii, 6, 9, 4).
   A5.I.5. One shallow open bowl, type VI (pls. xxxi, 4; liv, 3).
   A5.I.6, 12. Two deep bowls, one with dimpled base, type VIII (pls. xxxi, 7; liii, 1, 3).
   A5.I.15. One ear-lug of black bowl, type IX (pl. liv, 11).
   A5.I.7, 8. Two flanged cups with spouts, one inscribed, type X (pls. xxxiv, 4, 5; lv, 5, 8).
   — Two interesting sherds with plastic decoration in red-coated ware (pl. lvi, 16, 18, see pp. 128–9).
Stone. A5.I.9. One limestone tripod saucer (pls. xxxvii, 5; lvii, 2).
Metal. A5.I.14. Four bronze ring-beads, diam. *c.* 15–18 mm., made of strips of thin metal, *c.* 10 mm. wide, with butted or overlapping ends, unsoldered. Two smaller ditto, *c.* 5 and 8 mm. in diameter. Broken bits of at least two more. (Pl. xlv, 1. Desch, Analysis, specimen no. 2, bronze; see p. 106.)
   A5.I.13. Ear-ring, probably bronze, diam. 24 mm., made of drawn wire ± 3·5 mm. thick. Penannular (pl. xlv, 12).
   A5.I.13. Bangle, probably bronze, diam. *c.* 40 mm., but distorted; made of wire, ±3·5 mm. thick. Broken ends, but probably penannular (pl. xlv, 7).
   A5.I.13. Pin, probably bronze, length ±62 mm.: square section (pl. xlv, 11).
   About seventeen small tacks, bronze, with dome heads, ±8 mm. in diameter; and a nail, ±9 mm. long, also bronze (Desch, Analysis, specimen no. 4). These tacks (pl. xlv, 17), of which about eighty were found, mainly in groups I, II, V, X, may have been used as decorative studs in leather, or perhaps to fix metal sheeting on to a wooden core or framework. Most of them were

---

[1] As already explained, many of the small objects were found in the sieving outside; but even where this was not so, it has been impossible to include them in the plan.

[2] Record numbers A5.I.1, &c., mean Tomb A5, group I, item 1 in that group.

[3] Omitting fragments, unless of note.

[4] The object's number, 1 to 17 in the case of group I, is marked beside it in plan. Missing numbers refer to objects too small to show, too unimportant, or hidden.

[5] For pottery types see the Classification, Chap. XIII. Types from IX onwards are made of black 'stone ware' (cf. pp. 116–17).

caught in the sieves outside, and the possible evidence of their relative position in the soil is consequently not available to solve the question.

Beads. These include carnelians (Beck, no. 1); faience disks (Beck, no. 15; colour pl. xxxviii, 20), discoloured an olive-green to brown, but probably originally blue; red glass bicones and oblates (Beck, no. 16; colour pl. xxxviii, 6, 7); and the same in blue-green (Beck, no. 17; colour pl. xxxviii, 2, 8, 18); small shell disks (Beck, no. 25); and a number of pierced marine shells with apical or side perforation, listed by Dr. Wilfrid Jackson.

Shells. A5.I.14. Two valves of *Arca inflata* Reeve (pl. xli, 3). These seem to have been used as trays or saucers, for none is perforated, and were present in every group except two (IX and XI). None, however, was stained by cosmetic or unguent.

Obsidian microliths. One hundred and fifty were got in tomb A5, at burial level only. About half this number were collected *in situ*; the rest came from the sieves and were, like the shells, not individually numbered. Group I was particularly well stocked with them and yielded seventeen (see pp. 134–6 and pl. lviii, 1–55).

GROUP II. This lay also on the present threshold, alongside group I and so close that a single grouping might be justified. Like group I, it lay slightly above floor-level. It consisted of two fragmentary skulls, both with incomplete mandibles not in direct articulation, too crusted and rotten to preserve. One skull faced north-east and lay on its left side; the other rested on its base facing also north-east. With these were seven pots, three limestone saucers, and small miscellanea, of which a large disk bead, cut from a conus, and relics of an iron blade are the most conspicuous.

Pottery. A5.II.4, 8, 9. One pedestal bowl and two cups, type III (pls. xxx, 2, 9; lii, 1, 7).

    A5.II.5, 6, 7. Three deep bowls with dimpled bases, type VIII (pl. liii, 12, 9, 6).

    A5.II.10. One miniature cup in black 'stone ware', type XII (pl. lv, 17).

Stone. A5.II.1. One limestone tripod saucer (pls. xxxvii, 7; lvii, 3).

    A5.II.2. One limestone discoidal saucer (pls. xxxvii, 3; lvii, 6).

    A5.II.3. One limestone hemispherical saucer.

Metal. A5.II.11. Remains of an iron blade in fragments, *c.* 10·7 cm. long by 2.4 cm. wide, tapering to *c.* 1·3 cm. The metal is corroded through, but seems part of a straight knife or dagger.

    A5.II.12. A dart-shaped object, mainly iron, but the base of the pointed 'head' encircled by a thin bronze collar (Desch, Analysis, specimen 7; pl. xlv, 4). This combination of two metals recurs on a handle from A6 (see p. 88).

    A5.II.13. A needle or pin, probably bronze, *c.* 48 mm. long, but head broken. A flattened extremity suggests a needle.

    Nine or ten small bronze tacks as in group I.

Beads. Carnelians (Beck, no. 1); faience disks (Beck, no. 15); red and green glass bicones and oblates (Beck, nos. 16, 17); yellow glass bicone and barrel (Beck, no. 20); a striped yellow and green glass barrel (Beck, no. 23). Shell beads listed separately.

Pendants. A perforated limestone pebble (Beck, no. 6); a grey felspar oval pebble perforated (Beck, no. 5; pls. xl, 5; xlii, 25).

Shells. Three valves of *Arca inflata* Reeve, two being nested. A5.II.14 a large shell disk centrally perforated, ground down from a big cone shell, probably *Conus betulinus* L.; diam. *c.* 44 mm. (Beck, no. 25; pl. xli, 2). This ornament resembles the Ndoro or Mpanda worn by certain Bantu-speaking Africans as insignia of rank.

Obsidian microliths. About eight. Also a small core, type as pl. lix, 2, 3.

Bone polisher. Rods of steatite were found in various places (see pl. LXI, 1–3). The specimen in group II appears to be made of fossil bone and is *c.* 43 mm. long but broken. The surviving, functional end has been dressed by chips from one side (pl. LXI, 2).

GROUP III. This lay 1·50 m. or so inside the cave, isolated from other groups, and was on floor-level. There were no human remains with it. Six pots composed it and included two unique specimens, the chalice, type IV, and the lipped saucer or lamp, type VII. Miscellanea included a fly amulet in discoloured blue glaze and a minute scaraboid. The deep bowl, A5.III.1, overlay the chalice and a pedestal cup. It is notable that the chalice is incomplete, and no belonging fragments were found here or elsewhere: it must have been brought in already broken, unless the rest lies under the deposit section.

Pottery. A5.III.2. One pedestal cup, type III (pls. XXX, 7; LII, 2).
    A5.III.7. One chalice with internal rim, type IV (pls. XXXVII, 1; XLIX, 7).
    A5.III.3. One lipped saucer, type VII (pl. LIV, 7).
    A5.III.1. One deep bowl with dimpled base, type VIII.
    A5.III.5, 6. Two flanged cups with spouts and handles, one inscribed, type X (pls. XXXIII, 8; XXXV, 3; LV, 7).
    A5.III.4. One pedestal base reused as saucer (pl. LVI, 19).
Metal. A5.III.9. A ring, probably bronze, perhaps an ear-ring, diam. *c.* 23 mm., made of thick wire of circular section, with overlapping ends (Desch, Analysis, specimen 5; pl. XLV, 14).
Beads and Amulets. An agate barrel bead (Beck, no. 2; pl. XLII, 20).
A blue glaze amulet of debased Egyptian style, probably a fly, *c.* 6 mm. long, horizontally pierced (colour pl. XXXVIII, 27). Also a minute scaraboid, only 3 mm. long; discoloured whitish glaze. This was lost during an expert's examination in Cairo, and before the design on the underside had been made out.
Shells. A single valve of *Arca inflata*; a large cockle, *Cardium pseudolima* Lamk. (pl. XLI, 1), and various shell beads, including cowries with rubbed backs, listed separately.

GROUP IV. This lay about 1·50 m. inside the cave (*in situ*, pl. XXV, 1), about 15 cm. above floor-level. A skull cap with dissociated mandible retaining a single tooth lay on the left side facing east, with fragmentary bones in pulpy condition, amongst which the distal end of a femur, ribs, and four vertebrae, not in articulation, were identified. The pottery group was characterized by the remains of four tall goblets, three imperfect before burial.

Pottery. A5.IV.1, 2, 4, 5. Four goblets on tall stems, type I (pls. XXVII, 2; XLIX, 5).
    A5.IV.3. One pedestal bowl with ledge rim, type II (side and rim only).
    A5.IV.6. One pedestal cup, type III (crushed and incomplete).
Shells. A single valve of *Arca inflata*.

GROUP V. This group was at floor-level to the west of the entrance. A pair of crania, one immature, beside each other, were accompanied by eight pots. A single mandible, fragmentary and with one tooth only in place, lay under a pot and might have belonged to either cranium or to neither. The pots are of six different types and two are inscribed.

The word cut on the unguent cup (type X) is particularly welcome, for it reads 'perfume' and clinches the purpose of this class of singular stone ware vessel (see Ryckmans, no. 73, p. 179).

Pottery. A5.V.4. One goblet on tall stem, type I (pls. xxvii, 5; xlix, 3).

A5.V.9. One pedestal bowl with ledge rim, type II (pls. xxviii, 7; l, 4).

A5.V.6. One pedestal bowl, type III (not kept).

A5.V.1, 2. Two shallow open bowls, one inscribed, type VI (pls. xxxi, 5, 6; liv, 1, 6).

A5.V.7. One deep bowl with dimpled base, type VIII (pl. liii, 10).

A5.V.5. Flanged cup with spout and handle, inscribed, type X (pls. xxxiii, 9; xxxiv, 2; xxxv, 5; lv, 6).

Metal. An ear-ring, probably bronze, diam. *c*. 14 mm., made of drawn wire, penannular (as pl. xlv, 12).

About thirty small tacks (as pl. xlv, 17), bronze, as before, with dome heads.

Four pieces of thin bronze plating, about 11 mm. wide, the largest 24 mm., pierced by small tacks, held in position by corrosion. One plate has two tack heads in position, the others only one; they are too corroded to be sure if the same dome-headed variety was used (pl. xlv, 2; Desch, Analysis, specimen no. 4).

A gold-foil bead, *c*. 4 mm. in diameter, made of thin flat wire, *c*. 3 mm. wide, overlapped and apparently soldered (pl. xlv, 6).

Beads. About three dozen, including the common red glass bicones as before (Beck, no. 16), one blue and several green ditto, as before (Beck, nos. 17, 18); a blue glass cylinder (colour pl. xxxviii, 12), and small spheroid (colour pl. xxxviii, 3); an eye-bead, Indian red, with dark green? eyes encircled white (Beck, no. 22; colour pl. xxxviii, 4); about ten carnelians including two barrels, two disks, one rubbed bicone; one cylinder, and three spheroids; a black glass with white zones, oblate, imitating onyx (Beck, no. 24; colour pl. xxxviii, 10); a bone hollow cylinder, *c*. 25 mm. long by 14 mm. wide (Beck, no. 10; pl. xlii, 24).

Amulets and Pendants. A felspar pebble cut to the form of a shafted axe-head, with vertical perforation (Beck, no. 5; pls. xlii, 26; xl, 5); a drop pendant in black steatite, broken perforation (Beck, no. 17; pl. xlii, 28).

Shells. Two valves of *Arca inflata*, in addition to other shells, perforated for necklaces, listed separately.

Ivory or Bone Decorated Fragment (pl. xlv, 10). An anciently broken piece of some object, perhaps a box or hilt. Only about 27 mm. survives. The cross-section is plano-convex, 9 mm. thick. The convex surface is highly polished and bears two incised circles with a central dot; the lower face is smoothed. No other fragments were found, and as all the soil was sieved it must be assumed either that it reached the tomb as a fragment, caught up perhaps with other objects, or else that it alone of the original object survived an early plundering.

Microliths. About twenty-six, of which three are of chert, the rest of obsidian (pl. lviii, 1–55).

GROUP VI. This number was given to the bench cut in soft sandstone in the cave wall inside the entrance (pl. xxv, 2). It was 2·60 m. long by 50 to 60 cm. wide, and raised 0·35 m. above the floor. The group lying upon it consisted of a single incomplete skull cap, probably male (see Morant, p. 108, and pl. xlvi, 1), resting on its base with no lower jaw; a single tibia pressed up against the cave wall; nine pots and sherds of a tenth; and miscellanea scattered down the bench on a length of about 2 m. The group had been considerably crushed by falls from the wall.

The skull lay at the south-east end. Behind it was an earthenware saucer, resembling pl. LIV, 9, probably a low pedestal foot rubbed down and inverted. A pottery group of five vessels lay where the missing pelvis should have been, and beyond these again, three others, including a pedestal bowl with ledge rim inscribed with sixteen letters, *pointillé*, reading 'Waddum Abum—Mass Šamsum—Hawl 'Ab (?)' (pl. XXIX, 1).[1]

A bronze bangle, of the type pl. XLV, 5, 7, 8, lay near the skull. Another ornament was a blue glaze altar-shaped amulet (colour pl. XXXVIII, 13) found in the dust beneath the head. There were no beads.

> *Pottery*. A5.VI.4. One goblet on tall stem, type I (too smashed to keep).
> A5.VI.8. One pedestal bowl with inscribed ledge rim, type II (pls. XXVIII, 2; LI, 5).
> A5.VI.3. One pedestal cup, type III (too smashed to keep).
> A5.VI.9. One shallow open pedestal bowl, type V (pls. XXXI, 3; LII, 12).
> A5.VI.5. One shallow open bowl with rounded base, type VI (too smashed to keep).
> A5.VI.2. One deep bowl with dimpled base, type VIII (pl. LIII, 7).
> A5.VI.6, 10. Two flanged cups with spouts and handles, type X (pls. XXXIII, 6, 4; LV, 10, 3).
> A5.VI.1. Saucer, made of broken pedestal foot, inverted.
> *Metal*. A bracelet in three pieces, probably bronze (as pl. XLV, 5).
> *Amulet*. A discoloured blue glaze cube, *c*. 11 mm. long by 10 mm. broad and 6 mm. thick. The glaze, which is vivid peacock blue, has worn or corroded off the under side and one end; these show the white faience core. The upper face is plain except for a thin moulding at top and bottom. The sides are double-stepped or ribbed. The perforation is plain and vertical to the long axis. Though at first I was inclined to see in this amulet a debased *ded* column, I now think, with Mr. Beck, that it represents an altar—after all a more probable symbol in its south Arabian context. A standard altar amulet from Syria, of approximately the same date, in pale blue faience, is shown for comparison on the string of Syrian beads, pl. XL. In this the perforation is horizontal. (Colour pl. XXXVIII, 13; see also Beck, no. 14.)
> *Shells*. A single *Arca inflata* lay at the foot of the group, beside the little unguent cup A5.VI.10.

GROUP VII (pl. XXV, 2). This lay on the floor alongside the bench VI group and consisted of four skull caps, one immature, all lacking mandibles and, as seen in the plate, very fragmentary. Two imperfect lower jaws, with two and three teeth respectively, lay isolated. One skull cap only (darkened by shellac in the photograph) was saved, and Dr. Morant reports a male adult (pl. XLVII, 1). A heap of bones in hopeless condition, and as intermingled as spillikins, was mixed among the pots as though both had been unceremoniously dumped down together. Nevertheless, the skulls at least show a definite arrangement: three were in alinement facing north-west: the fourth, slightly in advance, likewise. With them were eight pots, six of which lay in a group before the crania, the other two beside them.

> *Pottery*. A5.VII.10. One goblet on tall stem, type I (too crushed to keep).
> A5.VII.7, 16. Two pedestal bowls with ledge rims, type II (pls. XXVIII, 4, 5; L, 3, 5).
> A5.VII.2. A pedestal and fragments, probably type II.
> A5.VII.8. One pedestal bowl, type III (pls. XXX, 1; LII, 8).
> A5.VII.1. One shallow open bowl with rounded base, type VI (pl. LIV, 4).

[1] Cf. Ryckmans, no. 57, p. 178.

A5.VII.6, 15. Two deep bowls with dimpled bases, type VIII (pls. xxxi, 8, 9; liii, 8, 5).

Beads and Pendants. This group was rich in beads. In glass the large red bicones and oblates (Beck, no. 16); the blue and green ditto (Beck, nos. 17, 18); the yellow barrels and oblates (Beck, no. 20); two flush crumbs (colour pl. xxxviii, 19; Beck, no. 19); small faience disks (Beck, no. 15); in stone, carnelians (Beck, no. 1); an agate tabular barrel (Beck, no. 2); a calcite large barrel (Beck, no. 8); in shell, small disks (Beck, no. 25); a spacing bead (Beck, no. 28), and numerous perforated sea-shells included in Dr. Jackson's list.

A white cylindrical object, tentatively bored at one end, appears to be a fossil coral or crinoid (Beck, no. 11).

Shells. Apart from species used as ornaments or amulets, group VII contained the usual *Arca* shells—two valves—and a large scallop valve (*Chlamys townsendi* (Sow), pl. xli, 4) found beneath the inverted pedestal bowl A5.VII.8.

Microliths and Core. Ten obsidian microliths; a fine obsidian core (pl. lix, 1) proves that the making of them was local.

Group VIII. This was a small group in linear arrangement close to the edge of the central deposit section, and possibly with outliers below it. A single imperfect cranium, without mandible, reported on by Dr. Morant, and probably male, lay on its base facing north-west. With it were four pots, a bronze wire ornament, and three *Arca* shells. This little group is notable for the presence of two pots in black 'stone ware', rare in type. One, A5.VIII.4, is a unique specimen, in perfect condition, inscribed 'Adîdat', perhaps the owner's name:[1] the other, A5.VIII.3, is one of the two miniature suspension bowls found, the other coming from tomb A6.

The bronze ornament, about 23 × 21 mm. in size, is seen in pl. xlv, 15, and is perhaps a clasp or brooch. An oblong border, incomplete on the fourth side, frames an open-work design composed of two letters, ⚭Ψ. Corrosion obscures technical details, but the ornament seems to be made of soldered wire rather than cut from a sheet *à jour*. At the back a broken hasp or other form of attachment springs from the lateral edge. Analysis reveals copper as the principal constituent of the metal (see Desch, Analysis, specimen no. 1, p. 106). I have not been able to trace with any degree of exactitude a parallel to this ornament. A rather larger bronze open-work plaque in Vienna has, however, possibly a distant relationship.[2]

Pottery. A5.VIII.1. One pedestal bowl with ledge rim, type II (pls. xxviii, 6; l, 6).

A5.VIII.2. One pedestal cup, type III (too crushed to keep).

A5.VIII.4. One open cup, inscribed, with tongue handle, type XI*a* (pls. xxxiv, 1; xxxv, 1; lv, 15).

A5.VIII.3. One miniature suspension bowl, type XIII (pl. lv, 18).

Metal. A5.VIII.5. Bronze ornament, described above (pl. xlv, 15).

Shells. Three valves of *Arca*.

Group IX. A collection of three cranial fragments, without lower jaws, two of which are reported on by Dr. Morant as being male and female respectively (p. 108). This pair had been placed on their left sides, touching, one behind the other and faced north-

---

[1] Cf. Ryckmans, no. 71, p. 179.   [2] *Handbuch der altarabischen Altertumskunde*, fig. 68.

east. The third, isolated, lay on its base facing north-west. With these were four pots, one in black 'stone ware' inscribed, a bronze bangle, beads, tacks, perforated shells (but no *Arca* valves), and microliths.

Pottery. A5.IX.4, 8. Two goblets on tall stems, inverted, type I (too crushed to keep).
    A5.IX.1. One pedestal cup, type III (pls. xxx, 4; LII, 11).
    A5.IX.2. One ear-lug bowl, inscribed, type IX (pls. xxxII, 3; LIV, 10).
Metal. A heavy bracelet or anklet, probably bronze (pl. XLV, 5), penannular, flattened in section and about 6 mm. wide.
    Bronze tacks (as pl. XLV, 17), five.
Beads. Red bicones and oblates (Beck, no. 16); blue and green ditto (Beck, nos. 17, 18); variously shaped yellow (Beck, no. 20); a dark purple cylinder with chamfered sides (Beck, no. 21, said to be rare); a flush crumb (Beck, no. 19). With these glass beads should be mentioned a pair of minute studs, probably obsidian, and used presumably as an inlay: they are short truncated cones. A chip shows the conchoidal fracture of glass (pl. XLV, 9).
Shells. Several cowries with rubbed backs, and a large *Oliva inflata* Lam. (pl. XLI, 41) are the most conspicuous of the shell beads, besides one with concave ends to fit against a spheroid (pl. XLIII, 22).
Microliths. Four in obsidian.

GROUP X. The numbers X and XII were given to a dispersed scatter of burial relics over the north-eastern part of the floor. No. X may cover three separate small groups, a point best decided individually by consulting the tomb-group plan, pl. LXXIX. Be that as it may, it includes seven skull fragments, eighteen pots, and miscellanea, including beads: also a nice scaraboid seal, A5X.16, the exact position of which, as it was found in a sieve, was doubtful, but which was somewhere near the position shown in plan. The isolation of this object and that of several of the pots, suggests that the earlier burials had been carelessly swept to the rear to make place for later comers nearer the entrance. A curious result of this unceremonious treatment had befallen one cranium (no. 18), which was tightly wedged inside the orifice of a goblet on tall stem. The formation of salt had further welded the two.

The human remains were in the usual bad state in addition to their fragmentary nature, and only two crania survived displacement, and none of the litter of other parts. These crania are pronounced by Dr. Morant to be male (see p. 108, and pls. XLVI, 3, 4; XLVII, 2, 6; XLVIII, 4). An immature skull cap was noted amongst the remaining five (no. 22). The postures of the six were varied. Four rested on their bases, three facing west, one north-west; the other two lay on their left sides facing north-east.

Pottery. A5.X.1, 3. Two goblets on tall stems, type I (pls. xxvII, 1, 4; XLIX, 1, 4).
    A5.X.9, 11. Two ditto (too crushed to keep).
    A5.X.2. One pedestal bowl with ledge rim, type II (pls. xxvIII, 3; L, 7).
    A5.X.4. One pedestal cup, type III (pls. xxx, 11; LII, 3).
    A5.X.7, 14. Two shallow open pedestal bowls, type V (pls. xxxI, 2, 1; LII, 14, 13).
    A5.X.12, 15. Two shallow open bowls with rounded bases, type VI (pl. LIV, 2, 5).

A5.X.3, 5, 8. Three deep bowls with dimpled bases, type VIII (pl. LIII, 4, 11, 2).

A5.X.17, 18. Two ear-lug bowls, type IX (pls. XXXII, 4, 8; LIV, 14).

A5.X.6, 13. Two flanged cups with spouts and handles, type X (pls. XXXIII, 3, 5; LV, 9, 1).

A5.X.10. Small cup with pinched flange lid, type XIV (pl. LV, 12).

Metal. A ring or ear-ring of thick wire, probably bronze, with overlapped ends (pl. XLV, 13). Four rings or ear-rings of wire, probably bronze, penannular (as pl. XLV, 12). Ten tacks (as pl. XLV, 17). Scraps of iron, probably nails, and bits of small objects probably of bronze.

Beads. The range, similar to that in other groups, included: in glass, red and green bicones, etc., as before; in faience, tiny disks; in stone, carnelian; in shell, small disks, and various perforated sea-shells, including cowries with rubbed backs, listed separately, and five larger shell rings, up to 24 mm. in diameter, made from the tops of *Conus acuminatus* (pl. XLI, 12–16).

Scaraboid (pl. XLIV, 9). This is oval in form, approximately 15 mm. long, and is made of brown-red stone, probably limestone, highly polished. A plain, large perforation is bored through the length. The back and sides are plain with bevelled angles. The inscribed face bears the name ⟨𝕏⟩ = Râqibum neatly cut across the centre inside two pairs of horizontal bars.[1] The two semi circular spaces at both ends are filled by winged objects the nature of which is rendered obscure by the attachment of four lines, suggesting legs: these may be the result of unintelligent copying of the winged-disk symbol. Apart from this lapse the workmanship is much above the level of painful incompetence usually exhibited in inscribed seals of south Arabian manufacture.

Shells. Fourteen *Arca* shell valves.

Microliths. Twenty-two, of which twenty were obsidian, the other two chert (pl. LVIII, 1–55). Three amorphous small bits of obsidian were also found, probably the residual from core shavings.

GROUP XI. This was a curious group, and, like X and XII, suggests a removal of earlier burials to the rear of the tomb to free the forepart for fresh claimants. But, if this be the true explanation, the procedure was very different. Instead of the contemptuous indifference shown in the redisposal of the ancestral remains in group X, in group XI the fifteen crania and bones were arranged carefully side by side in two rows running east and west. One row consisted of eight fragmentary skulls, the other of seven. None had lower jaws and were already incomplete when deposited. A greater regard for consistency in orientation had also been observed here than elsewhere. All except two faced south, south-east, or east. Eleven rested on their bases. Much time was spent on preparation for safe removal, but one by one the crania fell to pieces in the process. Eventually only four survived; these, nos. 1–4, lay side by side at the outer end of the first row, and presumably some accident of lesser humidity had rotted the bone less. They are reported on by Dr. Morant (p. 108, pls. XLVI, 5, 6; XLVII, 3; XLVIII, 2). The two central ones were children between eight and sixteen years old, flanked by remains, believed, on defective material, to be probably male and female respectively.

In yet another respect this group differed from the rest: it contained practically no equipment, and its two pieces of pottery have no counterpart. One is a small lid, pl. LVI, 20, with a conical pierced knob, fitting no pot found; the other is a tumbler-shaped pedestal pot in rough brown ware, provisionally classified with type III. It was incomplete and lay partly beneath cranium no. 4. (pl. LI, 8).

---

[1] Cf. Ryckmans, no. 55, p. 177.

GROUP XII. A loose group lying beyond X, consisting of three complete pots, two inscribed pot rims, a limestone tripod saucer, a hemispherical limestone saucer, and a roughly fashioned cup in gypsum. With these was a single skull cap, without lower jaw, reported on by Dr. Morant, fragmentary and probably male.

The most interesting features of this group are the two inscribed rims. Both belong to pedestal bowls with ledge rims, type II; but in both cases only the rim survived attached to a fragment of the shoulder. In the case of A5.XII.6 (pls. XXIX, 2; LI, 4) the rim was complete, and Professor Ryckmans reads ∏ᴴ⫯⊙ = Wadd 'Ab, evidently a magic formula.[1] The other rim, A5.XII.9 (pl. L, 2), is about a third of its full circumference, and the incomplete letters are meaningless.[2] Nevertheless, one is inclined to see in this careful preservation of these rims an intentionally pious or protective act.

Pottery. A5.XII.1. One goblet on tall stem, type I (pls. XXVII, 6; XLIX, 6).
    A5.XII.6, 9. Two inscribed rims from pedestal bowls, type II (pls. XXIX, 2; XXXV, 2; L, 2).
    A5.XII.8. One pedestal cup, type III (pls. XXX, 5; LII, 10).
    A5.XII.7. One shallow open bowl with rounded base, type VI (too crushed to keep).
Stone. A5.XII.4. One limestone tripod saucer (pls. XXXVII, 10; LVII, 4).
    A5.XII.2. One gypsum tumbler (pls. XXXVII, 2; LVII, 9).
    A5.XII.5. One limestone hemispherical saucer.
Shells. One *Arca* valve.
Metal. A bracelet, probably bronze (pl. XLV, 8).

The rear of the cave behind the deposit section was cleared, but contained nothing of note except potsherds of the usual types. Three isolated crania, nos. 40–2, lay south of the centre; no. 40 rested on its vertex; another, no. 39, lay on its left side on the outskirts of group XI. No. 41 was saved, and Dr. Morant reports it as probably female (pls. XLVI, 7; XLVII, 4; XLVIII 3). It was one of the three in the whole lot which rested on the right cheek, and it faced west.

Note on the Orientation of the Skulls

Contrary to a theoretic assumption that moon worshippers might face their dead to the west, it may, I think, be confidently asserted that in tomb A5 there was no fixed direction for the skulls. Two simple charts, one for the series of skulls resting on their bases, the other for those lying on their sides, will condense the evidence.

North-west, which accounts for the big majority in the base-posture series, is unrepresented in the side series. It should be noted that the seven oriented south, all occurred in group XI. In the side-posture series ten lay on their left cheek, three on their right. One skull not included in the analysis rested on its vertex. The cranium in a pot has been included in the base-posture series.

[1] Ryckmans, no. 56, p. 177.   [2] Idem, no. 75, p. 179.

Bases. Number 28.   *Sides. Number 13.*

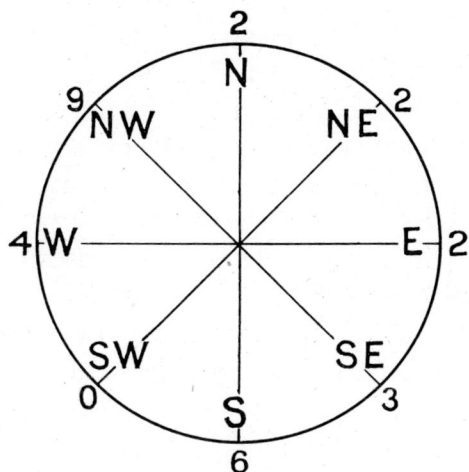

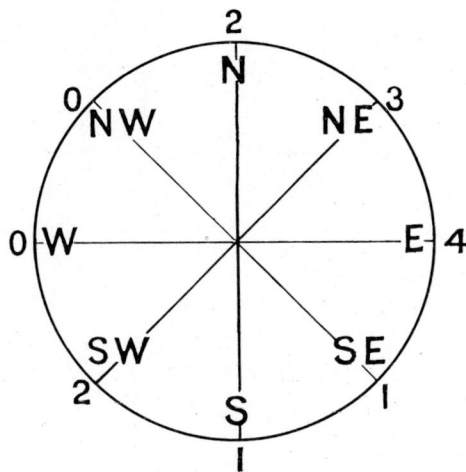

DISCUSSION AND CONCLUSIONS. Cave A5, for whatever purpose it may have been prepared, was, as we found it, an ossuary—a place of secondary and not primary interment. The single bench, however, possibly indicates an unfinished family sepulchre in origin: the cave seems far too large for a single burial. Just possibly, though I doubt it, it had formerly been a dwelling.

The facts which substantiate the ossuary interpretation are: (1) the undisturbed condition of the entrance fill and interior deposits; (2) the fragmentary nature of the human remains; (3) the incompleteness of many of the pots.

1. Robbery is possible; but that robbery, if any, must have been more or less contemporary with the burials, and amounted probably to petty pilfering rather than to methodical disturbance.

2. No primary collective burials, however disintegrated or disturbed, could yield such an incomplete assortment of human bones. All but seven lower jaws cannot have dematerialized; and the posture of the crania, lying in twenty-seven instances on their bases, and in another instance in a pot, is an impossibility had they been deposited in articulation. The two crania in group V lie too near the wall which they face to leave room for a skeleton, unless contracted. Moreover, only 90-odd loose teeth were found (mainly in the sieves) instead of over a thousand which forty-two not elderly heads should have had.[1] The crania were, in short, without a question, deposited separately from the skeletons and already incomplete.

No bones whatsoever were in articulation, or even in loosely related position: moreover, they were proportionately inadequate for the crania, and even the usually better-preserved parts of the skeleton, such as the metacarpals and metatarsals were present (incomplete) in groups I and II only. The bones, like the skulls, had been gathered

[1] Allowing for children and the few teeth remaining in position.

together carelessly and incompletely from elsewhere, and redeposited in positions bearing no relation to the anatomy of man.

3. The grave goods, also, seem to have been collected elsewhere and redeposited. Many of the chips and breaks are ancient and are not the crush-breaks of superposed weight, which cracks or flattens out but does not scatter. With the area covered by the deposit section unexamined, it is impossible to be certain to what extent seriously imperfect vessels were transferred as such. But among the more striking cases of fragmentary pots for which no related sherds were found was the chalice (type IV) in group III; the tall tumbler (variant of type III) in group XI; the two inscribed rims without bodies in group XII; the black stone ware inscribed fragment (type IX) in group I; and the decorated ivory fragment in group V. These are the most noteworthy instances, because the vessels are either unique specimens (i.e. the chalice and tumbler) or are otherwise easily recognizable, like the black stone ware, every scrap of which was collected.

An ossuary then, but of what kind?

The evidence seems to me to suggest that the re-burials were not a case of a single transfer *en masse* from some primary interment elsewhere, such as a cemetery, but that the remains reached the cavern at intervals, and often in twos or threes or more. It may be conceded that no samples of a normal cemetery would yield remains of consistently young individuals (probably all under 40 years, including 9 young adults and two children) such as Dr. Morant describes.

It is true, unfortunately, that he reports on only thirteen out of the total of forty-two; but it should be noted that these thirteen are drawn by the hazards of preservation from six out of twelve 'tomb groups', which reduces the chances of a misleading sample of the whole. Moreover, to Dr. Morant's list may be added my own observation of an additional six juveniles, too badly preserved to save.

We can rule out then, I think, cemetery clearance, for which in any case the numbers are quite insufficient. Nor are the remains accounted for as war casualties. Not only do the thirteen individuals saved and classified include three adult females, apart from the children (though in a land of savage tribal raids this need not necessarily be a valid argument), but, more conclusive, is the certainty that they reached the cave in fragmentary skeletal condition: nor were injuries to the head, apart from earth pressure and decay, present.

Something less usual than the cemetery or battle explanation is needed, but must be speculative until more information is obtained by further field-work on burial customs. In the meantime I venture a few perhaps not irrelevant observations on the layout of the so-called tomb groups, and on the physical peculiarities of the remains as described by Dr. Morant, which may be interconnected.

A glance at the plan, pl. LXXIX, shows that there is no order of arrangement. A crowd of six groups more or less block the entrance area, leaving large spaces to the rear and south unoccupied. Moreover, the layout of these six differs markedly from that of groups X and XII to the inner north, and of XI to the inner south. Nos. X and XII are scattered, not grouped, and XI is an alinement of skulls with practically no other remains, human or cultural. It seems legitimate from this to infer that what are now groups X to XII were originally deposited (perhaps in several smaller groups) also near the entrance, and were moved back out of the way when fresh floor space was needed for later arrivals.

The rearrangement was made with considerable care in the case of XI; and even in X and XII the crania were not just thrown farther back with their accompanying pots, but in four cases were set on their bases facing more or less the same way—a uniformity which could hardly have been accidental.[1] Moreover, the proportion of broken pots was not higher here than elsewhere: they were moved carefully, if my hypothesis is correct that they were moved at all. Skull 18 in group X seems to have made the journey balanced in the aperture of a large pot, and, undisturbed, was laid neatly, like an egg in an egg-cup, alongside no. 19. Why the close grouping was lost in this supposed shift does not explain itself, unless perhaps the interrelationship of individual to individual in these older groups having been forgotten, it was no longer thought necessary to respect it.

Group XI, escaping from this tentative interpretation, poses a separate question: still holding it one must suppose that, if likewise shifted from the front, the shifting was done by more pious hands and probably by different people from those who moved groups X and XII. The virtual lack of pottery with these strange rows of skulls also individualizes it. Possibly the considerable quantity of sherds lying where the compass arrow has been drawn in plan may have belonged; but if so their broken condition is still unexplained.

It must be admitted that there is no cultural support for the theory that different groups reached A5 at substantially different times. Quite the reverse, as the distribution table facing p. 88 makes clear. Comparing the potteries of groups I to V inclusive, at the entrance, with groups X and XII at the rear (group XI had only one pot and a lid), we find that the common pot types, I, II, III, VI, VIII, IX, X, occur in both places in reasonably proportionate numbers.[2]

	Tomb groups I to V	Tomb groups X and XII
Pottery type I	7	5
„ II	2	3
„ III	10	2
„ VI	3	3
„ VIII	7	3
„ IX	1	2
„ X	5	2

Nor do the beads show any recognizable differences in type.

If one subscribes, as I personally do, in the absence of more evidence, to the different

[1] Perhaps they made a mistake over skull 10 of group XII, and, keeping the direction, faced it the reverse way—easily done in that gloom.

[2] Types IV, V, VII, XI–XIV are omitted as being too scantily represented.

group-age theory, it is necessary to suppose either that the age difference is too small to be registered culturally, or that the same pot shapes and fabrics remained unchanged over a longish period—say anything up to a couple of hundred years. This is not improbable when we consider the time-range of an associated group of types (one or two are of little use) in far more progressive regions than the provincial backwaters of the Hadhramaut.

Be that as it may, apart from these suggested internal rearrangements, an impression is given by the other groups of a definite uniformity and continuity of method of disposal of the remains. Those little separate islands of from one to four crania, each with its battery of pots, consisting, as in life, of several different kinds—a water-cooler, a drinking-cup or beaker, and feeding and cooking bowls and dishes of various depths and shapes and functions—certainly produce the effect of domestic units gathered together in re-burial within the confines of a communal family vault after a period of primary burial elsewhere. During this transference, which may prove to be a normal stage in the burial rites of its date and place when more is known about them, and not an emergency measure, the bones, already decayed,[1] were still further reduced in number and hopelessly mixed.

The interrelationship of the individuals thus gathered together, though separate, is, I think, not incompatible with the physical evidence. Dr. Morant remarks on the unusual homogeneity of the series rescued from A5 (a homogeneity emphasized the more by the slight deviation from it recorded in the single skull from tomb A6) and thrown into greater prominence by the almost unprecedentedly low values the collective measurements present.

Since this is the first published series of ancient skulls from south Arabia, let alone approximately dated ones, it would be premature to speculate whether this homogeneity represents a local, tribal, or merely family feature, or is likely to embrace the racial characteristics of the whole region; more probably wide variations as elsewhere, and as now, may be expected.[2] Only when this is known from years of work, and after vastly greater archaeological data shall have been competently collected, shall we be able to endorse or discard these tentative conclusions.

---

[1] Mr. Philby, in *Land of Sheba*, p. 379, states that Pliny says the Sabaeans treated their dead as of no account, and threw out their corpses on dunghills and rubbish-heaps. No reference is given, and I cannot trace that Pliny ever said any such thing. Miss Jocelyn Toynbee has called my attention to Strabo, *Geography*, 16, 784, where he says of the Nabateans, 'They have the same regard for the dead as for dung'.

[2] A useful beginning on the present-day population will have been made when Dr. Huzayyin publishes his anthropometric material, collected in 1936 in Yemen and Hadhramaut. The great majority of the present-day Hadhramis I saw in the regions we visited, omitting the negro taint, were short- or medium-headed; but individuals, probably over the border line of long-headedness, were occasionally seen, though never approaching the extreme of the ancient inhabitants in A5.

X. THE TOMBS. A6

DISCOVERY. The second tomb was incompletely excavated between February 26 and March 3 inclusive, 1938. It lay under 50 m. west of A5 and was cut in a bend of the same scree-slope at approximately the same level of ±800 m. above sea. I had come on it while exploring the interior of a long-emptied cave of type similar to A5, now used as a fodder store by the local bedouin.

An irregular hole in the curving sandstone wall at ground-level, partly choked by deposit, looked interesting, and crawling through it I flashed a torch into the darkness. The dim outlines of another circular cave were seen, with a smooth sandy floor filling it to within about a metre of the roof. In the wall was a recessed bench. It appeared that the communicating hole was either an accidental crumbling of a former recess, pared too thin by the makers of the two adjoining caves, or else, and perhaps more probably, had been made by contemporary plunderers, unable to find the external entrance, or aware that demolition of the thin partition would be simpler and more secret than laborious clearance of the external approach. In any case it seemed worth investigating even if robbed, particularly as I wished to examine a tomb with good wall recesses and our time was nearly up.

EXCAVATIONS. EXTERNAL APPROACH. The position in the scree-slope of the external entrance was easy to calculate in theory. In practice it was a troublesome bit of work. The two photographs, pl. XXIII, 2, 3, show it before and after clearance. The disguise was perfect. The refilling of the approach passage, driven in this case at a gently declined angle into the scree, had been extremely thorough and well packed.

The fill of huge boulders and smaller rocks had to be levered loose with bars and picks, and the larger stones hauled clear by ropes. It held us up for nearly two ill-spared days.

The approach passage when cleared proved to be 5 m. long and between 1·20 and 1·60 m. wide, with sides tapering from 2·50 m. high at the inner end to nothing at the outer. These were raw natural walls of rough consolidated scree, with the underlying sandstone wedging in at the base.

Unlike the approach to A5, where nothing was found except the garnet beads on the surface, that of A6 contained several sherds which lay both in the pack and at floor-level. These included nothing new; but in the light of experience at A5 belonged to pottery types I (goblets on tall stems); II (pedestal bowls with ledge rims); and a fragment of X (stone ware flanged cup). Other fragments included a hollow pedestal of the type II or III build, and pieces of the common rough porous ware. These sherds certainly represent breakages by the actual tomb-cutters or (for those at passage level) perhaps by the mourners. They became of great value in consolidating the internal evidence.

ENTRANCE AND INTERIOR. The entrance aperture faced 10° west of south, and was an irregular rounded orifice, about 1·55 m. high by 1·60 wide. It was blocked by four huge undressed boulders packed with smaller stones, unmortared or plastered.

The interior, like A5, was a horseshoe-shaped cavity, measuring 8·00 m. from entrance to rear wall, and 8·50 m. in maximum width. The internal deposits were only 1·25–·35 m. deep, and consisted of 1 m. of a dry, pulverous yellow to reddish sandstone dust, devoid of archaeological interest, overlying about 30 cm. of a darker heavier version of the same material. This yielded all the finds.[1] The floor was sandstone and the roof slightly vaulted.

THE RECESSES. These were cut in the north and western arc of the wall only: their position is seen in plan, pl. LXXXI. They numbered probably six, two of them being super-imposed. They were empty, and were already empty when the deposits had formed to their full depth, for all were choked and overlaid by them except the upper one of the pair which was partly above their level. The type is seen in pl. XXVI, 2.

Recess I. This had been destroyed by the break-through, already mentioned, from the adjoining tomb, and no measurements were taken.

Recesses II, III. Two superimposed. The upper one measured 2 m. long by 0·60 wide by 0·50 deep. Its shelf was 1·35 m. above floor. The lower one was similar in dimensions: its sandstone roof (which formed the upper shelf) was 15 cm. thick.

Recess IV. Single. Length 2·20 m. by 0·60 wide by 0·50 m. deep. Height above floor 1·10 m.

Recesses V, VI. Both had probably been single, but were too ruined to measure as the soft sandstone rock had caved in: the dimensions seem to have been, judging by the length, the same as the others.

There was no hope in the remaining time of clearing the deposits fully, and an area approximately that shown in plan was untouched.

THE CONTENTS. *Human*. There was only one 'group' consisting of a skull, other bones, and grave goods. It lay on the floor close up below the wall at the east end of recess VI. The condition of the bones was better than any found in A5, and it is regrettable that these were the only human remains uncovered in A6, apart from useless scraps of bone meagrely present throughout the lowest level of the fill.

Dr. Morant reports this skull, which rested on its base facing north, to be female (see p. 108, and pls. XLVI, 8; XLVII, 7; XLVIII, 5). The mandible, which presumably belongs, lay 25 cm. away. With fragmentary bones, which also may belong to this individual, and include a left tibia and three lumbar vertebrae, was a second tibia, also left and probably also female, and a male sacrum and part of the pelvis. No trace of these other two mysterious individuals was found; they may lie in the unexcavated area, or may never have been brought to this sepulchre supposing it to be another place of secondary burial.

THE CONTENTS. *Grave Goods*. In a group with these peculiar remains, marked I on the plan, were the following:

[1] As in cave A5 this is regarded as floor-level (cf. p. 70).

Pottery. A6.I. Pedestal and broken side fragments of a large, ornamented pedestal bowl, classified (p. 117) as a variant of type I, and there described in detail. It has fortunately been possible to restore this handsome goblet, 28·2 cm. high, with complete certainty (pls. XXVIII, 1; L, 1).

A6.I. A deep bowl with dimpled base, type VIII*b* (pls. XXXI, 7; LIII, 13).

A6.I. An ear-lug bowl in black stone ware, type IX (pls. XXXII, 1, 5; LIV, 13). The lugs are not inscribed, and one is missing owing to crumbling of the rim.

Beads. Seven carnelians, including barrels and oblates, some with thick white patina (see Beck, no. 1, p. 97); an amethyst flattened barrel (Beck, no. 4; colour pl. XXXVIII, 16; section, pl. XLII, 17); a faience melon bead, discoloured blue-grey (Beck, no. 13; colour pl. XXXVIII, 5); five or six red glass bicones and oblates (Beck, no. 16; as colour pl. XXXVIII, 6, 7); shell disks (Beck, no. 25; section, pl. XLIII, 71, 72); and perforated marine shells, including cowry and Oliva.

Shells. Two valves of *Arca inflata* (as pl. XLI, 3).

The other objects found, apart from this single group, were completely scattered and fairly obviously the result of plundering; their exact positions were not plotted, but they are shown in their approximate positions on the plan, starting from the entrance and working counter-clockwise.

1. *Limestone Pedestal Cup* (pls. XXXVII, 4; LVII, 8). Ht. 6·1 cm. The cup is scored with shallow vertical lines, probably to simulate fluting. (For other details see p. 133.)

2. *Purple and White Wire-drawn Glass Vase* (pls. XLIV, 15; LVII, 10). Ht. 6·5 cm. Rim diam. 3·5 cm. Thickness ± 3 to 4 mm. Incomplete; in four fragments, lying a few centimetres apart, as though smashed in dropping: the pieces, however, fit, and build up about half the vase, making an irregular pear-shape with flat base. The moulding is rough, the surface undulating, the glass opaque. The vase was submitted to Dr. Plenderleith of the Research Laboratory, British Museum, who reports:

'The white pattern on the glass is certainly an opal glass which seems to have been pressed into the surface in the form of a paste or thick frit, and then the whole thing was fired like a piece of frit porcelain. It is a very interesting piece, and I have submitted it to some of my colleagues: they have not seen the technique before. There is agreement that it may have been made in imitation of glass of the Roman Imperial Period. You have no doubt noted the variation in thickness of the white design and that it contains blow holes and affects cracks in the same manner as the purple body of the ware with which, in fact, it probably differs little in composition.'

Professor C. G. Seligman kindly provided a specimen of medieval wire-drawn bichrome glass from Aidab, and Mr. Beck many other pieces from his own collections, ranging from ancient Egyptian, through Greek and Roman, to later times. But no real resemblance to the Hureidha vase could be traced in any of these, either in the appearance of the glass, nor even remotely with the shape. Finally an acknowledged glass expert, Mr. D. B. Harden of the Ashmolean Museum, confirmed the general opinion of its unique character. 'I am afraid that this glass has beaten me as far as finding parallels to it is concerned; but I have no hesitation in agreeing with Beck that it can be of the date you say it probably is, i.e. Persian or Ptolemaic.'

If I may venture a guess it would be that this vase and the purple, or purple and white, glass beads (Beck, no. 21) are related. Experts outside the British Museum do not agree that the technique itself is unusual.

3. *Spout-head of a Black Stone Ware Flanged Cup,* type X (pls. XXXIII, 2; XXXIV, 6; LV, 11). The

theriomorphic nature of the spout of some of these unguent vessels is particularly well seen in this specimen. A bull's head seems fairly certain in this case (see p. 125).

4. *Limestone Tripod Saucer* (pls. XXXVII, 8; LVII, 1). Ht. 5·2 cm. Like the pedestal cup, no. 1 above, this is scored with vertical lines. It seems to have been damaged before burial and lacks two of the stump legs. (For details see p. 133.)

5. *Handle* (pl. XLV 3). Length 3·8 cm. A loop of flat iron about 8 mm. wide, held together by a bronze band about 4 mm. wide (see Desch, Analysis, no. 8, p. 106). The curve of the iron shoulders below, broken off short, suggest that it might be the handle of a small mirror.

6. *Limestone Ointment Jar* (pls. XXXVII, 6; LVII, 7). Ht. 4·4 cm. A complete side fragment only. The vertical scorings are deep enough to constitute ribbings. The stone is translucent, and might popularly, and erroneously, be termed 'alabaster'. (For other details see p. 133.)

7. *Nozzle-spout and Side of a Black Stone Ware Cup*, type X (pl. LV, 2). Enough remains to reconstruct safely into a small unguent cup with dropper, similar, except for detail, to that in A5 group VI.6 (pl. LV, 10).

8. *Faience Scarab* (colour pl. XXXVIII, 1, and pl. XLIV, 10–12). Length 12 mm. A greeny-blue thin glaze, badly applied and partly worn off, exposes a brownish faience base. The plain perforation is longitudinal and emerges inside a well-defined theriomorphic nose. The work is debased, and little of the conventional beetle survives, except the here meaningless incisions round the lateral edges (see pl. XLIV, 12). It seems likely that a lion head was intended, the 'wing sheath' lines on the back being transfigured accordingly into a mane. The underside bears a plain diagonal, square-bordered, cross[1] (pl. XLIV, 11).

9. *Double-sided Seal in Black Kaolinite* (pl. XLIV, 4–8). Length 15 mm. Thickness 8 mm. Plain longitudinal perforation. The material was submitted to the Department of Mineralogy, British Museum, and Mr. Game reported: 'It is made from a clay mineral belonging to the Kaolinite group. It has a hard black outer skin which is possibly a low-temperature glaze. Because of this veneer the true character of the mineral puzzled us for quite a long time. It is not possible to say more about the hard veneer without flaking off a larger piece. Kaolinite is common from a great many localities, and no clue is therefore given as to its place of origin.'

The veneer referred to, best seen on the sides, is smooth, polished, and bears very fine striation marks of rubbing. It appears also in small areas on both faces untouched by the intaglio cutting.

10. *Single-sided Seal in Banded Agate, with Silver Mount* (colour pl. XXXVIII, 15, and pl. XLIV, 1–3). Length of seal stone 19 mm.; length of mount 35 mm.; thickness of seal stone 5 mm. Plain longitudinal perforation. The back is convex, pleasantly banded by the translucent stone. The fiddle-shaped mount holds the seal in a swivel, and consists of silver wire about 2 mm. thick. On the shoulders this has been reinforced by a neat overcast of similar wire. This mount, and a detachable silver wire hook suspended from it, suggests that the seal was worn as a pendant. Similar fiddle-shaped wire mounts in gold were noted in the Muncherjee Museum at Aden, but no comparable seal stones were seen there. The silver was examined spectrographically, and Dr. Desch's report will be found on p. 106, object no. 11.

Both seal stones, in view of their great importance for dating and culture-contacts, were submitted to Dr. Henri Frankfort, and his report is given in full, pp. 101–3.

11. *Silver Plaque Amulet* (pl. XLIV, 14). Length 2·9 cm. A thin, nearly square sheet of metal topped by an inverted triangle pierced for suspension. Two inscribed zones, separated and edged by three horizontal bands with diagonal hatching, bear the words H̱ilm on the upper line, ʿAwn T on the lower: these are discussed by Professor Ryckmans, p. 178, no. 58. The back is plain. The spectrographic analysis shows, as in the other silver objects, a heavy trace of tin (see

---

[1] This occurs also on a scaraboid in the Peabody Museum at Harvard, from the Yemen.

Analysis, p. 106, no. 10). Amulets of this form are fairly common in south Arabian collections from the Yemen, though this seems to be the first recorded in silver.

12. *Miniature Black Stone Ware Suspension Bowl, type XIII* (pl. LV, 19). Ht. 4·3 cm. Less than half was recovered, but this gives the form and the vertically pierced lug, as in the A5 specimen.

13. *Miniature Nozzled Cup in Black Stone Ware* (pl. LV, 14). Ht. 4·5 cm. It has a long dropper spout and a horizontal tongue handle. Though without the characteristic lid flange of type X, it has been provisionally classed as a variant.

Other objects found in A6 include:

14. *Fifteen Microlithic Implements*, all but two of obsidian, and of the same prevalently rectangular and trapezoid forms as in A5 (pl. LVIII, 56–70). Also eleven chips and flakes (pl. LVIII, 71–2) and one pyramidal obsidian core (pl. LIX, 3).

15. *Bronze Tacks.* Four specimens, identical with those in A5 (pl. XLV, 17).

16. *Beads.* In addition to those found with the ossuary group I, the following should be added.

Gold wire bead (pl. XLV, 6). This is a thin strip with overlapped ends, exactly like the A5 specimen. Both are so small and insignificant that one surmises that considerable numbers may have been used, perhaps to interspace carnelian or glass beads. If so they were very thoroughly plundered at, or shortly after, burial.

Agate flattened barrel bead (Beck, no. 2; colour pl. XXXVIII, 11; pl. XL, 2; section, pl. XLII, 19). This bead is slightly patinated.

Besides these most of the common types found in A5 were present in small numbers;[1] these are listed in the distribution table, below. Two small specimens of the shell drop-pendants, of the type pl. XLII, 27–8, may be added.

Sherds. These, apart from the black stone ware specified, consisted of the rough brown-red wares and red-coated finer pottery of A5. In cases where the shape could be identified they fell, without exception, into the classes proposed on the unbroken A5 material. They included certainly types I, II, III, and VIII.

[1] Carnelian, 14; faience disks, 22; red glass oblates and bicones, 16; green and blue ditto, 20; yellow ditto, 7; shell disk, 14; discoloured, uncertain, 10; zone bead, 1.

XI. THE TOMBS. DISCUSSION AND CONCLUSIONS

THE difficulty of interpreting the facts enumerated will not have escaped the attentive reader who has also studied the tomb plan. Exactitude about the inexact is no better than inexactitude about the exact; and it seems impossible, in the total absence of any guidance from similar (non-existent) archaeological work in south Arabia, to do more, without straining insufficient evidence intolerably, than indicate the various possibilities, without arriving at a fixed solution.

About the age of A6 relative to A5 there can be, however, little doubt. In spite of structural differences caused by the recessing of A6, it exhibits in all other respects such a close similarity in dimensions, shape, and mode of entrance that it would be unwise, I think, to assume a substantially different age in the construction of both, even were this less strongly supported than is the case by the contained material.

Identity of function, as an ossuary pure and simple, is, however, not so sure; much remains speculative owing to the (presumably) rifled condition of the contents and the large area unexcavated. But the absence of all but one small group of bones and pottery in the moiety cleared does not encourage the belief that many, if any, other groups comparable to A5 lie beneath the uncleared fill.

We are left to explain the relationship of:

(a) Six empty raised recesses, plundered (if ever used) before the deposits had fully formed.

(b) The association in a single floor group of a skull; a tibia which, being also female, may belong to the same individual; another tibia which does not; and part of a male pelvis—three individuals for certain, or perhaps four.

(c) A very thin scatter of isolated pots and valuables, all of small size, and sherds only of larger vessels—none even partly intact—more or less over the whole area excavated, combined with an equally meagre scatter of fragments of human bone.

It is less tempting than appears at first glance to attribute group I to the plundering of recesses: it is too closely similar in type to those in cave A5 which lacked recesses. Moreover, there is difficulty in supposing that plunderers would trouble to rearrange, in a compact group, a selection of the bones and grave goods dislodged in the course of recess looting. For these reasons, then, I decline to connect (a) and (b), even though it deprives me of one explanation for (a) without supplying another. I am prepared, then, to dispose of (b) by taking it at its face value—namely, a casual association of bones and grave goods transferred under conditions similar to those which operated at A5, from some other place of primary burial, and redeposited on the floor of A6.

Should we be justified then (having, perhaps rashly, eliminated (b) from further consideration) in equating (a) and (c)?—in supposing that the shreds of comminuted bone found in the riddling of the soil outside[1] represent all that remains of the former occupants of the recesses, plus what may still lie beneath the unexcavated area?

I hesitate to lay so great a burden of assumption on the undug deposits, for what the dug area produced was totally insufficient to make up a proportionately reasonable complement of skeletons. The equation could only, I think, be maintained as a fairly reasonable postulate if we assumed that the recesses themselves were used, not as full-length benches for the reception of complete bodies, but as shelves to accommodate parcels of human remains, already extremely fragmentary and brittle, gathered together from interment elsewhere. Given such pre-existing conditions, the violence of robbery, the throwing down on the floor, might perhaps explain the condition of the human residue, as well as the very completely smashed state of all the larger pots apart from those in group I, or otherwise enumerated in the inventory.

Could one be certain of all this, then A6, as well as A5, might be classed as an ossuary, though of a rather more elaborate kind, which the better quality of the grave goods that had escaped rifling would confirm.

Against this possibility which, on the whole, seems the least unsatisfactory, may be set the measurements of the recesses—2 to 2·20 m. long by 0·60 m. wide—which certainly suggest benches for complete, extended burials, and are unnecessarily long for parcels of disjointed and fragmentary bones.

On the other hand we have no real warrant, based on known evidence, for regarding these recesses as necessarily destined for any such purpose at all. Just conceivably they might be ledges for the placing of the funerary images of the deceased; statuettes, seldom exceeding 50 cm. high, which, though known by the hundreds in museums, chiefly from the Yemen, and obviously made in large numbers, have never yet been seen *in situ* by a reliable observer.[2] But that they were destined for niches seems assured by the unfinished state of their backs and head tops;[3] and that they were funerary equipment is generally agreed. That is one possibility, though I do not confidently advance it since neither cave-tomb yielded even a fragment of such a statuette; and their rarity in the Hureidha district seems attested by the fact that only one—seen in pl. xv, 2—was offered for sale there.

Yet another possibility, though remote all things considered, is that cave A6 was originally made for a dwelling;[4] admitting this, oblong recesses about 3 m. long by 0·50 m. wide, noted in houses at Petra, could be invoked as a reasonable parallel.[5] But this hypothesis only works on the assumption that such a dwelling was re-utilized later for interments (i.e. group I and the other floor remains human and cultural), and that

[1] They were too small to identify in the darkness of the cave. It may be noted that no parts of a skull were included, apart from two molars.

[2] I like to delude myself with the idea that Mohammed's ban on the fashioning of images was due to aesthetic distress at the result.

[3] A good short article by Dr. L. Legrain on those in the Pennsylvania University Museum appeared in the *American Journal of Archaeology*, July–Sept. 1934.

[4] Its darkness need not invalidate this possibility. Equally dark caves are still inhabited and have a certain attraction in torrid latitudes.

[5] G. and A. Horsfield, *Quarterly of the Department of Antiquities in Palestine*, vol. vii, pp. 16–18, fig. 1. But there is only a single elongated recess in each room, which is square. Small wall niches abound in the Petra houses.

the blocking of the entrance and approach dates from the latter stage—a cumbrous explanation.

Further essays in interpretation may best be left until future excavations supply more evidence. Archaeological literature abounds in the difficulties of rationalizing the imperfect records of disturbed tombs, and in particular those of the ossuary, fractional, or primary and secondary communal type.

In spite of these inherent difficulties, cave A6 is of quite exceptional importance for our dating evidence, which is not affected by them. The absolute and relative chronology of our other excavated sites, and all our pottery—itself the indispensable link with future excavations—is mainly dependent on it.[1] We are on sure ground, ignoring the problems of *why* things were as we found them, in asserting that A6 had been used as a sepulchre, and that the position and condition of the objects in it stamp their mark on it as a plundered one. We may further assert that the plundering took place through the hole in the western partition wall, and that it occurred before the deposits had formed, for the trifles remaining were scattered on the floor. The true entrance was intact, and the sherds in the *dromos*—a key position—link it culturally with the wares in A5. Similar potteries recur inside, and the three ceramic fabrics noted at A5—the coarse porous, the red slip-coated, and the black stone ware—were here repeated. Though mainly in sherds, vessels of classes I, II, III, VIII, IX, X, XIII occurred for certain. The only deviation from A5 lies with the big decorated goblet in group I (pls. XXVIII, 1; L, 1). This is a more ambitious ceramic achievement, though badly executed.

Other objects, too, give a general impression of a somewhat higher status than does A5. The limestone ointment jar (no. 6) and tripod saucer (no. 4) are in fine crystalline translucent stone, resembling alabaster, and both are pseudo-fluted. The little limestone pedestal cup (no. 1), though in coarser stone, is nicely shaped and worked. The variegated glass bottle (no. 2), so far unique, was undoubtedly a treasure. The suggested mirror handle (no. 5) belonged at any rate to some presumably 'luxury' article; its technique of bronze and iron recalls a similar combination noted in the dart-shaped object in A5.II.12 (p. 73). The silver inscribed amulet (no. 11) also contributes to this impression, which the pair of import stamp-seals (nos. 9, 10) finally enhances.

It is difficult to resist the conclusion that these last three objects and the fragment of the stone ware suspension bowl (no. 12) were originally associated with recesses. Three lay suspiciously at the foot of the two-tiered recess. As no one, apart from burial rites, would intentionally leave a valuable seal, complete with silver mount, on a dusty floor, the positions of these objects provide independent, and I think strong, evidence for a former burial of some kind in one or both of the recesses. These, I surmise, were subsequently looted; the objects fell into the dust below and in the darkness were lost. The ransacking must have been thorough. If the positions of the other few surviving articles may be used as evidence, one may guess that not only the recesses but the cavern

---

[1] 'Mainly' because Mr. Beck's bead dating for A5, without the confirmation of the import seals in A6, has given us an elastic, independent, estimate.

in its whole periphery was inspected. The objects lost, or discarded as valueless, tend to lie in patches, nos. 1 to 5 in one, and 6 to 8 in another; and it is not improbable, I think, that this denotes the irritable rejection of unwanted articles: in flinging aside (perhaps from the other side of the cave) there would be an unconscious tendency to throw the same length and in the same direction.

THE DATING OF A5 AND A6. The intimate cultural interrelations of A5 and A6 seem conclusively demonstrated by the tabular comparison of the contents set out opposite p. 88.

The date is co-determined within its self-imposed limits of uncertainty by the beads in both, and the pair of foreign seals in A6 with their three mythological designs. Rarely has the chance association of imports from distant sources provided more convergent results; nor two much-travelled stamp-seals conspired in their final resting-place to tell so closely the same story.

Mr. Beck, for his part, affirms 'a distinct resemblance to beads from the Eastern Mediterranean which are dated to the 7th–5th centuries B.C.'

Dr. Frankfort, having expounded the difficult problems of borrowed style and subject inherent in stamp-seal dating and provenance, discharges, nevertheless, in his conclusions a double barrel of independent evidence each of which hits the same mark. The agate seal was 'produced somewhere outside Mesopotamia under the influence of Achaemenian seals'. For the black kaolinite double-sided seal 'we may postulate an Achaemenian prototype for one of the two designs', whereas the inverted mythology of the other 'is such as may occur in a peripheral region. . . . It is remarkable that our independent analyses of the two seals converge upon the same conclusion, namely that they were cut in a region directly or indirectly influenced by Achaemenian glyptic . . . the consistency of the evidence makes it probable that the tomb . . . dates to Achaemenian times.'

Seventh- to fifth-century affinities therefore are present on one line of evidence; sixth to fourth on the other. They provide a fixed upper dating limit, but leave us to guess at the lower. Time-lag and trade drift are impossible factors to estimate without a large body of diverse material, added to which must be placed in our case the uncertainty which envelopes the time-span covered by our two tombs.

XII. EXPERTS' REPORTS

INTRODUCTORY REMARKS TO THE BEAD REPORT

THE beads collected in the Hureidha tombs A5 and A6, and a few we found on the surface of the pre-Islamic ruins at Gheibun (Meshḥed, Wadi Do'an) and Sūne (Wadi 'Adim), were submitted for examination to Mr. Beck, who had already handled those found by Dr. Huzayyin a year earlier at Gheibun.

Our beads were on exhibition at the Fitzwilliam Museum in the late summer and autumn of 1938, and consequently Mr. Beck, also occupied till then on other tasks, began work on them only in October. His examination was ended before completion, at the New Year 1939, by his illness and departure to Algeria in search of recovery. That hope was disappointed, and on his return in the spring of 1939 continuation of the interrupted work proved impossible. His report is now published as it stood, without the microscopic sections and analyses originally intended. The essentials, however, are there, and Mr. Beck's unrivalled command of his subject, and unequalled range of experience in it, gives his report a greater value, perhaps, than a more detailed contribution from other hands.

The choice of beads drawn in section (pls. XLII, XLIII) is, therefore, my own. In their arrangement I have deliberately disregarded the typological classifications based on shape and proportions laid down in Mr. Beck's standard work[1] and in Mr. Brunton's publications.[2] My south Arabian collection is too small to respond to formal classification. It numbers under 500 specimens, omitting the numerous shell beads; and I have, in pls. XLII, XLIII, grouped the beads in their colour and composition class regardless of form. In so doing the order of Mr. Beck's report is followed. I have also disregarded, with regret, the use of the Ostwald Colour Scale, advocated by Mr. Oliver Myers,[3] for the majority of the glass beads from the tombs are corroded and discoloured beyond recognition, short of fracture, of their original tint (colour pl. XXXVIII, 17, shows the cobalt-blue colour of the broken surface of a brown corroded bead). Samples of the better-preserved beads and amulets are given in the colour plate.

Pls. XXXIX, XL show, as supplements to the section drawings, strings of the chief sorts of beads life-size. In order to facilitate cross-references I have numbered them in accordance with the notation added for convenience to Mr. Beck's report. It must be made clear that the stringing is a photographic and exhibition convenience. No strings, not even of three or four beads, were found in related order; and the interspacing, for instance, of carnelians with shell disks in string no. 1 of pl. XL is designed only to outline the shapes better and has no other authority.

---

[1] 'Classification and Nomenclature of Beads and Pendants', *Archaeologia*, vol. lxxvii.

[2] Especially, *Qau and Badari II*.

[3] *Cemeteries of Armant I*.

The bottom string on pl. xl is a set of dated beads from Syria, used by Mr. Beck together with others in his Syrian collection, for comparison, and as a 'control' over the affinities and dating of the south Arabian beads. Mrs. Beck in a letter dated December 18, 1939, says: 'In looking out beads to send to Dr. Huzayyin I went more carefully into the Syrian beads in my husband's collection. Each of your types seems to be there except the cuprous oxide bicones.[1] I discovered a little red eye-bead, identical with yours,[2] but the eyes are undoubtedly of green glass. Probably the eyes in yours are dark green though they look almost black.' It should be noted on the photograph of this Syrian string that the axe and altar amulets recur in the Hureidha tombs.

The absence from the Syrian collections of the large red, green, and blue bicones and oblates (nos. 16, 17, 18 of the report) is arresting when other resemblances are so close. In my collection they form a high proportion of the total of glass beads, and we found them on the surface of the Gheibun and Sūne ruins. They appear to be uncommon, however, in other regions of south-west Arabia, unless the evidence of native riflings is completely deceptive, as it may well be. The extensive bead collections in the Muncherjee Museum of Aden,[3] said to be mainly Baihan plunder, include only one or two of the red variety; none, as far as I could see through a glass case, of the blues and greens. Rathjens and von Wissmann published none from the Yemen;[4] but one or two bicones, perhaps of our type, figure in photographs kindly sent me by the Peabody Museum at Harvard, got by Dr. Coon, and another on a string published by Dr. Legrain, both from the Yemen.[5]

Perforated sea-shells were a very important element in the pre-Islamic necklaces of Hureidha. Large numbers of a minute *Columbella*, only 6 or 7 mm. long (pl. xli, 61), had been used (also noted at Sūne), as well as larger shells of about seventeen different kinds listed by Dr. Wilfrid Jackson. Sea-shell pendants, too, such as pl. xlii, 27, had evidently a special significance, for they were carefully imitated in stone (pl. xlii, 28) even to the reproduction of the columnar whorl. The numerous shell disks, large and small, are also cut from sea-shells, and neither Mr. Beck nor Dr. Jackson noted any ostrich shell—an interesting pointer in the direction of contacts, with the sands of the Great Desert nearer on the north than the Indian Ocean on the south. The stones include none not, in all probability, of south Arabian origin. The areas of old granites and crystalline schists shown on O. H. Little's map, and which extend round to the head of the Wadi Hadhramaut, probably yield the amethyst, garnet, felspars, carnelian, and agate.

---

[1] Nos. 6, 7, colour pl. xxxviii.
[2] No. 4, colour pl. xxxviii.
[3] These have no archaeological value: they have no history, and unrelated beads are strung together regardless of date or association.

[4] In *Südarabien Reise* a bicone is figured, pl. 167*d*: the text (p. 207) describes it as 'gelbroten durchsichtigen Stein'; conceivably it may be weathered glass.
[5] L. Legrain, *American Journal of Archaeology*, July–Sept. 1934, fig. 10.

REPORT NO. 134. COLLECTION OF BEADS FROM HADHRAMAUT, CAVE SEPULCHRES AT HUREIDHA, AND RUIN FIELDS AT SŪNE AND GHEIBUN

By H. C. BECK, F.S.A.

The types and materials of these beads show a distinct resemblance to beads from the eastern Mediterranean which are dated to the seventh to fifth centuries B.C.; but it is interesting to note that no amber is used. This seems to suggest that the Amber Route, which reached the eastern Mediterranean and the Crimea, was not at this relatively late date carried on as far south as south Arabia.

Although the dating of the collection as a whole evidently seems to belong to a few centuries B.C., there are one or two beads among the carnelians where the boring of the perforation is much more roughly done than in beads of that date. These may belong to an earlier civilization.[1]

Practically all the beads can be matched by specimens from Syria. The beads from Gheibun and Sūne may be of the same civilization as those of the cave sepulchres at Hureidha (A5 and A6), but it is difficult to say so definitely on account of the relatively small number of beads found. On the whole they are in better condition and show greater skill in workmanship than those from the tomb sites.

Materials. Carnelian, faience, glass, and shell are the materials used in the greatest quantities, but there are individual beads of agate, granite, amethyst, felspar, limestone, steatite, calcite; as well as a few very corroded copper or bronze ones,[2] and two small gold ones. These are made out of a thin strip of metal with the ends overlapping but not attached, and are cylindrical (see pl. XLVI, 1, 6).

Shapes. These are represented chiefly by bicones and spheroids: there are also a great many oblates, several disks, a few cylinders, two segmented beads, two zone beads, and only one melon bead.

Pendants. There are a number of pendants, mostly of shell (pl. XLII, 27, 31). Two are of felspar (pl. XLII, 25, 26), one is of steatite (pl. XLII, 28), and one of limestone. This is a pebble with a V-perforation in it.[3]

1. *Carnelian Beads* (pl. XL, string no. 1; colour pl. XXXVIII, 14, 21; sections, pl. XLII, 1–15). The appearance of these beads shows that they have been worked on in very different ways. Some are only roughly chipped into shape and have had a groove ground across the end to assist in starting the perforation, such as appears on beads made in pre-dynastic Egyptian periods when this device was frequently used. These are

[1] Though the tombs cover, I believe, a certain span of time, I do not think the collective evidence from pottery and other objects supports this suggestion. I should prefer to invoke the explanation of different levels of workmanship in this backward civilization—differences found equally in pots of the same type. On the other hand, we have, independent of dating associations, a few objects, such as the bronze flat axe (p. 144), the jade celts (p. 144), and the thin black rippled sherd (p. 145), which in other lands would certainly be attributed to an older civilization. If such they truly are (but there is no evidence) it is possible the primitive carnelian beads were handed down. G. C. T.

[2] Bronze. See Desch Report, no. 2, p. 106.

[3] The only limestone pebble I can trace (pl. XL, 6) has not got a V-perforation. G. C. T.

drilled from one end, with the result that the pressure of the drill causes considerable fracture on the end of the perforation.

Other beads show much greater skill in workmanship. Most of them are barrel-shaped or spheroid, one is very roughly faceted, while some even show attempts at intaglio carving or etching.[1] A considerable number shows traces of white patination which may be due to etching or to cremation, or to some special quality of the soil in which the beads were buried. In the latter case one would expect a larger proportion of the beads to be affected. On the other hand, in the string from A6 this patination is so much more in evidence that there seems no doubt that it was intentionally produced with a view to decoration. Another reason for this theory is that the white lines in many cases do not follow the natural structure of the material. There are, however, one or two on a string from A6 which are so much patinated that they show quite definite signs of burning. These are so completely whitened that it is not easy to tell if they are carnelian or agate.[2]

2. *Agate* (pl. xl, 2, colour pl. xxxviii, 11; section, pl. xlii, 18–20, 29). There are two agate beads from A5. One is a large barrel (A5.III, pl. xlii, 20). This is a well-known form of roughly made agate bead. Most of these probably come from India, but beads of similar material and shape are also found in other countries[3] (see H. C. Beck, 'A Note on certain Agate Beads', *Antiquaries Journal*, vol. x, no. 2).

The other is a tabular barrel (A5.VII, pl. xlii, 21) which seems to be the remains of a seal which has been burnt. From A6 (pl. xlii, 19; colour pl. xxxviii, 11) there is a flattened barrel with a certain amount of patination on it.

3. *Granite* (pl. xxxix, top string, no. 3; colour pl. xxxviii, 23). This is a spheroid of granite from surface finds at Gheibun (see under 'Gheibun').

4. *Amethyst* (pl. xl, 4; colour pl. xxxviii, 16; section, pl. xlii, 17). There is a flattened barrel bead from A6.

5. *Felspar* (pl. xl, 5; section, pl. xlii, 25, 26). There are two pendants of felspar. One is a small one in the form of an axe-head (A5.V); the other is irregular in shape (A5.II).

6. *Limestone.* There is one pendant made of a pebble (A5.II).[4] This has a V-perforation which is decidedly rare and only found in primitive cultures. It is probably best known among the Bronze Age beads of jet and amber.

---

[1] I am not convinced of this. G. C. T.

[2] Cremation can be ruled out for lack of supporting evidence, although an agate bead also shows signs of burning. Etching is possible, though none show a pattern. Etched carnelians are still worn in the Hadhramaut. I tried to buy a small pendant of this type from a bedouin at Hureidha (who was wearing it round his neck solo), but failed to offer enough: he evidently valued it. Presumably they come from India. On the whole I think soil contact is the likelier explanation of our patinated carnelians. Those I collected from surface sites were not affected in this manner. G. C. T.

[3] That the Hadhramis shaped their own beads from nodules is suggested by the unperforated unpolished barrel found at Gheibun (pl. xlii, 29). The agate may well be local, from the areas of old crystalline rocks to the south and west. The Yemen as a source of supply seems, I believe, to have been overlooked in attributing beads to India. G. C. T.

[4] There is doubt about the identification. Pl. xl, 6, is a limestone pebble pendant, but does not seem to show the perforation noted above. It has a large plain hole, due, I think, to natural causes, i.e. the weathering of a fossil. Mr. Beck's pendant must have been mislaid. G. C. T.

7. *Steatite* (section, pl. XLII, 28). Another pendant (A5.V) is of black steatite: this is a drop pendant.[1] Sp. gr. 9·61.

8. *Calcite* (pl. XL, 8; section, pl. XLII, 23). This is a roughly made irregular barrel-shape with a large perforation (A5.VII). Sp. gr. 2·72.

9. *Garnet* (section, pl. XLII, 16). There are six very small spheroid beads of this material, which is not common either in Mesopotamia or in Egypt. These beads are particularly well made and perfect in structure, and it is rather significant that they should have been found outside the sepulchre (A5). Sp. gr. 3·5. (See p. 70 for position.)

10. *Bone* (section, pl. XLII, 24). There is a large bead made from a hollow bone, cylindrical (A5.V).

The two very small segmented ones are interesting as they are unusual and suggest the type found in the Bronze Age. These have sp. gr. 1·1 and 1·5.

11. *Fossil*[2] (A5.VII). There is a white cylindrical object about 1 inch long, with a curious structure which may be fossil. The surface is irregularly pitted with tiny rosettes which are natural. An attempt has been made to perforate this cylinder at one end. Sp. gr. is 2·31.

12. *Faience.* There are a number of beads which look as if they were made of the material called 'faience' in Egypt. A microscopic examination, however, shows that they contain very few of the sharp crystalline fragments which are so characteristic of the Egyptian 'faience', where as much as 95 per cent. of the material usually consists of powdered quartz. In the Hadhramaut beads so large a proportion is isotropic that their consistency is more like glass, and in this way suggests the kind of material used in China which Professor Seligman and H. C. Beck have called 'glass faience' (cf. C. G. Seligman and H. C. Beck, 'Far Eastern Glass: Some Western Origins', *Bulletin XII. Museum of Far Eastern Antiquities*, Stockholm).

13. *Faience. Melon bead* (colour pl. XXXVIII, 5). The only one in the collection. (From A6.)

14. *Faience. Bead in the form of an Altar* (colour pl. XXXVIII, 13). (From A5.VI.)[3]

15. *Faience. Disk beads* (colour pl. XXXVIII, 20; pl. XL, 15, string; sections, pl. XLIII, 33–6). A number of very small disk beads (A5 and A6).

16. *Glass. Red glass* (colour pl. XXXVIII, 6, 7; pl. XXXIX, string 16; sections, pl. XLIII, 37–45, 60). The colouring of the red is due to cuprous oxide which appears in larger quantities in some beads than in others. This would account for the differences in specific gravity, which varies from 2·32 to 3·00. The cuprous oxide crystals are unusually fine and free from deposit of metallic copper, which shows that the beads have been made at a low temperature, at any rate under 1,000° C. In some cases there are a number of crystals of the yellow form of cuprous oxide. Cuprous oxide glass corrodes so

[1] Imitating a shell pendant; see p. 95.
[2] Perhaps a crinoid? G. C. T.
[3] A Syrian altar bead is photographed for comparison, pl. XL. Mine has probably been painted upside down in the colour plate. In any case its perforation is vertical; that of the Syrian specimen, horizontal. Both are blue faience, the A5 specimen brighter and greener. G. C. T.

extensively that in some cases red beads have been taken to be green.[1] The layer of corrosion can be as much as ½ mm. thick. (From A5, A6, Gheibun.)

17. *Green Glass* (colour pl. XXXVIII, 2, 3, 8, 18; pl. XXXIX, string 17; sections, pl. XLIII, 46–52, 61). The green glass is probably also made with copper, with a little iron included which gives the green tinge. Most of the green beads are so corroded that they do not appear to be translucent. The corrosion covers in many cases a large portion of the surface. There are one or two small beads which are transparent. (From A5, A6, Sūne; and Gheibun.)

18. *Blue Glass* (colour pl. XXXVIII, 12, 17, 25; sections, pl. XLIII, 53, 54). When copper alone is used for colouring the glass is blue, distinctly lighter in tone than the dark blue produced by cobalt. There are several specimens of this blue copper glass. This is a light glass with specific gravity varying from 2·00 to 2·4. (From A5, A6, Gheibun.)

19. *Mixed Glass, Flush Crumbs* (colour pl. XXXVIII, 19; section, pl. XLIII, 55).[2] A good many of the beads are made of two glasses mixed together. These glasses have melted in such a way that flakes of one glass appear sprinkled on the other, making a flush-crumb bead. All of these beads are considerably corroded. The corrosion is caused by chemical action between the two glasses. (From A5.)

20. *Yellow and Orange Glass* (colour pl. XXXVIII, 28; sections, pl. XLIII, 56–9). This glass is coloured by iron which appears to be carried in an amorphous form. In some cases in similar glass, instead of the amorphous mass small crystals of spinel are evident, and it may be that these amorphous masses are also a form of spinel. This is a light glass with sp. gr. 2·3 to 2·5. It is probably free from lead. There is a considerable number of yellow glass beads of which the larger ones are specially corroded, and a few small orange ones. (From A5, A6, Gheibun.)

21. *Black Glass and Purple and White Glass* (colour pl. XXXVIII, 10 top left; section, pl. XLIII, 62, 69; pl. XXXIX, 21). There are a few specimens of this glass and also one bead of purple and white glass worked together, pl. XXXIX, 21. This is a rather rare glass. Oenoche made of it are generally found to have come from the Mediterranean, but I have not previously seen a bead. (From A5, Gheibun, Sūne.)

22. *Eye-bead* (colour pl. XXXVIII, 4; section, pl. XLIII, 63). One only in the collection. It is a very unusual type, as it is rare to have the base made of red glass. One is known from Cumae, but the glass of the Cumae bead has a much lower sp. gr., 2·43, whereas this one has a high sp. gr. of 3·02 and probably contains lead. This bead is noticeably small, being only 0·2 in. in diameter. It had probably seven stratified eyes of dark blue and white glass, the centre of the eyes being dark blue.[3] (From A5.V.)

23. *Yellow and Green bead* (colour pl. XXXVIII, 22; section, pl. XLIII, 64). There is a small barrel bead of green and yellow glass. The yellow glass is laid on the top of the

---

[1] This is very likely in the present case. G. C. T.

[2] These are not confined to any special shape or colour. The bright blue bicone, colour pl. XXXVIII, 25, is a flush crumb. But I have had difficulty in identifying 'a great many', and can, with certainty, trace only three or four

specimens in A5, groups VII and IX, and one at Gheibun. Mr. Beck's experienced eye would find more. G. C. T.

[3] See Mrs. Beck's remarks on p. 95. It is not possible to say if the eyes are dark blue or green; they are, in their present condition, nearly black. G. C. T.

green in a thin strip so that it looks like an enamel. Sp. gr. is 2·00. These beads are found very frequently in Egypt, where they are called Roman, though they appear both at earlier and later periods. (From A5.II.)

24. *Zone beads* (colour pl. XXXVIII, 10 bottom left, right; pl. XL, 24; sections, pl. XLIII, 65, 66). There are two beads of black glass with white zones. One is barrel-shaped, and the other a small oblate. Sp. gr. 2·4. Similar beads have been found during the Etruscan period in Italy and at a still earlier date at Tell-el-Amarna (1400 B.C.). (From A5.V, A6.)

25. *Shell Disk Beads* (pl. XLI, 2, 12–17, 23; sections, pl. XLIII, 70–2). There is a large proportion of beads and pendants made from partial or complete shells. The most noteworthy is a disk bead cut from a large cone shell (pl. XLI, 2, see Jackson, p. 104, *Conus betulinus* L.). This bead has a diameter of 1¾ in. and closely resembles the disk beads now worn in the South Sea islands. Of the smaller disk beads the majority, if not all, are cut out of sea-shell and not out of ostrich egg-shell. Among these there are one or two which have been blackened artificially (see pl. XLI, 23). (A5, A6, Gheibun, Sūne.)

26. *Pusiostoma mendicaria* (see *Engina mendicaria* Lamk. of Shell Report). These are extremely common in the Middle East.

27. *Cowries.* A large number with rubbed-down backs (see Shell Report).

28. *Shell Pendants, Spacer, and Concave-ended bead* (sections, pl. XLII, 27, 30, 31). There are four drop pendants (of the type pl. XLII, 27). Three of these are surface finds at Gheibun, one at Sūne. A steatite copy has been noted from A5 (see no. 7 above). A spacing bead is seen on pls. XL, 28, centre, XLII, 30, (from A5.VII). There is also a shell bead with concave ends to fit against a spheroid (pls. XL, 28, left, XLII, 22; from A5).

BEADS FROM GHEIBUN, NEAR MESHHED.[1]

There is one string from Gheibun in which nearly all the types found in the Hureidha tombs are represented.[2] There are also three different types which are unusual.

3. *Granite bead* (colour pl. XXXVIII, 23; pl. XXXIX, 3). This is a spheroid of grey granite similar to the granite found at Ur, where it was only occasionally used.[3] The bead is very well made and polished.

21. *Purple and White Glass* (pl. XXXIX, 21; section, pl. XLIII, 69). Another distinctive bead is a small oblate made of purple and white glass combined.[4]

29. *Red and Green Glass* (colour pl. XXXVIII, 26; section, pl. XLIII, 68). One small

[1] These were collected by E. W. Gardner and myself on a short visit. All were surface finds. At the time I did not know that Dr. Huzayyin had collected there a year before. His series is more extensive and includes two fine blue eye-beads. Our collection adds little to his except the granite bead (no. 3, above). G. C. T.

[2] Nos. 1, 2, 15, 16, 18, 19, 20, 21, 25 of the Hureidha

series were found in our short search in addition to the others referred to above. G. C. T.

[3] For the probable source see p. 95. G. C. T.

[4] The purple and white (no. 21) from A5 is vaguely zoned by the white (see pl. XL, 21). In the Gheibun bead it is speckled.

spherical bead of red glass, with dark green spirals inlaid, is of particular interest as this type seems confined to Gheibun, Dr. Huzayyin having also found a larger one on the same site. It is made, however, of the same glass as the cuprous oxide beads from the Hureidha tombs. The design recalls the type of bead made in south England in Anglo-Saxon times, and dating to between A.D. 500 and 700. Identical beads are found in Syria dating to the Roman period and possibly earlier.

30. *Transparent Green Glass* (colour pl. XXXVIII, 24; pl. XXXIX, 30; section, pl. XLIII, 67). A tabular barrel bead, very well preserved. Sp. gr. 2·24.

Note by G. C. T. The barrel-shaped, unperforated lump of banded agate shown in section, pl. XLII, 29, and not seen by Mr. Beck, is interesting, for it indicates that these beads need not too easily be regarded as imports. It is unpolished, but seems to have been rubbed by an abrasive, for flat chamfers mark the sides. The banding of the stone runs longitudinally, and one side is white, the other brown.

BEADS FROM SŪNE.

There is not enough material to tell how these ruins compare with the others as to period, but it shows a general resemblance to the other finds. The copper or bronze beads (type, pl. XLV, 1) are larger and relatively more numerous. There is one faience spacing bead (colour pl. XXXVIII, 29) and a particularly well-made shell drop pendant (section, pl. XLII, 27).

NOTE ON TWO SEAL STONES

By DR. HENRI FRANKFORT

Engraved stones discovered in a newly explored part of the Near East will as a rule establish connexions with better-known regions. It is well to remember, however, that the degree of enlightenment which we may derive from them varies greatly. On the one hand there are recognizable exports, such as the cylinders found in the fourth stratum at Sialk in central Iran, which are Mesopotamian products of the Jemdet Nasr period.[1] On the other hand we find non-Mesopotamian or non-Egyptian objects made under the influence of the leading centres, but too careless in their imitation or too independent in their iconography for precise deductions to be drawn from them. One of the three cylinder seals discovered at Tepe Hissar in NE. Iran[2] vaguely suggests affinities with Elamite seals of the Jemdet Nasr period; the group, as a whole, remains enigmatical and the chronological position of the objects with which they were found is still a matter of surmise. We are not even entitled to assume that the seals were made on the spot; they may have reached Tepe Hissar from the west, or from any site on the periphery of Mesopotamia. We shall see that the seals from the Hadhramaut are in the same category.

[1] R. Ghirshman, *Fouilles de Sialk*, i, pl. XCIV.   [2] Erich F. Schmidt, *Excavations of Tepe Hissar*, p. 198.

Now the glyptic of the peripheral regions presents a definite problem.[1]   Its dependence
on Mesopotamian seals is fundamental. Further development consists either in a more
or less garbled repetition of the derived motives, or in an increasing measure of independ-
ence, new and original themes displacing the derivations. In either case we gain an
ins'ght into the peculiarities of the region where the seals are found, but our ability to
date a newly discovered peripheral style is dependent upon the derivative elements.
The best we can hope for is that they reflect a particular phase of Mesopotamian glyptic
in some detail.

The shape of one of the two seals from the Hadhramaut provides a first indication
of its affinities. The somewhat conical domed seal of agate (pl. XLIV, 1, 3) assumes a form
used during Assyrian, Neo-Babylonian, and Achaemenian times. Stratified or otherwise
dated specimens are exceedingly rare, and while the style or subject of the seal cylinders
enables us to some extent to distinguish between the three periods, the stamp-seals are
hardly ever subdivided.

Our agate seal contains, however, some features significant also in this respect. The
design shows a standing figure facing left on the impression and wrapped entirely in a
long robe (pl. XLIV, 2). It is due to the prolongation of the lower horizontal line at the
waist until it touches a petal of the flower (a result of careless cutting) that the figure
appears at first sight to place one foot upon the plant in a well-known attitude of conflict,
never found, however, in a similar context. The creature holds an indistinct object in
one hand and lifts the other above its head. Its features are very curious and certainly
not human: rather bird-like. But the gesture of the arm is characteristic for a lion-headed
monster brandishing a dagger. This appears already on seals of the Akkadian period;[2]
again in the time of Hammurabi[3] on Assyrian seals and reliefs;[4] and on an Achaemenian
seal.[5] An eagle-headed demon, on the other hand, is common on Assyrian monuments,
but it does not hold a weapon.

It is probable that our seal-cutter blurred the leonine features, and perhaps more
likely, confused the two monsters and rendered the bird-headed demon in the other's
attitude. In either case it is improbable that he was an Assyrian for whom features and
pose would have had a definite meaning.

The manner in which the figure is cut—a drill hole at the shoulders and straight lines
marking back and front—is peculiar to certain Neo-Babylonian seals, and may be also
late Assyrian or Achaemenian.[6] But the last-named period is suggested by the plant,
for it has no resemblance to the Assyrian or Neo-Babylonian renderings of the sacred
tree, and may be interpreted as the Soma plant in a Zoroastrian context. It is repeatedly
depicted, sometimes with five and sometimes with three petals.[7] A combination of three

[1] Frankfort, *Cylinder Seals*, pp. 224 ff.

[2] Ibid., pl. XXII *f.*

[3] Ibid., pl. XXVIII *c*, and 174 ff.

[4] Gadd, *Stones of Assyria*, pls. 17, 32; and also in his
British Museum publication on *Assyrian Sculpture*, pp. 49 ff.
L. Delaporte, *Catalogue des Cylindres Orientaux de la Biblio-
thèque Nationale*, pl. XXXV, 543 *c.*

[5] Von der Osten, *Ancient Oriental Seals in the Collection
of Mrs. Agnes Baldwin Brett*, pl. XII, 139: called Assyrian or
Achaemenian, but shown to be the latter by the design on
face C.

[6] Delaporte, loc. cit., pls. XXXVI, 557; XXXVII, 600, 603.

[7] Ibid., pl. XXXVII, 604–11.

of these lotus-like plants is accompanied by an inscription in Pahlavi [1] another indication of its Achaemenian background. Above the plant may appear a crescent, a winged disk, or a god in a crescent, and the accompanying figure is, on Achaemenian seals, always human and rendered in an attitude of worship.

The appearance, on our seal, of an aggressive monster instead of a praying man is on a par with the confusion of leonine and bird-headed monster; both represent mistakes such as normally arise in a peripheral region. It would seem, then, that this seal was produced somewhere outside Mesopotamia under the influence of Achaemenian seals.

The other seal is an oval of black stone engraved on both faces (pl. XLIV, 4–8). This shape is less characteristic than that of the first, which has a definite connexion with Mesopotamia. The designs of the black seal are similarly non-Mesopotamian, in the technique of their cutting as well as their contents. Both faces (pl. XLIV, 4–7) show a variant of the age-old scene of combat between a hero and two beasts. On one side (pl. XLIV, 4, 5) a winged personage holds two animals by the hind legs. This group is common on Syrian and Cypriote seals of the last third of the second millennium B.C.;[2] but it is rare in Mesopotamia until Neo-Babylonian times,[3] when an archaizing tendency led to the revival of various extinct themes. On Achaemenian seals it is common, but there the Persian king appears usually as the master of the two animals. Two seals are known, however, where lions are cut in the usual Achaemenian style, and the central figure is not wearing the royal cidaris but a round skull-cap, and is, moreover, winged.[4] We may therefore postulate an Achaemenian prototype for one of the two designs on our seal.

The other design (pl. XLIV, 6, 7) is most peculiar, for it is an inversion of the theme. Instead of the hero dominating two beasts, we see two lions towering over a small crouching man. Here again the change is such as may occur in a peripheral region where the design is not established by tradition, and may well be modified by indigenous mythology.[5]

It is remarkable that our independent analyses of the two seals converge upon the same conclusion, namely, that they were cut in a region directly or indirectly influenced by Achaemenian glyptic. This does not imply that they were made in the Hadhramaut; caravans or coastal traffic may have brought them from the Persian Gulf. But in any case the consistency of the evidence makes it probable that the tomb discovered by Miss Caton Thompson dates to Achaemenian times.

---

[1] *The Art Bulletin*, xiii, no. 2 (Chicago, 1931); Von der Osten, *The Ancient Seals from the Near East in the Metropolitan Museum*, no. 100.

[2] Frankfort, op. cit., pls. XLIV, I; XLV, G. J.

[3] *Ibid.*, pl. XXXVI, I. On Assyrian seals the animals are not held upside down.

[4] Delaporte, op. cit., pl. XXXVIII, 637, 638.

[5] Another S. Arabian example is reproduced from Grohmann, *Göttersymbole*, in *Handbuch der altarabischen Altertumskunde*, fig. 68, where the crouching figure is dwarfed by two rampant ibex. G.C.T.

REPORT ON MARINE SHELLS

By J. WILFRID JACKSON, D.SC., F.S.A., F.G.S.

(Manchester Museum)

During the excavations at Hureidha in the Western Hadhramaut in 1937–8 numerous marine shells were met with in the tombs. These have been submitted to me by Miss G. Caton Thompson, F.S.A., the excavator. Many have been perforated and used as beads: others are more or less perfect. The report is as follows:

One valve of large Scallop or Pecten, *Chlamys townsendi* (Sow.). (From A5.VII.3, pl. xli, 4.) Found living in the Persian Gulf and around Aden. Recorded from ancient Egyptian graves at Karnak.

Umbonal part of a large Cockle, *Cardium pseudolima* Lamk. (From A5.III.8, pl. xli, 1.) Found living in Indian Ocean, around Aden, etc.

One valve of smaller Cockle, *Cardium rubicundum* Reeve. (From A6.) Recorded living from Gulf of Suez, Red Sea, Aden, etc. Also fossil from Raised Beaches east of Gebel Esh, Red Sea.

Valves of large Ark-shells, *Arca inflata* Reeve. (From A5 and A6, pl. xli, 3.) Recorded from Aden, etc.

Ground-down top of large Cone-shell, probably *Conus betulinus* L., perforated in the centre for threading. (From A5.II.12, pl. xli, 2.) This species is found locally. (See also Beck, no. 25, p. 100.)

One shell of *Nerita polita* L., with side perforation. (From A5.I, pl. xli, 11.) Found living at Aden, in Red Sea, etc. Recorded from ancient Egyptian graves at Badari (Badarian, Pan-grave, &c.), Qau-el-Kebir (6th and 16th dyn.), Balabish (Pan-grave), &c. Also at Beersheba (Colt Expedition).

Two shells of *Conus acuminatus* Hwass., with apical perforation. (From A5, pl. xli, 46, 48.) Living at Aden, Gulf of Akaba, Red Sea, etc.

Twelve shells of *Engina mendicaria* Lamk., some with apical perforation, others with hole at one side. (From A5, pl. xli, 18–21, 26, 28, 30, 32, 34, 37, 40, 43.) Occurs at Aden, Red Sea, Indian Ocean, etc. Recorded from ancient graves at Gerar, and from Karnak, Koptos, Balabish (Pan-grave), Qau-el-Kebir (12th dyn. and Roman). (See also Beck, no. 26, p. 100.)

One shell of *Oliva inflata* Lamk., with apical perforation. (From A5, pl. xli, 41.) Living in the Red Sea, Aden, Persian Gulf; and fossil in Raised Beaches of the Red Sea. Has been recorded from graves at Badari.

Sixteen shells of *Oliva ispidula* L., all with apical perforation. (From A5, A6, pl. xli, 9, 10, 35, 39, 42, 45, 47, 49, 50, 52–4, 57, 59, 60.) Occurs living in the Red Sea, Makran coast, Indian Ocean, &c.; also fossil in Raised Beaches of the Red Sea.

One shell of *Ficula (Pyrula) ficus* Lamk., with apical perforation. (From A5, pl. xli, 51.) Living in the Red Sea, Persian Gulf, Makran coast, Indian Ocean, etc.

One immature shell of *Trochus radiatus* Gmel., with side perforation. (From A5, pl. XLI, 58.) Occurs in the Red Sea, Persian Gulf, Indian Ocean.

Two shells of *Marginella terveriana* Petit., with apical perforation. (From A5, pl. XLI, 62.) Occurs at Aden and the Red Sea.

Two[1] shells of *Columbella alizonae* M. and S., with apical perforation. (From A5, pl. XLI, 61.) Occurs n Persian Gulf, etc.

One shell of *Nassa obockiensis* Jouss?, with side perforation. (From A5, pl. XLI, 44.) Occurs at Aden, in the Red Sea, etc.

One shell of *Pleurotoma* (*Surcula*) *catena* Reeve, with side perforation. (From A5.I, pl. XLI, 56.) Occurs at Aden, etc.

One shell of *Cypraea erosa* L., rubbed down on the back. (From A5, pl. XLI, 33.) Living in the Red Sea, Aden, Indo-Pacific; and fossil in the Raised Beaches of Red Sea. Recorded from ancient Egyptian graves at Ballas.

Two shells of *Cypraea moneta* L., rubbed down on the back. (From A5, pl. XLI, 27, 29.) Occurs in the Red Sea, Aden, Indian Ocean, etc. Recorded from ancient graves at Karnak, El Amrah (pre-dynastic), &c., and from Beth-Pelet, Palestine.

Three shells of *Cypraea turdus* Lamk., rubbed down on the backs. (From A5, A6, pl. XLI, 25, 31, 38.) Occurs in the Red Sea, Persian Gulf, Indian Ocean, etc.; and fossil in the Raised Beaches of Red Sea. A specimen, similarly rubbed, was found at Beersheba (Colt Expedition).

One shell of *Cypraea helvola* L. (From A5.) Recorded living in the Red Sea, Aden, Indo-Pacific; and fossil in the Red Sea Raised Beaches.

Two shells of *Cypraea annulus* L., rubbed down on the backs. (From A5, pl. XLI, 22, 36.) Occurs in the Red Sea, Indian Ocean, etc.; recorded fossil from Raised Beaches of the Red Sea. In ancient graves at Karnak, Koptos, Nagada (pre- or proto-dynastic), Abydos (18th dyn.), Medum (22nd dyn.), Badari, Qau-el-Kebir (6th dyn., Roman); and Gerar, Palestine. Also in ancient graves at Shusha in Transcaucasia.

The custom of rubbing down the backs of the ring- and money-cowry, *C. annulus* and *moneta*, is still in vogue amongst east African people.[2] In Liberia these small white cowries are used in fortune-telling. (See also Beck, no. 27, p. 100.)

In addition to the above there are a number of very small shell rings or disks, probably made from a small species of *Conus*. (From A5 and A6, pl. XLI, 7, 8, 23; and on pl. XL, inter-threaded with carnelian beads. See also Beck, no. 25, p. 100. A blackened specimen is seen in pl. XLI, 23.)

---

[1] Very large numbers of these small shells were caught in the sieves: they were mostly broken in the riddling, being very fragile. They must have been strung in long chains and necklaces. G. C. T.

[2] It has indeed a record in Africa of about 7,000 years— a longer record perhaps than any other ornament or amulet— for it occurs in the Amratian, the Badarian, and in late Capsian deposits farther west. G. C. T.

REPORT BY THE NATIONAL PHYSICAL LABORATORY, METALLURGY DEPARTMENT, ON SPECTROGRAPHIC ANALYSIS OF OBJECTS FROM HUREIDHA, SUBMITTED BY G. CATON THOMPSON, 18 MAY 1939

The objects were examined by the method used in previous analyses. The resulting spectrograms showed the presence of the following elements:[1]

X indicates principal constituent.
xxxx „ element present in analytical quantity.
xxx „ heavy trace of element present.
xx „ trace of element present.
x „ faint trace of element present.

	1. Ornament A5.VIII.5 (pl. XLV, 15)	2. Bead A5.I.14 (pl. XLV, 1)	3. Nail A5.V (pl. XLV, 2)	4. Tacks A5.II (pl. XLV, 17)	5. Ear-ring A5.III.9 (pl. XLV, 14)	6. Pin A5.I.13 (pl. XLV, 11)
Au (Gold) . .	x	..	..	..	..	..
Ag (Silver) . .	xxx	xxx	x	xxx	xx	xxx
Cu (Copper) . .	X	X	X	X	X	X
Pb (Lead) . .	xxxx	x	..	xxx	xxx	x
Sn (Tin) . .	xxxx	xxxx	xx	xxxx	xx	x
Ni (Nickel) . .	xxx	x	..	xx	xx	xxx
Fe (Iron) . .	xxxx	xxx	xxx	xxx	xxx	xxx
As (Arsenic) . .	xxx	x	..	xxx	..	xxx
Si (Silicon) . .	xx	xx	xx	xx	xx	x
Sb (Antimony) .	..	..	..	..	..	..

	7. Dart-shaped object A5.II.12 (pl. XLV, 4)	8. Handle A6 (pl. XLV, 3)	9. Bangle A5.XII (pl. XLV, 8)	10. Plaque amulet A6 (pl. XLIV, 14)	11. Mount of seal A6 (pl. XLIV, 1–3)
Au (Gold) . .	..	..	..	..	..
Ag (Silver) . .	x	xx	x	X	X
Cu (Copper) . .	xxxx	X	X	xxxx	xxxx
Pb (Lead) . .	..	xxx	..	xxxx	xxx
Sn (Tin) . .	xxx	xxx	xxx	xxx	xxx
Ni (Nickel) . .	..	x	x	x	xxx
Fe (Iron) . .	X	xxx	xxx	..	..
As (Arsenic) . .	xx	x	x	..	..
Si (Silicon) . .	xxxx	xxx	x	..	..
Sb (Antimony) .	..	..	..	..	..

In addition to these eleven objects from the tombs, I submitted four others bought at or near Hureidha. One is the flat axe (pl. LXI, 9; see p. 144), another is the cruciform ornament shown in pl. XLV, 16. The other two are a silver ring, not figured here, and

[1] To make the report clearer the field numbers and illustration of the objects have been added to the analysis number. G. C. T.

one of three inscribed oval seals bought by F. Stark, also not figured as I believe them to be forgeries[1] and rejected them when offered for sale.

			12. *Flat axe* (*pl.* LXI, *9*)	13. *Ornament* (*pl.* XLV, *16*)	14. *Ring*	15. *Seal*
Au (Gold)	.	.	..	..	XXXX	..
Ag (Silver)	.	.	XXX	XXX	X	XX
Cu (Copper)	.	.	X	X	XXXX	..
Pb (Lead) .	.	.	XXXX	XXX	XXXX	XXXX
Sn (Tin) .	.	.	XXXX	XXXX	XXXX	XXXX
Ni (Nickel)	.	.	XXX	XXX	XX	XXX
Fe (Iron) .	.	.	X	XXX	X	X
As (Arsenic)	.	.	..	XXX	XXX	..
Si (Silicon)	.	.	..	XXX	XXX	..
Sb (Antimony)	.	.	..	..	..	..

Dr. C. H. Desch, who kindly superintended the analyses, makes the following comments:

Nos. 2, 4, 12, 13 are bronze.

No. 7 is iron which has been made by smelting and not from a meteorite, as it is free from nickel.

Nos. 10–11. Silver. In no. 11, tin may be about 1–2 per cent., lead <1 per cent., nickel <0·1 per cent. These are estimates from a comparison with copper alloys free from silver. The presence of so much tin in the silver objects (see also no. 14) is rather unusual, and this may be a means of tracing their origin.

No. 14 is an impure silver. The quantities of arsenic and nickel are not high. Little importance is to be attached to iron and silicon as they probably come from the soil in which the objects were embedded.

No. 15. Bronze. No bismuth or antimony.

A DESCRIPTION OF HUMAN REMAINS EXCAVATED BY MISS G. CATON THOMPSON AT HUREIDHA

By DR. G. M. MORANT

These skeletal remains comprise fourteen crania (most of which are incomplete and only one of which has a mandible), a nearly complete mandible, five fragments of other mandibles, the sacrum and right side of the pelvis of an individual, three vertebrae of an individual, and two tibiae of two other individuals. They were discovered in artificial caves which had probably been used as sepulchres for a considerable period, and are believed to relate to the last few centuries before the Christian era. The bones are in a bad state of preservation. They were light in colour when found and most are now brown owing to treatment with shellac. The specimens could not have been saved without treatment of that kind, but it has made observation of anatomical details and location of craniometric 'points' difficult.

[1] Professor Ryckmans is of the same opinion.

The following remarks on the crania relate principally to sex and age at death. Unless otherwise stated, the coronal, sagittal, and lambdoid sutures appear to be completely open externally.

(1) A5.VI.13. Incomplete calotte of an adult: probably male. This specimen appears to be slightly distorted by earth pressure in the grave (pl. XLVI, 1).

(2) A5.VII.11. Incomplete calvaria of an adult: male. Slight distortion due to earth pressure is evident. An *os épactal* is present (pl. XLVII, 1).

(3) A5.VIII.7. Cranium of an adult with the right temporal bone and right side of the facial skeleton defective: probably male. The sagittal suture was closing and the coronal and lambdoid were apparently beginning to close. Several teeth had been lost before death (pls. XLVI, 2; XLVII, 5; XLVIII, 1).

(4) A5.IX.6. Calotte of an adult: female.

(5) A5.IX.7. Incomplete cranium of an adult: male. This specimen is markedly distorted by earth pressure and no measurements of any value can be taken. Most teeth were present at death.

(6) A5.X.19. Calvaria of an adult with the base partly defective: male. The coronal and sagittal sutures were apparently beginning to close (pls. XLVI, 4; XLVII, 2).

(7) A5.X.18. Cranium of an adult: male. The sagittal suture was closing. Three molars had been lost before death (pls. XLVI, 3; XLVII, 6; XLVIII, 4).

(8) A5.XI.1. Cranium of an adult with the calvaria and facial skeleton largely defective on the right side: probably female. Several teeth had been lost before death (pls. XLVI, 5; XLVII, 3; XLVIII, 2).

(9) A5.XI.2. Calotte of a child, probably from eight to fourteen years old at death. Interparietal bones are present, the *os pentagonale* and right *os triangulare* being separate and of the usual shapes.

(10) A5.XI.3. Calvaria of a child with frontal bone and base defective, probably from twelve to sixteen years old at death. This specimen is distorted to some extent by earth pressure (pl. XLVI, 6).

(11) A5.XI.4. Cranium of an adult in fragments, no further reconstruction being possible: probably male. No measurements of any value can be taken. The calvarial sutures were probably open.

(12) A5.XII.10. Incomplete calotte of an adult: probably male. This specimen was probably distorted by earth pressure and it is too imperfect to measure.

(13) A5.41. Cranium of an adult with the base and facial skeleton partly defective: probably female. It is probable that no teeth had been lost before death (pls. XLVI, 7; XLVII, 4; XLVIII, 3).

(14) A6.I. Skull of an adult: female. The calvarial sutures appear to have been completely open. It is unlikely that any teeth had been lost before death. Appearance of the lower third molar on the left side was delayed: the crown of the tooth can be seen in its crypt below the alveolar margin, while the other three third molars appear to have been fully erupted (pls. XLVI, 8; XLVII, 7; XLVIII, 5).

Of the fourteen crania, two are immature, eight adult male, and four adult female. There are nine young adults and the other three are middle-aged: the oldest was probably less than forty years old at death. The age constitution of the small sample is remarkable on account of the absence of aged individuals. No rare anatomical anomalies were observed. It may be noted that no one of the fourteen specimens is metopic.

Judging from a qualitative examination of the skulls, the series appears to be remarkably homogeneous, and the differences observed are no greater than those expected in the case of individuals belonging to the same community. The most aberrant specimen is A6.I, and it is the only one from site A6, all the others having come from another site (A5). It is peculiar on account of the unusual height of the premaxillary region, from the nasal aperture to the upper teeth, but it is not clearly distinguished in any other respects. This skull is orthognathous and the form of its nasal region does not suggest negroid admixture. Little significance can be attached to the peculiarity noted. Considered together, and as a series coming from the Near East, the skulls are remarkable on account of the small size, feeble muscular development, and low cephalic index of the type. In these respects they show little variation.

Individual measurements of eleven of the specimens are given in Tables 1 and 2, the other three being too defective to provide any measurements of value. Characters are denoted by

TABLE 1
Calvarial measurements of skulls from the Hadhramaut

	A5.VI.13 ♂?	A5.VII.11 ♂	A5.VIII.7 ♂?	A5.X.19 ♂	A5.X.18 ♂	A5.IX.6 ♀	A5.XI.1 ♀?	A5.41 ♀?	A6.1 ♀	A5.XI.2 Juv.	A5.XI.3 Juv.
Glabella-occ. length (L: M.1)	181?	187?	184	185·5	184	..	178	172	175?	174	174·5?
Max. parietal breadth (B: M.8)	124·5	128?	125·5	141?	129	..	..	122·5?	123?	123	119?
Min. frontal breadth (B': M.9)	..	..	87·7	90·0	91·8	88·2	86·6	88·4	90·7	86·2	..
Max. frontal breadth (B'': M.10)	108	113·5?	104·5	115·5	111	112·5?	..	108·5	102?	106	..
Biasterionic breadth (M.12)	..	107?	106?	107·5?	110·5	..	..	99·5	..	..	..
Basio-bregmatic height (H': M.17)	..	..	134·5	..	121·5	..	..	122·5?	126·5	..	..
Chord nasion to bregma (S'_1: M.29)	..	..	117·8	111·2	107·4	102·9	104·2	104·5	103·0	107·9	..
Chord bregma to lambda (S'_2: M.30)	124·6	123·0?	113·2	118·5	116·1	111·7	116·1	108·2	110·0	119·9	110·3
Chord lambda to opisthion (S'_3: M.31)	..	88·9	96·0	..	93·4	..	92·0	96·9?	94·9	..	92·2?
Arc nasion to bregma (S_1: M.26)	..	..	135	128·5	121·5	125	116	119·5	117·5	129?	..
Arc bregma to lambda (S_2: M.27)	140·5	140?	124·5	136	131·5	122	132·5	121·5	122	133	122·5
Arc lambda to opisthion (S_3: M.28)	..	112	115	..	116	..	112	119?	115	..	111?
Arc nasion to opisthion (S: M.25)	..	..	375	..	369	..	361	360?	354·5	..	..
Horizontal circumference (U: M.23a)	..	..	505?	517	502	..	..	478	485?	485?	..
Trans. arc through bregma ($\beta Q'$: M.24)	..	..	302?	311	295	..	..	287	288?	..	..
Length of *for. mag.* (*fml*: M.7)	..	..	36·7	..	36·0	..	..	32·1?	32·2	..	..
Breadth of *for. mag.* (*fmb*: M.16)	..	..	27·4	..	26·7	..	..	..	28·1	..	..
Chord nasion to basion (LB: M.5)	..	..	100·1	..	97·1	..	..	88·9?	95·4	..	..
100 B/L	68·8?	68·4?	68·2	76·0?	70·1	..	..	71·2?	70·3?	70·7	68·2?
100 H'/L	..	..	73·1	..	66·0	..	..	71·2?	72·3?	..	..
100 B/H'	..	..	93·3	..	106·2	..	..	100·0?	97·2?	..	..
Occipital index (Pearson's)	..	56·6	60·2	..	57·4	..	58·8	58·2?	59·2	..	59·7?
100 *fmb/fml*	..	..	74·7	..	74·2	..	..	..	87·3	..	..

TABLE 2

Facial measurements of skulls from the Hadhramaut

	A5.VIII.7 ♂?	A5.X.18 ♂	A5.XI.1 ♀?	A5.41 ♀?	A6.1 ♀
Bizygomatic breadth (J: M.45)	..	121	..	..	115·5?
Mid-facial breadth (GB: M.46)	..	96·9	..	..	87·9?
Upper facial height ($G'H$: M.48)	67·0?	64·7	..	..	73·4?
Chord nasion to alveolar point (GL)	99·0?	104·7	..	..	91·3?
Nasal height (NH, L)	51·3	48·1	47·1?	43·1	49·2?
Nasal breadth (NB: M.54)	25·4	26·9	25·1?	20·9	23·5
Orbital breadth (O_1L: M.51)	38·8?	40·4	40·4?	38·1	40·1?
Orbital height (O_2L: M.52)	31·2	28·1	32·9	29·7	31·4?
Palatal length (G'_1: M.62)	..	49·9	..	43·2?	45·7
Palatal breadth (G_2: M.63)	..	..	..	33·8?	33·2?
Simotic chord (SC: M.57)	10·0	12·0	11·2?	11·9?	..
Subtense to simotic chord (SS)	6·3?	4·2	..	5·5?	..
100 $G'H/GB$	..	66·8	..	..	83·5?
100 $NB/NH, L$	49·5	55·9	53·3?	48·5	47·8?
100 $O_2/O_1, L$	80·4?	69·6	81·4?	78·0	78·3?
100 G_2/G'_1	..	..	..	78·2?	72·6?
100 SS/SC	63·0?	35·0	..	46·2?	..
$N\angle$	69·5°?	78·0°	..	..	64·0°?
$A\angle$	71·5°?	65·0°	..	..	70·0°?
$B\angle$	39·0°?	37·0°	..	..	46·0°?
Alveolar profile angle ($P\angle$)	83°?	81·5°	..	..	85°?

the usual biometric symbols and also by the numbers in Rudolf Martin's list. The impression that the type is small is confirmed, as many of the chords and arcs—and particularly the maximum calvarial breadths—have exceptionally low values. The average cephalic indices are 70·3 for the 5 male, 70·7 for the 2 female, and 69·5 for the 2 juvenile skulls. These three means are remarkably close. On the average the indices for both female adult and juvenile skulls are about one unit greater than that for male specimens representing the same population. Accepting these differences, an estimate of 69·8 for males based on all nine skulls is obtained. There appear to be no adequately long cranial series from any part of the world except the Pacific which have given a male mean cephalic index below 70. The lowest recorded values for European, north African, and Indian series are between 71 and 72. An index of 69·8 for the skull may be supposed to correspond to one of 71·8 for the living.

There are no published descriptions of series of skulls from Arabia, and comparisons with data available for isolated specimens would not be profitable. Measurements taken by Bertram Thomas of thirty-seven adults and five children belonging to ten south Arabian tribes are treated by Sir Arthur Keith and Dr. W. M. Krogman.[1] The lowest cephalic index recorded for these individuals is 78·2, so there is a complete separation of the range for them from that for the Hadhramaut skulls. In the same paper the averages are given for series previously measured of south Arabian men. The averages given for these are:

[1] Bertram Thomas, *Arabia Felix* (Appendix I, 'The Racial Characters of the Southern Arabs'), London, 1932.

Muscat 78·3, Sheher 80·9, and Yemen 81·1. The comparative material is by no means extensive, but it suggests that there may have been a population in the Hadhramaut in late pre-Christian times which was markedly different from any found in the region to-day. This appears to have been of a very distinctive type on account of its low cephalic index.

Plates XLVI–XLVIII reproduce photographs of the more complete skulls orientated as nearly as possible so that the Frankfort horizontal plane of the specimen was parallel or perpendicular to the focal plane of the camera.

The associated sacrum and left side of the pelvis (no. A6.I) are male. Both tibiae (no. A6.I), which are left and feebly developed, are probably female. One has a maximum length (excluding the spine) of 334 mm., giving a reconstructed stature of 1,533 mm. (5 ft. 0¼ in.): the other is imperfect and it must have been about 1 cm. longer. The three lumbar vertebrae probably belonged to the same individual: two are fused together as the result of *arthritis deformans*, and the margins of the other are affected by the same condition.

Clearance of scree masking entrance to A6

Entrance to A6 before clearance

The same after clearance. Crosses mark the same
points in both views

Entrance to tomb A5, with section of infilling in background

Tomb A5 with deposits to rear and side in relation to burial level

Tomb A5. Burial group IV

Tomb A5. Bench group VI, and burial group VII on floor alongside

CAVE TOMBS

Interior of A5 after clearance. Deposit section on left. Men seated on bench VI

Niched tomb occupied by bedouin family

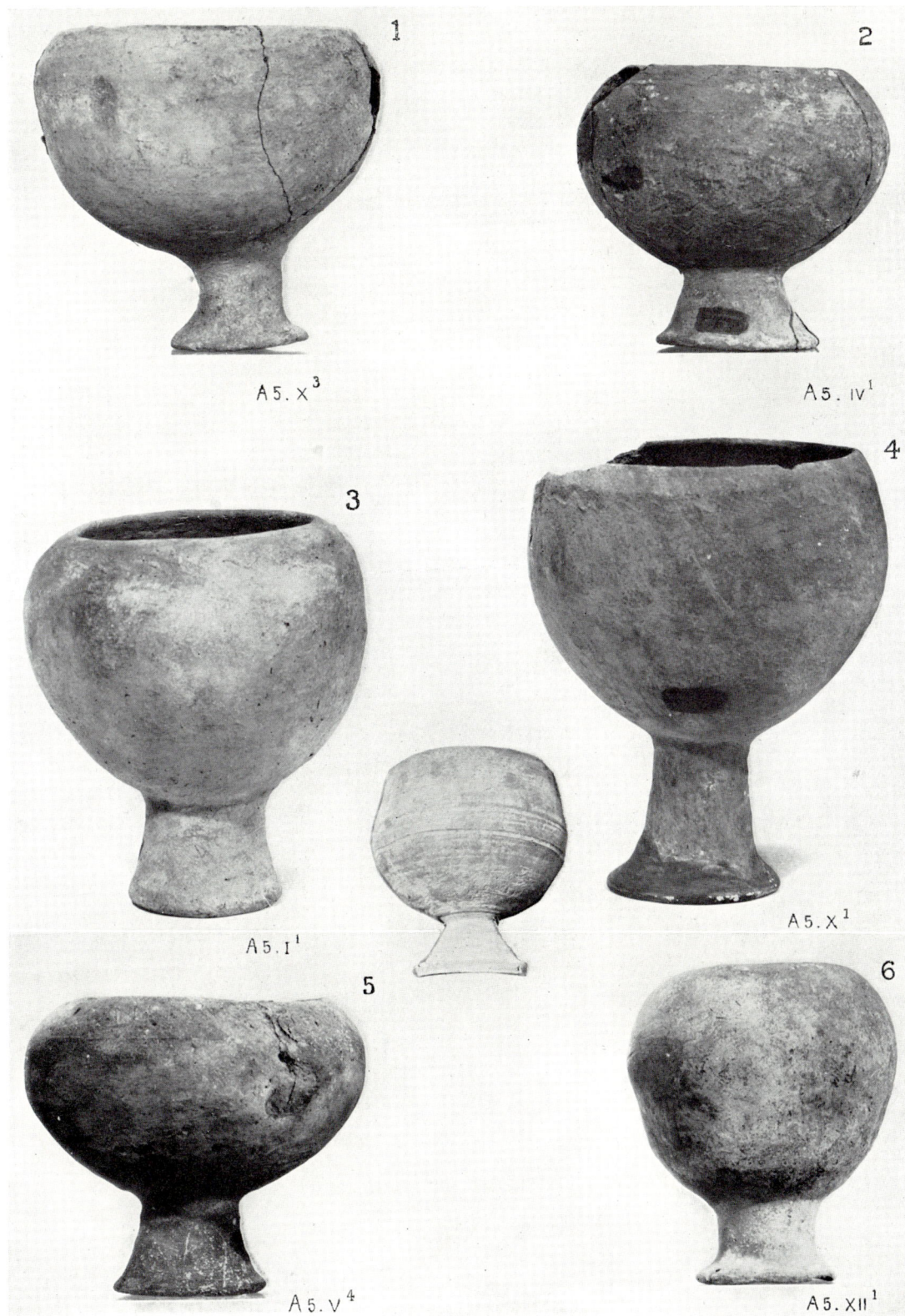

1   A5. x³

2   A5. ıv¹

3   A5. ı¹

4   A5. x¹

5   A5. v⁴

6   A5. xıı¹

Goblets on tall stems, type I. (Inset) a modern water cooler

Pedestal bowls with ledge rims, type II No. 1, a variant type

Inscribed ledge rims of Pedestal bowls, type II

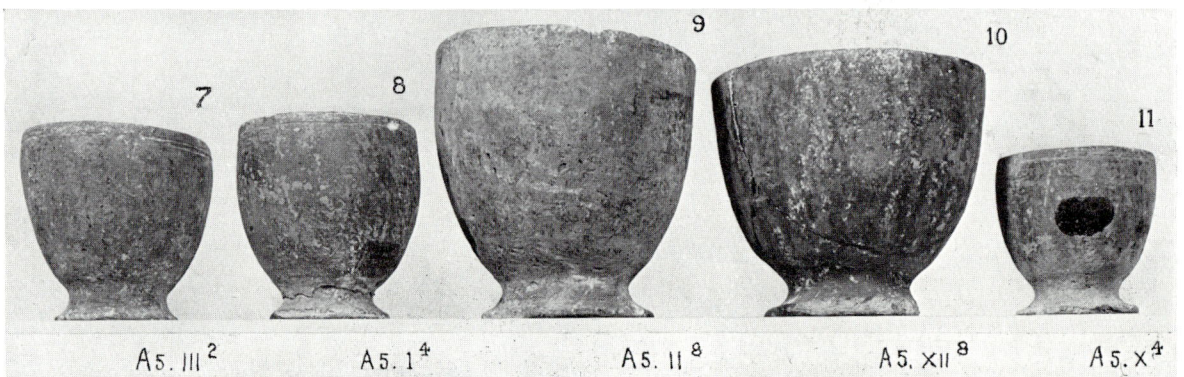

Pedestal bowls and cups, type III

Erratum. No. 6, read A5.1³

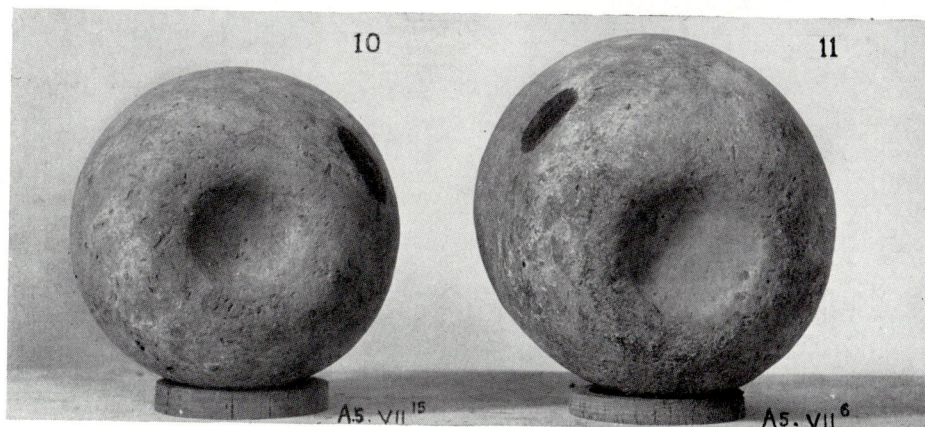

Nos. 1–3. Shallow open pedestal bowls, type V
Nos. 4–6. Shallow open bowls with rounded bases, type VI
Nos. 7–9. Deep bowls with dimpled bases, type VIII
Nos. 10, 11. Dimpled bases of type VIII

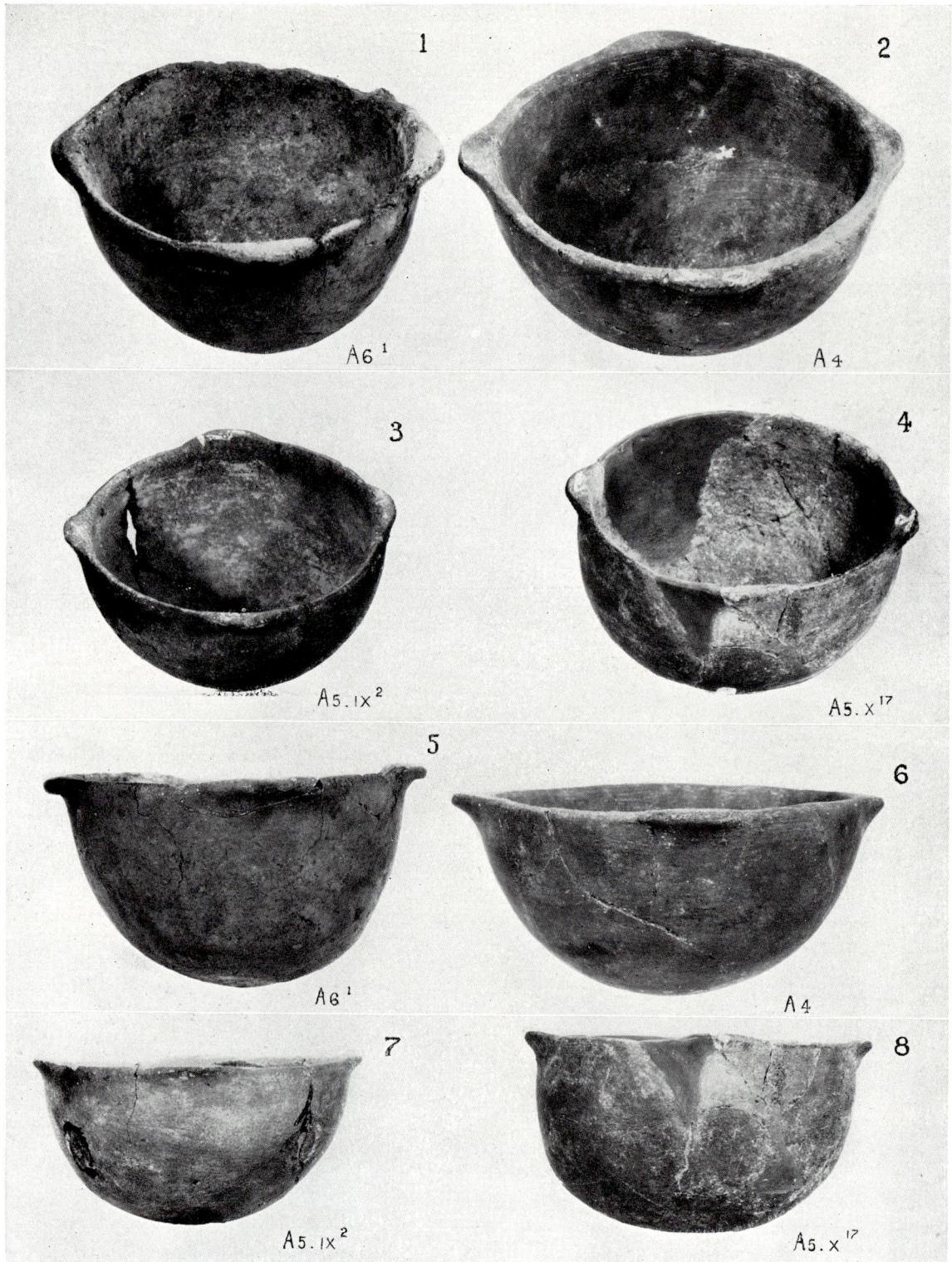

Eared bowls in black or grey stone ware, type IX

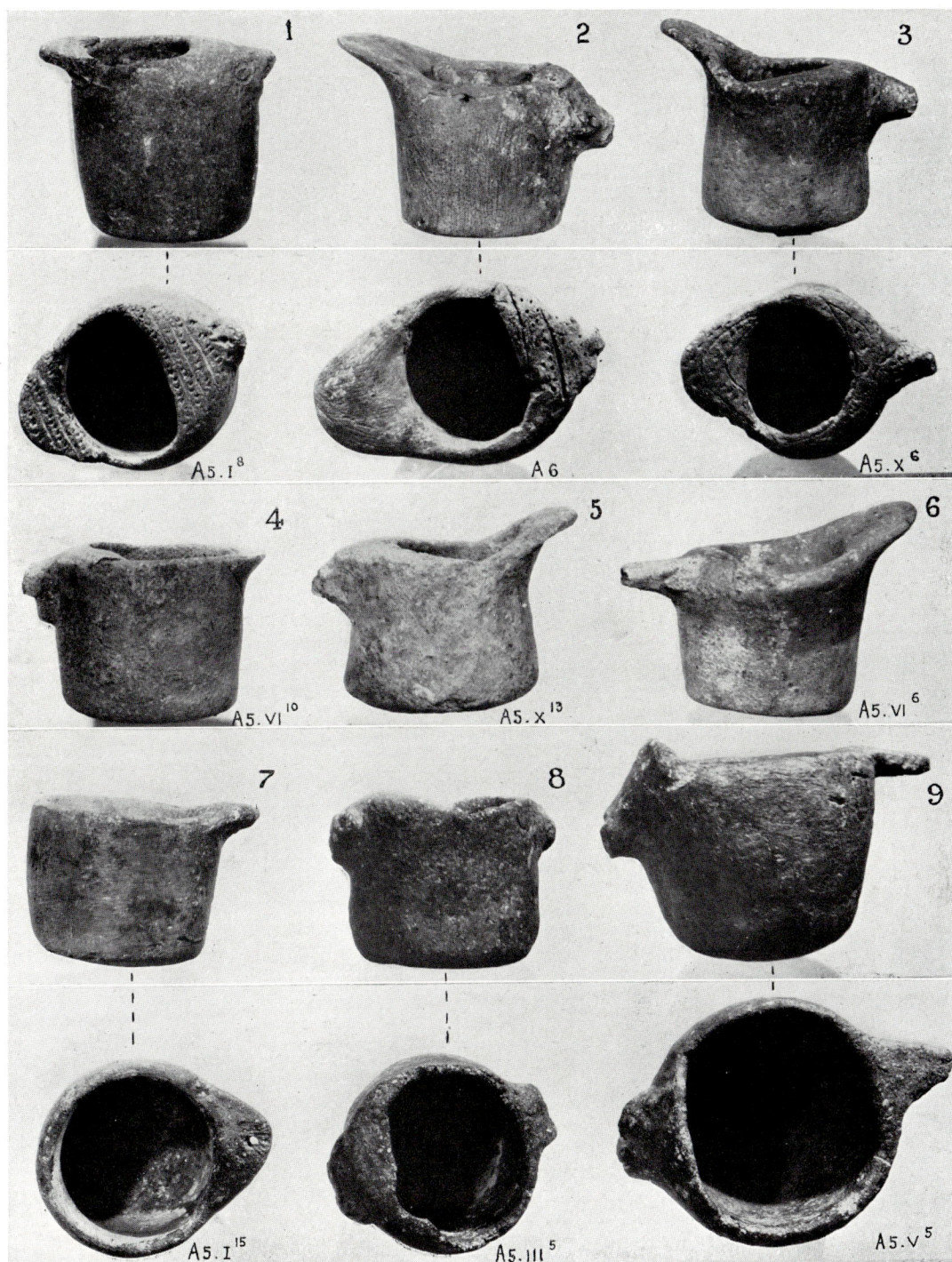

Nos. 1–6, 8, 9. Flanged cups with spouts and tongue handles in stone ware, type X
No. 7. Open cup with tongue handle in stone ware, type XI*a*

Flanged and other cups in stone ware. Nos. 1–4 inscribed. Nos. 5–7 with theriomorphic spouts

Inscriptions on stone ware, and pottery sherds

Erratum. No. 4, read A5.1¹⁵

A4 B

2

3

4

A4. SURFACE

A4 - A5 SURFACE

5

A4. C

A4. SURFACE

6

7

A3. SURFACE

GHEIBUN SURFACE

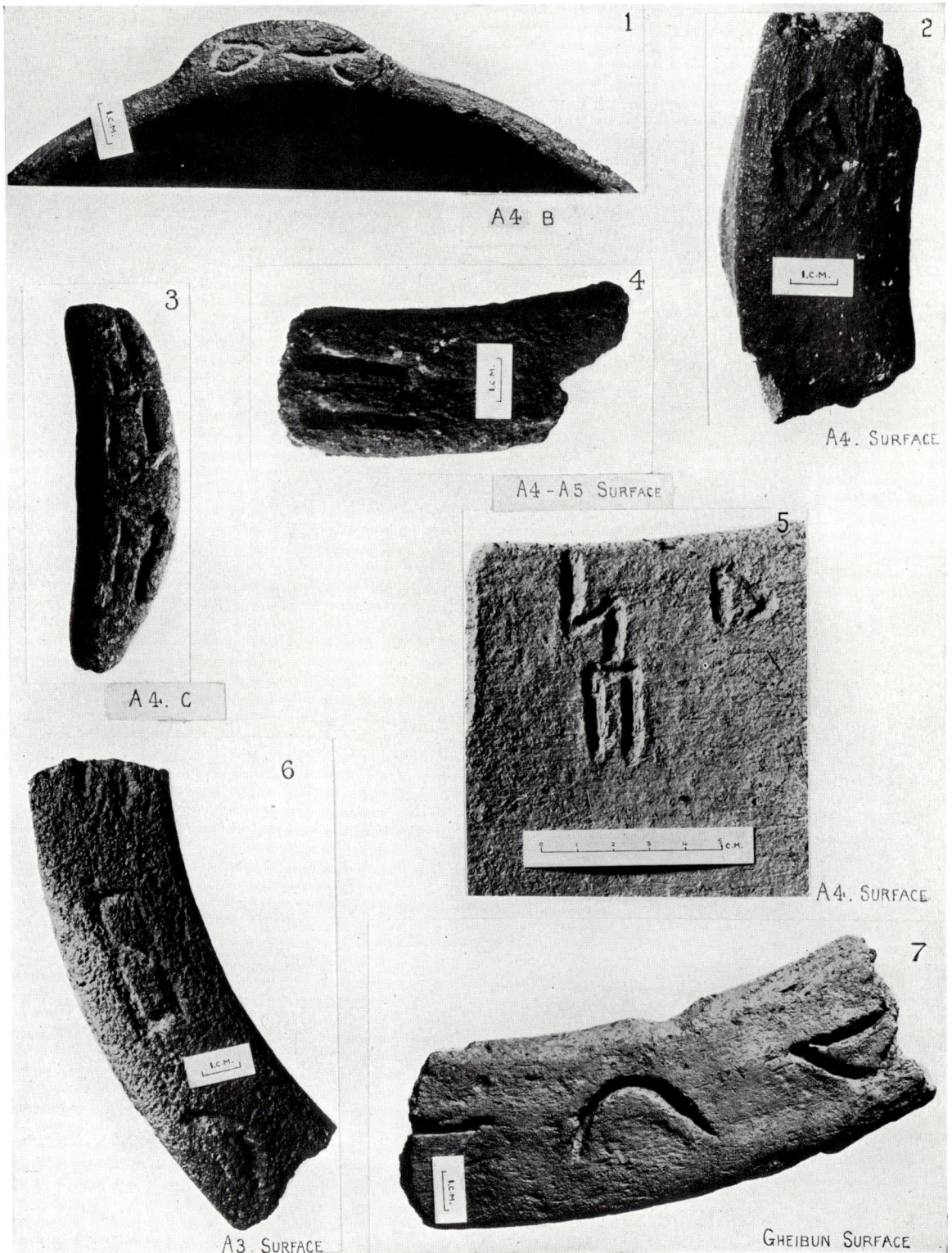

Miscellaneous pottery inscriptions or monograms

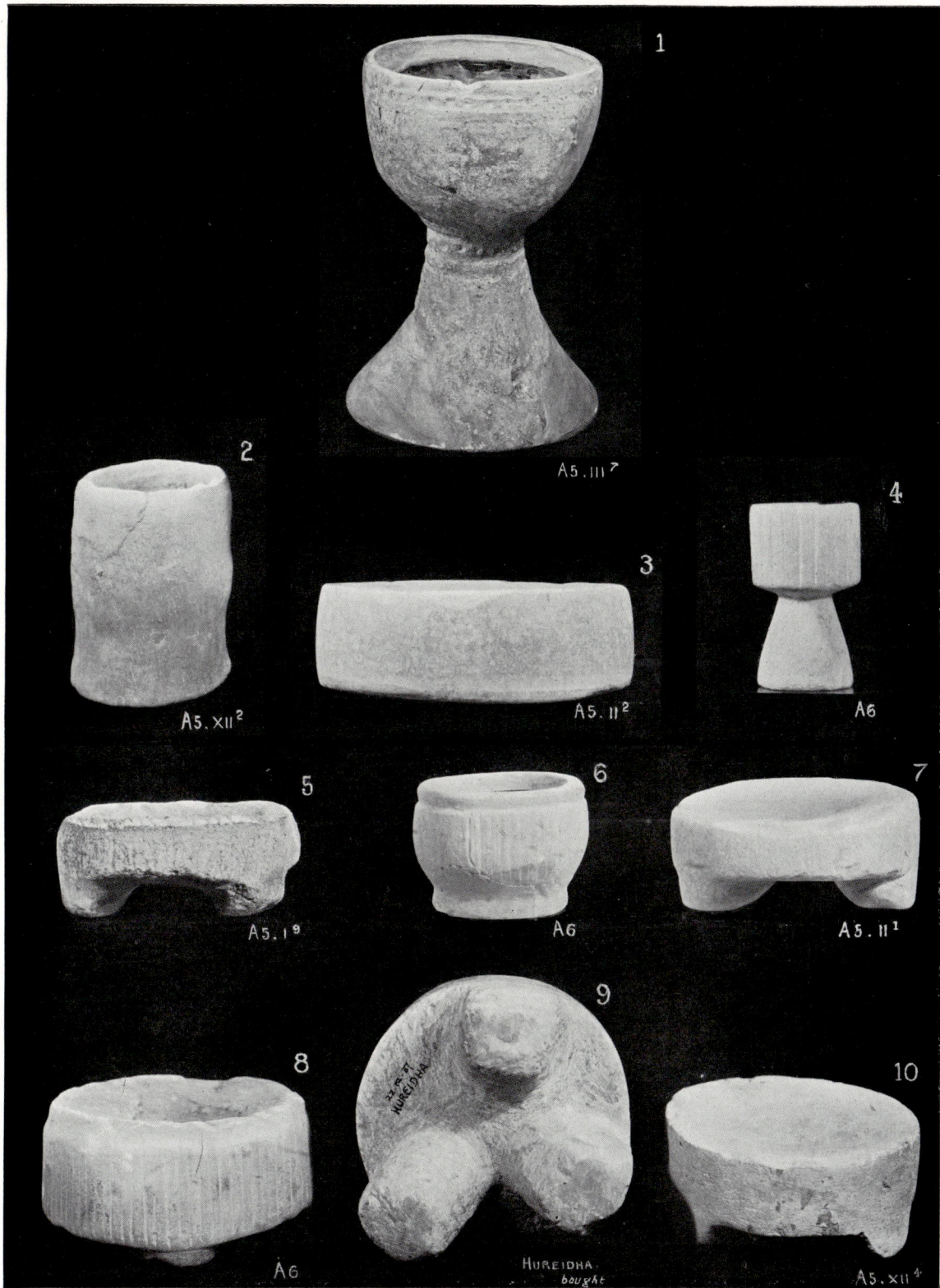

No. 1. Pottery chalice (height 12·6 cm.), type IV
No. 2. Gypsum tumbler
Nos. 3–10. Cups and tripod saucers in crystalline limestone

TOMB CONTENTS—GHEIBUN AND SŪNE

Types of beads, amulets, and agate seal in silver mount (painting by Mrs. Austin Kennett)
(Scale 1:1, except No. 4 twice natural size)

Top string, beads from surface at Gheibun. Bottom three strings glass beads from tombs A5 and A6

Faience, stone, and shell disk beads from A5 and A6. Syrian string for comparison

Marine shell beads and valve saucers

1 No. 1. Carnelian. A5, A6.
   Pl. XL, 1.

2 No. 1. Carnelian. A5, A6.
   Pl. XL, 1.
   Colour Pl. XXXVIII,
   21.

3 No. 1. Carnelian. A5, V.
   Colour Pl. XXXVIII,
   14.

4 No. 1. Carnelian. A5, A6.
   Pl. XL, 1

5 No. 1. Carnelian. A5, A6.
   Pl. XL, 1.

6 No. 1. Carnelian. A5.
   Pl. XL, 1.

7 No. 1. Carnelian. A5, II.
   Pl. XL, 1.

8 No. 1. Carnelian. A5, II.
   Pl. XL, 1.

9 No. 1. Carnelian. A5, II.
   Pl. XL, 1.

10 No. 1. Carnelian. A5, A6.
   Pl. XL, 1.

11 No. 1. Carnelian. A5, A6.
   Pl. XL, 1.

12 No. 1. Carnelian. A5, A6.
   Pl. XL, 1.

13 No. 1. Carnelian. A5, A6.
   Pl. XL, 1.

14 No. 1. Carnelian. A6.
   Pl. XL, 1.

15 No. 1. Carnelian. A5.
   Pl. XL, 1.

16 No. 9. Garnet. Outside
   A5 only.

17 No. 4. Amethyst. A6 only.
   Pl. XL, 4.
   Colour Pl. XXXVIII,
   16.

18 No. 2. Agate. A6.

19 No. 2. Agate. A6.
   Pl. XL, 2.
   Colour Pl. XXXVIII,
   11.

20 No. 2. Agate. A5, III.
   Pl. XL, 2.

21 No. 2. Burnt agate. A5,
   VII.
   Pl. XL, 2.

22 No. 27. Sea-shell. A5, IX.
   Pl. XL, 28.

23 No. 8. Calcite. A5, VII.
   Pl. XL, 8.

24 No. 10. Bone. A5, V.

25 No. 5. Felspar. A5, II.
   Pl. XL, 5.

26 No. 5. Felspar. A5, V.
   Pl. XL, 5.

27 No. 28. Sea-shell. A6.
   Sūne, surface. Also
   Gheibun.

28 No. 7. Black steatite. A5,
   V.

29 No. 2. Banded agate, unpolished and unperfo-
   rated. Gheibun, surface.

30 No. 28. Sea-shell spacer.
   A5, VII.
   Pl. XL, 29.

31 No. 28. Sea-shell. A5.
   Pl. XL, 28.

BEADS AND PENDANTS IN STONE, BONE, AND SEA-SHELL

32

33

34

35

36

37

38

39

40

41

42

43

44

45

No. 13. Faience. A6.
Discoloured blue melon.
Colour Pl. XXXVIII, 5.

No. 15. Faience. A5, A6.
Discoloured blue.
Colour Pl. XXXVIII,
20.

Pl. XL, 15.

do.

do.

No. 16. Glass. A5, A6.
Indian red.
Colour Pl. XXXVIII, 6,
7.
Pl. XXXIX, 16.

No. 16. Glass. A5, A6.
Indian red.
Colour Pl. XXXVIII, 6,
7.
Pl. XXXIX, 16.

No. 16. Glass. A5, A6.
Indian red.
Pl. XXXIX, 16.

No. 16. Glass. A5, A6.
Indian red
Pl. XXXIX, 16.

No. 16. Glass. A5.
Indian red.
Pl. XXXIX, 16.

No. 16. Glass. A5, A6.
Indian red.
Pl. XXXIX, 16.

No. 16. Glass. A5.
Indian red.
Pl. XXXIX, 16.

No. 16. Glass. A5.
Indian red.
Pl. XXXIX, 16.

No. 16. Glass. A5.
Indian red.
Pl. XXXIX, 16.

46

47

48

49

50

51

52

53

54

55

56

57

58

59

No. 17. Glass. A5, A6.
Discoloured green, blue-
green.
Colour Pl. XXXVIII, 8.

No. 17. Glass. A5, A6.
Discoloured green, blue-
green.
Pl. XXXIX, 17.

No. 17. Glass. A5, A6.
Discoloured green, blue-
green.
Colour Pl. XXXVIII,
18.

No. 17. Glass. A5, A6.
Discoloured green.
Colour Pl. XXXVIII, 2.

No. 17. Glass. A5.
Discoloured green.
Pl. XXXIX, 17.

No. 17. Glass. A5, V.
Dark green.
Colour Pl. XXXVIII, 3.

No. 17. Glass. A5.
Discoloured green.
Pl. XXXIX, 17.

No. 18. Glass. A6.
Blue.
Colour Pl. XXXVIII,
25.

No. 18. Glass. A5.
Discoloured blue.
Colour Pl. XXXVIII,
12.

No. 19. Flush-crumb glass.
A5.
Green-yellow.
Colour Pl. XXXVIII,
19.

No. 20. Glass. A5, A6.
Orange, yellow, cream.
Colour Pl. XXXVIII,
28.

No. 20. Glass. A5, A6.
Orange, yellow.
Colour Pl. XXXVIII,
28.

do.

do.

60

61

62

63

64

65

66

67

68

69

70

71

72

No. 16. Glass. A5, A6.
Indian red.
Pl. XXXIX, 16.

No. 17. A5.
Green-blue?
Pl. XXXIX, 16.

No. 21. Glass. A5, IX.
Purple glass.
Pl. XL, 21.

No. 22. Glass. Eye-bead.
A5, V.
Indian red ground.
Colour Pl. XXXVIII, 4.

No. 23. Glass. A5, II.
Parti-colour yellow and
green.
Colour Pl. XXXVIII,
22.

No. 24c. Glass. A5, V.
Black and white zone.
Colour Pl. XXXVIII,
10.

No. 24b. Glass. A6.
Black and white zone.
Colour Pl. XXXVIII,
10.
Pl. XL, 24.

No. 30. Glass. Gheibun.
Green.
Colour Pl. XXXVIII, 24.
Pl. XXXIX, 30.

No. 29. Glass. Gheibun.
Indian red, inlaid dark
spirals.
Colour Pl. XXXVIII, 26.

No. 21. Glass. Gheibun.
Purple and white.
Pl. XXXIX, 21.

No. 25. Sea-shell. A6.
Dark grey.

No. 25. Sea-shell. A5, A6.
White.

No. 25. Sea-shell. A5, A6.
White. Interspaced with
Carnelian.
Pl. XL, 1.

BEADS IN FAIENCE AND GLASS. SEA-SHELL DISKS

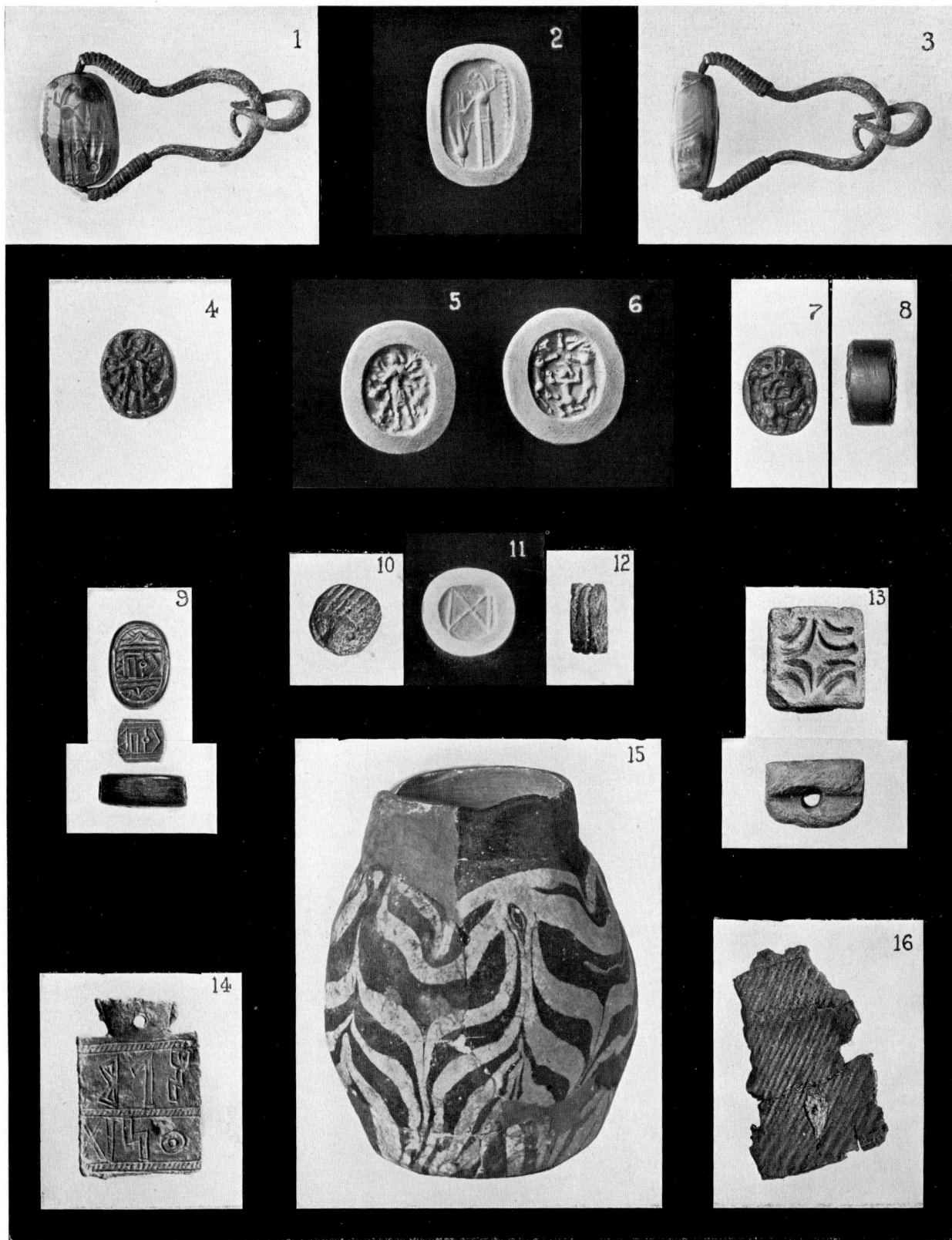

1–3. Agate seal. 4–8. Kaolinite seal. 9. Red limestone seal. 10–12. Faience scarab. 13. Limestone seal (bought).
14. Silver amulet. 15. Glass vase. 16. Ripple sherd from surface

(Scale 1 : 1, except No. 13, 1 : 2)

1

A5.1[14]

5

6

A5. V   A 6

A5.1X

12

A5.1[13]

13

A5. X

2

A5. V

7

A5.1[13]

14

A5.111[9]

3

A 6

8

9

A5.1X

A5. X11

15

A5.V111[5]

16

BOUGHT

4

A5.11[12]

10

A5 V

11

A5.1[13]

17

A5.1

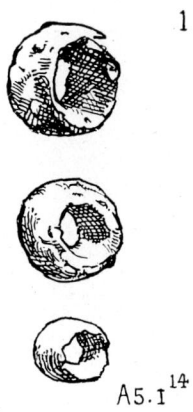

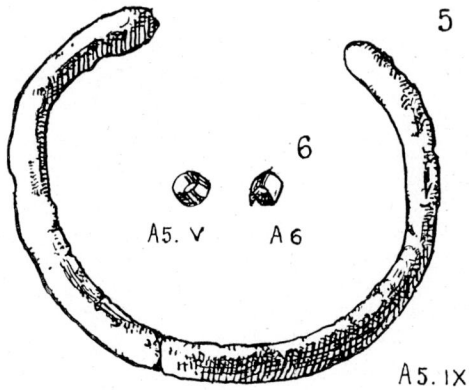

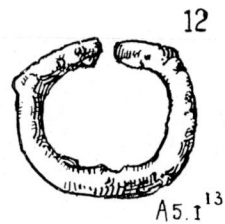

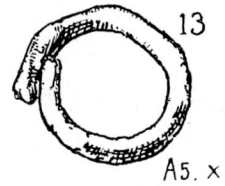

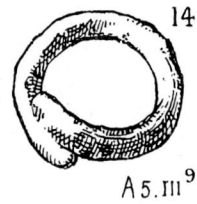

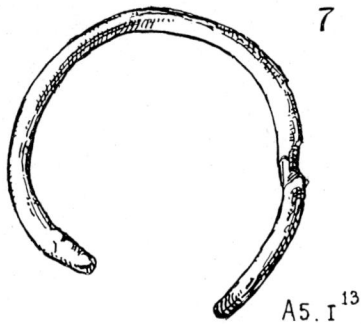

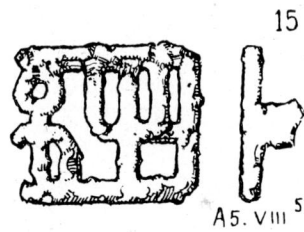

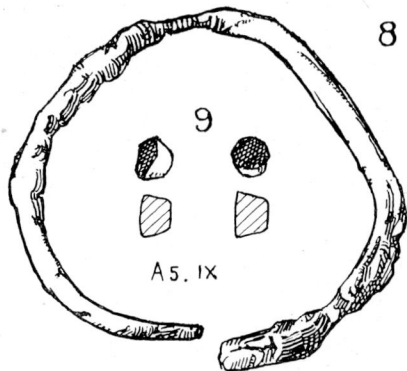

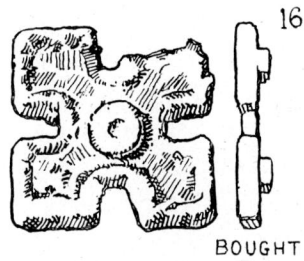

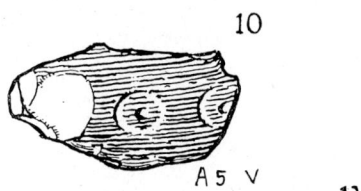

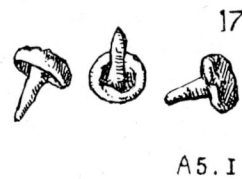

Metal objects: No. 9, obsidian; No. 10, ivory or bone
(Scale 1 : 1)

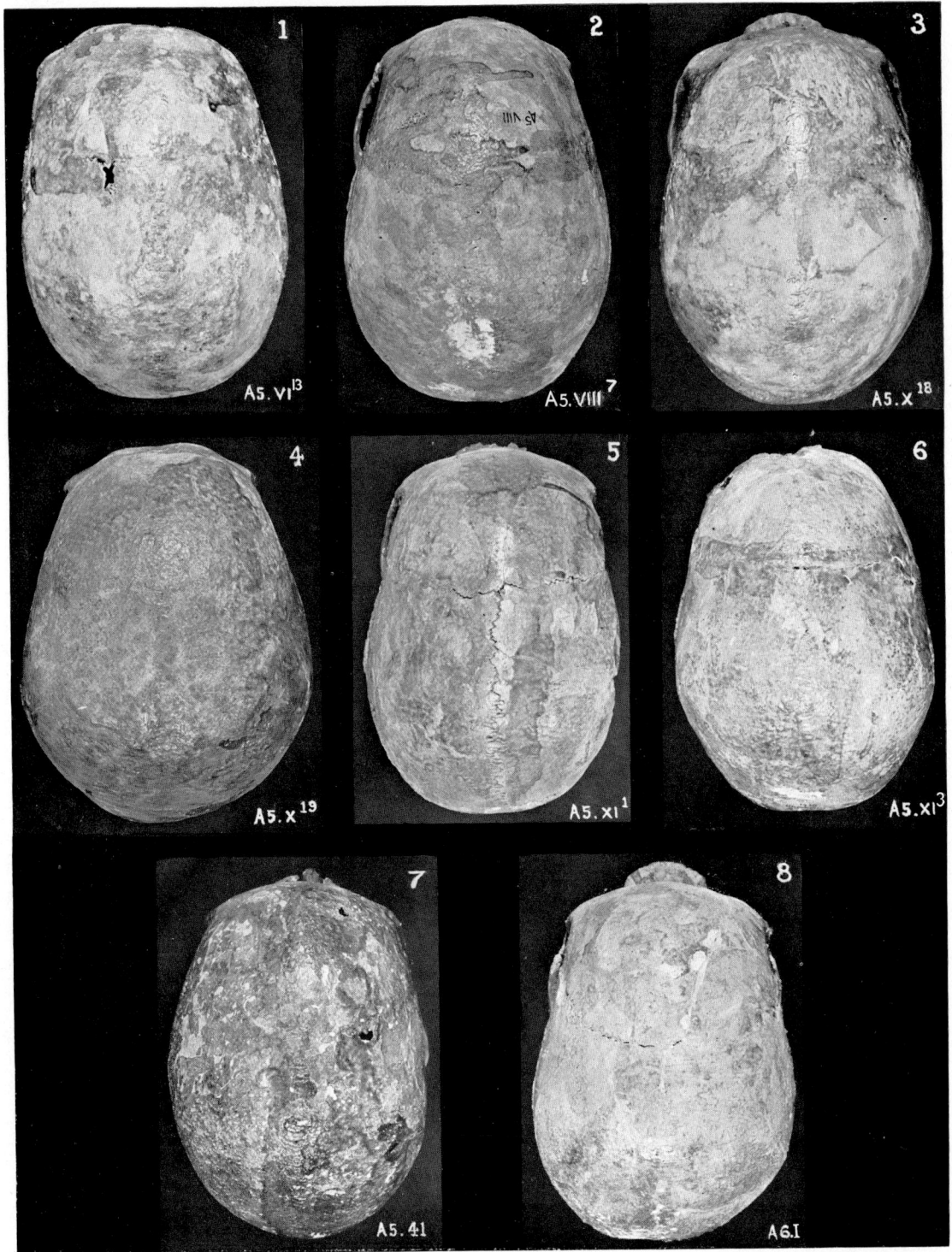

Norma verticalis

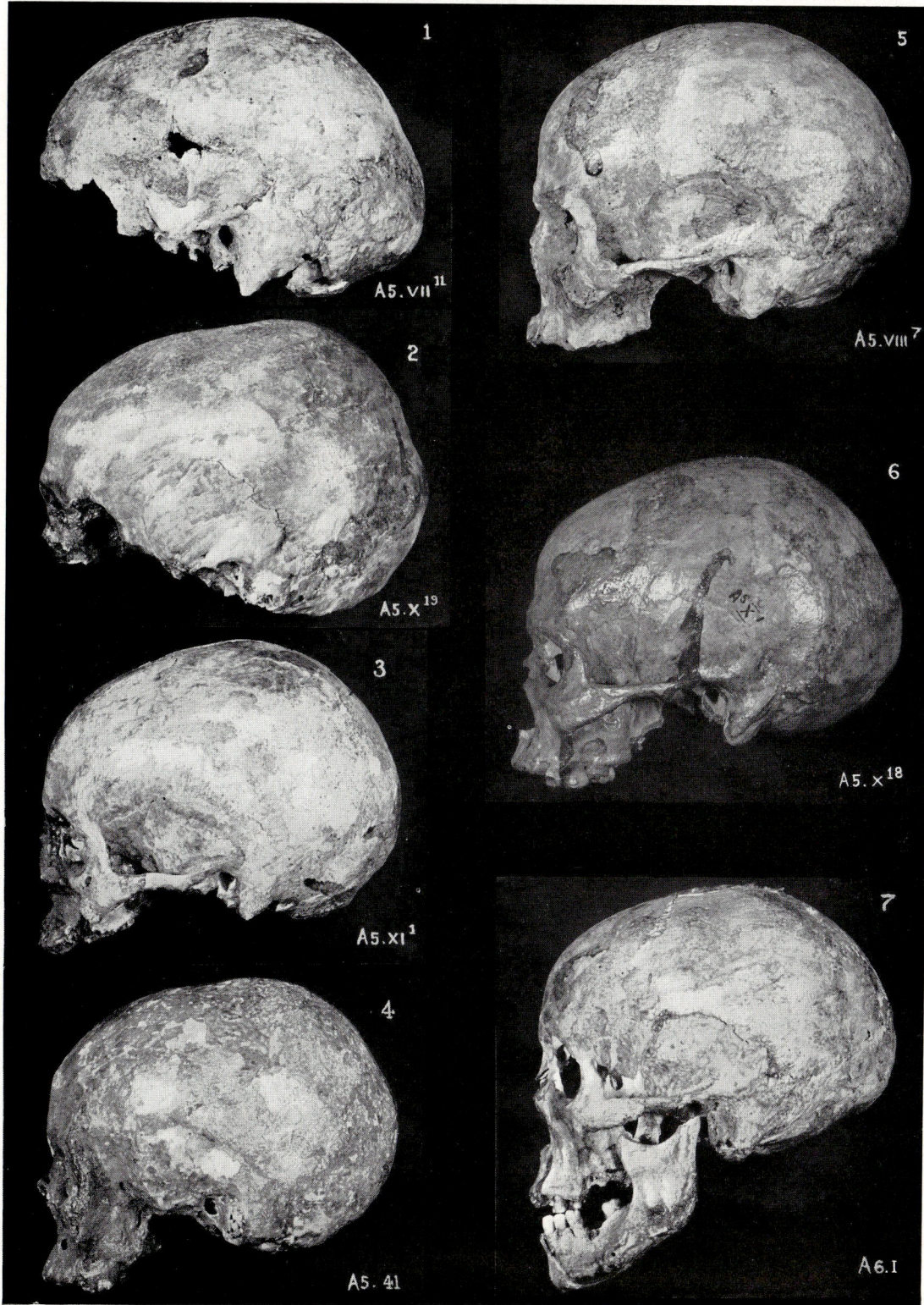

1   A5.VII ^{11}

2   A5.X ^{19}

3   A5.XI ^{1}

4   A5.41

5   A5.VIII ^{7}

6   A5.X ^{18}

7   A6.I

Norma lateralis

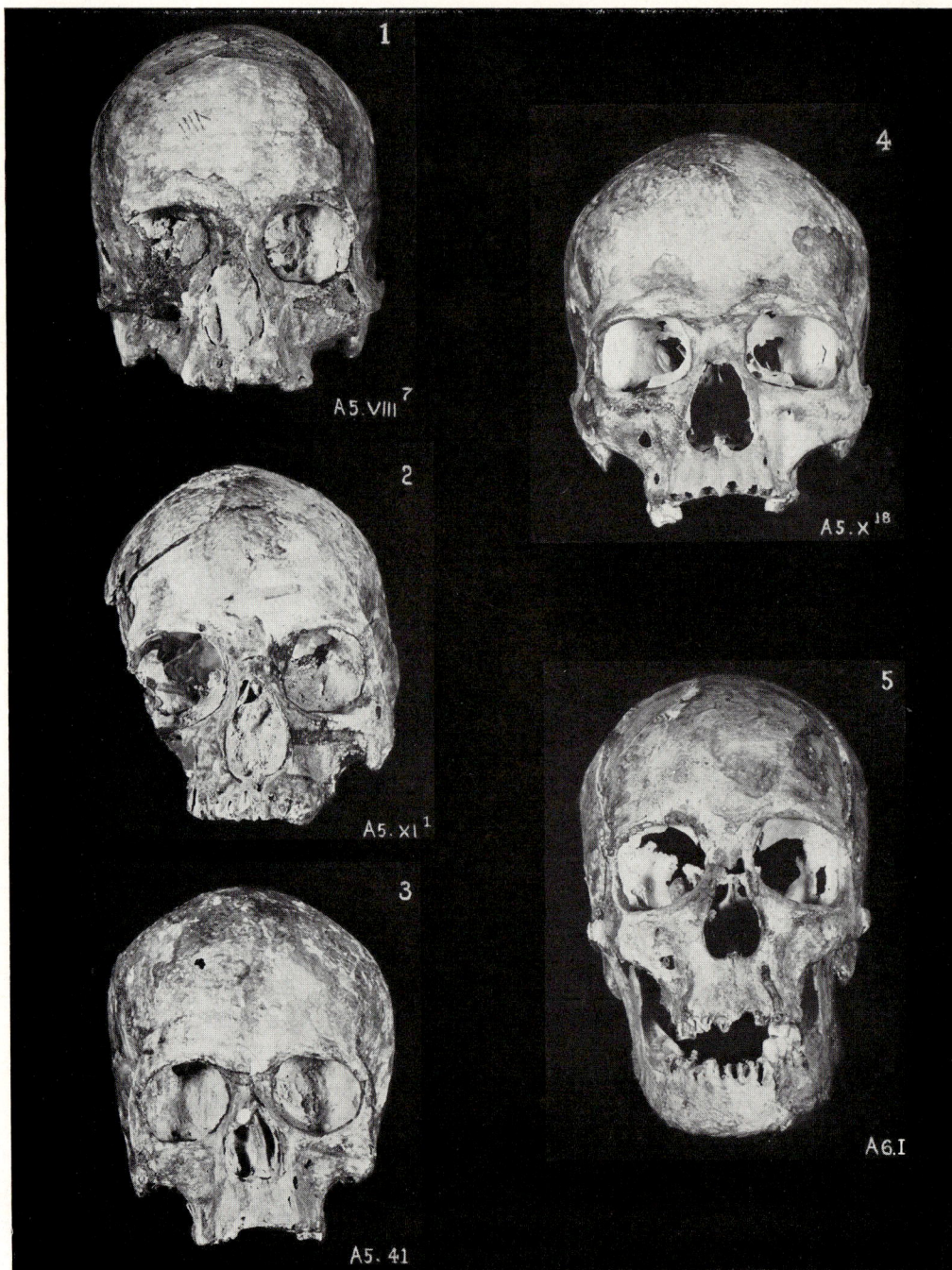

Norma facialis

PART IV
TYPOLOGY

XIII. CLASSIFICATION OF THE TOMB POTTERY

THE vessels recovered from tombs A5 and A6 number ninety-three, of which eighty-seven were more or less intact. Sufficient, therefore, was procured for classification and the establishment at last of a small introductory corpus of south Arabian wares, of which nothing previously was known, based on material found *in situ* in controlled excavations, and forming associated groups within the limits of its dating range. These have been used, therefore, as the standard of comparison for the fragmentary pottery found in the Moon Temple and at the farmstead A4.

The material has been classified here into fifteen forms: subdivisions within these may be needed when more material has been found: at present slightly aberrant types have been treated as 'variations' from the nearest class.

These forms comprise three well-defined fabrics: two normal ceramics; one a curious black ware I have termed 'stone ware', which has puzzled the experts who have examined it. It is likely eventually to become important for distribution questions.

The first of the ceramics is a porous, pinky-buff pottery, mainly used for water-coolers and storage-jars. The second is a brick-red slipped or washed pottery, mainly used for smaller drinking-cups and bowls. The third, the 'stone ware', is black or grey, and was reserved for a special type of ear-lug bowl, and for small spouted unguent vessels and other miniature vases, all destined probably to contain fatty substances. The clay of the first two is similar in origin and is probably local; the difference between them lies in the greater coarseness of the particles in the more porous ware, its higher chaff content, and greater thickness which has decreased the effect of firing. Moreover, the surface has not been treated, as in the second variety, with a slip coating.

I am indebted to Dr. H. W. Webb, D.Sc., F.I.C., of the Ceramic Testing Laboratory, North Staffordshire Technical College, Stoke-on-Trent, for the following observations on five samples of the slip-coated ware, and the 'stone ware' submitted to him.

'*Specimens 1–3* (the slip-coated ware). They are made from a sandy, rather refractory clay, and have been fired to a temperature I should estimate at about 900°–950° C. From the character of the ware I should suggest it was made by the operation potters call 'pressing', with the exception that the clay was not rotated during the process.[1] The pressing would be done from plastic clay, put inside a wooden or stone vessel of the right shape, and worked by hand to the shape of the vessel. In drying it would release itself by shrinkage. There is evidence for this in the comparative smoothness of the outside of the pieces, compared with the inside, and the texture of the ware itself. Where slip coatings have been used, it is reasonably certain these were made from a clay with or without added haematite. Such red clay slips could readily be obtained by shaking up certain

---

[1] Having the advantage of the study of complete vessels, I suggest that primitive rotation, particularly on rim and pedestal, can in many cases be detected. G. C. T.

clayey sands and clayey haematites with water, and using the supernatant liquid which contains a suspension of very fine clay, which is usually red burning.

'There is very little evidence for the method of application of the red slip, but it is quite consistent with the clay having been dipped in the slip when partly dry and subsequently fired. A fault we call 'black core' caused by unburnt carbonaceous material in the clay is so prevalent that I am inclined to think the pots were put inside a closed muffle of clay when being fired, and not exposed to the gases from the burning fuel.'

The technical difficulty of establishing the exact nature of the black ware will be apparent from the following. Dr. Webb's first report on two characteristic sherds was that they were not ceramics and had not been fired, but were cut from a porphyritic basic igneous rock of a probably partially weathered and soft type. The abnormal drab colour of one of the specimens, similar in other respects, he considered to be due to the stone having stood for a long time on a hot hearth.

Previous to this I had submitted samples to Dr. Leonard Hawkes, F.G.S., who gave the following petrological description. 'Variously sized angular fragments of a tremolite-chlorite-talc-schist with small quartz grains set irregularly in a dense (?) clay matrix.[1] It is improbable that it is a natural rock. There are no petrological indications of baking, but in view of the nature of the material this cannot be conclusive evidence against possible heat treatment.'

I next re-submitted three more samples of complete vessels to Dr. Webb's laboratory, including one of those examined by Dr. Hawkes. In the light of these it was considered that the vessels were not of stone, but an artificial product which had (presumably) undergone a certain amount of light baking. Nothing like them had been seen before. The report ends, 'There is a chance that they are made from clayey material due to the intense weathering (under conditions approaching tropical) of igneous and metamorphic rocks. But I have a suspicion that the talc-schist pieces are put in deliberately to make a kind of "plum pudding", and are not part of the original deposit.'[2]

I had already formed an independent opinion that we were dealing with clever imitations of stone vases; the forms are those of stone, as well as the resemblances of the fabric. There is in the Hureidha vicinity, as far as I know, no geological formation to supply a rock or derivative clay of this mineral nature. The provenance is, therefore, almost certainly not local; but only a few days' camel journey south or south-west would reach areas of basic igneous rocks. The material is very soft and rotten, and seems likely to come from some secondary supply derived from the break-down of the igneous rock. The 'dense (?) clay matrix' noted by Dr. Hawkes is consistent with this view; on the other hand, the angularity of the larger minerals hardly supports it, and Dr. Williamson's suggestion of deliberate additions of selected crystals is attractive. Perhaps a combination of both possibilities is nearest the mark. But I feel sure some unidentified treatment

---

[1] In view of the kaolinite rock of which the A6.9 seal is made (cf. p. 88) I submitted a sample to Mr. P. M. Game of the Department of Mineralogy, British Museum, who had made the kaolinite determination. He states that the matrix is not determinable with certainty, but is certainly not kaolinite. In his opinion there is no doubt that the material is not a naturally formed rock.

[2] From Dr. W. O. Williamson.

of the material, to give it tensile strength and cohesion, has still to be accounted for. Further light would perhaps be thrown on the problem by the expert examination of all our two dozen-odd specimens, instead of the six handled between them by Dr. Webb and Dr. Hawkes.[1]

It was a pleasing shock to discover that this 'stone ware'[2] is not restricted to south Arabia. Mr. Oliver Myers discovered a small open cup with lugs in similar material measuring $8 \times 6 \cdot 5$ cm. at Armant. The circumstances of its find did not, unfortunately, give any dating evidence beyond the probability that it was 'late'.

In the following pages all descriptions of wares and technique are my own, unless Dr. Webb's authority is specifically quoted.

I. GOBLETS ON TALL STEMS (*pls.* XXVII, 1–6; XLIX, 1–6)

Form. The deep globular bowl incurves to a plain rim, and is mounted on a long, deeply hollowed stem with splayed foot.

Ware. Rough-finished without slip or wash,[3] but probably wet-smoothed. The colour is pinky-buff, brindled with redder or greyer firing patches. The clay is coarse, friable, and contains chaffs and grits; the core is grey through insufficient firing. The porosity of A5.I.1 was tested, and within twenty minutes moisture oozed from the walls.

Technique. All are asymmetric in some respect; one or two, such as A5.X.3 absurdly so. The pots are hand-made, with hints, given by horizontal striae, that rim and foot may have been turned in some primitive fashion on a support of some kind. There is no evidence that the stem was made separately.

Decoration. All possess a zigzag (angular), or wavy (curvilinear), band, lightly scored freehand below the rim with a blunt tool in the wet. In two cases (pl. XLIX, 3, 5) the band, doubled or tripled, adorns the goblet belly also.

Variants. Parts of the side and complete stem of a large, ornate, hollow-stemmed goblet were found in tomb A6. The restoration, seen in pls. XXVIII, 1; L, 1, is certain. The bowl is more open and set on a relatively shorter, thicker stem, which ends in a widely splayed base. Diameter and height are approximately equal. Another distinction is an angular moulding pinched horizontally out from the wall, which encircles the base of the cup. The space below this and down the stem is incised with closely set wavy lines, which become zigzags on the stem. The ware resembles that of the other members of this type.

Comment. The modern Hadhramaut water-cooler (pl. XXVII, centre), which in well-

---

[1] Archaeologists will appreciate the difficulty of getting adequately long series of analyses for their different materials. Experts, though wonderfully patient and helpful in dealing with the ever-increasing questions referred to them by the field archaeologist, are busy people, charged primarily with work of their own. Many most generously give their services *gratis*; but others cannot and should not, and the burden of specialists' fees, covering all materials, bears heavily on those responsible for conscientious publication.

[2] I am aware I am appropriating a term already given to a certain type of fabric. But the robbery is convenient and apt.

[3] It has been authoritatively stated by Dr. Ritchie (*Cemeteries of Armant*) that no distinction without analysis is possible. It seems best, therefore, to use the word 'coating' in cases where one or the other is certain. Friction-treated surfaces, pebble-burnished, rubbed, or wet-smoothed, will be specified when tolerably sure.

ordered houses stands brimming in a draughty window, is a deep goblet on hollow pedestal in porous buff or red ware. Though less incurved and shorter stemmed, it is near enough to the ancient pattern to denote functional and, presumably, traditional relationship. The table below shows that in tomb A5 these water-coolers were present in eight burial groups out of twelve.

Number noted. In tomb A5 sixteen.[1] In tomb A6 one (variant). Number kept, seven.

Inventory no.[2]	Height	Rim diam.[3]	Foot diam.	Condition	Plates	Allocation	Additional no. not kept in each group
A5.I.1	23·5	14·3	9·0	Complete	XXVII, 3; XLIX, 2	Cambridge	1
A5.IV.1	17·2	12·0	9·7	Crush break, slight restoration	XXVII, 2; XLIX, 5	Aden Gov.	3
A5.V.4	18·5	15·1	9·1	Workman's break, slight restoration	XXVII, 5; XLIX, 3	,,	..
A5.VI.4	..	..	..	..	..	..	1
A5.VII.10	..	..	..	..	..	..	1
A5.IX.4, 8	..	..	..	..	..	..	2
A5.X.1	28·1	18·8	10·9	Restored foot and rim	XXVII, 4; XLIX, 1	Ashmolean	2
A5.X.3	20·5	17·0	8·6	Crush break, body restoration	XXVII, 1; XLIX, 4	Aden Gov.	..
A5.XII.1	19·2	10·5	9·0	Complete, chipped	XXVII, 6; XLIX, 6	,,	..
A6	28·2	28·0	13·5	Restored from fragments constituting one side	XXVIII, 1; L, 1	Cambridge	..

II. PEDESTAL BOWLS WITH LEDGE RIMS (*pls.* XXVIII, 2–7; L, 2–7; LI, 1–7)

Form. The bowl is oval, set on a short hollow pedestal with splayed foot. The rims are characterized by broadening out into a flat ledge varying from 1·8 to 3·4 cm. wide. Below this is a moulding more or less accentuated (pl. L, 4–6), or a decorative band (pl. L, 2, 3, 7).

Ware. Rough finished, without applied coating (with one exception), but perhaps wet-smoothed. The colour is pale pinky-buff, mottled with redder or greyer firing patches. The core is grey, the firing temperature low. The clay is friable and contains grits and chaff. The single exception is A5.VI.8, the smallest of this class. This is dark brown to dark grey and shows remains of pebble burnish on an applied coat, orange-brown in colour fading to grey. The tested porosity of these vessels varied, due possibly to different states of preservation of the surfaces. A5.VI.8 which, being burnished, looked watertight, held its contents for six hours and then leaked rapidly. A5.VIII.1 showed, after twenty-four hours, damp patches only. A5.VII.16, after twenty-six hours, remained impermeable.

Technique. Similar to class I. The wide ledge rim seems to have been made by folding back and squeezing out the 'slack' of the edge, and was not applied separately.

Decoration. Five specimens have a single band of stabbed drop-shaped incisions

[1] For this and other pottery types the full number includes all recognizable fragments too incomplete, crushed, or disintegrated for preservation or reconstruction.

[2] The number of each type in any one 'tomb group' (see p. 71) may thus be seen. The position of each will be found on the plan, pl. LXXIX, but I have not, in the last column, given the inventory numbers of the specimens not kept.

[3] Overall measurements unless otherwise stated.

below the rim; in one case only, A5.XII.9 (pl. L, 2), this is reinforced by a light zigzag. The ledge rims of three bear inscriptions (pls. L, 2; LI, 4, 5). The longest of these, A5.VI.8, is done in light pointillé (detail in pl. XXIX, 1); the others are boldly incised in the wet (detail in pl. XXIX, 2). Pointillé was favoured in south Arabia, for it appears in an inscription on an alabaster or limestone saucer rim in the Pennsylvania Museum,[1] and in rock graffiti here published (pls. LXIX, LXX). It seems likely that the flat broad rim is a stone form adapted to pottery. Decipherment of these inscriptions is given on p. 177–8; they are magic invocations.

Variants. A5.VII.7 (pl. L, 3) has a modified rim.

Comments. The wide brims prevent easy pouring, and these vessels are probably store-jars. In spite of the inscriptions they are not specifically funerary wares, for fragments of similar but larger jars were found in and on the Temple deposits (pl. LI, 2), on the farmstead site (pl. LI, 1, 6), as well as on the surface in other places. Nor is it a local, Wadi 'Amd form only, for pl. LI, 3 shows a rim we picked up on the Gheibun ruin-field in the Wadi Do'an, and Dr. Huzayyin found others there the preceding year. The type occurred in over half of the A5 tomb groups.

Number noted. In tomb A5 nine. In tomb A6 none. Number kept, eight.

Inventory no.	Height	Rim diam.[2]	Ledge width	Inscribed	Condition	Plates	Allocation
A5.IV	..	..	2·6	..	Rim and side only	..	..
A5.V.9	18·6	13·3	2·4	..	Complete	XXVIII, 7; L, 4	Aden Gov.
A5.VI.8	16·0	9·1	1·8	p. 178, no. 57	Chipped foot	XXVIII, 2; LI, 5	Cambridge
A5.VII.7	18·6	13·8	1·2	..	Complete	XXVIII, 4; L, 3	,,
A5.VII.16	·18·3	10·5	2·4	..	,,	XXVIII, 5; L, 5	Ashmolean
A5.VIII.1	21·7	12·4	2·5	..	Chipped foot	XXVIII, 6; L, 6	Cambridge
A5.X.2	23·6	16·6	2·0	..	Crush break restored	XXVIII, 3; L, 7	Aden Gov.
A5.XII.6	..	12·1	3·4	p. 177, no. 56	Rim only	XXIX, 2; LI, 4	,,
A5.XII.9	..	16·8	2·2	p. 179, no. 75	Rim and part side	XXXV, 2; L, 2	,,

III. PEDESTAL BOWLS AND CUPS (*pls.* XXX, 1, 3–11; LII, 2–11)

Form. The bowl is oval in profile and in most cases the rim is the widest diametric measurement. Straight, slightly flared, and incurving rims are all present in this class, though all are thin and plain. The bowls stand on low pedestals with splayed foot. The sizes vary from tiny cups only 6·7 cm. high to a goblet of 17·7 cm.

Ware. Less friable than the preceding types and, being thinner, better fired. Contains chaff. Seven or eight retain a brick-red coating outside and in, smooth but not polished. Dr. Webb describes this ware as a 'sandy marl' and adds 'Black cored through insufficient air in firing. Easy (badly) fired. Soft in texture. Coated with a fine, red burning, clay slip'. Others, now rough, drab-pink, probably possessed originally a coating also, for the surviving coatings in some specimens are flaking, and leave a similar under-face. A5.IX.1 was tested for permeability and oozed after two hours.

[1] L. Legrain, *American Journal Archaeology*, vol. xxxviii, no. 3, 1934, fig. 7. Also same specimen in Ryckmans, *Muséon*, tome xlviii, 1935, pl. IV. 146, and nos. 142 and 144.

[2] Aperture diameter; the ledge width added gives the overall measurement.

Technique. Hand-made, with possible rotation on rim and foot. Many are grotesquely asymmetric.

Decoration. Five have a vague incised line defining the rim. Two others bear in addition a wavy line below this.

Variants. Two vessels, both larger and of abnormal shape, are provisionally included, until the discovery of others shall establish their claim to a separate class. One is the globular bowl, pls. xxx, 2; lii, 1. The other is the tall tumbler, pl. li, 8. Both are of rough, pinky-buff to brown ware, with chaff, badly fired.

Comment. In several cases rims and bases are rubbed as though in service before interment. A modern drinking-cup, with similar brick-red coating, bought in Terim market, suggests the use to which the pre-Islamic series was put (pl. lii, 5). The modern decoration consists of patterned groups of white paint dots, carelessly executed. All the tomb-groups in A5 yielded one or more examples of these vessels.

Number noted. In tomb A5 seventeen. In tomb A6 none. Number kept, eleven.

Inventory no.	Height	Rim diam.	Condition	Plates	Allocation	Additional no. not kept in each group
A5.I.2	16·9	13·2	Workman's break, repaired	xxx, 3; lii, 6	Aden Gov.	I
A5.I.3	13·8	12·1	,, ,, ,,	xxx, 6; lii, 9	Ashmolean	..
A5.I.4	8·2	7·4	Repaired foot, worn	xxx, 8; lii, 4	,,	..
A5.II.4	24·7	21·8	Complete, worn	xxx, 2; lii, 1	Aden Gov.	I
A5.II.8	10·7	10·6	,, ,,	xxx, 9; lii, 7	,,	..
A5.III.2	7·5	7·4	,, ,,	xxx, 7; lii, 2	Cambridge	..
A5.IV.6	..	..	..	..	..	I
A5.V.6	15·4	14·0	Smashed in transit	..	..	..
A5.VI.3	..	..	..	..	..	I
A5.VII.8	17·2–18·2	15·1	Crush break, mended	xxx, 1; lii, 8	Aden Gov.	..
A5.VIII.2	..	..	..	..	..	I
A5.IX.1	14·0	12·7	Complete, cracked, worn	xxx, 4; lii, 11	Cambridge	..
A5.X.4	6·7	6·4	Restored patch, worn	xxx, 11; lii, 3	Aden Gov.	..
A5.XI.5	27·0	16·6	Restored from one side	li, 8	,,	..
A5.XII.8	10·9	11·1	Crush break, restored	xxx, 5; lii, 10	,,	..

IV. CHALICE WITH INTERNAL RIM (*pls.* xxxvii, 1; xlix, 7)

Form. This is represented by fragments only, which fortunately build up into a complete side from rim to base and make restoration conclusive. The chalice is biconical and consists of a rounded cup with contracted base set on a tall hollow pedestal splaying to a base nearly as wide as the cup brim. A concave internal rim indicates a former lid. This was not found, but may have resembled that shown on pl. lvi, 20.

Ware. Red-brown, rough, with no surviving coating. Mica grains gleam in the clay.

Technique. Hand-made, apparently in one piece.

Decoration. A double belt of shallow dots encircles the waist. The pedestal has vague flutings. A dotted belt and horizontal scoring defines the rim.

Numbers noted. One only, in A5.

Inventory no.	Height	Rim diam.	Foot diam.	Plate	Allocation
A5.III.7	12·6	8·5	8·0	XXXVII, 1; XLIX, 7	Cambridge

V. SHALLOW OPEN PEDESTAL BOWLS (pls. XXXI, 1–3; LII, 12–14)

Form. These are wide, open, straight-sided bowls with cups only 5 cm. deep by 12 to 13 cm. wide, incurving sharply to a squat, low, hollow pedestal. The rims are plain.

Ware. A brick-red coating, similar to class III, covers outside and inside. This coat is flaking off: it is smooth but not polished. The reddish-brown rough pottery is leavened with grits and chaff.

Technique. Hand-made, probably turned.

Decoration. None.

Comment. A rare form. Of the three found, two were together.

Number noted. In tomb A5 three. In tomb A6 none. Number kept, three.

Inventory no.	Plate	Rim diam.	Foot diam.	Condition	Plate	Allocation
A5.VI.9	6·7	13·1 by 13·0	8·6	Chipped foot and rim	XXXI, 3; LII, 12	Cambridge
A5.X.7	7·3	12·9	8·4	Workman's break to rim	XXXI, 2; LII, 14	Aden Gov.
A5.X.14	7·1	13·1	8·5	Complete, worn	XXXI, 1; LII, 13	Ashmolean

VI. SHALLOW OPEN BOWLS WITH ROUNDED BASES (pls. XXXI, 4–6; LIV, 1–6)

Form. The series is characterized by straight to outward-inclined sides, and in all except one specimen, by a sharp, almost keeled angle between side and base, which is seen in its most accentuated form in pl. LIV, 1. Owing to convexity of base the bowls rock on a flat surface and were probably meant to stand on a ring-stand (or broken, inverted pedestal), or on sand.

Ware. Four bear traces of a brick-red coating on the interior, with more doubtful external traces. The colour of the clay beneath is pinky-buff with or without firing mottlings. Chaff and grits are ingredients. Fractures reveal a badly fired grey core. One specimen (pl. LIV, 2) is dark grey in colour, but this is probably due to secondary causes.

Technique. Hand-made; horizontal striations here again suggest some form of slow turn-table. But the rims are far from being true circles in most cases.

Decoration. One only has the common incised line below the rim, and this specimen, A5.V.1 (pls. XXXI, 5; LIV, 1), has in addition the letter 4 cut in the wet clay.

Variants. A small round-bottomed bowl, A5.X.15 (pl. LIV, 5), differs from the rest in its incurved rim and smoothly curved sides. It is also in finer, better-fired red ware, formerly red-coated outside and in.

R

Number noted. In tomb A5 eight. In tomb A6 none. Number kept, six.

Inventory no.	Height	Rim diam.	Condition	Plate	Allocation	Additional no. not kept in each group
A5.I.5	6·6	15·6 × 14·9	Complete	XXXI, 4; LIV, 3	Ashmolean	..
A5.V.1	6·5	15·3 × 16·2	,,	XXXI, 5; LIV, 1	Cambridge	..
A5.V.2	6·5	15·5 × 16·0	,,	XXXI, 6; LIV, 6	Aden Gov.	..
A5.VI.5	..	..	..	..	..	I
A5.VII.1	5·3	14·5 × 14·0	Complete	LIV, 4	Aden Gov.	..
A5.X.12	6·3	15·2 × 15·0	,,	LIV, 2	,,	..
A5.X.15	4·0	11·5 × 11·0	Workman's break, restored	LIV, 5	,,	..
A5.XII.7	..	..	..	..	..	I

VII. LIPPED SAUCER (*pl.* LIV, 7)

Form. Shallow, with sides sloping abruptly to an acutely convex base. The rim is drawn out into a single projecting lip, and is not of level height.

Ware. Rough-faced dull red; dark grey core with chaff. Traces of a former red coating.

Technique. Hand-made, badly fired.

Comment. A single specimen was found. The saucer might be a lamp; the modern Terim coffee roaster is not dissimilar though furnished with a long projecting handle.

Number noted. One only, in tomb A5.

Inventory no.	Height	Rim diam.	Condition	Plate	Allocation
A5.III.3	4·6	10·6	Lip anciently half broken	LIV, 7	Aden Gov.

VIII. DEEP BOWLS WITH DIMPLED BOTTOMS (*pls.* XXXI, 7–11; LIII, 1–13)

Form. These bowls, whilst falling into two varieties, are essentially a single series grading into each other. Though deep, the height in all cases is less than the diameter. Both varieties share, with one exception, the peculiarity of a marked indentation or dimple in the centre of the bottom which forces up the interior (the exterior view is seen, pl. XXXI, 10–11). In variety *a* the curvature of the sides and base is gently rounded with slightly inclined rims in six out of eight specimens (pl. LIII, 3–6), and the maximum diameter lies towards the middle of the bowl. In two cases, however, intermediate between varieties *a* and *b*, the rims are straight or slightly everted (pl. LIII, 7–8). In variety *b* the maximum diameter lies at the rim (pl. LIII, 9–13), the basal curvature is more angular, and the sides are vertical or inclined slightly outwards to the rim.

Ware. All are in pinky-buff to purply-red or grey-brown ware, with darker firing patches. The surface is rough, but in five specimens traces of a former brick-red applied coating still survives; chaff and grits are present in the clay, which Dr. Webb refers to as a 'marl'.

Technique. In five cases horizontal striae are noticeable, as though the damp surface had been rotated (perhaps against a cloth). In one case finger-marks are visible (pl. XXXI, 7). Several are grotesquely asymmetric and all are hand-made.

Decoration. A single lightly incised line below the brim appears in eight out of thirteen pots.

Variants. A globular bowl, A5.X.8 (pl. LIII, 2), is both larger and more enclosed than the others, but the dimpled base is similar. A5.I.12 (pl. LIII, 1) is another variant, and is hemispherical in form with a plain convex base.

Comment. The bowls occurred in seven out of twelve groups in A5.

Number noted. In tomb A5, variety *a*, seven; variety *b*, six. In tomb A6, variety *b*, one. Number kept, thirteen.

Inventory no.	Height	Rim diam.	Variety	Condition	Plate	Allocation
A5.I.6	8·8	10·8	*a*	Complete	XXXI, 7; LIII, 3	Ashmolean
A5.I.12	8·2	9·6	*a*	Complete, chipped	LIII, 1	Aden Gov.
A5.II.5	12·4 × 11·2	15 × 15·6	*b*	Workman's break, repaired	LIII, 12	,,
A5.II.6	10·0	16·0	*b*	Complete, crumbling rim	LIII, 9	,,
A5.II.7	8·1 × 7·5	8·3 × 8·8	*a*	Complete	LIII, 6	,,
A5.III.1	..	..	*b*	Crushed and not kept	..	..
A5.V.7	6·3	8·4	*b*	Complete, chipped	LIII, 10	Cambridge
A5.VI.2	10·9 × 10·5	12 × 13	*a*	Workman's break, repaired	LIII, 7	Aden Gov.
A5.VII.6	10·3 × 10·1	13·5	*a*	Complete, cracked	XXXI, 8; LIII, 8	,,
A5.VII.15	10·1 × 9·8	12 × 11·6	*a*	Complete	XXXI, 9; LIII, 5	Cambridge
A5.X.3	9·6 × 8·7	10·8 × 11·1	*a*	,,	LIII, 4	Aden Gov.
A5.X.5	10·3 × 9·5	14·7	*b*	,,	LIII, 11	,,
A5.X.8	14·1	8·2	Variant	Fragmentary base	LIII, 2	,,
A6.I	11·7 × 11·0	15·5	*b*	Crush crack, complete	LIII, 13	Cambridge

IX. EAR-LUG BOWLS IN STONE WARE (*pls.* XXXII, 1–8; LIV, 10, 11, 13–14)

Form. The rim diameter is nearly twice the height, and the sides curve in to a rounded base. The plain rim is pinched out into four small flattened ears which, in four out of five bowls, have been incised with single letters.

Ware. In the absence of agreed conclusions about the nature of this material I propose to call it 'stone ware'. Discussion concerning it need not be repeated.[1] It is dull black to dark grey in colour, with a rather greasy feeling (due to stored fat?), and is extremely friable. Broken edges crumble easily. The proportion of coarse minerals to argillaceous matrix differs in each bowl, but all show a micaceous sparkle. The fragment, A5.I.15, consisting of a side and single lug (pl. LIV, 11), is a dull pink outside, toning to dark grey in. This is believed by Dr. Webb to be due to standing on a heated surface (see p. 116). A similar pink hue is apparent also in one area of A5.X.17 (pls. XXXII, 4, 8; LIV, 14).

Technique. Rubbing striae are visible on the exterior. The surfaces undulate, and the shape is asymmetric.

Decoration. A5.IX.2 (pl. LIV, 10) has a letter on each ear, ҷ and ҷ, and two unidentifiable. A5.X.17 (pls. LIV, 14; XXXII, 4) has opposite ears incised with well-cut letters

---

[1] Cf. p. 116.

R 2

ʾ and ʾ, the other two being damaged. A5.I.15 (pl. LIV, 11) bears a ⴼ on its single surviving lug. A6. is uninscribed.

Comments. The modern 'burma' for holding grease is, in some cases, made of a heavy black material, in form not unlike the ancient bowls and with rounded base. Fragments of ear-lug bowls were found in the farmstead site;[1] and 'stone ware' fragments were present in the Temple deposits.[2]

Number noted. In tomb A5, two complete, and fragments of two more. In tomb A6 one. Number kept, all.

Inventory no.	Height	Rim diam.	Ear-lugs	Condition	Plate	Allocation
A5.I.15	..	..	Single, lettered	Ear and part of side only	LIV, 11	Aden Gov.
A5.IX.2	8·5	16 × 15·5	Four, lettered	Crush break, mended and restored	XXXII, 3, 7; LIV, 10	Cambridge
A5.X.17	10·0	16·0	Two, lettered, one missing, one damaged	Crush break, restored	XXXII, 4, 8; LIV, 14	,,
A5.X.18	..	..	..	Irreparably damaged	..	..
A6.I	11·4	18·5 × 18	Three, unlettered, one missing	Perished rim	XXXII, 1, 5; LIV, 13	Ashmolean

X. FLANGED CUPS WITH SPOUTS AND HANDLES IN STONE WARE
(*pls.* XXXIII, 1–6, 8, 9; XXXIV, 2–7; LV, 1–11, 14)

Form. In the twelve specimens found—not all complete—there are sufficient minor variations in shape to hint at a future subdivision when more of these very interesting little pots are known. For the present it seems sufficient to treat them as an homogeneous group, as functionally they are, with emphasis on individual differences. They may be described as small, more or less straight-sided cups, averaging 6·1 cm. high (maximum variability within 2·7 cm.), with minute tubular spouts, solid tongue-handles, more or less raked, degenerating into rim lugs, and tops partially enclosed by a flanged lid, resembling the modern feeding-cup in all essentials. Variations of form are seen in bases, spouts, and handles.

Bases. One series (four out of ten) is convex-bottomed; the other (six out of ten) flat-bottomed.[3] The first series includes slightly curved bases (examples, pls. LV, 1, 9; XXXIII, 3, 5) and the extreme convexity of pl. LV, 14. The second series may be rectilinear with the sides (examples, pls. LV, 3; XXXIII, 4) or flat-bottomed with rounded angles to the side walls (examples, pls. LV, 7, 8; XXXIII, 8).

Spouts. All are tiny, horizontal, and down-sloping passages through the relatively thick walls of the vessels, prolonged into a projecting spout. These in most cases have been damaged, but it seems admissible to separate them into two styles. The one is a short, clumsy spout-head, sometimes modelled theriomorphically (pl. XXXIV, 5–7), or in plainer fashion; in one case the aperture and passage are doubled. The other, known in two incomplete specimens, one from each tomb, is thin, tubular, and projecting as much as 3·8 cm. (pl. LV, 2, 10). Though fragmentary, these nozzle-

---

[1] Cf. pp. 141–3.   [2] Cf. pp. 25, 39.   [3] Two are incomplete in this part.

spouted cups include the major part of the vessels' side and the reconstruction is fairly certain.

Handles. These range from broad raked tongues, such as pls. XXXIII, 3, 5; LV, 1, 9; horizontal tongues, such as pls. LV, 6; XXXIII, 9; to small rim lugs, such as pls. LV, 3, 8; XXXIII, 1, 4.

Ware. The colour in nine cases is dark grey to dull black; the exceptions are pl. XXXIV, 5, which is mud-coloured, and pl. LV, 5, which is greyish-brown with a redder brown under-surface. The material is peculiar and is so heavily charged with very coarse grits that an impression of stone is created both to eye and touch. All contain mica in varying degrees, and in some cases, particularly in specimens A5.I.7 and A5.X.13 (pls. XXXIV, 4; XXXIII, 5), the surface glistens with it, so that the workmen believed them to contain gold.

Technique. The vessels are roughly hand-made; the ware is crumbly and insufficiently fired. Some specimens bear traces of wet-smoothing, others are roughly finished. The action of heat on the mineral constituents is not apparent.

There is no evidence that the flange lids, drawn partially over the apertures, were attached separately; they seem to be folded over from the walls. There are, on the other hand, indications that the spout was applied. The best example is A5.I.7 (pl. LV, 5), where it is missing, and the break occurs flush with the walls of the vessel. A5.III.6 (pl. LV, 13) is another instance of this.

Decoration. Half the cups are inscribed, have ornamental or symbolic spouts, or decorated flanges, lids, or handles.

Inscriptions. Three cups, all from tomb A5, are inscribed in the wet (pls. XXXIV, 2, 3; XXXV, 3). A5.I.7 (pl. XXXIV, 3, 4) shows three neatly executed letters and a terminal stroke, | X ⴼ 𐩣, done with a fine point. Professor Ryckmans gives the translation 'cent' and suggests a serial number, as it seems quantitatively too high to indicate the cup's capacity.[1] Might it not refer, however, to the value of the contents? A5.V.5 shows a carelessly executed ⟩▥◦, done with a blunt tool (pls. XXXIV, 2; XXXV, 5). Professor Ryckmans reads 'perfume'.[2] A5.III.5 (pl. XXXV, 3) bears the letter 𐩺, also bluntly incised. An initial or potter's mark is proposed.[3] These three inscriptions are placed respectively beside the handle, one on the right of it, two on the left.

Ornamental or symbolic spout-heads. Definitely theriomorphic heads form the spouts in three cases, two from tomb A5, one from A6 (pl. XXXIV, 5–7); these do not occur on the inscribed cups. They are rough in execution and have lost the spout-tips; but the modelling and incised detail unmistakably portray animal heads. What animal? A5.I.8 (pls. XXXIV, 5; LV, 8) shows a pair of diamond-shaped incisions on each side of the spout. These seem to me ears rather than eyes, for if we are right in supposing a bull's head these would be round or oval, and set lower on the part of the spout unfortunately broken.

---

[1] Cf. Ryckmans, p. 179. F. Stark has unfortunately published, without any authority, her own translation, 'māt = he died.' *Winter in Arabia*, p. 122.

[2] Cf. Ryckmans, p. 179.

[3] Cf. Ryckmans, p. 179.

On the lid flange above there are four bands of irregular pointillé dots separated by lines (best seen in pl. LV, 8), and pointillé also on the snout or muzzle. The spout-head of A5.X.6 (pls. XXXIV, 7; LV, 9) shows oval eyes, and a triangular pointillé pattern on the forehead bounded by lines: the lid flange bears a crescentic incision following the plastic curve of the rim, filled with vague dots. This last I take to be the horns of a bull, already suggested by the triangular forelock (best seen in pl. LV, 9). The raked tongue-handle bears two bands of pointillé bounded by lines on its upper surface. A6 (pls. XXXIV, 6; LV, 11) has two deeply punched eye sockets which have gouged up the unfired clay. Pointillé dots cover the forehead. The lid flange continues these in two rows held within lines. Only the spout-head and part of the lid flange survive in this specimen, and it cannot, therefore, be certain if conventionalized horns are intended; but with the other example as guidance this seems likely. I think that bulls' heads, the symbol of the Moon God, are without much doubt intended in all three cases.

An interesting spout variant is that of A5.VI.6 (pls. LV, 10; XXXIII, 6); the long tubular nozzle is flanked by shorter projections which give the appearance of an elephant's trunk with tusks.

Comment. With the inscription on A5.V.5 to tell us in plain Semitic what the vessel held, we need hardly argue the case for the use of this series as unguent cups. The tiny spout proclaims a precious liquid or semi-liquid poured drop by drop; the lid flange the care taken to see that none was spilt in the pouring. The exact 'perfume' used and the significance attached to it must, however, remain a matter for speculation. The cups on removal from the soil had no smell or incrusted deposit which could be collected for analysis. Was the pouring a libation to the dead, purification of the dead or of the living after contact with the dead, or anointment? Was it merely therapeutic? The answer is

Number noted. In tomb A5 nine. In tomb A6 three. Number kept, twelve.

Inventory no.	Height	Spout detail	Inscribed	Condition	Plate	Allocation
A5.I.7	6·4	Single, broken		Sound, missing spout	XXXIV, 3, 4; LV, 5	Cambridge
A5.I.8	6·5	Single, theriomorphic	..	Sound, spout-tip missing, handle restored	XXXIII,1; XXXIV, 5; LV, 8	Aden Gov.
A5.III.5	5·6	Single, theriomorphic		Poor, handle and spout broken	XXXIII, 8; XXXV, 3; LV, 7	,,
A5.III.6	5·6	Single, broken	..	Crumbling, spout missing	LV, 13	,,
A5.V.5	7·8	Double		Sound, broken spout-head	XXXIII, 9; XXXV, 5; LV, 6	,,
A5.VI.6	5·1	Tubular nozzle 2 cm. long	..	Spout and side complete, rest restored	XXXIII, 6; LV, 10	Cambridge
A5.VI.10	6·1	Single	..	Sound, damaged spout	XXXIII, 4; LV, 3	Ashmolean
A5.X.6	6·3	Single, theriomorphic	..	Sound	XXXIII, 3; XXXIV, 7; LV, 9	Cambridge
A5.X.13	6·1	Single, complete	..	Sound, rough drab ware	XXXIII, 5; LV, 1	Aden Gov.
A6	?	Single, theriomorphic	..	Incomplete, restored	XXXIII, 2; LV, 11	,,
A6	4·5	Tubular nozzle	..	Sound	LV, 14	,,
A6	?	Tubular nozzle 3·8 cm. long	..	Incomplete, restored	LV, 2	,,

not facilitated by the presence of a fragment of a similar cup inside a room of the farmstead (p. 142 and pl. LV, 4). In tomb A5 they occurred in five tomb groups out of twelve, and in four instances were in pairs. Tomb A6 yielded three specimens.

XI*a*. OPEN CUP, UNSPOUTED, WITH TONGUE-HANDLE IN STONE WARE
(*pls.* XXXV, 1; XXXIV, 1; LV, 15)

Form. A single specimen from tomb A5. It is a flat-bottomed cup widening to a plain rim. A single tongue-handle is raked.

Ware. Black soft stone ware full of angular coarse grits and mica. The surface is smooth and almost lustrous.

Technique. Hand-made.

Decoration. To the left of the handle XHHo is incised with a blunt point in the wet, untidily. Professor Ryckmans suggests the proprietor's name.[1] The word, however, was traced before firing, so if the name is that of the owner the cup was 'made to order'. Perhaps it was the potter's name.

Inventory no.	Height	Inscribed	Condition	Plate	Allocation
A5.VIII.4	7·1	XHHo	Sound, complete	XXXV, 1; XXXIV, 1; LV, 15	Cambridge

XI*b*. OPEN CUPS, UNSPOUTED, WITH PIERCED TONGUE-HANDLE IN STONE WARE (*pls.* XXXIII, 7; LV, 16)

Form. This is speculative, being based on two separate handles attached to fragmentary sides. A5.I.15 (pl. XXXIII, 7) consists of a broad tongue-handle centrally perforated and the complete side and part of a flat base. This gives us a form similar to, though smaller than the type XI*a*. The difference lies in the perforation; and on the assumption that the corresponding but missing half would also be dissimilar. For perforation of the handle suggests suspension, and suspension suggests equipoise. Hence in the reconstruction a counterbalancing pierced handle has been tentatively added. A similar perforated handle was found in tomb A6.

Ware. Black or dark grey, gritty, micaceous, stone ware.

Technique. The perforation is circular and vertical. Hand-made.

Number noted. In tomb A5, group I, one. In tomb A6 one. *Allocation*, Aden Gov.

XII. MINIATURE CUP IN STONE WARE (*pl.* LV, 17)

Form. An open bowl of irregular height, contracting to a thick rounded base.

Ware. Heavy dark grey stone ware with large quartz grits and mica.

Technique. Hand-made and very rough.

Inventory no.	Height	Rim diam.	Condition	Plate	Allocation
A5.II.10	6·1	7·1	Workman's break at rim	LV, 17	Aden Gov.

[1] Cf. Ryckmans, p. 179.

XIII. MINIATURE SUSPENSION BOWLS IN STONE WARE (*pl.* LV, 18, 19)

Form. Oblate, with flattened bases. One of the pair, A5.VIII.3 (pl. LV, 18), has the curious 'dimple' on the bottom with corresponding internal hump which characterizes the bowls of type VIII.[1] The plain rims are inclined. A pair of pierced lugs on each side are perforated vertically.

Ware. Both are dark grey to black, friable, and heavy with coarse grits and mica.

Technique. Roughly hand-modelled and very lightly fired.

Comment. Appear to be imitations of stone bowls with lugs.

Number noted. In tomb A5 one. In tomb A6 one. Number kept, both.

Inventory no.	Height	Condition	Plate	Allocation
A5.VIII.3	6·4–5·8	Crumbling; one lug lost	LV, 18	Aden Gov.
A6	4·3	A single side and part of base. Reconstructed	LV, 19	Cambridge

XIV. SMALL CUP WITH PINCHED FLANGE LID IN STONE WARE
(*pl.* LV, 12)

Form. A general resemblance to the unguent cups, type X, but lacking the handle. The lid flange also differs and is pinched into a crinkled outline. The side is perforated, but lacks a spout.

Ware. Black, soft, full of mica and quartz grits.

Technique. Roughly hand-modelled and lightly fired.

Inventory no.	Height	Condition	Plate	Allocation
A5.X.10	5·4	Poor	LV, 12	Ashmolean

XV. CONICAL PIERCED LID (*pl.* LVI, 20)

A single lid was found in the excavations at all sites. It came from tomb A5, group XI.

Form. It is small, 4·5 cm. in diameter, surmounted by a conical knob horizontally pierced, and is fitted with an internal rim.

Ware. Coarse buff to pink, well fired.

Comment. It fits no pot we found, but if larger the type might complete the chalice with internal rim, class IV.

Allocation. Cambridge.

SHERDS (*pl.* LVI, 16, 17, 18)

Three sherds, which do not fit into any of these pottery types, were found in tomb A5. All came from A5.1, the group at the entrance, and would thus appear to be the latest objects buried in the tomb.

Pl. LVI, *16*, shows a rim fragment, 7 mm. thick, in fine red ware with an applied brick-

---

[1] This is evidence against 'foreign' origin for this stone ware.

red coating on both faces. The rim is defined by a deeply incised line, and distinction is added by a raised square, projecting about 7 mm., which alternates with oblong raised panels.

Pl. LVI, *18*, is also a rim fragment, 6 mm. thick, in well-fired, brick-red applied coated ware. A solitary flat discoidal stud, projecting about 4 mm., whets the curiosity for the complete vessel.

Pl. LVI, *17*. This bowl-rim fragment, which in shape conforms to type I of our classification, is, unlike that type, made in rough-faced dark grey ware, nearly black on the inner face. This appears not to be secondary discoloration.

Pl. LVI, *19*. Mention should be made of a number of broken short pedestal bases which in many cases had been rubbed down to make saucers. The specimen figured is in red-coated, semi-burnished ware.

DESCRIPTION OF THE TEMPLE POTTERY

No complete vessels were found in the Moon God Temple, A3, nor were sherds abundant. Consequently until the tombs yielded later the pottery described above, the Temple wares had remained unintelligible fragments of more or less speculative forms. Many of these were subsequently typed to their tomb counterparts, leaving no doubt that the same forms characterized both places, though many included in the tomb groups were absent in the Temple, where shallow open bowls predominated. There has been no need, therefore, to multiply the pottery plates, beyond the addition, on pl. LVI, 1–11, of a few sherds, important because of their position in the Temple deposits and illustrative of the fact that they tended on the whole to be rather finer in texture than the grave goods. Further references to the Temple pottery will be found in the stratigraphical description of that building.

Pl. LVI, *1*. From the east outer corner deposits, 2·08 m. below the period C pavement.[1] Reconstructed from 6 cm. of rim, complete side, and basal curve. A deep, open bowl with rounded bottom, about 6·4 cm. high. Rim thickness 4 mm. The ware is thin, hard, hand-made, with grey core, and a brick-red applied coating both sides, horizontally rubbed. The shape falls into tomb-class VI, but its proportions are slightly different.

Pl. LVI, *2*. From the fill of area VII, at 0·65 m. below the period C pavement.[2] Reconstructed from 10 cm. of rim, side, and basal curve. An open bowl with rounded bottom and the angularity of basal curve noted in tomb-class VI, for instance in the bowl A5.X.12 (pl. LIV, 2). The walls of the Temple specimen are, however, thinner, with a rim thickness of 6 mm. The ware is reddish-buff with a brick-red applied coating, horizontally rubbed.

Pl. LVI, *3*. From the east outer corner deposits, 2·30 m. below the period C pavement.[3] Reconstructed from 5 cm. of rim, side, and curve to base. A shallow open bowl with rounded bottom and slight angularity of basal curve. The ware is hard and well fired,

---

[1] Cf. p. 25.   [2] Cf. p. 36.   [3] Cf. p. 25.

with a brick-red applied coating outside and in, horizontally rubbed. A vague, lightly scored line below the rim. The bowl belongs to tomb-class VI.

Pl. LVI, *4*. From the fill of area VI, 0·40 m. below the period C pavement.[1] Reconstructed from 10 cm. of rim, side, and basal curve. A shallow open bowl with rounded base and non-angular curve to walls. The ware is thin, rim thickness only 3 mm., and bears a brick-red applied coating on both faces, horizontally rubbed. Tomb-class VI.

Pl. LVI, *5*. From the fill of area VI, 2 m. below the period C pavement.[2] Reconstructed from 11 cm. of rim and 8·5 cm. of side without base. The rim is 7 mm. thick with angular moulding: below it a scored line. The rim profile most resembles the pedestal bowls of tomb-class II (pl. L), but the ware is thinner, with a red applied coating on both sides, horizontally rubbed.

Pl. LVI, *6*. From the fill of area VI, 0·85 m. below the period C pavement.[3] Reconstructed from 7·7 cm. of rim and part of side. A shallow open bowl of very fine, brick-red applied coated ware, horizontally smoothed. The rim is 5 mm. thick with a scored line below. A raised moulded band, 6 mm. wide, encircles the side below and broadens out interestingly just where the break interrupts its development. This band is pinched up from the walls and is not applied. The plastic band on the tomb sherd, A5.I (pl. LVI, 16), is recalled.

Pl. LVI, *7*. From the east outer corner, 2 m. below the period C pavement.[4] A rim fragment, 3·8 cm. long, 9 mm. thick. Rough red-brown ware with red applied coating. The profile resembles that of tomb-class VIII*b* (the deep bowls), particularly A6.I (pl. LIII, 13).

Pl. LVI, *8*. From the fill of area VII, 3·35 m. below the period C pavement.[5] A rim fragment, 3·8 cm. long, 8 mm. thick tapering to the edge. Hard, smooth, red, shading to grey, without coating; grey core. Scored line. The profile and ware fall into tomb-class VIII*b*, particularly A5.X.5 (pl. LIII, 11).

Pl. LVI, *9*. From the east outer corner, 2 m. below the period C pavement.[6] Rim fragment, 4·6 cm. long, 11 mm. thick. Hard, rough-faced red ware, horizontally wet-smoothed; grey core. The section has no exact parallel in the tomb series, though allied probably to class VIII*a*, the deep bowls.

Pl. LVI, *10*. From the east outer corner, 1·30 m. below the period C pavement.[7] A rim fragment, 4·4 cm. long, in rough-faced red-brown ware. The profile has no exact parallel in the tomb pottery.

Pl. LVI, *11*. From the east outer corner, 2 m. below the period C pavement.[8] Rim fragment, 5·6 cm. long, 6 mm. thick. Hard red-coated ware, horizontally smoothed both sides. A deeply scored line below the angular moulding of the rim. The profile has no exact parallel in the tomb series, but apart from the sharp inclination of the side (which may be exaggerated in the section drawing) it resembles tomb-class VIII*b*.

Pl. LI, *2*. From the surface outside south-west wall. Rim fragment, 13 cm. long, of

[1] Cf. p. 36.   [2] Cf. p. 36.   [3] Cf. p. 36.   [4] Cf. p. 25.
[5] Cf. p. 36.   [6] Cf. p. 25.   [7] Cf. p. 25.   [8] Cf. p. 25.

large pedestal bowl with ledge rim, 3·5 cm. broad; this bears two letters incised in the wet and part of a third (see Ryckmans, no. 82, p. 180). The pot is considerably larger and the rim moulding bolder than any of the pedestal bowls of tomb-class II, to which, however, it belongs. The suggestion on p. 119 that these vessels are store-jars gains probability by the occurrence on the surface deposits beside the Temple at Gheibun of a similar large specimen (pl. LI, 3); another even larger lay by the farmstead A4 (pl. LI, 1).

Pl. LIV, 8. From the votive group A3.20.[1] A pedestal base rubbed down to serve as a makeshift offering saucer. The diameter, 22·7 cm., is far larger than any of the pedestals of tomb-class II, with which it may be compared. But its dimensions would be suitable for a large storage-jar such as pl. LI, 2. The ware is badly fired mud colour, hand-made.

Pl. LIV, 9. From the same votive group A3.20.[2] A rough saucer, not certainly a pedestal base in origin, diameter 9·9 cm., in reddish-buff coarse ware.

In addition to these figured items, presented as type specimens of many examples, the Temple deposits yielded also broken rims and bases of the drinking-cups, tomb-class III, and two scraps of the black or dark grey stone ware with mica and quartz ingredients which characterizes tomb-classes IX–XIV. Unfortunately, owing probably to the crumbling nature of this ware, these sherds are too small for identification of form.[3]

The Temple, then, produced sherds recognized as belonging to vessels of tomb-classes I,[4] II, III, VI, VIII, and a black ware which resembles tomb-classes IX–XIV. The missing types are IV, the unique chalice; V, the shallow open pedestal bowls; VII, the unique lipped saucer. We believe it legitimate, therefore, to infer that Temple and tombs are closely related in epoch and were the work of the same populace.

[1] Cf. p. 51. [2] Cf. p. 51. [3] Cf. pp. 25, 30.
[4] For this single specimen of an earlier vessel re-used, see p. 47.

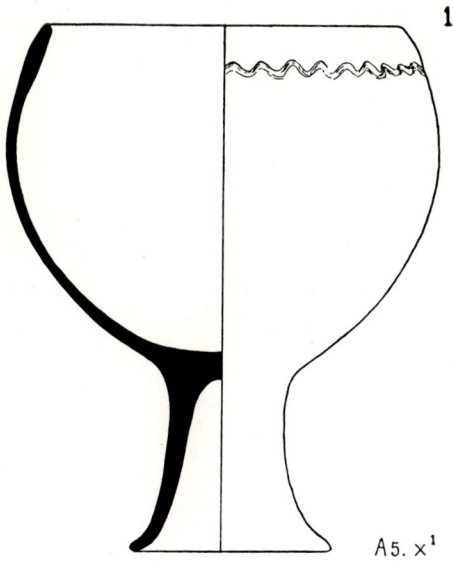

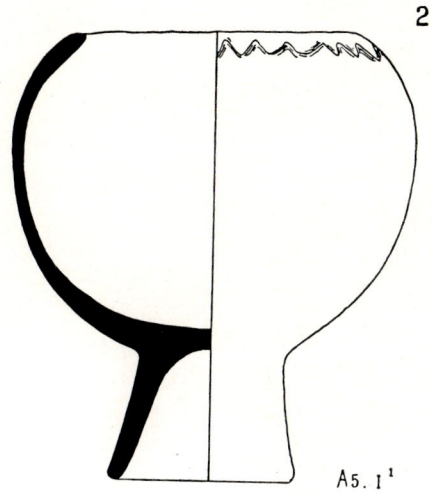

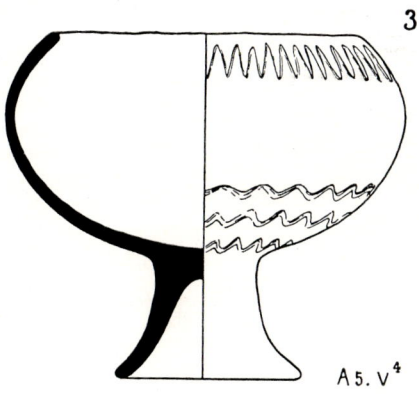

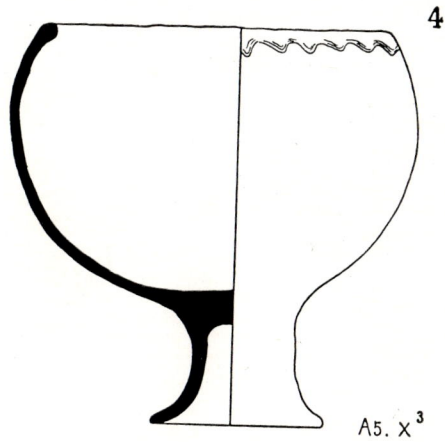

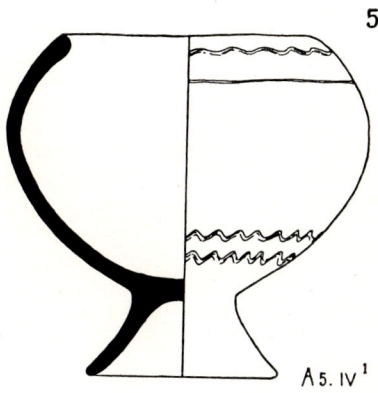

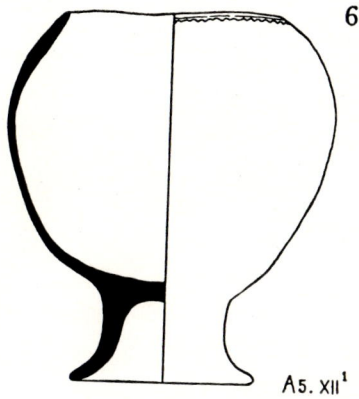

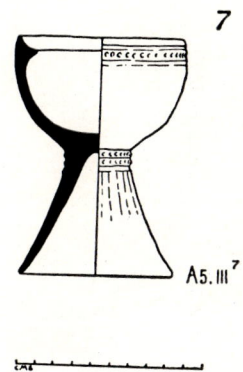

Goblets on tall stems, type I. No. 7. Chalice with internal rim, type IV
(Scale 1 : 4)

1

A6. 2

2

A5. XII^9

3

A5. VII^7

4

A5. V^9

5

A5. VII^{16}

6

A5. VIII^1

7

A5. X^2

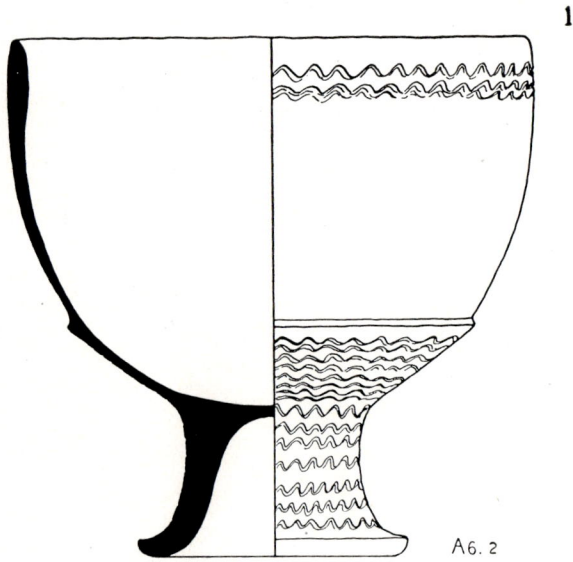

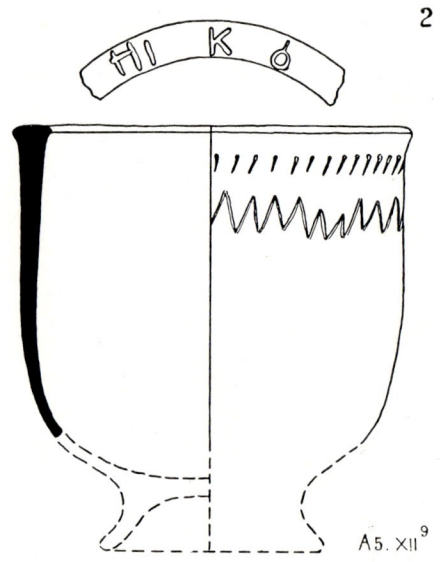

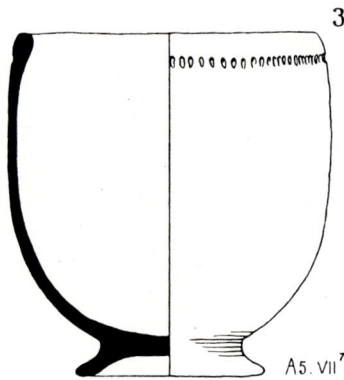

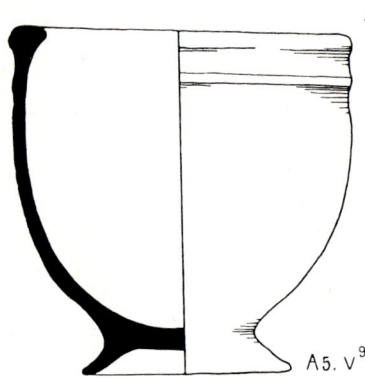

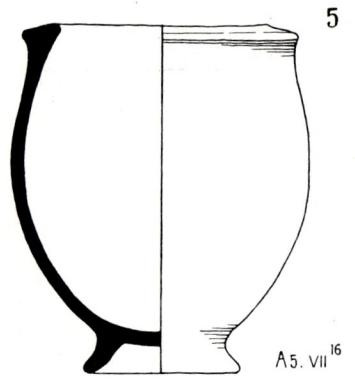

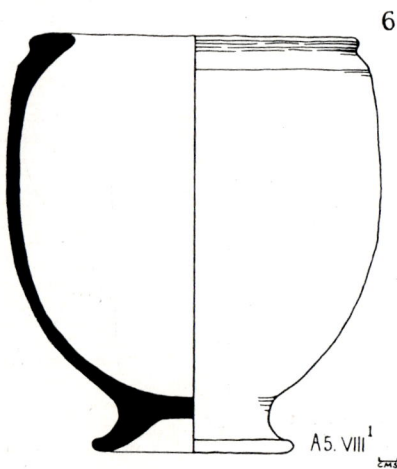

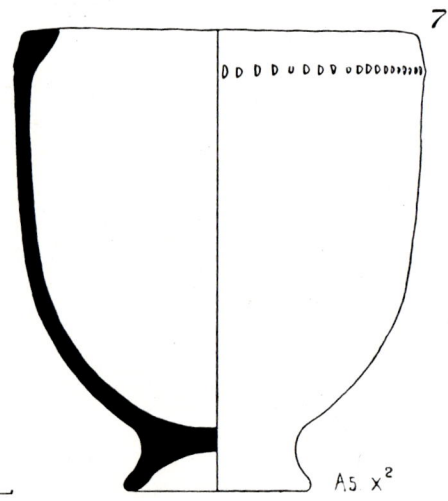

Pedestal bowls with ledge rims, type II. No. 1. Variant of type I

(Scale 1 : 4)

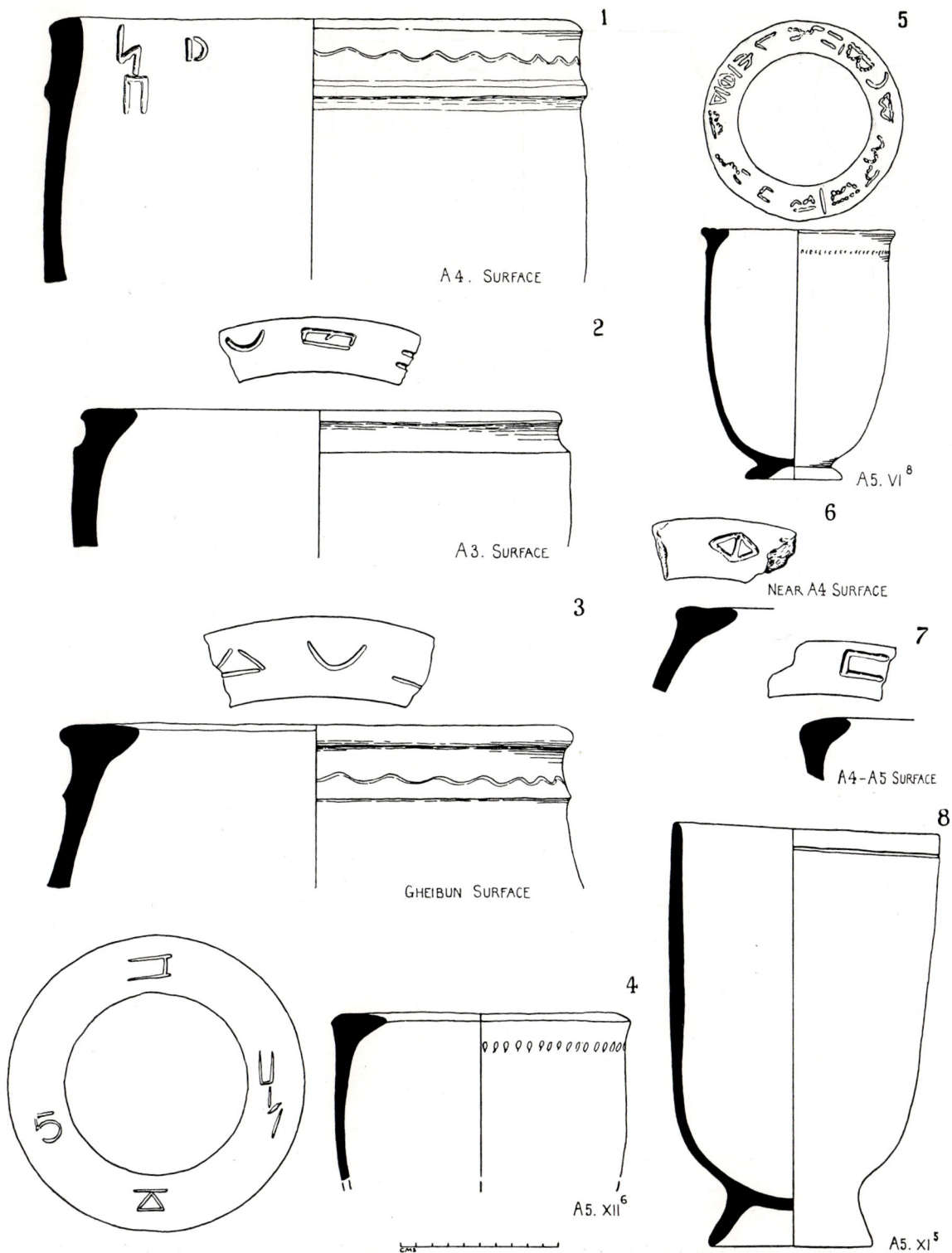

1

A 4. SURFACE

2

A3. SURFACE

3

GHEIBUN SURFACE

4

A5. XII⁶

5

A5. VI⁸

6

NEAR A4 SURFACE

7

A4-A5 SURFACE

8

A5. XI⁵

Pedestal bowls with ledge rims, type II. No. 8. Variant of type III

(Scale 1 : 4)

2

A5.III²

1

A5. II⁴

3

A5. X⁴

4

A5. I⁴

5

TERIM [modern]

8

A5. VII⁸

6

A5. I²

7

A5. II⁸

10

A5. XII⁸

9

A5. I³

11

A5. IX¹

12

A5. VI⁹

13

A5. X¹⁴

14

A5. X⁷

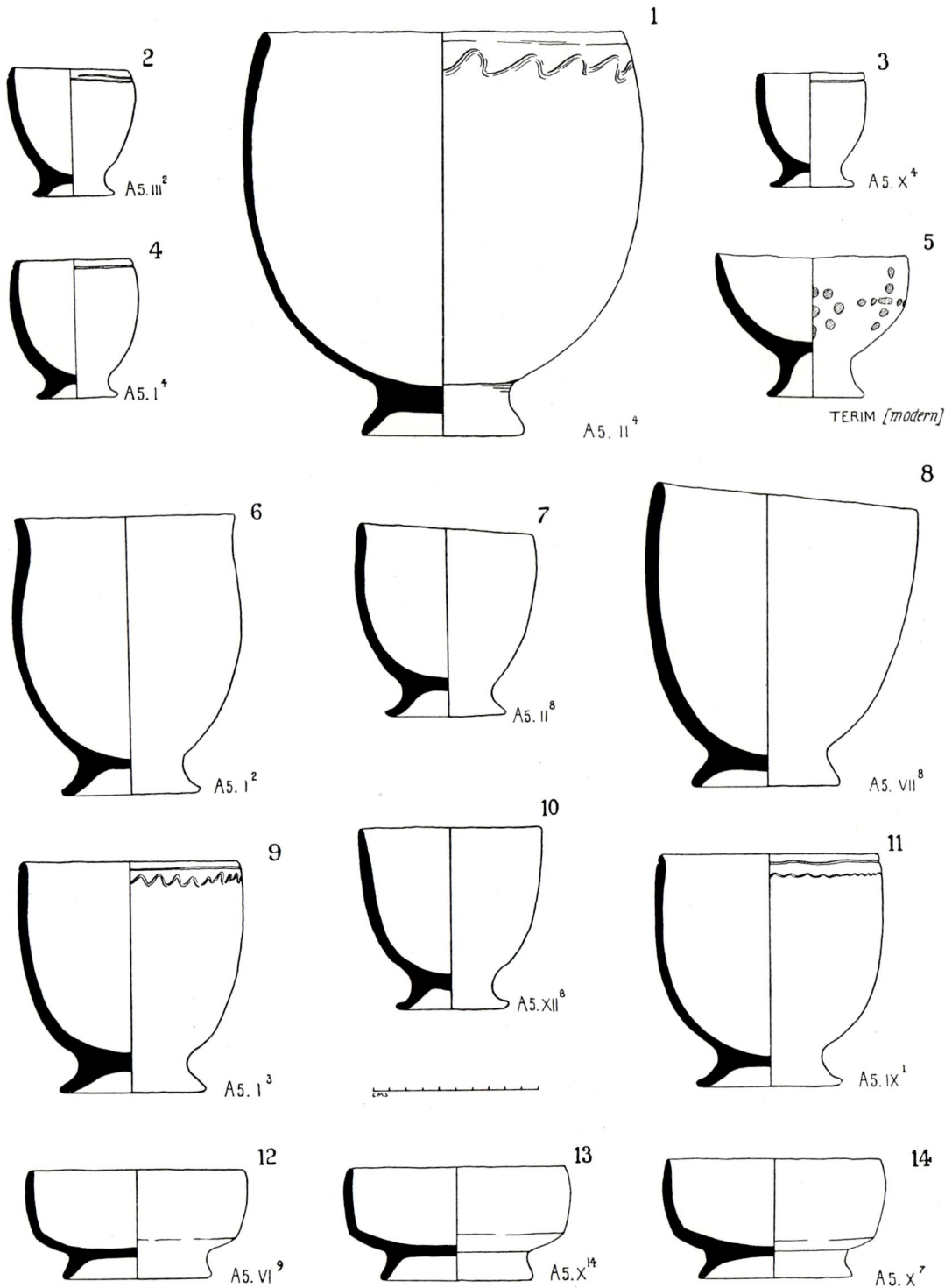

1–11. Pedestal bowls and cups, type III. 12–14. Shallow wide pedestal bowls, type V
(Scale 1 : 4)

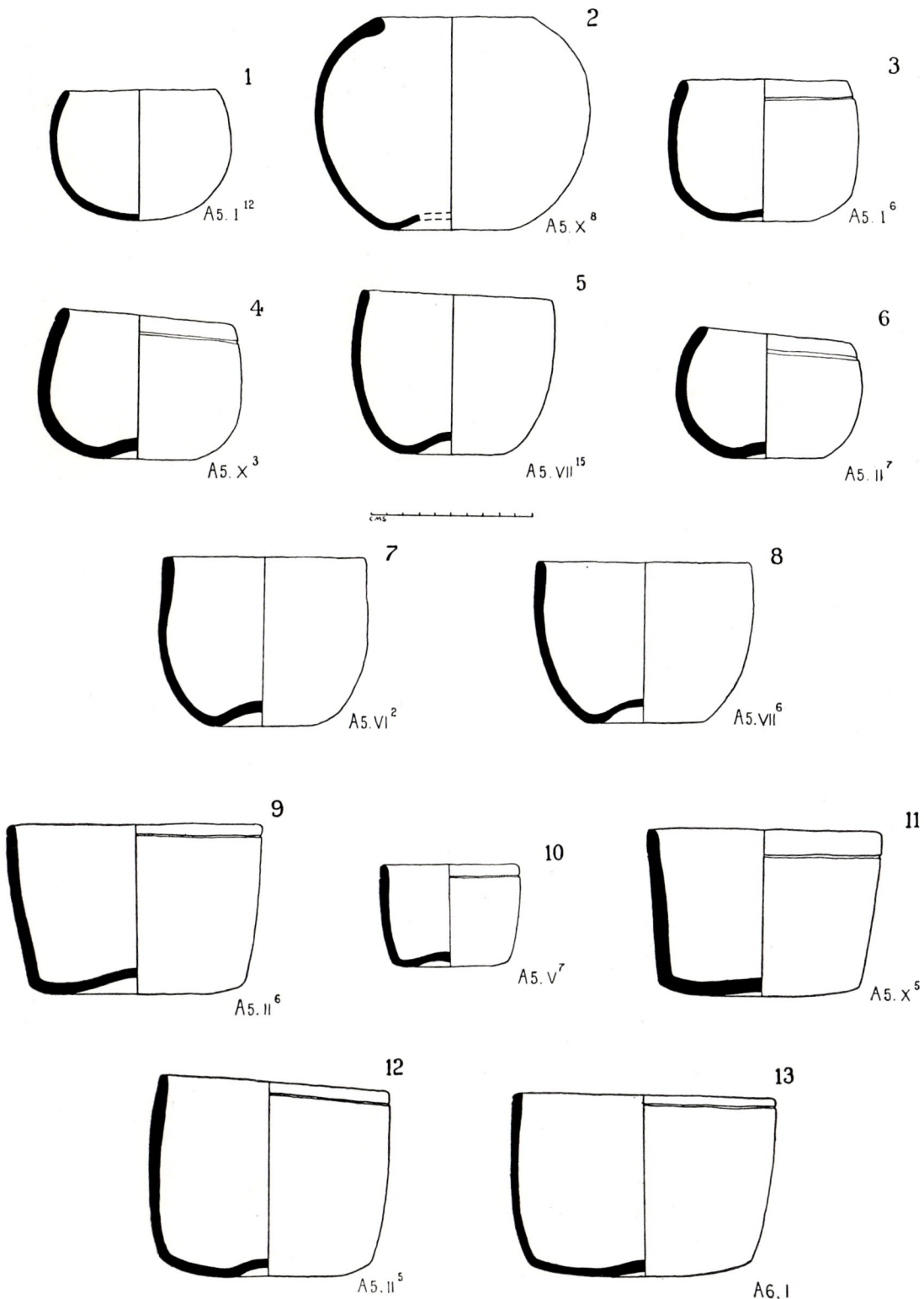

1–8. Deep bowls, type VIII*a*. 9–13. Deep bowls, type VIII*b*

(Scale 1 : 4)

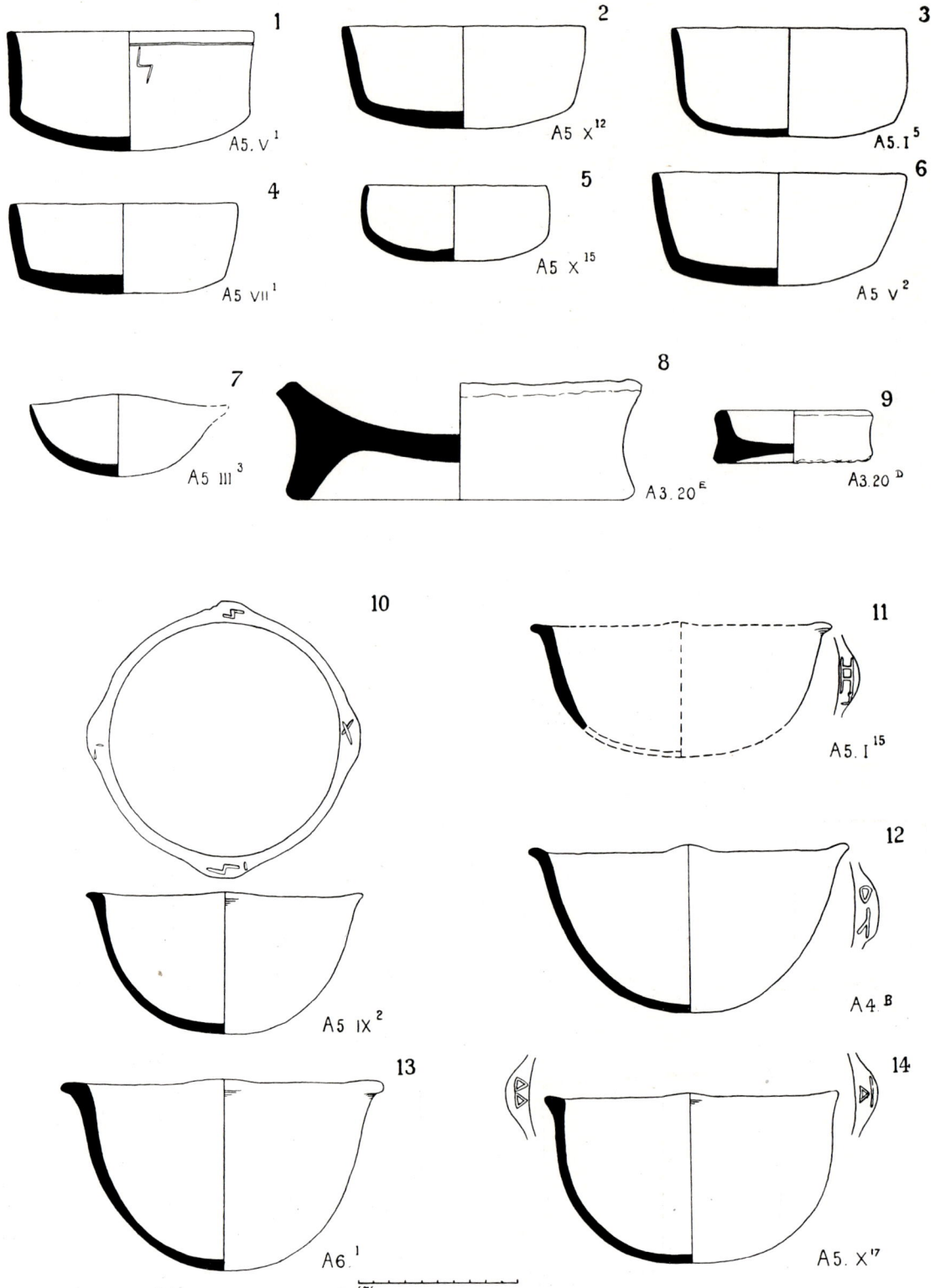

1–6. Shallow wide bowls with rounded bases, type VI. 7. Lipped saucer, type VII. 8–9. Pedestal bases reused as saucers. 10–14. Eared bowls in stone ware, type IX

(Scale 1 : 4)

Stone ware unguent cups and bowls, types X–XIV

(Scale 1 : 4)

1

A3. E. CORNER
2·08 m. below pavement

2

A3. AREA VII
fill 0·65 m.

3

A3. E. CORNER
*2·30 m. below pavement
level*

4

A3. AREA VI
fill 0·40 m

5

A3. AREA VI
fill 2 m.

6

A3. AREA VI
fill 0·85 m.

7

A3. E. CORNER
2 m. below pavement

8

A3. AREA VII
fill. 3·35 m.

9

A3. E. CORNER
2 m. below pavement

10

A3. E. CORNER
1·30 m. below pavement

11

A3. E. CORNER
2 m. below pavement

12

A 4.
B. WALL 4

13

A4. C. Wall 8

14

A4. C. Wall 6

15

A4. C. Wall 8

16

A5. I

17

A5 I

18

A5. I

19

A5. III [4]

20

A5. XI [2]

21

N. CLIFF SITE

22

N. CLIFF SITE

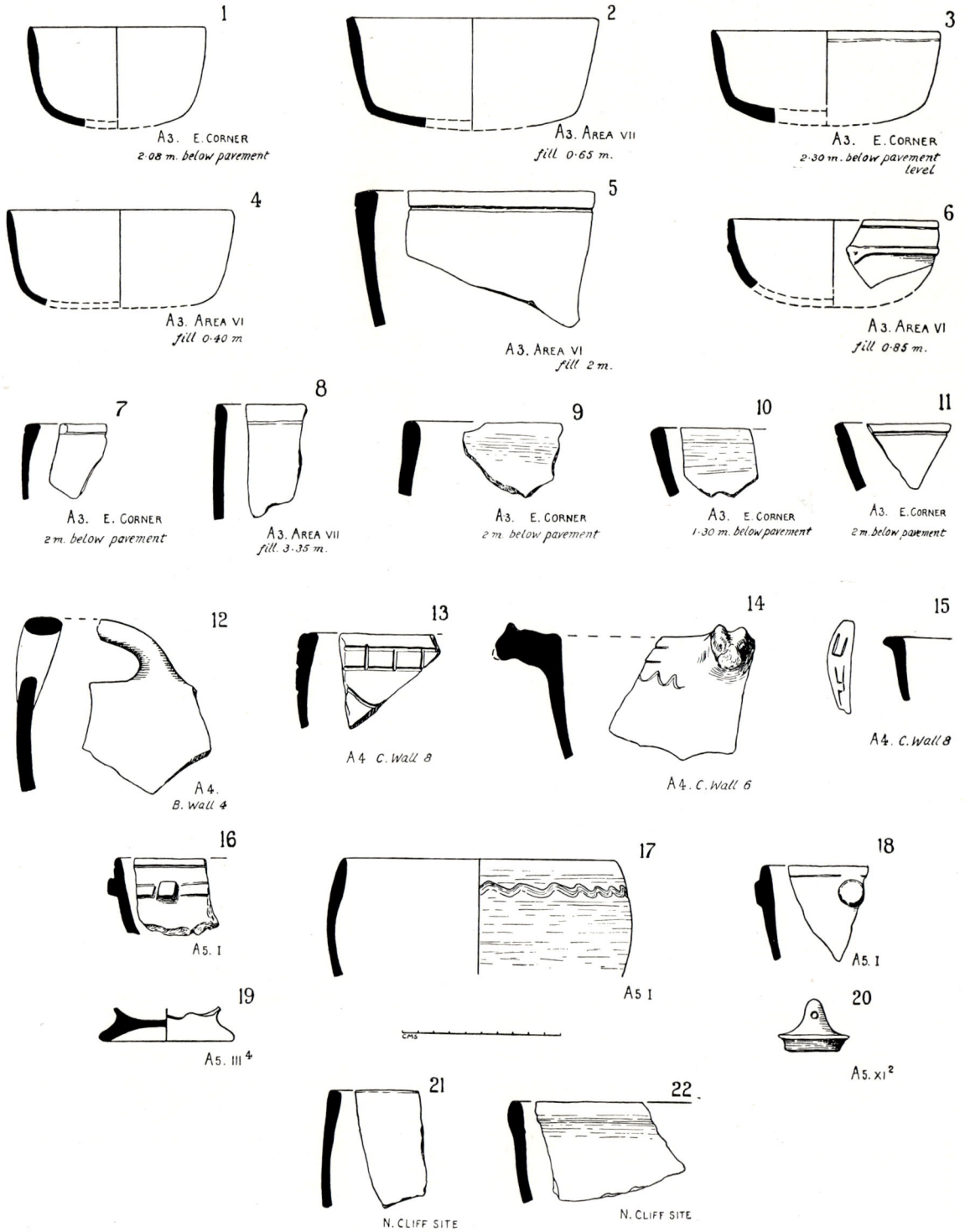

Sherds, some reconstructed, from Temple, Tombs, and Farmstead
(Scale 1 : 4)

XIV. STONE OBJECTS FROM TOMBS A5 AND A6

1. LIMESTONE OR MARBLE

OFFERING SAUCERS. Numbers of cylindrical objects of crystalline limestone with slightly concave tops were found in the tombs, such as pls. XXXVII, 3, and LVII, 6. Others were more hemispherical in shape. Only four of these had tripod legs; a fifth was bought locally. The hollows were not stained by incense, and unless the objects are cosmetic mortars—and no corresponding pestles or pebbles were found—they are probably offering saucers. None was found in the Temple.

Pls. XXXVII, *3;* LVII, *6.* A5.II.2. Diam. 10·2 cm.; ht. 3·45 cm. Undecorated. Fine crystalline limestone mottled grey.

Pls. XXXVII, *5;* LVII, *2.* A5.I.9. Diam. 7·3 cm.; ht. 3·4 cm. including tripod knobs 1·1 cm. high. Deep concavity. Decoration on sides of vertical scratches. Crystalline limestone.

Pls. XXXVII, *7;* LVII, *3.* A5.II.1. Diam. 8·3 cm.; ht. 3·9 cm. Undecorated. Fine crystalline limestone.

Pls. XXXVII, *8;* LVII, *1.* A6. Diam. 8·7 cm.; ht. 5·2 cm. One tripod knob alone remains; the others had been broken before the object was placed in the tomb. Decorated sides, with close-set vertical lines. Translucent crystalline limestone.

Pls. XXXVII, *9;* LVII, *5.* Bought locally. Diam. 9 cm.; ht. 6·4 cm. Coarse crystalline limestone.

Pls. XXXVII, *10;* LVII, *4.* A5.XII.4. Diam. 8·1 cm.; ht. 3·5 cm. Undecorated. Translucent crystalline limestone.

CUPS. The remaining objects include a tumbler-shaped cup, a pedestal cup, and a squat pot.

Pls. XXXVII, *2;* LVII, *9.* A5.XII.2. Tumbler, ht. 7·3 cm. Diam. at rim 5·5 cm. The shape is irregular, and diagonal tool-marks show on walls and flat base. The cup is hollowed for about two-thirds of its height. The material is gypsum.

Pls. XXXVII, *4;* LVII, *8.* A6. Pedestal cup, 6·1 cm. high. Rim diam. 3·7 cm. The cup is irregular in thickness and only 2·5 cm. deep. The pedestal is conical and only slightly hollowed. The chalice is decorated with vertical incisions, irregularly spaced. In coarse crystalline limestone.

Pls. XXXVII, *6;* LVII, *7.* A6. Ointment pot, 4·4 cm. high. Rim diam. 5·4 cm. The ring base slightly hollowed. The rim is moulded and below it vertical incisions form a ribbing. The pot is reconstructed from a complete side. In translucent crystalline limestone.

These objects show no sign of rotatory action as on many Egyptian limestone or gypsum vases: they appear, by the tool-marks, to have been shaped with chisels, about 6 mm. wide. The series includes no 'alabaster' (calcium carbonate) except the rough gypsum tumbler, A5.XII.2. The translucent white marble or crystalline limestone might, however, be erroneously described as 'alabaster', without analysis.

2. OBSIDIAN IMPLEMENTS

The material consists of 269 microliths, some figured on pls. LVIII, LX, and 4 large cores (figured pl. LIX) and 20 smaller ones, as well as a quantity of waste and core residuals. It came from the surface of four pre-Islamic sites: Sūne in the Wadi ʿAdim; Shibam, at a small pre-Islamic mound about 3 km. west of the town; Gheibun, near Meshḥed; and in the Wadi ʿAmd near Hureidha on the anciently irrigated plain around the Moon Temple. In addition to these collections, of no conclusive value in establishing the synchronism of the microliths with the deposits on which they lay, we found them *in situ* with the burial groups in tombs A5 and A6; and a core and two flakes were got also in the Temple deposits.[1]

The recorded connexion of these obsidian tools with pre-Islamic sites thus covers a large area in the Hadhramaut, and we may deduce that they still formed the normal equipment of everyday life in this region a few centuries or less before the Christian era, when more advanced countries had ceased to use them. They were absent at old Arab sites I searched—Usaila near Aden, Senahiye and Maryama in the Wadi Hadhramaut, and at ʿAndal in the Wadi ʿAmd.

Obsidian flakes had already several times been recorded on the ruin-mounds at Gheibun;[2] but though the presumption of their synchronism was strong, it had lacked the conclusive evidence. This was supplied by their presence in considerable numbers in the Hureidha tombs, intimately mixed with the tomb groups.

The tools consist of microliths, restricted to three main types: trapezoids, such as pl. LVIII, 8, 18, 21; rectangles, such as pl. LVIII, 1, 4, 59, 60; and lunates, such as pl. LVIII, 37, 46. The first two are far the most numerous; but the three types grade into each other, and I have therefore not attempted a more elaborate subdivision. The tools are struck from a prepared core; their upper faces bear one or more flake-ridges parallel or oblique to the long axis. The marginal 'batter' is usually, but not invariably, struck from the under-face: it is restricted to the edge and does not impinge upon the under-face, as in the Helouan-Natufian industries. In a few cases, such as pls. LVIII, 58, 60, or LX, 32, the retouch is confined to the ends only.

Each series from the different sites includes a small number of simple larger flakes, such as pl. LX, 54. The maximum length of these, 5·1 cm., is reached in a blade from tomb A5. Other flakes without retouch are figured, pl. LX, 24–9, and 50–5. No. 52, however, with its thick lateral edge partly cortex-covered, is probably a core paring rather than a backed tool. I am not satisfied that any implement is an intentional burin, though pl. LX, 50, has a burin-like facet.[3] The micro-burin is absent.

The larger cores, or rather scraper-cores, are shown on pl. LIX. They include pyramidal (pl. LIX, 2, 3), multiple (pl. LIX, 1), and carinated types (pl. LIX, 4). Amongst

---

[1] Cf. p. 37.
[2] Van der Meulen and H. von Wissmann, *Hadramaut*, 1932, p. 86, 'Little bits of rough dark glass'; W. H. Ingrams, *Journ. R. Central Asian Soc.*, July 1936, p. 393; F. Stark, *Southern Gates of Arabia*, 1936, p. 166; S. Huzayyin, *Nature*, Sept. 18, 1937, p. 573.
[3] Dr. Huzayyin, however, in conversation, said his Gheibun collection included burins.

the smaller specimens, many of which are probably residuals, pared down to their last limit, are small pyramidals, under 2 cm. high; and one neat little oval tortoise-core, only 2 cm. long, with a minute ventral flake scar. The smallest of all is a mere button, about 1 cm. in diameter; but as obsidian was used for ornamental studs or inlay,[1] it is possible this is a rough-out for such a purpose.

The series from such far-separated sites as Sūne and the Wadi 'Amd show no differences, though the tombs contained a proportionately higher number of well-defined lunates. But a comparison with surface collections, hurriedly picked up, is not permissible. All series contain a few chert microliths of similar types, some of which are figured. The absence of scrapers may be noted with surprise.

TOMB A5. Trapezoid, rectangular, and lunate microliths   .   129 (55 fig. pl. LVIII)
              Flakes and waste   18
              Lame écaillée   1
              Cores   .   .   .   .   2 (1 fig. pl. LIX, 1)

About half these were recovered from sieves outside the tomb. Those observed *in situ* were not grouped in a manner which could give a clue as to their use (i.e. in sickles, arrow-shafts). Possibly they were razors. The cores came from tomb groups II and VII.

TOMB A6. Trapezoid, rectangular, and lunate microliths   .   15 (fig. pl. LVIII, 56–70)
              Flakes and waste   .   .   .   .   .   .   11 (fig. pl. LVIII, 71, 72)
              Core   .   .   .   .   1 (fig. pl. LIX, 3)

The fine steep-ended scraper or push-plane of obsidian, pl. LIX, 4, was bought locally. It is fresh and unweathered, and there is reason to think it came from a cave-tomb near A5.

MOON TEMPLE. Pyramidal core, in inter-façade deposits, 4 m. below latest pavement.
              Probably phase 'A' (fig. pl. LIX, 2).
              Chip, ditto.
              Waste flake, in inter-façade deposits, 4.30 m. below latest pavement.
              Probably phase 'A'.[2]

The surface collections, picked up on pre-Islamic sites, are as follows:

HUREIDHA. IRRIGATION AREA. Trapezoid, rectangular, and lunate microliths   .   16
                        Pressure-flaked fragment   1
                        Waste, various   2
                        Cores, mainly residuals   6

SŪNE.   Trapezoid, rectangular, and lunate microliths   .   .   25 (pl. LX, 30–49)
        Flakes and waste   .   .   .   .   .   .   37 (pl. LX, 50–5)
        Cores (obsidian)   5
        Cores (chert)   .   .   .   .   .   .   3 (type pl. LIX, 2, 3)

SHIBAM.   Trapezoid, rectangular, and lunate microliths   .   .   84 (pl. LX, 1–23)
        Flakes and waste   .   .   .   .   .   .   12 (pl. LX, 24–8)
        Cores, including a micro tortoise-core   .   .   .   7 (pl. LX, 29)
        Amorphous core trimmings   10

Wind scour has changed the lustrous surface of the obsidian to a dead opaque aspect on all exposed specimens.

SOURCE OF THE OBSIDIAN. The rocks at Hureidha and other sites listed are Eocene and

---

[1] Cf. p. 78, tomb A5.   [2] Cf. p. 37.

Cretaceous sediments, and neither the older igneous nor more recent volcanic series were met away from the coast. There is no doubt the obsidian comes from within the Hadhramaut borders, and in all probability from its south-westerly regions. The bedouins still use chert strike-a-lights,[1] but their use of obsidian has not so far been recorded.

There was no evidence of blade industries in the Palaeolithic flake implements collected in the Hadhramaut, apart from a single end-scraper in the 10-m. (Levallois) gravels of the Wadi ʻAmd. In their noticeable absence it is difficult to believe the obsidian and chert microliths to be an indigenous growth. It seems more probable that the true parentage lies in east Africa, the contacts of which with south Arabia must go back long before the few centuries B.C. covered by our Hureidha specimens.

[1] W. H. Ingrams, *Geog. Journ.*, Dec. 1936, p. 539.

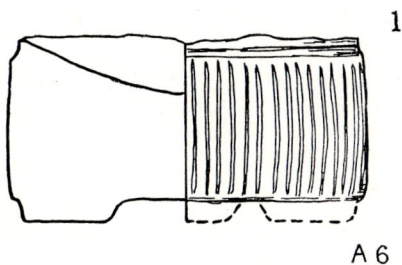

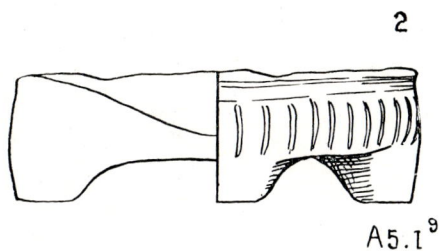

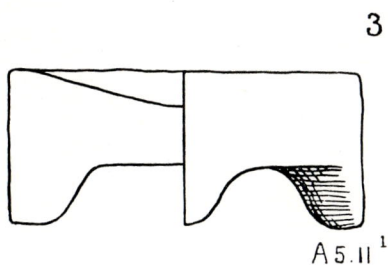

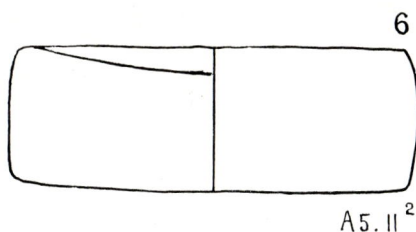

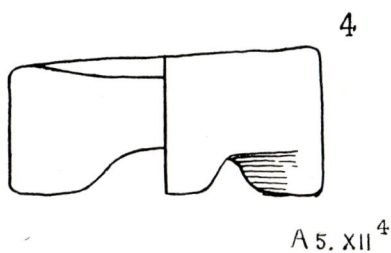

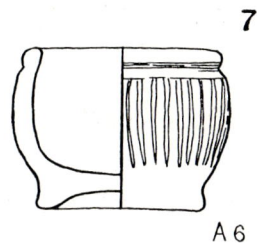

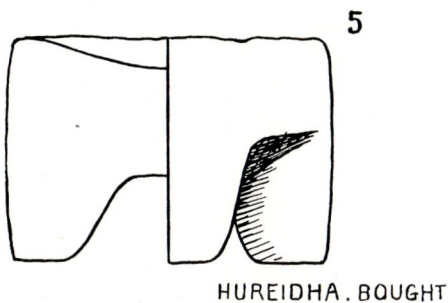

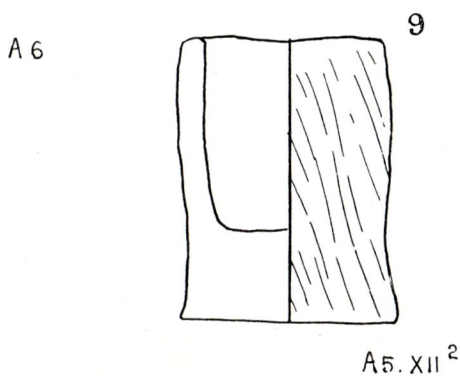

Nos. 1–8. Offering saucers and cups in crystalline limestone. No. 9. Gypsum tumbler. No. 10. Wire-drawn purple and white glass vase

(Scale 1 : 2)

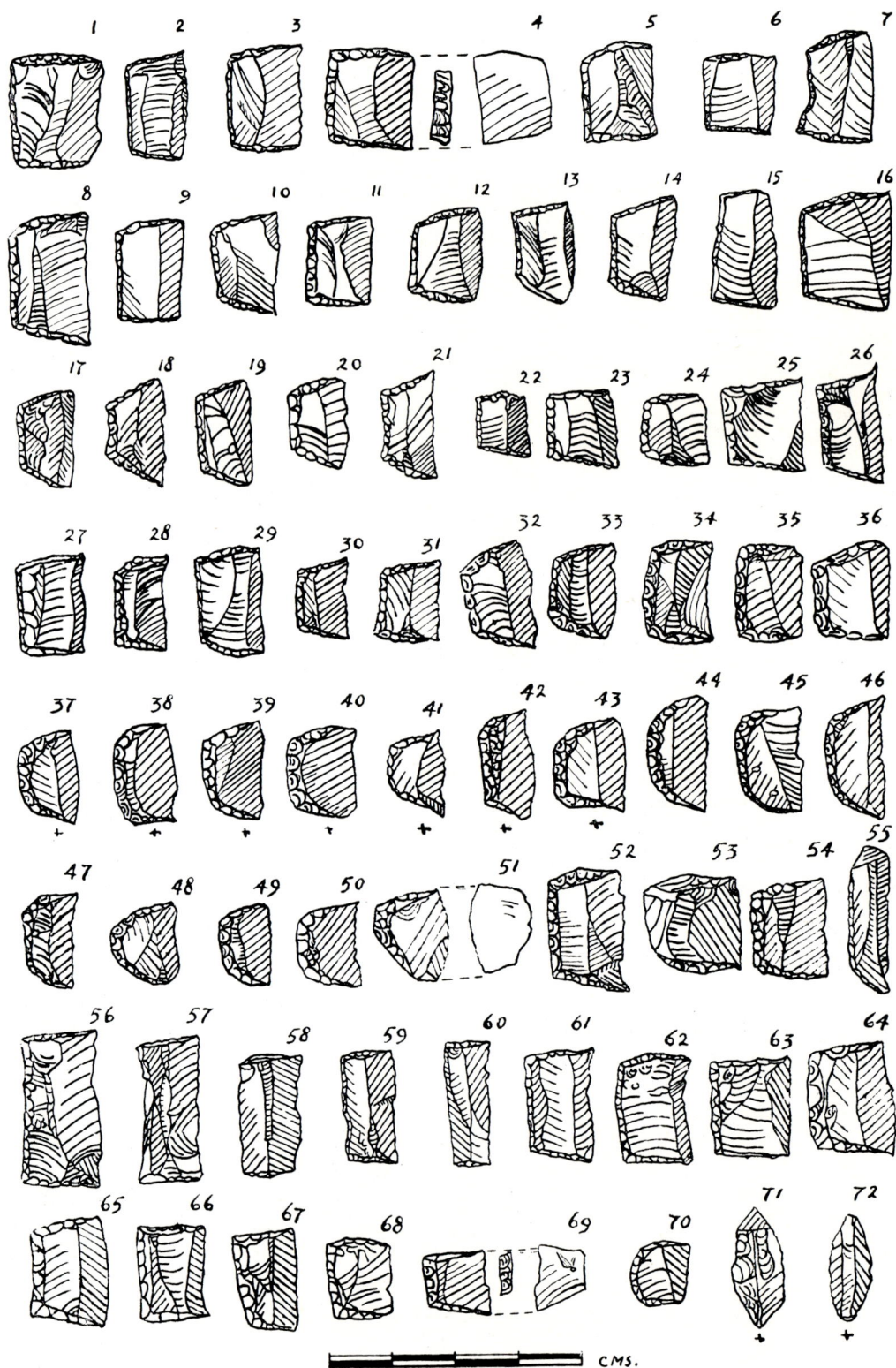

Obsidian and chert microliths

1–55. From tomb A5. Those marked with a cross are of chert. 56–72. From tomb A6

(Scale 1 : 1)

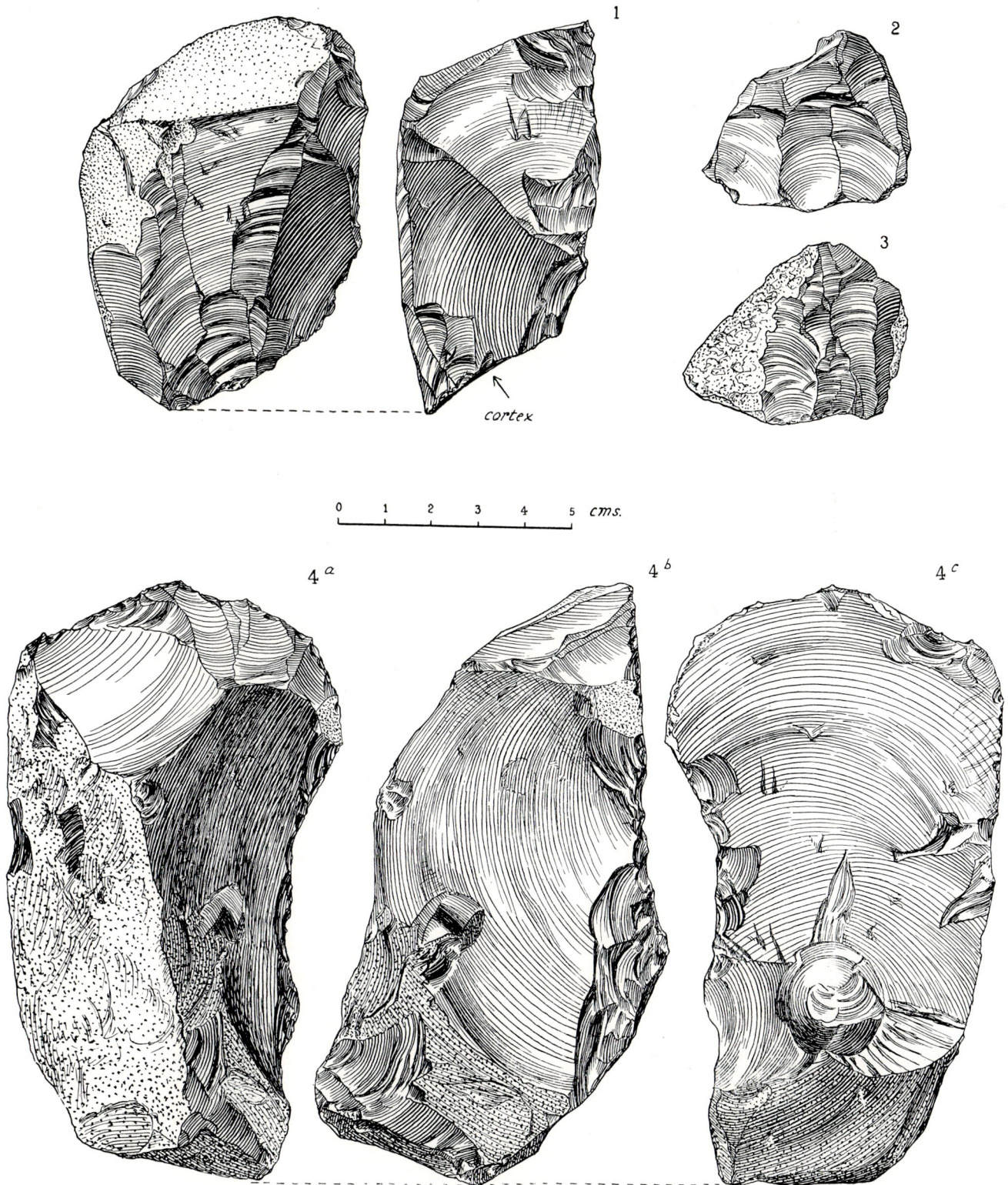

Obsidian cores

1. From A5.VII.   2. From A3, area VI.   4 metres.   3. From A6.   4. Bought at Hureidha near tomb A5
(Scale approx. 3 : 4)

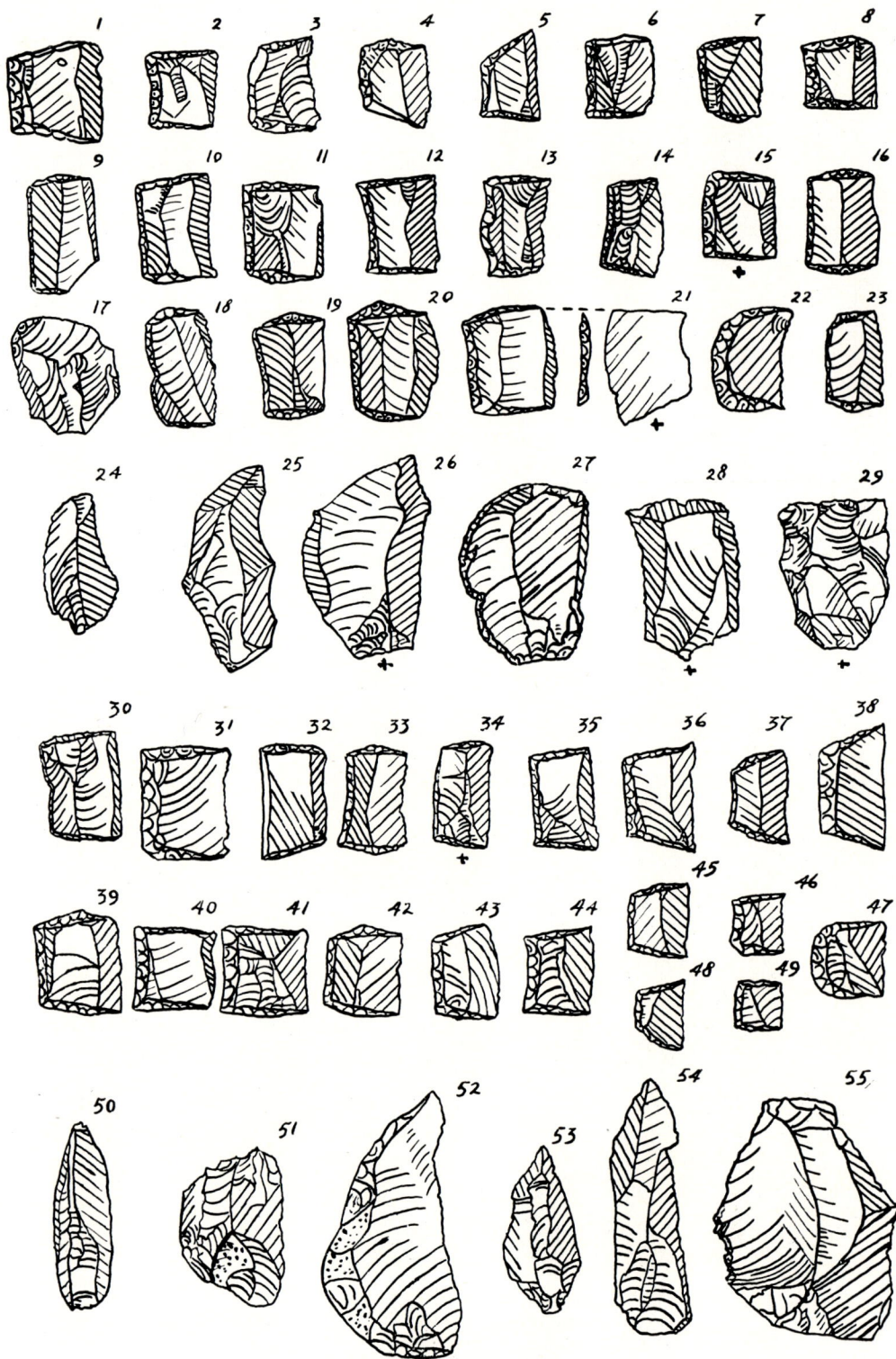

Obsidian and chert microliths

1–29. From Shibam. 30–55. From Sūne. Those in chert marked with a cross

(Scale 1 : 1)

PART V
VARIA

XV. THE FARMSTEAD A4

SYNOPSIS. A mud-brick dwelling-house near the Temple, apparently a lowly farm building, was partially excavated. The well-preserved ground walls and hard mud floors show four irregularly sized rooms. Structural features identified included fragments of a collapsed ceiling, wood reinforcement to treads, mud-brick benches, and two sizes of mud bricks. The stone foundations, usual in modern buildings, were absent. The contents indicated occupation more or less of the Temple and tomb period.

SOME 130 m. north of the Moon Temple, on the same ridge of higher ground, a raised drift of sand mingled with limestone chips, particles of mud brick, and weathered sherds, including the inscribed fragments, pls. XXXVI, 2, 4, 5; LI, 1, 6, suggested that a building lay beneath. As I was anxious, before starting work on the tombs, to study the layout and equipment of a common dwelling of the Temple period, a trench was cut through it. Loose mud bricks, fragments of decayed wood, a broken mealing-stone, and sherds turned up in dung-discoloured sand. Accordingly three days, January 15–17, 1938, were allotted to further clearance by twenty-two men and boys, which was all the time that could be spared.

The resultant plan, pl. LXXVIII, is obviously not that of a complete building, and of the walls, no. 7 and possibly 9 and 10 are outer walls, the remainder being the partitions of the other parts of the *dar*; but it suffices to indicate a straggling complex of rooms, passages, or perhaps alley-ways, erected evidently with little regard to true alinement. The walls were cleared on both sides, more or less in the order numerically shown (two gangs worked simultaneously on separate areas), and the rooms and passages, alphabetically numbered, were then emptied (except F) to floor-level.

THE WALLS. These were of friable sun-dried mud brick containing chaff. Owing to the weathered surfaces measurements of the bricks were difficult to get; but two sizes were distinguished, a smaller one of about 26 × 22 × 12 cm., and a larger of about 45 × 32 × 9 cm. which was used in wall 10. Mr. Ingrams quotes 41 × 23 × '4 finger's widths' as a standard size of modern Hadhramaut brick.[1] Early Ptolemaic mud bricks in the Fayum, possibly not far removed from the A4 specimens as to date, measured 35·5 × 18 × 12·7 cm.[2] O. Myers quotes 37 × 20 × 11 cm. as the largest of the Old to Middle Kingdom series measured at Armant,[3] and G. Brunton gives 34 × 15 × 7·5 cm. for the same period at Qau, and 39 × 17·8 × 8·8 cm. for the Second Intermediate–New Kingdom.[4] It is evident the south Arabian brick differed radically in dimensions from those used in Egypt. At Chagar Bazar in Syria M. E. L. Mallowan comments on the unusually large size—37 × 17 × 9 cm. and 37 sq. × 8·5 cm. being the normal dimensions at that site in the second millennium B.C. or earlier—and he notes that the ancient builders

---

[1] 'House Building in the Hadhramaut', *Geog. Journ.*, Apr. 1935, p. 371.
[2] *The Desert Fayum*, p. 146.

[3] *The Cemeteries of Armant*, I, p. 25.
[4] *Qau and Badari*, I, p. 146.

of the historic periods on the Ḥabur generally used a large size of mud brick which is still in vogue there to-day; the brickwork of Assyria, he adds, is on the whole larger than that of Babylonia.[1] I have not been able to trace such a long thin brick as the old and modern south Arabian specimens elsewhere (see also p. 21).

They were laid in mud mortar, and the wall surfaces had also been smeared with wet mud, which added to the difficulty of determining the bond. Many of the walls were 25–6 cm. thick (nos. 1, 2, part of 3, 4, 6, 7, 9, 12–14), which suggests a header arrangement, but others were up to 40 cm. (part of 3, 5, 8, 10, 11) which could only be got by other combinations. Wall 10 alone was made of the larger bricks. Unlike modern buildings the house lacked a stone foundation of rubble masonry; the mud brick rested directly on the silt plain, and evidently the site lay, as the contours of the plan, pl. LXXII, suggest, above the surrounding irrigated level. But even so the fact is surprising. The maximum height of standing wall above floor-level was 1·50 m. (in wall 4). The top of this lay only 20 cm. below the surface. There is no doubt that internally the walls had been whitewashed. This was not seen actually on them, but there were traces of white powder in the fill, notably in rooms B and C and below wall 2 in A: it was conspicuous against the skirting, as though it had flaked off by degrees after the place had been abandoned.

Rooms A AND F. Size of A, 5·20 × 3·20 m. Max. ht. of walls 1·40 m. Min. ht. 0·55 m. Size of F, 4·90 × 3·10 m. Max. ht. of walls 1·30 m.

The cross-wall between A and F consisted of a single line of bricks, which in the dotted length was doubtfully traced. The projecting internal wall, no. 1, ended abruptly in the centre of the room as though incomplete. Room A was cleared to floor-level, which consisted of rammed mud. Whitewash was noted below wall 2 only. Large quantities of goat dung covered the floor, piling in heaps at the wall angles. It was abundant also throughout the fill. A rough sandstone mealing-stone below wall 10 was the only equipment, and some sherds of rough red-brown ware (see Inventory). The single entrance lay at the angles of walls 1 and 2. This was an opening into room B, 1·30 m. wide, which had been roughly blocked with mud brick flush with the partition at some later time. The floor-level of room B was about 8 cm. higher, and the mud step had been strengthened by a wooden pole: the decayed ends of this, pushed into the mud-brick walls on either side, alone remained.[2]

Room F was not cleared except for a narrow trench to free the walls. Here, too, goat dung lay at floor-level and above, and it seems likely that A and F, built perhaps originally as two living-rooms, had eventually been used as pens.

Room B. Size 3·5 × 2·2 m., but not a true rectangle. Max. ht. of walls 1·50 m. Min. ht. 0·80 m. Floor of rammed mud. Traces of whitewash in fill. Entrance 80 cm. wide in partition wall 4, in addition to the opening into room A at right angles to it.

---

[1] *Iraq*, vol. iii, pt. i, 1936, p. 15.
[2] Dr. Nelson Glueck instances similar reinforcement of the tread at Ezion-Geber (*Asia*, Sept. 1939, p. 531). I have recorded them also in early Ptolemaic houses in the northern Fayum (*The Desert Fayum*, p. 146).

This entrance had also been blocked to a height of 60 cm. with mud brick at a later date. At opposite ends of the room were benches of solid mud brick fitted against the angle of the walls 2–10 and 5–10. These benches were about 32 cm. wide by 80 long by 43 high—a comfortable sitting height, though perhaps not made with that intent, but rather as a ledge for utensils, in which the rooms seemed otherwise deficient. The finds here included:

Two limestone saddle querns, flat oval slabs about 30 cm. long, slightly hollowed by friction on one face. No mealing-stones were found.

A small fragment of a rough heavy limestone trough, engraved in monumental style with the incomplete letters ⋔𝐇𝚼.

A rim sherd, about 3 cm. long, 1 cm. thick, in coarse red-brown ware, with traces of internal polish. From the rim springs a broken flat loop-handle (pl. LVI, 12). Nothing similar was found elsewhere, and this is the only evidence for loop-handles discovered.

Inscribed ear of a stone ware bowl, tomb type IX (see p. 123), of which three complete specimens were got in the tombs. The letters are badly drawn in the wet clay but appear to be ○𝚼 [1] (pls. XXXVI, 1; LIV, 12). A second inscribed ear, not apparently belonging to the same bowl, was found in room C.

In the sand fill, about 1 m. above floor-level, a square limestone brick, 13 × 12 cm., with a central narrow panel in low relief originally scalloped as pl. XX, 2, but much worn (see p. 56).

From room B came the sole evidence for a ceiling. The supposed remnant lay in the fill of loose sand at about 1·10 m. above floor-level, and 20–30 cm. below the existing top of wall 10 alongside it. It consisted of about two dozen lengths of twigs, 26–30 cm. long, which lay in parallel order though unbound. The ceilings of the modern Hadhramaut house are made of rough rafters of local *sidr* wood, supported on square wooden pillars and filled in with small slats or twigs neatly disposed in rows, often arrayed in herring-bone pattern. I have little doubt the A4 twigs were the vestiges of a similar ceiling, fallen in after abandonment, and after the more valuable timbers had been removed.

ROOM C. Size 2·50 × 1·90 m., but not a true rectangle. Max. ht. of walls, nos. 6, 8, 12, 1·40 m. Floor of rammed mud. Traces of whitewash in fill alongside walls. Entrance 70 cm. wide in wall 6, blocked by mud brick to a height of 80 cm. This entrance in any case must have been partly obstructed by a mud bench 1·30 m. long, which projected 30 cm. Unlike those in room B, this bench was 90 cm. high. In the angle of walls 5 and 12 a semicircular kerb of moulded mud, 80 cm. thick: the interior of this was not raised nor discoloured by heat; possibly a store- or water-jar stood here.

The interesting objects in this room, apart from the normal sherds, were:

Pl. LVI, *13*. A rim sherd, 5·8 cm. long, 1 cm. thick, in red ware, formerly slipped and polished. Below the rim a trellis pattern, four squares of which survive, formed by deep broad cuts in the wet clay. Part of an incised loop appears below. The design may well be copied from stonework, particularly that which frequently adorns the capitals of ancient columns in the Yemen.[2]

---

[1] Cf. Ryckmans, Inscription 77, p. 179.   [2] *Vorislamische Altertümer*, figs. 12–14, 61, 62, 68, 88, 89.

Pl. LVI, *14.* A rim sherd, 6 cm. long, 6 mm. thick, in dark brown-grey ware, unpolished. From the rim projects an animal-headed free handle, with short prick ears; the muzzle is unfortunately broken. Below, the end of a wavy incised line and two plain scorings, all horizontal, are truncated by the old fracture. The sherd, which has no parallel in our collection, is astonishingly like one in Schliemann's collection from Hissarlik, published by E. J. Forsdyke,[1] with which, of course, it can have no connexion whatsoever.[2]

Pls. XXXVI, *3;* LVI, *15.* The inscribed ear-lug of a deep bowl in black stone ware, tomb type IX, bearing two letters ⋂ℏ. See inscription no. 78, p. 179.

Pl. LV, *4.* Side fragment of stone ware pot, tomb type X.[3]

A white crystalline limestone cylindrical mortar or saucer, 8·5 cm. in diameter, hollowed on one face (as pls. XXXVII, 3; LVII, 6, from tomb A5).

A plain limestone flag, 24 × 17 × 7 cm., dressed smoothly and diagonally as in the Temple paving, from which it probably came.

PASSAGES D AND E. These were narrow passages or blind alleys, the excavation of, which could not be completed in the allotted time. Passage D, running parallel to A and B, was 1·40 m. wide at its south-east end, and had widened another 20 cm. at the point where we discontinued clearance, 4·30 m. onwards. Passage E, running at right angles to D was 1·20 m. wide and was cleared on a length of 4·50 m. without reaching its opening. A blocked entrance, 90 cm. wide, connected with D, but neither had direct access to rooms A, B, or C. It is doubtful, therefore, if they were open alleys separating different houses, for had that been so entrances off them might have been expected. More rooms, which might elucidate this question, certainly exist outside walls 3, 8, 13, and 11–14; but insufficient objects were being found to tempt further work at the expense of more urgent information.

SHERDS FROM A4 ADDITIONAL TO THOSE SPECIFIED.

Room A. 1. Rim of pedestal bowl with ledge rim, tomb type II.
  2. Ditto, from a larger jar.
  3. Rim and side of deep bowl with dimpled base, tomb type VIII*b*.
Outside wall 7. Room A. 4. Half of shallow bowl with rounded base, tomb type VI, in rough red-brown ware.
Room B. 5. Rim of pedestal bowl with ledge rim, tomb type II.
  6. Side fragment of ditto, perhaps belonging.
  7. Rim and top side of goblet on tall stem, tomb type I.
  8. Ring base from large pot, probably tomb type II or III, used as dish.
Room C. 9. Fragment of side of shallow bowl, rounded base, tomb type VI, but rough red ware.
  10. Rim and side of shallow bowl, slightly keeled rounded base, tomb type VI, but rough red ware.
  11. Rim and side of shallow bowl, incised line below rim, tomb type VI, but rough red ware.
  12. Rim and side of deep bowl, tomb type VIII*a*.

[1] *A Catalogue of Greek and Etruscan Vases in the British Museum*, vol. i, pt. i, 1925, A6.9, fig. 21.
[2] Since writing the above a second example has come to light from south Arabia. It is in the collection of the Peabody Museum at Harvard, to which I am indebted for the photograph. The Harvard specimen, from the Yemen, represents undoubtedly a bovine head.
[3] Cf. p. 127.

Passage E. 13. Rim fragment of pedestal bowl with ledge rim, tomb type II, decorated band of oval incisions.

Passage D. 14. Rim and side of deep bowl, tomb type VIII*b*.

The ware throughout is hand-made. These fourteen fragments were the only sherds large enough to type; but pottery was scarce—about seventy sherds in all—and the occupants of the dwelling must have been mainly dependent, as at present, on water-skins. They yield us, however, five of the fourteen types of pottery recovered from tombs A5 and A6, and the two distinctive wares—namely the black stone ware of type IX, as well as the rough red-brown to pinky-buff wares of the other classes: the haematite slip on the trellis-patterned sherd in room C is identical with the red polished surfaces of tomb types III, V, VI, VIII.

DATE RELATIVE TO TEMPLE AND TOMBS. The pottery evidence warrants, I believe, the assumption that A4 is more or less contemporary with the tombs. Its relation to the Temple is less clear, for the comparative material is too meagre. The sherd, no. 9 from room C, is practically identical with that from area VII infilling in the Temple (pl. LVI, 2), and A4 sherds, nos. 4, 10, 11, similarly of shallow bowls type VI, fall into the same series as the Temple bowls illustrated, pl. LVI, 1–4, though coarser. The decorated limestone brick from the filling of room B, though probably a part of the Temple architecture,[1] can hardly have reached its secondary position until the house (and perhaps the Temple) was abandoned. The limestone flag on the floor of room C might, if certainly from the Temple, argue for an occupation of A4 not earlier than the Temple 'C' phase or the Shrine-builders' period, when destruction as well as reconstruction of that edifice was in progress. But it might also be argued that a limestone slab could have been filched at any time from the sacred building during pavement repairs. The dating evidence, then, must be content with a claim of general contemporaneity with Temple and tombs.

FUNCTION OF A4. We have named the place a farmstead because of its position on the plain in the midst of remains of the irrigation channels and cultivated plots. As seen on the map, pl. LXXII, it lies close to and somewhat above the main canal. That flocks were herded in rooms A and F is evident, though certainty that this happened from the start is not possible. The blocked entrances reflect a continuation of that practice after the building was otherwise abandoned.

The absence of window openings in walls which stood high enough still to show them had they existed,[2] suggests that we have to do with the ground-floor of a one- or two-storied house.[3]

---

[1] Cf. p. 56.

[2] The modern window is set only a few inches above floor-level in deference to a community which sits on the ground.

[3] The modern ground-floor has no windows, for protection.

XVI. MISCELLANEOUS UNDATED OBJECTS[1]

BRONZE AXE (pl. LXI, 9). Bought from a local bedouin at Hureidha, and stated to have been found in the vicinity. No corroboration of this was obtained. The condition does not suggest a recent disinterment. The length is 19·2 cm., the weight 2 lb. 1 oz. The implement typologically is a flat axe without stop-ridge or flanges; it was apparently cast in an open mould. The cutting-edge is splayed and convex, and set at an adze-like slant. It is sharp and undamaged. The sides taper gently to the rectangular butt, which, owing to battering (probably in fairly recent times), has expanded. Original hammer-shaping of the hot metal is displayed on both sides of the shaft (well seen in Mr. Water-house's profile drawing), and this has forced up the lateral edges into incipient, accidental flanges. The shaft sides nearer the butt show heavy subsequent battering. The colour is dark copper with green patinated flecks. The metal, spectrographically analysed, is a true bronze.[2]

CHERT KNIFE (pl. LXI, 8). From the scree outside tomb A5. It was found in the circumstances related on p. 67. Length 11·3 cm. Thickness ±7 mm. The chert is brindled grey, the cortex sand-coloured. Chert nodules of good quality large enough to produce such a knife were very rare in our locality. Both faces are pressure-flaked, but without symmetry of direction. The edges are minutely serrated. A date contemporary with the tomb is not impossible in a land which was making scraper-cores and microliths far on in the first millennium B.C.

POLISHED JADE AXE (pl. LXI, 7). Bought at Hureidha. Length 7 cm. Section, a thick oval with rounded butt and sides. The cutting-edge is blunt and slightly battered. The butt and both lateral edges, also, have been bruised. The colour is dark jade green.

MINIATURE POLISHED JADE AXE (pl. LXI, 5). Bought at Hureidha. Length 2·9 cm. The section is a pointed oval. The wide cutting-edge has angular corners; the sides are bevelled. The conical butt is shattered and may have been fitted into an amuletic pendant. The colour is jade green, paler than the last.

MINIATURE POLISHED JADE AXE (pl. LXI, 6). Bought at Hureidha and stated to be a local find. Length 3 cm. The specimen is oblong with a thin oval section. The sharp narrow cutting-edge is straight, with slightly bevelled corners. The butt is tapered and may have been rubbed in an amulet mount. The colour is jade green, slightly bluer than the preceding.

Dr. Leonard Hawkes, F.G.S., kindly examined these three axes, and considers them to be true jade. Their specific gravity is between 2·97 and 3·00, which seems to preclude jadeite, with a specific gravity of 3·3. Neither a chemical nor microscopic analysis could, however, be made without destroying the specimens.

---

[1] Objects in this section are in the Fitzwilliam Museum, Cambridge.   [2] Cf. Report, p. 107.

A jade axe, got in Wadi Do'an, is recorded by Mr. W. H. Lee Warner in 1931;[1] and a 'jadeite' bead is specified in a collection of mixed beads of 'agate, carnelian, glass and paste' from the Yemen probably, but without known history, in the Pennsylvania University Museum.[2] The source of the jade is unknown. It occurs in metamorphosed rocks of unusual type, and until the rocks of south-west Arabia have been geologically mapped and examined it may be unwise to assume that our specimens came necessarily from the known jade localities in Turkestan, Siberia, or Kashmir.[3]

Grooved Schist Rubber (pl. lxi, 4). From the irrigated area, surface, near A3. The bar, 9 cm. long, bears three wedge-shaped longitudinal grooves. It has certainly acted as a rubber or sharpener of some kind.

Two Fragments of Black Pottery (pl. xliv, 16). From the surface near A4. The ware is unlike anything found in excavation. It is much thinner—2·5 mm. approx.—and externally has a smooth, lustrous surface, with a fine cloth-impressed ripple pattern on the under-face. It appears to be a carbonaceous ware, and the core is evenly black.

Search in the vicinity for the remainder of this extremely interesting and possibly important vase failed to produce another scrap. As the two pieces combined measure only 3·9 by 2·5 cm., the form cannot be determined; but the rimless, tiny fragments show a strong curvature and must belong to a small delicate vase. It has the undefined 'feel' of something much older than the potteries we otherwise discovered.

---

[1] 'Notes on the Hadhramaut', *Geog. Journ.*, Mar. 1931, p. 217.

[2] *American Journ. of Archaeology*, July–Sept. 1934, p. 337, and fig. 10.

[3] Mr. P. M. Game, of the Department of Mineralogy, British Museum, in correspondence, remarks that there is no reference to the occurrence of such rocks in Arabia, but very little is yet known in detail of the geological formations.

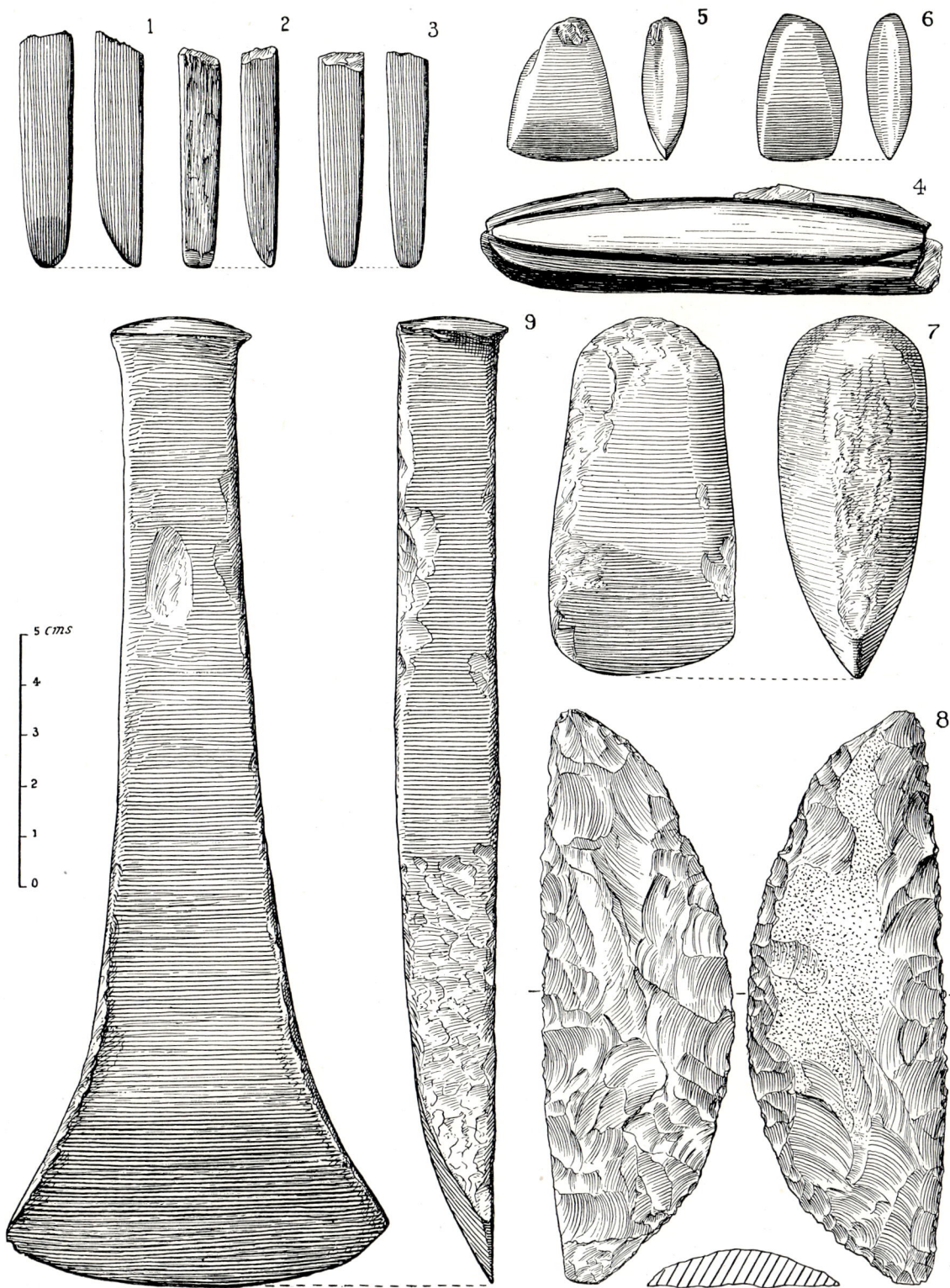

1–3. Schist and bone 'pencils'. 4. Schist rubber. 5–7. Jade axes. 8. Chert knife. 9. Bronze axe
(Scale approx. 3 : 4)

PART VI

DISCUSSION AND CONCLUSIONS

XVII. FINAL DISCUSSION AND SOME CONCLUSIONS

IT would be folly to overstrain the limited evidence of one small site incompletely excavated, by attempting prematurely to fit it into its larger historic setting. For the time being Hureidha must remain an isolated unit of archaeological fact; and not till a dozen or more sites have been systematically worked *and published* can it be possible even to begin the task of piecing together the obscure and practically undated history of the ancient kingdoms of south-west Arabia.

Biometrically the crania, remarkable as they are, are totally insufficient in number to be material for racial conclusions. All one can say is that the view that the Armenian type of brachycephaly portrayed on the ancient south Arabian coins was early and went deep[1] is not corroborated by our specimens. At the same time no correspondence in physical type need necessarily be expected between the Yemen and the Hadhramaut; or between the tribal peasants of Hureidha and a ruling class elsewhere. The regal coinage of the Yemen, in any case, is considerably later than the period I envisage as probable for the Hadhramaut skulls.[2]

Epigraphically the inscriptions make no contact with events recorded elsewhere.

Archaeologically, apart from a few recognizable imports which can do no more—but that is much—than fix an upper dating limit, and the perilous deductions to be drawn from a derived and probably eclectic architectural style, nothing in the absence of coins was, or could be, found to tell us with which centuries we were dealing, before the rise of Islam in south Arabia put an end, nominally if not actually, to such pagan things as astral worship, and the images and baetyls we unearthed in the latest of our Moon Temple structures.[3]

With the warning, therefore, that any suggestions to follow are provisional and subjective, a few comments may perhaps be justified, more with the intention of aerating ideas than in the assurance of ultimate confirmation.

MODE OF LIFE. We may, I think safely, envisage our little community at Hureidha as a population mainly, as now, living on the fruits of diligent, if sparse, agriculture and the products of their flocks.[4] A security from tribal enmities, denied in modern times to their descendants who, for safety, have clustered their little town on rising ground

[1] A view advanced by Mr. Bertram Thomas in *Journ. Royal Asiatic Society*, July 1937, p. 494, in a review of *The Arabs of Central Iraq*, by Henry Field.

[2] G. F. Hill, *Catalogue of Greek Coins of Arabia, Mesopotamia, and Persia*, p. lxvi, states: 'On the whole we shall not be far wrong in assigning the coinage of this class to a period about A.D. 50, and lasting about a century'.

[3] K. Hitti, *History of the Arabs*, p. 66, states that in 628, the sixth year of the Hijrah, the fifth Persian satrap of the Yemen embraced Islam. Its spread to the Hadhramaut may

be a few years later. Cf. W. H. Ingrams, *Report on the Hadhramaut*, pp. 23–4, who summarizes local tradition concerning this event. Survivals of a pre-Islamic terminology for the deity are reported by Bertram Thomas. The Hadara tribesmen, although Moslems, seldom know the Qur'an, or make the pilgrimage to Mecca ('Four Strange Tongues from South Arabia. The Hadara Group', p. 55, from *Proceedings British Academy*, vol. xxiii).

[4] I say 'flocks', not 'herds', because we found no bovine bones.

beneath the protecting fortress of the cliffs, seems to have been theirs. From first to last the Temple stood, white, exposed, and unprotected, dominating from its high stylobate the contemporary village, the houses of which may lie still buried on its north-east outskirts. It may be noted that in the whole course of excavation nothing which was certainly a weapon was found. A scrap of iron in a tomb may have been a knife,[1] the dart-shaped object might be a javelin-head;[2] but there the doubtful inventory ends; and on graffito slabs we find, not the curved knife—the *djambiya*—so faithfully reproduced in numerous rock engravings elsewhere,[3] but a camel and a foot, of doubtless prophylactic symbolism.[4] This is not to imply that weapons did not exist. Of course they must have done; but a combative attitude was not, apparently, customary.

Social organization seems to have been based on the tribal system, and the headman of the Ramay clan could enforce maintenance works on the Temple and town from the community.[5]

CULTURE CONTACTS. That a close contact with the coast existed is proved by the numbers of shells of different sorts, which were threaded and worn whole, probably as charms, or rubbed down into disks or columnar amulets large and small. The absence of ostrich egg in these disks emphasizes interestingly the southern contacts at the expense of the northern. And to the coastal regions, too, must be attributed the obsidian so plentifully worked, perhaps by African slaves.[6]

Hitherto it has been customary to attribute in south Arabia all cultural influence from outside to Hellenism. This may be frequently justified. The penetration of Greek influence, direct or oblique, up till now demonstrated from the rather better-explored Yemen, is undoubted, and is particularly clearly attested by coins imitative of comparatively late Attic types of the fourth century (*circa* 393–322 B.C.), which in south Arabia can be scarcely earlier than the third.[7] Further, a Corinthian column fragment, seen by Glaser near Jerim,[8] suggests that Levantine masons or Hellenized Arabs might sometimes have been structurally employed; to whom might be attributed also the tendril decorations in stone reliefs found both in Yemen[9] and Hadhramaut.[10] Bronze heads also, human and leonine, though of uncertain date, proclaim the inspiration of the Mediterranean world.[11] Recently, too, has been brought to light in native hands in the Wadi Jardan a bronze statuette of a well-known Peloponnesian type, dating to the middle or latter part of the sixth century B.C.[12]

---

[1] Cf. p. 73.

[2] Cf. p. 73 and pl. XLV, 4.

[3] As examples, Rathjens and von Wissmann, *Südarabien Reise*, Band ii, photos. 119, 120, from Ḥugga.

[4] Cf. pp. 52, 53 and pl. XIX.

[5] Cf. inscriptions 4, 10, and 26, 38. The name is not found among present tribes.

[6] Since the blade culture, from which microliths are derived, seems alien to the Hadhramaut.

[7] G. F. Hill, op. cit., p. xlviii. Tetradrachms, however, are expressly excluded into a suspense account.

[8] Nielsen, *Handbuch der altarabischen Altertumskunde*, p. 148, fig. 37.

[9] Rathjens and von Wissmann, *Südarabien Reise*, Band ii, photo. 27, from Ḥugga.

[10] Unpublished. Brought from Shabwa by the Hon. R. B. Hamilton. The finest example, in Istanbul, is figured by Nielsen, op. cit., fig. 62, and comes probably from Yemen.

[11] *The British Museum Quarterly*, vol. xi, 1936–7, pp. 153–6, and pls. XL, XLI, XLII. Also Rathjens and von Wissmann, op. cit., p. 89, figs. 51–5.

[12] Photographed on the spot, but not acquired, by the

Contacts with Greek culture therefore, whatever the channel, are now well established, not only, as hitherto, for the Hellenistic or Roman periods. To these, in the opinion of some, will now be added the architectural style of the Moon Temple. I shall, however, propose that perhaps the Persian Empire, or its Oriental Hellenistic successor, may have played in the Hadhramaut an even greater part.

The modern architecture of the Hadhramaut has rightly been regarded as surprising and unique. But the strength of ancient Iranian tradition was the first unheralded thing which struck me as I viewed the inland towns. The houses portrayed on the bronze from Van in the British Museum, with their tiers of narrow windows rising to a flat roof adorned with a parapet of latticed stucco surmounted by a cresting of stepped pyramidal design, seemed to spring to a living reality. Even the 'parabolic' arch of many of the doorways, and the narrow, deeply recessed light or drain-shafts breaking up the high wall-surfaces from roof to ground by long vertical strips of shadow, are portrayed on the Van example.[1] The Persian origin of the narrow oblong wood capitals which support the posts in Hadhramaut rooms has been correctly noted elsewhere.[2] The Iranian *Qanat* water-conduit system has been already mentioned.[3] In combination they witness, I believe, to a deeply rooted culture connexion with old Iran, which, in the backwaters of the Hadhramaut, has survived to the present day.

The recognized period of Persian domination in south Arabia begins as late as the sixth century A.D. and there may lie the mainspring. But contacts also in Sasanian times[4] and before[5] may probably safely be assumed. And substance is now added to the surmise by the discovery of the pair of stamp seals in Tomb A6 at Hureidha, which, if not Persian, were made under the influence of Achaemenid models. To date such imports in the land of their adoption is a dangerous task.[6] The associated pottery is new to archaeology and cannot, at this early stage, give the guidance it will ultimately do. Limited by the extreme upper dating of the middle sixth century B.C. imposed by the seals, I can find no satisfactory parallel for it—neither in Palestine during the post-exilic period nor in Transjordan during the Nabatean; neither in the last Egyptian and Ptolemaic dynasties nor in contemporary Mesopotamia. The isolated pottery vessels from the Yemen are not of our shapes, and from photographs look later;[7] nor can my

Hon. R. B. Hamilton, thanks to whom the precious records reached me. Without the actual object closer dating must be withheld. Measures have been taken to retrieve the bronze, if still possible.

[1] The bronze is reproduced in E. Herzfeld, *Archaeological History of Iran*, 1935, p. 8.

[2] F. Stark, 'Two Months in the Hadhramaut', *Geog. Journ.*, Feb. 1936, p. 119. Also, *Seen in the Hadhramaut*, 1938, p. 79 and plate. The Van bronze may readily be compared with Hadhramaut architecture in that picture book.

[3] Cf. p. 10. Sir Aurel Stein states that tradition in Persia ascribes great antiquity to their construction, connecting it with the beginning of Persian domination in the Near East. Cf. 'Archaeological Reconnaissance in Southern Persia', *Geog. Journ.*, Feb. 1934.

[4] The splendid ibex-handled lamp in Vienna, figured by Nielsen, op. cit., fig. 66, may well be referred to this source.

[5] G. F. Hill, op. cit., p. liv, quotes, unapprovingly, Mordtmann's reading of an Arsacid name on a coin, and his reference to the fact that the writer of the *Periplus Maris Erythraei* states that part of the coast of Hadhramaut belonged to Persia before Sasanian times. Herodotus, Book iii, 86–8, remarks that the Arabians were never reduced to the subjection of Persia but were united in friendship.

[6] For instance in the Seleucid and Parthian periods, old seals were prized. A number of Sumerian seals were found in Parthian levels at Seleucia. See *Berytus*, vol. i, 1934, pp. 12–18.

[7] Rathjens and von Wissmann, op. cit., figs. 30–6. Also some unpublished pots from Yemen in the Peabody Museum,

Hadhramaut collection produce the handleless amphorae figured on coins from the old Sabaean kingdom.[1] Bahrein, too, fails to provide satisfactory connexions, and the glazed ware, said to date there to 300 B.C. or rather earlier, cannot be paralleled by my finds.[2]

From Ezion-Geber on the Gulf of 'Aqaba, of a rather earlier, post-Solomonic period, Dr. Nelson Glueck has kindly sent me unpublished pottery drawings for comparison. But there again, both individual forms, and the assemblage as a whole, fail to correspond sufficiently to suggest ceramic connexions.[3] All one may note is that the Arabian series from all sources, including Hureidha, is characterized by a striking absence of loop handles, so much favoured in other countries in the last pre-Christian centuries.

Judged by the Hureidha pottery, I think this lack may be explained by the fact that though water-coolers—porous drinking vessels—were common, no water-pitchers for filling at a well-head or spring are represented. Water was carried, as now, in skins.

Taken as a whole my pottery bears the stamp of two discordant things: one, the extreme primitiveness of the hand-made technique and ill-controlled firing; the other, the mature shapes—long, hollow stems and splayed pedestals, internal rim, plastic ornament, and theriomorphic modelling—far too ambitious to be successfully executed by such unskilled hands. In combination they suggest a craft learned late in local history, for which there was little traditional aptitude. On the other hand, the manipulation of stone would seem to have been inbred in the culture, resulting in that curious semi-ceramic product the 'stone ware'. This, moreover, is not apparently a purely local invention. From the ruins at Hugga and Haz in Yemen are recorded dark-grey vessels, hewn, it is said, out of natural stone of crystalline aspect like graphite.[4] These are in Berlin, and without proper examination it cannot be certain that the material is, as I suspect, 'stone ware'. The same authors illustrate spouted 'lamps' in dark-grey lime-stone,[5] which, though shallower, recall the Hureidha spouted 'stone ware' unguent vessels. Be that as it may, a small pot of characteristic 'stone ware' has been found at Armant in Upper Egypt, unluckily in an undated, though probably 'late', context. It may well be that precious balms were exported from south Arabia to Egypt in their original containers, as ginger travels from China.

So much for the pottery. It is mainly a local product which, for the time being, cannot satisfactorily be related to its foreign source, or more probably sources, of inspiration.

Certain of the stone vessels are more responsive. These are the square, four-legged incense-burners in limestone—miniature fire altars—found, with one exception, in an

---

Harvard, which, with low ring bases and everted lips, correspond with the Rathjens specimens, not with mine.

[1] G. F. Hill, op. cit., pls. VIII, IX, X. These amphorae, supporting an owl, are long and narrow, with pointed base and wide rim; some have double loop handles. The style is foreign to anything found at Hureidha.

[2] E. Mackay, *Bahrein*, p. 29.

[3] In spite of the fact that two jars, inscribed in south Arabic characters, have been found there, dating to the first part of the eighth century B.C. Cf. Nelson Glueck, *Asia Mag.*, Oct. 1938 and Sept. 1939. G. Ryckmans, in *Revue Biblique*, April 1939, p. 247, expresses the view that the letters on one example are Minaean; and he thinks the jar came from a Minaean colony in Hejaz, not S. Arabia.

[4] Rathjens and von Wissmann, op. cit., pp. 83–4. According to Rihani, *Arabian Peaks and Deserts*, p. 167, mica is abundant in Yemen, and is referred to by Yāqūt.

[5] Idem, photos. 42, 43.

extramural shrine of the Moon Temple.[1] Their relative date there is thus securely fixed to the C or post-C phase; for the single exception within the Temple itself lay *in situ* in the C phase extension, with which it might be either contemporary or later.[2]

This style of incense-burner has been found in Palestine, and in particular a cave-tomb at Gezer, with *arcosolia*, bench graves, and two bulls' heads in relief on the wall, provides so close a parallel to the Hureidha burners that a connexion is certain.[3] The Gezer specimen is of soft limestone, rectangular, standing on four square-cut legs, with a similar shallow trough; its outer sides are adorned, like ours, with a linear criss-cross pattern, which, on the legs, is similarly expressed by a diagonal cross. No mention, however, is made of the reddened surface visible on our series. Though the tomb had been rifled, no doubt exists as to its Seleucid date;[4] and, with one older exception, all the incense-burners of this type found at Gezer, including some scratched with rude naturalistic scenes, are attributed to Hellenistic times.[5]

This accords with my opinion as to the relative dating of the building phases in the Hureidha temple. Phase C or post-C, which alone yielded these objects, would therefore be later—possibly very considerably later—than 300 B.C. In this connexion it may be significant that tombs A5 and A6, broadly correlated through their pottery with phases A and B of the Temple,[6] produced no incense-burners of this type.

Assessment of the architectural influences creative of the Moon Temple is not easy, though partial assimilation of foreign models is manifest. Its 'orientation' as well as its tutelary deity are rooted collaterally far back in Babylonia, from whence the Persian Empire, chronologically nearer our problem, derived, through Assyria, some at least of its earlier stimuli. The high, rubble-filled platform of the Hadhramaut temple, and the imitative rustic copings, already present in the earliest building,[7] might derive equally from Achaemenian Persia, Phoenicia, or Asiatic Greece; and the extent to which buildings in south Arabia were indebted to the Near Eastern Asiatic world of the last five and a half centuries before Christ is well exemplified at Marib, where Glaser reported evidence for leaden clamps upon the masonry.[8]

Finally, bearing in mind the seventh- to fifth-century affinities with Syria proclaimed for the tomb beads; and the sixth- to fourth-century affinities with peripheral Persia proclaimed for the seals, I assume, until corrected, though on all too slender material, that the dating probabilities for the tombs and phases A and B of the Moon Temple are contained somewhere within the middle or later years of the Persian Empire—in the middle fifth to fourth centuries B.C.; whereas phases C and post-C (if this last be truly an aftermath) of the Temple, doubtfully represented in the tombs, are Seleucid.

Nothing would be permanently gained by attempting to place the ancient Madhâb

---

[1] Cf. pp. 49, 50 and pls. XII, XVI, XVII.
[2] Cf. p. 36 and pls. XVI, 3; XVII, 2.
[3] R. A. S. Macalister, *The Excavations of Gezer*, 1912, vol. i, pp. 355–8, and fig. 185.
[4] *Quarterly Statement of the Palestine Exploration Fund*, 1900, pp. 22–26.

[5] *The Excavations of Gezer*, vol. ii, p. 444.
[6] Cf. pp. 25, 39–40, 129–31.
[7] Cf. pp. 22, 30.
[8] Nielsen, *Handbuch der altarabischen Altertumskunde*, p. 146.

of our pioneer excavations on or off a still hypothetical Incense Route, that seductive thoroughfare of speculation so zealously explored of recent years by ready writers regardless of the essential requirement of an archaeological distribution map; and prone, moreover, to over-simplify the excursion by assuming the synchronism of the few surface ruins which appear as yet on the very incomplete topographical surveys of southern Arabia. One may reflect that if the European transcontinental Amber Route, trading a virtually imperishable substance, has taken some seventy years of expert team-work to establish with even the semblance of finality, and which has now been shown by means of distribution plottings of key objects to have followed different courses at different times according to the tastes, and economic and other fluctuating conditions, of the period, the ramifications of the Incense Route, trading perishable commodities in conditions of constant instability, are unlikely to be resolved by anything less than severely practical archaeology.

PART VII
EPIGRAPHY
by
PROF. G. RYCKMANS

EPIGRAPHY

NOTE BY THE EXCAVATOR. Cross references in footnotes should facilitate correlation with the excavatory detail of each Temple inscription. The fifty-eight stones were recorded by means both of wet squeezes and photographs, unless disintegrated or very fragmentary, when a hand copy alone was made. The freestone is coarse and brittle. Several slabs were smothered in plaster, the removal of which by dilute hydrochloric acid was difficult. Twenty-two inscriptions, in bad preservation, in small fragments or *in situ* were left in the Temple. Fourteen, more important, were transferred to the Mansab's house. Nine were left at the Residency, Mukalla, and thirteen were sent to England. These last have been distributed to the Musée Biblique at Louvain, the Fitzwilliam Museum, and the Ashmolean. The inscriptions without exception are sunk carvings; guide-lines are conspicuous on many. Two stones only bear decorative borders, and these are done in low relief. Five slabs still show traces, like the Temple incense-burners, of a red artificial colouring, perhaps haematite, which doubtless adorned a larger number or all.

The rock graffiti near Seiyun and Shibam were on low level boulders, fallen from the cliffs, and which I found in rambles. At neither place do they mark any special geographical feature such as a track to the high desert, or water.

F. Stark has twice stated (*A Winter in Arabia*, p. 192, and *Journal R. Asiatic Soc.*, July 1939, p. 482) that I did not consider some graffiti, found by her at Hureidha, 'worth photographing'. I had, as she then well knew, only one roll of exposures left (supplies from Cairo having failed to arrive), and these were necessarily kept for my last week's tomb excavations.

I. INSCRIPTIONS DU TEMPLE DE ḤUREYḌA[1]

Caton Thompson 1. Ḥureyḍa A3.1. A Ḥureyḍa, chez Sayyid Ḥasan al-'Aṭṭas. Fragment, caractères archaïques. Copie, fac-simile.[2] Photographie *in situ*, pls. LXII, 5; VIII, 1.

$$\cdots \text{𐩣𐩩𐩨𐩠} \qquad \ldots une\ image\ et \ldots (?)$$

A rapprocher de 𐩥𐩣𐩡?, 'image', cf. CIH 723, etc. L'inscription peut faire allusion à la dédicace d'une stèle représentant le dédicant.

Caton Thompson 2. Ḥureyḍa A3.2. A la Résidence de Mukalla. Brisée à droite et à gauche. Caractères de type archaïque évolué vers un type plus récent.[3] Photographie, pl. LXIII, 2.

$$\text{𐩤𐩠𐩱𐩬} \cdots \cdots\ \text{1} \qquad \ldots fi]ls\ de\ \check{S}ib\hat{a}m,\ a\ d\acute{e}[di\acute{e}\ \grave{a}$$
$$\text{𐩠𐩥𐩩𐩬} \qquad\qquad\ \text{2} \qquad S\hat{\imath}n]\ sa\ [personne]\ et\ ses\ enfants.$$

𐩱𐩬, cf. RNP, i, p. 205. 𐩤𐩠𐩠, etc., cf. RES 4064.

[1] ABRÉVIATIONS: CIH = *Corpus Inscriptionum Semiticarum*, pars iv, Inscriptiones Ḥimyariticas atque Sabaeas continens; RES = *Répertoire d'Épigraphie sémitique*; RNP = G. RYCKMANS, *Les Noms propres sud-sémitiques*, i–iii, Louvain, 1934–5, où l'on trouvera la liste des autres abréviations et des sigles usités dans la présente étude. Sauf indication contraire, le dialecte est ḥaḍramoutique.

[2] Cf. p. 33.   [3] Cf. p. 33.

Caton Thompson 3. Ḥureyḍa A3.3. A la Résidence de Mukalla. Brisée à droite. Caractères archaïques. Dialecte sabéen?[1] Photographie, pl. LXIII, 1.

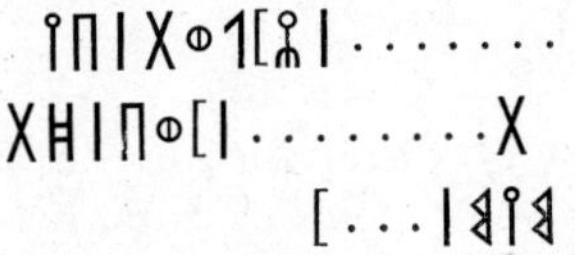

� 1	... *la fa*]*çade antérieure du tem-*
.... 2	*ple* ....] *et par Ḏât-Ḥi-*
[... 3	*myam* ...].

X⊙ʕᵐ, cf. RES 2776, 2; cf. Caton Thompson 10, 2: ..., 'la façade antérieure (du temple) de Maḏâbum'. ... est une divinité sabéenne (cf. RNP, i, p. 14), connue aussi en qatabanite, cf. RES 4332, 2; RYCKMANS 159 (*Le Muséon*, l, 1937, p. 242); si la présente inscription n'est pas sabéenne, comme Caton Thompson 17*b*, la mention de cette divinité se présenterait pour la première fois en ḥaḍramoutique.

Caton Thompson 4. Ḥureyḍa A3.4. A Ḥureyḍa, chez Sayyid Ḥasan al-ʿAṭṭas. Brisée en bas. Caractères évolués vers un type récent.[2] Photographie, pl. LXIII, 3.

[inscription]	1
[inscription]	2
[inscription]	3
[inscription]	4
[inscription]	5
[inscription]	6
[inscription]	7
[inscription]	8
[inscription]	9
[inscription]	10
[inscription]	11
........) .. ⊓ . ⅃ .. ◊ ..	12

L. 1. ..., cf. RNP, i, p. 168. ..., cf. le n. pr. حَابِس, IBN DOR. 235; Ḥâbis, WÜST., *Reg.*, p. 193. ..., cf. Caton Thompson 10, 1–2; ces mentions de kabîr (RES 2687) sont les premières qui se présentent dans les textes ḥaḍramoutiques.

L. 2. ..., épithète d'un second personnage? (cf. le suffixe du duel à l. 6). D'autre part, l'emploi du pluriel en apposition avec deux noms (cf. le mot qui suit, ...), ainsi que dans un verbe qui a deux sujets (cf. ... à la l. 3) est d'usage fréquent; cf. RES 4663, 1, etc.; Caton Thompson 49, 2–3 (?). La deuxième lettre de ... est un ..., à angles aigus; cette lettre présente la même forme partout ailleurs dans l'inscription, excepté dans ..., à la l. 3, où la forme est arrondie. C'est un exemple de l'état de transition dans l'évolution paléographique de cette lettre. Le ◊ se retrouve, mutilé, à la l. 12. ..., duel (voir ci-dessus): forme du pluriel en ⊙; cf. ⊙)Υ⊙: RES 2726, 3;

[1] Cf. p. 33.   [2] Cf. p. 34.

3591, 1; CIH 418, 2–3; ⊙)ᚷᚕ: RES 3591, 1; la désinence ⊙ se présente aussi dans le duel génitif en qatabanite, cf. RES 4094, 3: ⊙ᚻᚖᚌ; voir aussi Rhodokanakis, *Ḳat. Texte*, i, pp. 126–7. ᚺᚖᚻ, 'élite'? cf. ar. آمن, 'la meilleure partie'; soqoṭrî, *'imhen*, 'part' (Leslau, *Lexique soqoṭrî*, pp. 64–5). On pourrait rapprocher aussi ᚺᚖᚻ de l'éth. *'emna*, ar. من. En sab. ᚕᚺᚖᚻ signifie 'garde du corps' (RES 3945, 13, 18); en min. ᚺᚕᚖᚺᚖᚻᛁᚖᚖᚻ se dit d'une classe de femmes vouées à la divinité (RES 2813, 2, etc.).

L. 3. ᚌᚠᚻᚌ est l'ancien nom de la ville de Ḥureyḍa, dont Sîn était la divinité tutélaire, cf. ll. 3–4; Caton Thompson 54, 2. Madâbum est aussi le nom du temple, cf. Caton Thompson 10, 2. Le nom de Maḏâb est déjà connu comme celui d'une localité près de Ḏur'ân, d'un wâdî dans le Djôf, et aussi, en minéen, comme élément d'un édifice; cf. RNP, i, p. 331.

L. 4. ᚖᚺᚕᚌ, ar. سند, 'appuyer'; le ᚖᚺᚕᚌ est la stèle érigée au dieu en dédicace ou en action de grâces; cf. Rhodokanakis, dans *W.Z.K.M.* xliii (1936), p. 50, note 1. Par métonymie, le ᚖᚺᚕᚌ est aussi l'inscription gravée sur la stèle; cf. RES 2633, 6: ᚖᚖᚕᚌᛁᚖᚕᛁᚙᚙᚻ. En arabe, le mot *musnad* a fini par désigner les anciennes inscriptions attribuées aux 'himyarites'; cf. Hamdânî, *Iklîl*, d'après RES 3181*bis*–3194. ᚻᚔᚗ, 'accomplir', cf. Ryckmans 162, 6 (*Le Muséon*, l, 1937, pp. 245–6); 169, 4 (ibid., pp. 248–9; cf. RES 3854).

L. 5. ᚌᛁᚖᚕᚕᚠ, cf. RES 3945, 14: ᚌᛁᚖᚌ, 'pour la deuxième fois'; alternance du ᚕ ḥaḍramoutique et du ᚗ sabéen, cf. RES 2687, 5: ᚖᚖᛁᚖᚕ—⊙ᚌᚻᚠᚌ⊙ᚗ, 'le jour de Ḏû-Samâwî'? Cf. ⊙ᚗᚻᚠ, sans ᚗ, RES 3247 (CIH 972), jour de la fête de cette divinité, ou plutôt un nom de mois, la divinité Ḏû-Samâwî (RNP, i, p. 24) n'étant pas attestée en ḥaḍramoutique, ce qui rendrait sa mention d'autant plus surprenante dans une inscription dédiée à Sîn. Voir une construction analogue dans RES 3104, 3–4:)⊙ᚗᚠᛁᚌⵔᚕᛁᚌⵔᚠᚠ, 'au neuvième jour (du mois) Ḏû-Ṯawr'. Le ⊙ final n'est pas certain dans ⊙ᚗᚻᚠ; lire peut-être, mais moins probablement ⵔᚗᚻᚠ, nom de mois, cf. RNP, i, p. 380. ᚕᚖᚕᚻ, alternance de ᚕ et ᚗ, cf. *supra* et Caton Thompson 10, 2; RES 4213.

L. 6. ᚌᚻᛁ se dit de la construction en plein, et non en creux; cf. RES 2687, 3; 3869, 2: 'exécuter en construction massive'. ᚕᚖᚌᚻ, cf. RES 3308, 1; 3610, 12, 13, 'part, dépôt'? cf. soqoṭrî *'imhen* (ci-dessus, l. 2); ar. الأمانة, 'ce qui est confié, dépôt'. Il s'agit des ressources au moyen desquelles sont effectués les travaux, ressources appartenant aux ᚺᚖᚻ et constituant leur part, ou constituées par un dépôt, formé par des redevances. ᚕᚠ⊙ᚗ, nom du puits; ar. شعبة, 'crevasse, fente dans un rocher'; ce nom convient à une anfractuosité de rocher aménagée en puits.

L. 7. ᚕᚠᚗⵔᚻ, forme causative de ᚠᚗⵔ, 'renouveler', d'après Rhodokanakis, dans *W.Z.K.M.* xliii (1936), p. 40, *ad* CIH 448, 2, 3 (sabéen: ᚠᚗⵔᚖ). Nous traduisons, après ᚕᚖᚕᚻ, par 'refaire' d'après Dozy, cité par Rhodokanakis. Le suffixe ḥaḍramoutique ᚕ pour ᚻ; voir la même alternance dans ⊙ᚕᚻ, Rhodokanakis, dans *W.Z.K.M.* xxxix (1932), p. 223. Le suffixe se présente sous la forme ᚕ à la l. 9 (ᚕᚠ), tandis qu'il se présente sous la forme ᚻ à la l. 4 (ᚻᚔᚗ) et à la l. 5 (ᚺᚖᚺᚕᚺᚖᚻ). ᚌᚕᛁᚕ), 'largeur, ampleur', cf. ᚕⵔᛁᚖ, 'élargir', CIH 117, 2, etc.; ᚕᚕⵔᛁᚖ, 'ampleur', CIH 610, 10; ar. أروح, 'large'.))ᚖᚌ, ar. درّ, 'ruisseler, tomber, couler en abondance (lait, pluie)'; cf. CIH 615, 8: ⊙ᚌᛁᚖ))ᚖ (CIH: 'incrementum'); RES 3306, 3:))ᚖ? Le subst.))ᚖᚌ pourrait se rapporter à un conduit destiné à amener l'eau dans le puits.

L. 8. ᚖᚖᚗᚌ, 'bassin, réservoir', cf. RES 4197*bis*, 2. ᚌᚠᚕ⊙ᚻ, plur. brisé, cf. ar. عتب, 'inégalité, aspérité du sol, seuil, marche soit les', marches de l'escalier qui mène au fond de la citerne, soit les parois de la citerne aménagées elles-mêmes en degrés. Voir des types d'escaliers et de citernes à degrés dans RATHJENS et VON WISSMANN, *Vorislamische Altertümer*, p. 146, phot. 92, et p. 147, phot. 94 (Stufenzisterne); voir aussi une citerne à degrés avec un escalier, p. 152, phot. 100, 101.

L. 8–9. 𐩣𐩬𐩤𐩬, le 𐩬 final appartient à la racine, comme l'indique le mot suivant, tandis que dans RES 4230 c, 2: 𐩣𐩬𐩤𐩬𐩣 | 𐩣𐩬𐩬, où le 𐩣 marque la mimation, et où ce subst. est dérivé de قصّ ou de 𐩣𐩬𐩬. Ici la racine est قصم, 'casser, rompre'; cf. قِصَم, 'morceau'; en relation avec 𐩬𐩩𐩤𐩬, 'pierre équarrie', pour les parties apparentes de la maçonnerie (RES 2687, 4), traduisons 𐩣𐩬𐩤𐩬, 'pierre brute, cassée', destinée au gros-œuvre non apparent. 𐩭𐩬𐩣𐩬𐩣, cf. CIH 309, 4: 𐩬𐩬𐩬𐩬 | . . . | 𐩬𐩬𐩬, 'il ordonna la construction' (RHODOKANAKIS, *Ḳat. Texte*, i, p. 39, note 1). Pour le suffixe 𐩭, voir l. 7. 𐩬𐩬, alternance de 𐩬 ḥaḍr. et o sab., cf. RES 2687, 5.

L. 10. 𐩭𐩬𐩣𐩬, 'sommet', cf. ar. قومة, 'taille, stature', comme قمّة de قم; cf. CIH 338, 16 (= Gl. 1209, 12–13): 𐩬𐩬𐩬 | 𐩬𐩬𐩬 | 𐩬𐩬𐩬𐩬) | 𐩬𐩬, 'de sa base au sommet' (RHODOKANAKIS, dans *W.Z.K.M.* xxxix, 1932, p. 176), du rad. قم (ibid., p. 186).

L. 11. 𐩬𐩬𐩬, cf. Caton Thompson 10, 3; CIH 539, 3; RES 3951, 3–4.

1 *'Asamum, fils de Ḥabîsum, kabî[r de Ramay*
2 *et . . .]* *'Aqnum, aristocrates de la vil-*
3 *le de Maḏâbum, ont dédié à Sîn Ḏû-*
4 *Maḏâbim cette inscription, et s'en sont acquittés*
5 *au deuxième jour de Ḏû-Samâw. Et ils ont renouvelé et*
6 *bâti en construction massive avec leur part (?) le puits Shu'-*
7 *bat, et ils l'ont refait en largeur, et le con-*
8 *duit, et le bassin, et les degrés. Et (ils l'ont bâti) en gros œuvre*
9 *et en pierres équarries. Et ils ont ordonné ce (travail) jusqu'au*
10 *sommet du puits de la ville de Maḏâ-*
11 *bum, et avec la participation de (la tribu) de Ramay, et . . . .*

Caton Thompson 5. Ḥureyḍa A3.5. Fragment. Copie, fac-similé.[1]

𐩬𐩬𐩬𐩬 | 𐩬𐩬𐩬(𐩬 | 𐩬)𐩬𐩬[𐩬 | 𐩬𐩬𐩬 | 𐩬𐩬𐩬 · · ·

. . . a dédié à Sîn] sa [per]sonne, et ses enfants, et son établissement (?).

𐩬𐩬𐩬, voir le verbe, RES 2657; hébr. יָשַׁב.

Caton Thompson 6. Ḥureyḍa A3.6. Fragment. Copie, fac-similé.[2]

𐩬𐩬 | 𐩬𐩬𐩬𐩬   *Shibâmum, fils de . . . .*

Cf. RNP, ii, p. 126.

Caton Thompson 7. Ḥureyḍa A3.7. Cambridge, Fitzwilliam Museum. Autel à libations.

[1] Cf. p. 34.   [2] Cf. p. 29.

Inscriptions à caractères archaïques sur les parois antérieure et latérales de la table. Celle-ci est brisée à l'angle arrière gauche.[1] Photographies, pls. XVIII, 3; *in situ*, VIII, 1.

Il s'agit d'un autel à libations et non d'un autel à sacrifices sanglants. Les parois latérales de la table mesurent 0,25 m. de longueur sur 0,09 m. de hauteur. La table repose sur une pyramide tronquée,[2] comme celle de l'autel à libations ḥaḍramoutique RES 3512 (voir aussi RHODOKANAKIS, dans *W.Z.K.M.* xliii, 1936, pp. 55–7) dont on trouvera la description chez RYCKMANS, *Le Muséon*, xl, 1927, p. 169. Les autels à sacrifices sanglants étaient établis à même le sol, cf. CIH 288, reproduit par MORDTMANN et MITTWOCH, *Himj. Inschr. Berlin*, 1932, p. 33; cf. HÖFNER et RHODOKANAKIS, dans *W.Z.K.M.* xliii, 1936, p. 217, qui comparent cet autel avec ceux du haut-lieu de Zibb 'Atûf à Petra, dont le plan est reproduit par NIELSEN, *Die altarabische Mondreligion*, 1904, fig. 30.

D'après le croquis, la surface supérieure de la pierre présente un évidement qui se prolonge en rigole dans un saillant, dont l'extrémité est sculptée en bucrane à la façon des gargouilles reproduites par RATHJENS et VON WISSMANN, *Vorisl. Altertümer*, p. 55, phot. 23 et p. 56, phot. 24. Voir aussi la gargouille du Musée d'Aden, RYCKMANS, *Le Muséon*, lii (1939), no 227, p. 76.

𐩺𐩬𐩠𐩡𐩡𐩤𐩡𐩺 𐩠𐩠 𐩵 𐩩𐩠𐩡𐩤𐩬𐩡𐩠𐩠𐩬𐩰   *Ḥasamum, fils de 'Ilqaṯam, a dédié [à Sîn.*

𐩠𐩠𐩬𐩰, cf. RES 4400, 2. 𐩠𐩠𐩵𐩩𐩠, le 𐩵 est tracé de la même main sur la paroi latérale du saillant en gargouille, ce qui permet de supposer qu'il appartient à l'inscription. Cf. 𐩠𐩠𐩵, RNP, i, p. 195, et 𐩠𐩵𐩵, Caton Thompson 54, 1. En excluant le 𐩵, on lirait 𐩠𐩠𐩩𐩠, '*Iltamma*? Cf. ‎؟, 'raffermir, consolider', ou '*Alṯam*, élatif, cf. 𐩠𐩠𐩩 et ses dérivés, RNP, i, p. 123; l'élatif se présente toutefois plus fréquemment comme épithète dans les n. pr. sud-ar. 𐩩𐩬𐩵𐩰, préformante 𐩰, cf. RES 4181; Caton Thompson 29; 31; 36; 37; 44.

Caton Thompson 8. Ḥureyḍa A3.8. Copie, fac-simile.[3]

𐩩𐩬𐩵𐩠 ···   *... a dédié*

𐩠𐩷𐩠𐩵𐩬[𐩡𐩬𐩵𐩠   *à Sîn sa] personne.*

Caton Thompson 9. Ḥureyḍa A3.9. Encastrée dans un pavement. Au registre supérieur, dans un cadre, quatre bucranes stylisés portant un fruit (?) entre les cornes, cf. GROHMANN, *Göttersymbole*, p. 33; Caton Thompson 49; sous les panneaux supérieur et inférieur du cadre, une frise à métopes rectangulaires. Caractères évoluant vers un type récent.[4] Photographies, pls. LXII, 1; LXIII, 4; *in situ*, VII, 1.

---

[1] Cf. p. 24.
[2] This is a misapprehension, due to the fact that for photography it was lifted up on to the stone pillar at the foot of which it lay. G. C. T. (See p. 24.)
[3] Cf. p. 30.   [4] Cf. p. 42.

𐩺𐩫𐩬𐩵𐩶𐩬𐩪𐩭𐩲   1   *'Iḫtašam le Garbite,*

𐩠𐩩𐩱𐩺𐩠𐩩𐩫𐩬𐩩𐩠   2   *fils de Madhiqum, a*

𐩠𐩵𐩱𐩩𐩫𐩩𐩠𐩩𐩫𐩩   3   *dédié à Sîn cette inscrip-*

𐩠𐩬𐩩𐩠𐩭𐩲𐩩𐩠𐩺𐩠   4   *tion, et il a voué à la sujé-*

𐩠𐩠𐩩𐩠𐩫𐩩𐩠𐩩𐩠𐩠   5   *tion de Sîn son âme*

𐩠𐩠𐩠𐩠𐩲   6   *et ses sens.*

L. 1. 𐩱𐩵𐩭𐩲, cf. 𐩱𐩵𐩲, RNP, i, p. 107. 𐩠𐩺𐩩𐩬𐩵𐩩, nom gentilice avec le déterminatif 𐩠𐩺 ḥaḍra-moutique; cf. 𐩠𐩺𐩩𐩬𐩵𐩩: RNP, ii, p. 44.

L. 2. 𐩱𐩱𐩺𐩠𐩱, cf. ar. ذحق, 'être écorché et dépouillé de la cuticule extérieure' (se dit de la langue, à la suite de quelque maladie). La racine ذحق est apparentée à ذحج, 'peler, dépouiller de son écorce'; l'arabe connaît le n. pr., مذحِج, Ibn Dor. 237; voir aussi en sud-ar. le n. pr. d'homme ou d'édifice: 𐩱𐩩𐩺𐩠𐩱, Ryckmans 159, 2, qatab. (dans *Le Muséon*, l, 1937, p. 242).

L. 3. 𐩠𐩺𐩠𐩱𐩱, cf. Caton Thompson 4, 4: 𐩠𐩺𐩠𐩱𐩭; alternance de 𐩱 et 𐩭.

Ll. 4–6. 𐩠𐩭𐩲, etc., cf. RES 2693, 4–5: 𐩠𐩠𐩠𐩲|𐩠𐩠𐩷𐩱|···|𐩺𐩩𐩱|𐩠𐩠𐩬𐩩|𐩠𐩭𐩲; voir aussi RES 2869, 7 min. et Caton Thompson 33, 34.

Caton Thompson 10. Ḥureyḍa A3.10+26. A la Résidence de Mukalla. A droite de la l. 1, un espace de deux lettres mutilé, probablement un monogramme ou un symbole. Quelques cassures dans la l. 3. Caractères apparentés à ceux de Caton Thompson 4, mais évolués vers un type plus récent. Le trait du ⊙ est horizontal.[1] Photographie, pl. LXIV, 1.

𐩠𐩩𐩠𐩺𐩱𐩵𐩩𐩩𐩵𐩱𐩱𐩲𐩩𐩠𐩬𐩩𐩩𐩠𐩩𐩬   1

𐩠𐩠𐩲𐩩𐩩𐩺𐩬𐩱𐩬𐩠𐩱𐩭𐩲𐩩𐩱𐩭𐩠𐩺𐩠𐩩𐩱𐩵𐩩𐩵𐩬   2

𐩩𐩱𐩵𐩩𐩬𐩵𐩬𐩲𐩩𐩺𐩭𐩩𐩱𐩱   3

L. 1. 𐩩𐩠𐩫𐩬, cf. RNP, ii, p. 38. 𐩵𐩱𐩠𐩱𐩲, cf. RNP, i, p. 223. 𐩠𐩺𐩩𐩱𐩵𐩩, gentilice comme 𐩠𐩺𐩩𐩬𐩵𐩩, Caton Thompson 9, 1. Ce nom est apparenté à celui de la tribu 𐩩𐩱𐩵, cf. l. 2 et 3. 𐩵𐩬𐩠, etc., cf. Caton Thompson 4, 1.

L. 2. 𐩭𐩠𐩺𐩠, cf. Caton Thompson 4, 5. 𐩭𐩲𐩩𐩱, cf. Caton Thompson 3, 1. 𐩱𐩬𐩠𐩱, cf. Caton Thompson 4, 3–4, 10–11. 𐩩𐩺𐩬, particule 𐩬 suivie de l'élément d'indétermination ḥaḍramoutique 𐩩𐩺, en minéen 𐩩𐩠; cf. Rhodokanakis, *Studien*, ii, p. 171; id., *Ḳat. Texte*, i, pp. 125–6. Dans RES 2687, 5, la formule se rapproche de très près de celle qui se présente ici: 𐩠𐩺𐩩𐩠𐩭𐩱𐩱𐩠𐩠𐩲𐩠𐩩𐩩𐩠𐩺𐩵𐩩𐩩𐩺𐩬, 'la deuxième (année de l'éponymat) de Yašraḥ'il Dû-'Aḍîdim'. 𐩱𐩠𐩠𐩲, comme dans Caton Thompson 24, 2–3, n. pr. d'homme; RES 2687, 5, clan. Ici on lirait plutôt 𐩱𐩠𐩠𐩲, mais le trait horizontal qui caractérise le ⊙ dans la présente inscription, pourrait n'être qu'un renforcement de la ligne horizontale qui marque la section médiane des lettres pour faciliter le tracé au lapicide. Cette ligne est également accentuée au début de la l. 2.

[1] Cf. p. 54.

L. 3. 𐩦𐩡𐩻𐩠𐩬, alternance du 𐩻 et du 𐩯 en ḥaḍramoutique, voir ci-dessus et Caton Thompson 4, 5. 𐩥𐩨𐩦𐩧𐩫, cf. Caton Thompson 4, 11.

1 *Bin'il, fils de 'Ammḏamar, le Yarmite, Ka-*
2 *bîr de Ramay, a renouvelé la façade antérieure (du temple) de Maḏâbum, la*
3 *troisième (année de l'éponymat de) 'Aḏîḏum, et avec la participation de (la tribu) Ramay.*

Caton Thompson 11. Ḥureyḍa A3.11. A Ḥureyḍa, chez Sayyid Ḥasan al-'Aṭṭas. Brisée à droite. Caractères archaïques.[1] Photographie, pl. LXIV, 2.

......|]𐩨𐩬|𐩺𐩠𐩬	1	*...fils de Yuhan-*
...|𐩠]𐩤𐩬𐩺|𐩢𐩥𐩡	2	*...a dé]dié à Ḥawl.*

L. 1. On connaît en sud-ar. le n. pr. 𐩺𐩠𐩬𐩪, RNP, i, p. 74, et l'épithète 𐩺𐩠𐩬𐩲𐩣, cf. RNP, ii, p. 70.

L. 2. 𐩠]𐩤𐩬𐩺 plutôt que 𐩪]𐩤𐩬𐩺, d'après les textes paléographiquement apparentés. Cf. Caton Thompson 7; 21; 29; 31; 36; 37; 44. 𐩢𐩥𐩡, dieu lunaire ḥaḍramoutique, à identifier probablement avec Sîn. Ḥawl est la divinité lunaire caractérisée par une idée de récurrence périodique. Cf. RNP, i, p. 12. Voir des dédicaces à Ḥawl, RES 4067; Caton Thompson 32.

Caton Thompson 12. Ḥureyḍa A3.12. A la Résidence de Mukalla. Brisée à gauche. Caractères archaïques.[2] Photographie, pl. LXIV, 5.

𐩺𐩹𐩢𐩣|𐩨𐩬[|...|𐩥...|𐩠𐩤	1	*Yaḏḥam, fils de[... et ... ont*
𐩬𐩺𐩥|𐩪𐩺𐩬	2	*dédié à Sîn.*

L. 1. 𐩺𐩹𐩢𐩣, n. pr. inconnu; cf. ar. ذحم = ذام, 'blâmer', ou زحم, 'serrer' avec alternance de 𐩹 et 𐩸? Cf. Caton Thompson 10, 2–3: 𐩲𐩹𐩹𐩣.

L. 2. 𐩠𐩤]𐩬𐩺𐩥, la préformante 𐩠 est probable; cf. Caton Thompson 11. Le lapicide avait oublié le 𐩥, dont il a surchargé le trait de séparation qu'il avait déjà gravé.

Caton Thompson 13. Ḥureyḍa A3.13. Fragment. Copie, fac-simile.[3]

...𐩪𐩺𐩬...   *...Sîn...*

Caton Thompson 14. Ḥureyḍa A3.14. Graffites de différentes mains. Ces graffites étaient probablement tracés sur des pierres faisant partie du mur extérieur du temple.[4] Cf. Caton Thompson 14*bis*; 22; 22*bis*; RYCKMANS 294–301 (dans *Le Muséon*, lii, 1939, pp. 108–10). Photographie, pl. LXIV, 3.

(*a*) En haut.	Wasm?	𐩦𐩣𐩩	*Šamît?*
	Wasm?	𐩭𐩡𐩮𐩺	*Ḫalṣay?*

[1] Cf. p. 54. [2] Cf. p. 54. [3] Cf. p. 54. [4] Cf. p. 53.

ᕽ⟨ᛃ⟩, cf. RNP, ii, p. 129. ᚠᛝᛝᚼ, cf. RNP, ii, p. 65. Le ᛝ appartient au type thamoudéen; cf. Freya Stark 36 (34). La lecture de ce dernier nom est douteuse.

(*b*) Sous le graffite précédent. Boustrophédon?

ᛀ . . . ᛁ ᛁ . . .

ᛁᛏᛁᙂᙅᛏ 2 *Ḏû-Ḥaḥay'il.*

ᛁᛏᛁᙂᙅ, du type des noms ᛝᛟᛁᙂᙅ, ᕽᛝᛟᛁᙂᙅ, cf. RNP, i, p. 228. Le ᛁ forme monogramme avec le ᛏ qui le précède; il est marqué par un crochet qui se rattache à la base verticale gauche du ᛏ; cf. Caton Thompson 22*b* et 22*bis c.*

(*c*) A droite du précédent, négligemment tracé.

ᛃ⟩ᙅ⟩ *Šahrum.*

Le ᙅ renversé, avec la fourche en angle aigu, de type thamoudéen.

(*d*) Sous le précédent, dextérogyre.

→ ᚲᛜᛟ◊ᕽᚲ *Nawfatân.*

Le ◊ est douteux. Cf. ᚼᛟᛜᚼ, RNP, i, p. 138.

(*e*) A droite du précédent.

ᑎᛁᛜ *'Ayb*(?).

Voir les dérivés de ᑎᛁᛜ, RNP, ii, p. 15. Le nom pourrait être mutilé au début.

Caton Thompson 14bis. Ḥureyḍa A3.14bis. Cambridge, Fitzwilliam Museum. Graffites de différentes mains.[1] Au milieu, un chameau de profil. Photographie, pl. XIX.

(*a*) ᙂᛃ◊ᙅ ᛁ *A élargi (ou Hafšaḥ)*

⟩ᛑᛁ 2 *Yagûr.*

ᙂᛃ◊ᙅ, cf. ar. فشح, 'écarter'; فسح, 'élargir, rendre plus spacieux'. Les deux racines sont apparentées; l'accadien *pasû*, II, 'se développer, s'élargir', correspond phonétiquement à l'ar. فشح. ᙂᛃ◊ᙅ est probablement une forme verbale dans Freya Stark 43 (34) *a* (Ḥureyḍa), inscription près de l'entrée d'une caverne, et qui pourrait se rapporter à des travaux d'élargissement de celle-ci.[2] Au cas où ᙂᛃ◊ᙅ serait ici une forme verbale, ⟩ᛑᛁ connu seulement comme épithète ou comme n. pr. d'édifice (cf. RNP, ii, p. 68), devrait être un n. pr. d'homme. Au cas où ᙂᛃ◊ᙅ serait un n. pr., ⟩ᛑᛁ serait épithète. Ce dernier mot se trouve plus bas à gauche, et non d'alignement du précédent, mais il est de la même main.

(*b*) A gauche du précédent. Tracé faible.

ᛒᛁ⟩(?) *Riyyâm?*

N. pr. d'homme? Cf. RES 4465? Entre le ᛁ et le ᛒ, un grand ᛒ isolé, d'une autre main.

---

[1] Cf. p. 53. [2] Cf. p. 157, excavator's note.

(*c*) Sous le ventre du chameau.

𐩵𐩠𐩯𐩺   *Rabbânum.*

Cf. RNP, ii, p. 122.

(*d*) Entre les pattes du chameau.

𐩣𐩺𐩦𐩺   *Ġufrum.*

Cf. RNP, ii, p. 114. Sous le 𐩦, une autruche de profil vers la droite. A sa droite, deux lettres: 𐩠𐩣.

Caton Thompson 15. Ḥureyḍa *A3.15.* Copie, fac-simile.[1]

𐩲𐩬𐩠𐩠𐩪   1   *'Amm 'an[as*

··𐩦𐩲   2   ...

Cf. RNP, ii, p. 108; Caton Thompson 49, 1.

Caton Thompson 16. Ḥureyḍa *A3.16.* Sur une paroi. Caractères archaïques.[2] Photographie, pl. LXIV, 4.

···𐩬𐩺𐩠𐩺𐩺𐩲𐩠𐩬𐩠𐩺𐩺   *Ha[lakyaṭi' a dé[dié* ....

Voir les composés de 𐩬𐩠𐩺, RNP, ii, p. 49.

Caton Thompson 16a. Ḥureyḍa *A3.16a.* Sur une marche de l'escalier. Caractères archaïques.[3] Photographie, pl. LXIV, 4.

···𐩣𐩺𐩠𐩯···   *...fils de Ṭ* ....

Caton Thompson 17a. Ḥureyḍa *A3.17a.* Sur la paroi d'une dalle. Caractères archaïques.[4] Photographie *in situ*, pl. LXII, 4.

𐩦𐩠𐩦𐩯𐩺𐩯𐩺𐩠𐩺···   *... (a dédié à) Sîn sa personne.*

Caton Thompson 17b. Ḥureyḍa *A3.17b.* Sur les parois d'une dalle. Une ligne sur chaque paroi. Sabéen. Copie, fac-simile.[5] Photographies *in situ*, pls. LXII, 4, XI top inset.

𐩯𐩠𐩺𐩺··𐩺𐩦𐩦𐩺𐩯𐩠𐩣𐩺𐩬𐩺𐩯(𐩦)   1   (*Ṣ)adiq'il, fils de Mayfa'um, [tribu de?] Haysân*

𐩻𐩺𐩦𐩨𐩠𐩺𐩺𐩺𐩺   2   *a dédié à 'Almaqah*

𐩦··𐩠   3   (*une statue*)?

L. 1. 𐩨𐩠𐩺𐩦, copie: 𐩨𐩠𐩺𐩠. 𐩦𐩲𐩵𐩺𐩦, cf. RNP, i, p. 112. 𐩯𐩠𐩺𐩺, nom de la tribu, précédé de 𐩠𐩯? Cf. ar. هيس, 'disperser, mettre en fuite'; أَهْيَس, 'courageux'.

L. 2. La dédicace est faite à 'Almaqah, dieu lunaire sabéen. Elle est faite par un sabéen qui invoque le dieu lunaire sous le nom qui lui est donné dans le pays de Saba. Voir les inscriptions

---

[1] Cf. p. 54.   [2] Cf. p. 41.   [3] Cf. p. 41.   [4] Cf. p. 52.   [5] Cf. p. 52.

Y

de Délos dédiées par un minéen à Wadd (RES 3570) et par un ḥaḍramoutique à Sîn (RES 3952).

L. 3. Lire (𐩻)[𐩡𐩣]𐩣, 'une statue'? Cf. CIH 336, 9–10, etc.

Caton Thompson 18. Ḥureyḍa 18. Fragment détérioré. Copie, fac-simile.[1]

…𐩣(𐩽)𐩠[𐩤]𐩬𐩹 … *mar a dédié* ….

Copie: 𐩣𐩧𐩠.𐩬𐩹.

Caton Thompson 20. Ḥureyḍa A3.20. Fragment inséré dans la paroi latérale de l'autel.[2] Pl. XII, 1, *in situ*.

…]𐩲𐩧𐩽𐩠𐩤[𐩬𐩹𐩽𐩪𐩹𐩬 …] *ḍ-r, a dédié à Sîn.*

𐩲𐩧 … est vraisemblablement la finale d'un nom propre.

Caton Thompson 21. Ḥureyḍa A3.21. A Ḥureyḍa, chez Sayyid Ḥasan al-ʿAṭṭas. Brisée à droite et à gauche. Caractères archaïques.[3] Photographie, pl. LXV, 1.

…𐩸𐩣𐩧𐩽𐩨𐩬𐩽𐩯𐩦… 1 … *ḏamar, fils de F–Š … (et)*

…𐩢𐩹𐩰𐩡𐩽𐩠𐩤𐩬[𐩹𐩥… 2 *Ḥay'il, [ont] dédié ….*

L. 1. 𐩸𐩣𐩧…, finale d'un nom composé, cf. RNP, ii, p. 6. 𐩯𐩦…. Aucun nom commençant par ces lettres n'est connu en sud-ar. Rapprocher de 𐩯𐩹𐩦? Cf. RES 4316.

L. 2. Le premier nom est probablement 𐩢𐩹𐩰𐩡, cf. RNP, ii, p. 59. Lire peut-être 𐩠]𐩢𐩹𐩰𐩡? Cf. Caton Thompson 14*b*.

Caton Thompson 22. Ḥureyḍa A3.22. A Cambridge, Fitzwilliam Museum. Graffites, cf. Caton Thompson 14.[4] Photographie, pl. XIX.

(*a*) En bas, à gauche:

→ 𐩣𐩧𐩴 1 *Mârid*

𐩹𐩯𐩦(?) 2 *Yafûš?*

L. 1, dextérogyre, quoique le 𐩧 soit sinistrogyre. 𐩣𐩧𐩴, cf. RNP, ii, p. 90.

L. 2, en monogramme; le 𐩦 est couché en-dessous du 𐩯. 𐩹𐩯𐩦, cf. RNP, ii, p. 74. On pourrait lire aussi 𐩹𐩦𐩯, cf. RNP, ii, p. 75.

(*b*) Plus haut:

𐩳𐩱𐩦𐩣 *Gaʿšum*

N. pr. inconnu. On pourrait lire aussi 𐩳𐩯𐩦𐩣.

(*c*) Dans l'empreinte d'un pied droit:

𐩥𐩴𐩰𐩡 1 *Wadd'il*

𐩠𐩥𐩦 2 *a tra-*

𐩢 3 *cé.*

[1] Cf. p. 54. [2] Cf. p. 46. [3] Cf. p.52. [4] Cf. p. 52.

L. 1. 𐩥𐩴𐩰𐩡, cf. RNP, ii, p. 52. Le 𐩥 ressemble à un 𐩱 archaïque avec une ligne médiane oblique. Le 𐩡 final forme monogramme avec le 𐩰 qui le précède; cf. Caton Thompson 14*b*; 22*b*. La lecture 𐩥𐩴𐩰𐩡 est plus probable que celle de 𐩱𐩴𐩰𐩡 (cf. RNP, ii, p. 114). Ce dernier nom qui se présente en safaïtique, est inconnu en sud-ar. De plus, le trait médian ne s'expliquerait pas dans le 𐩱, tandis que l'on retrouve des 𐩥 à angles aigus avec trait médian oblique en safaïtique, et avec trait médian vertical en liḥyanite (cf. JS 8 liḥ., etc.).

L. 2–3. 𐩯𐩥𐩦𐩢. Le 𐩥 comme ci-dessus. Pour le même motif, on ne lit pas 𐩯𐩱𐩦𐩢, cf. Caton Thompson 14*bis a*. Le verbe وشح signifie 'ceindre, orner, parer' (et aussi 'frapper par le milieu du corps', cf. RES 3101). Le verbe peut très bien se rapporter au dessin du pied. On trouve une représentation analogue dans le graffite Freya Stark 325.

Caton Thompson 23. *Ḥureyḍa A3.23*. A Louvain, au Musée biblique de l'Université. Louvain 5.[1] Graffites, cf. Caton Thompson 14. Photographie, pl. LXV, 3. *In situ*, pl. XIII, 1.

(*a*) A gauche, gravées avec soin, deux lettres: 𐩰𐩺; initiales? Cf. RYCKMANS, dans *Revue Biblique*, 1939, p. 248.

(*b*) Au centre, caractères récents:

𐩢𐩣𐩰𐩡	1	*Ḥam'il*
𐩦𐩣𐩪	2	*Šams.*

L. 1. Le 𐩡 final forme monogramme avec le 𐩰 qui le précède; cf. Caton Thompson 14*b*. Voir RNP, ii, p. 60 (liḥyanite).

L. 2. 𐩦𐩣𐩪, les lettres sont quelque peu encrassées, mais la lecture sur la pierre est certaine.

(*c*) A droite, traces, sur trois lignes, des dernières lettres d'un graffite:

... 𐩥𐩰𐩣
... 𐩰
... 𐩯𐩥𐩣

Caton Thompson 24. *Ḥureyḍa A3.24*. A la Résidence de Mukalla. Caractères archaïques. quelque peu évolués.[2] Photographie, pl. LXV, 2.

𐩰𐩡𐩥𐩲𐩧	1	*'Ilwaḍar,*
𐩨𐩬 | 𐩱𐩸𐩸	2	*fils de 'Aḏîḏu-*
𐩣	3	*m.*

L. 1. Nom nouveau. Cf. ḥadr. وضر, 'bloquer' (avec des pierres les trous entre les briques); وَضَرَة, 'moellon, brique cassée' (LANDBERG, *Ḥaḍramout*, pp. 404, 736); cf. ar. وضرى, 'gros rocher arraché d'un côté de la montagne'; وضراء, 'marque de tribu en forme de serre de corbeau'. Ce nom

[1] Cf. p. 54. [2] Cf. p. 54.

pourrait contenir une allusion à une représentation de 'Il dans un bloc de rocher. C'est ainsi que la divinité préislamique al-Fals était représentée par un bloc rocheux.[1]

L. 2. Cf. Caton Thompson 10, 2.

Caton Thompson 25. Ḥureyḍa A3.25. A Ḥureyḍa chez Sayyid Ḥasan al-ʿAṭṭas. Fragment. Copie, fac-simile.[2]

$$\cdots \circ|\text{ᔭ}\Pi|\circ\text{ᔭ}\text{Y}\text{)}\text{ᔭ}\text{ᕼ} \qquad \textit{'Amrhumû, fils de } \cdots$$

⊙ᔭY)ᔭᕼ, 'leur oracle' (des dieux), formation analogue à celle de ⊙ᔭYᕼ∏○, RNP, i, p. 155; ⊙ᔭYΨ∏ᔭ, RNP, ii, p. 116; voir aussi Caton Thompson 31; 43.

Caton Thompson 27a, b, c, d. Ḥureyḍa A3.27. A la Résidence de Mukalla. Fragments. Copie, fac-simile.[3]

(*a*)   Ψ)Hᶦ   *Yaḏraḥ*

Le nom est probablement incomplet par la fin. Voir les dérivés et composés de Ψ)H, RNP, ii, pp. 6, 47.

(*b*)   ○ᔭ)   *Râmiʿ*

Cf. RNP, i, p. 201.

(*c*)   ⋯ᶦᔭ]ᛰY|ᔭX⋯   ⋯ *zum a dé[dié* ⋯

(*d*)   ⋯ᕼᔭ|ᔭ∏|ᔭ⋯   ⋯ *m, fils de M–S* ⋯

          ᔭᶦᕼ ᶦ[ᔭᛰY   *a dé]dié à Sîn.*

Caton Thompson 27f. Ḥureyḍa A3.27f. A la Résidence de Mukalla. Stèle portant des graffites.[4] Photographie, pl. LXV, 4.

Au centre:

          ᔭᕼHᔭ(?)   *Maḏʿan?*

Voir les dérivés de ᔭᕼH, RNP, ii, p. 5. Le ᔭ forme un monogramme avec le H qui le suit. Cf. Caton Thompson 14*b*; 22*bc*.

En bas, à l'envers:

                              ⋯○Y|ᔭ∏

Au dessus du H, en travers:

                              ⋯ᛰᶦXX○⋯

Caton Thompson 28. Ḥureyḍa A3.28. A Ḥureyḍa, chez Sayyid Ḥasan al-ʿAṭṭas. Brisée

---

[1] Au sujet d'al-Fals, cf. IBN EL KALBI, *Kitâb el Aṣnâm*, texte arabe édité par Ahmed ZEKI Pacha, Le Caire, 1924 p. 59.

[2] Cf. p. 54.
[3] Cf. p. 48.
[4] Cf. p. 48.

en haut. Caractères évolués de l'archaïque vers un type plus récent.[1] Photographie, pl. LXV, 5. *In situ*, pl. XII, 1.

ᚠ○|ᚺᚾ 1   *fils de ʿUqâ-*

ᚺᚠᚼ|ᚾ 2   *b, a dédi-*

ᚼᛁᚼ|ᛁ 3   *é à Sîn*

ᚼᚼ◊ᚺ 4   *sa personne.*

ᚾᚠ○ est connu en safaïtique. Cf. RNP, i, p. 170.

Caton Thompson 29. Ḥureyḍa *A3.29b.* A Louvain, au Musée biblique de l'Université. Louvain 6. Caractères archaïques. La pierre portant l'inscription paraît avoir été remployée.[2] Photographies, pls. LXVI, 1; *in situ*, X, 1.

|○ᛞ᚜>ᛒ|ᚺᚾ|ᛞᛞᚼ○ 1   *ʾAsamum, fils de Ḍarrsamaʿ,*

ᚼᛁᚼ|ᛁᛞᚺᛁY 2   *a dédié à Sîn.*

ᛞᛞᚼ○, cf. Caton Thompson 4, 1. ○ᛞᚼ)ᛒ, voir le n. pr. ᛞᚾ>)ᛒ, et les dérivés de))ᛒ, RNP, ii, p. 17.

Caton Thompson 29b. Ḥureyḍa *A3.29b.* Fragment sur la paroi latérale de l'autel.[3] Photographie *in situ*, pl. XI, 2 and lower inset.

A l'envers:

··· |ᚼᛁᚠᛞ| ···   *... le bassin ....*

Cf. Caton Thompson 4, 8.

Caton Thompson 30. Ḥureyḍa *A3.30.* Fragment. Copie, fac-similé.[4] Photographie *in situ*, pl. V, 2.

A l'envers: ··· ᚼ○ᛁᛁ○○◊ ···

Le premier mot doit être restitué probablement: ᛞ○○◊[ᛁ], [*Ya*]*fiʿʿamm*, nom nouveau; on connaît le n. pr. ○◊ᛁᛞ○.

Caton Thompson 31. Ḥureyḍa *A3.31.* A la Résidence de Mukalla. Caractères archaïques.[5] Photographies, pls. LXVI, 2; *in situ*, X, 2.

ᚼᚻ|ᚺᚾ|○ᛞYᛞᚤ 1   Ḥamhumû, *fils de Ḏaʾ-*

ᛁᚼ|ᛁᚼᚠY|ᛞ)) 2   *rârum, a dédié à Sî-*

ᚼᚼ◊ᚼᚼ 3   *n sa personne.*

L. 1. ○ᛞYᛞᚤ, cf. RES 4561; pour l'élément ○ᛞY, cf. Caton Thompson 25; 43. ᛞ))ᚼᚻ, cf. ar. ذائر (rac. ذأر), 'audacieux, rebelle, récalcitrant'.

---

[1] p. 48.   [2] Cf. p. 45.   [3] Cf. p. 45.   [4] Cf. p. 46.   [5] Cf. p. 44.

Caton Thompson 32. Ḥureyḍa *A3.32.* Fragment. Copie, fac-simile.[1]

〔...〕　　　　　... ont [dé]dié à Ḥaw[l.

Cf. Caton Thompson 11, 2.

Caton Thompson 33. Ḥureyḍa *A3.33.* A Cambridge, Fitzwilliam Museum. Brisée en haut et en bas. Caractères relativement récents.[2] Photographie, pl. LXVI, 4.

[〔...〕]　　　　　　　[... a dédié à]
　〔...〕 1　　　　　Sîn son âme
　〔...〕 2　　　　　et ses sens
　〔...〕 3　　　　　et ses en-
　[〔...〕]　　　　　[fants].

Cf. RES 2697, 5–6; Caton Thompson 9, 4–6.

Caton Thompson 34. Ḥureyḍa *A3.34.* A Ḥureyḍa, chez Sayyid Ḥasan al-ʿAṭṭas. Brisée à droite et à gauche. Caractères archaïques.[3] Photographie, pl. LXVI, 3.

...〔...〕...

... ont] dédié à Sîn, et ont voué à [sa] sujé[tion ....

Cf. Caton Thompson 9, 4–6.

Caton Thompson 35. Ḥureyḍa *A3.35.* Fragment dans un mur à l'envers. Copie fac-simile.[4]

〔...〕

Caton Thompson 36. Ḥureyḍa *A3.36.* A Ḥureyḍa, chez Sayyid Ḥasan al-ʿAṭṭas. Brisée à droite et probablement à gauche. Caractères archaïques.[5] Photographie, pl. LXV, 6.

...〔...〕... 1　　　　... ḫ'alay, fils de M-ṣ ...
...〔...〕... 2　　　　(et) ... ḫ-num ont dédié ....

L. 1. 〔...〕 ..., on connaît 〔...〕 et 〔...〕, composés de 〔...〕, cf. RNP, ii, p. 15.

Caton Thompson 37. Ḥureyḍa *A3.37.* A la Résidence de Mukalla. Brisée à gauche. Caractères archaïques légèrement évolués.[6] Photographie, pl. LXVI, 5.

...〔...〕 1　　　　Bašar'il, fils de ...
　〔...〕 2　　　　a dédié à Sîn.

〔...〕, cf. le n. pr. de divinité et d'homme 〔...〕 et ses dérivés, RNP, ii, pp. 4, 41.

---

[1] Cf. p. 53.　　　[2] Cf. pl 54.　　　[3] Cf. p. 55.　　　[4] Cf. p. 52.　　　[5] Cf. p. 55.　　　[6] Cf. p. 55.

Caton Thompson 38. *Ḥureyḍa A3.38.* Oxford, Ashmolean Museum. Dalle, découpée d'une plus grande pierre. Mesures: 28,8 × 9,8 cm.[1] Dessin, pl. LXVII, 3.

Face antérieure.   𝛔𝛎) *Ramay* (?).

Cf. le n. pr. de tribu, 4, 11, et 10, 2, 3. Le mot est peut-être incomplet par le début.

Face latérale. Un 𝛿, et, en dessous, en direction verticale, un 𝑘 de type thamoudien précédé d'un trait et suivi de deux traits, ou un ⋈ mal tracé, entre deux traits.

Caton Thompson 41. *Ḥureyḍa A3.41.* A Cambridge, Fitzwilliam Museum. Brisée à gauche. Caractères archaïques.[2] Photographies, pls. LXVII, 1; *in situ,* X, 1.

   𝟙𝟜𝟨𝚼𝟙 · · ·]𝟙𝟜𝚷)𝛿𝖧𝚼𝛿𝒉   *Sumhuḏamar, fils de* [... *a dédié à*
   𝟜𝟙𝒉   *Sîn.*

Pour les composés de)𝛿𝖧, voir RNP, ii, p. 6; pour l'élément 𝚼𝛿𝒉, cf. RNP, ii, pp. 99–100.

Caton Thompson 42. *Ḥureyḍa A3.42.* A la Résidence de Mukalla. Brisée à gauche. Caractères archaïques.[3] Photographie, pl. LXVII, 2.

         𝛿𝛿𝖧𝚼𝟙𝟜𝚷 · · ·   ... *fils de Haḍîmum.*

Cf. ar. هضيم, 'mince' (de taille).

Caton Thompson 43. *Ḥureyḍa A3.43.* Fragment. Copie, fac-simile.[4]

      · · · 𝟙𝟜𝚷𝟙◉𝛿𝚼𝛿·) 1   *R.mhumû, fils de* ...
      𝟙𝟜𝟨𝚼𝟙𝛿) · · ·   2   ... *rum, a dédi[é* ....

Cf. Caton Thompson 25; 31.

Caton Thompson 44. *Ḥureyḍa A3.44.* A Ḥureyḍa, chez Sayyid Ḥasan al-'Aṭṭas. Brisée à droite?[5] Boustrophédon. Caractères archaïques.[6] Photographie, pl. LXVII, 4.

      𝟙𝟙𝟜𝟨𝚼𝟙𝟜𝚷 ←   1   *B-y-n a dédié*
      → 𝒉𝟙𝑟   2   *à Sîn.*

𝟜𝟙𝚷, incomplet par le début?

Caton Thompson 45. *Ḥureyḍa A3.45.* Fragment. Copie, fac-simile.[7]

   · · 𝟙𝟙𝟜𝟨𝚼𝟙𝛿𝟹𝟟𝟙𝟜◯𝚷𝟙𝛿𝚷·𝟨   *Q.bum, fils de Gušam, a dédié* ....

𝟜𝚷, la copie porte un trait après le 𝚷. 𝛿𝟹𝟟, cf. RNP, i, p. 290 (tribu) et 328 (habitation).

---

[1] Cf. p. 54.   [2] Cf. p. 45.   [3] Cf. p. 56.
[4] Cf. p. 56.   [5] Cf. p. 56.   [6] Cf. p. 174.
                                  [7] Cf. p. 34.

II. CHRONOLOGIE DES INSCRIPTIONS DU TEMPLE DE ḤUREYḌA

La présente tentative de classement est basée sur les données paléographiques, confirmées par quelques faits relevant de la phonétique; elle est limitée à la chronologie relative des inscriptions. Celles-ci ne fournissent aucune donnée de chronologie absolue. Le petit nombre d'inscriptions ḥaḍramoutiques connues ne constitue pas d'autre part une documentation suffisante pour situer synchroniquement les matériaux nouveaux dans un cadre chronologique quelque peu précis.[1] Les résultats archéologiques des fouilles de Ḥureyḍa, eux aussi, ne peuvent être exploités que du point de vue de la chronologie relative, faute de points de repère qui seront un jour établis, espérons-le, par des campagnes sur d'autres chantiers. Et même, de ce point de vue limité, il est très délicat d'établir la succession chronologique des inscriptions d'après les stratifications dans lesquelles elles ont été découvertes, à cause des remaniements qu'a subis le monument, et du remploi manifeste de plusieurs pierres portant des inscriptions.

Les fouilles de Ḥureyḍa sont un premier pas dans la voie de l'exploration systématique des richesses épigraphiques et archéologiques que récèle le Ḥaḍramout. L'appoint de données précises concernant la provenance, la destination et la localisation exacte d'un lot relativement considérable d'inscriptions sur un site archéologique déterminé, est un facteur de progrès dont il est superflu de souligner l'importance.

Nous ne tenons compte dans ce classement que des inscriptions photographiées, en négligeant les copies.

Le boustrophédon n° 44 est assurément un des textes les plus anciens. La ligne médiane du Ⴠ est horizontale et présente à peu près la même longueur que celle des deux verticales. La hauteur de la hampe du Ⴤ est égale à celle de la fourche dont le bas est légèrement arrondi; le trait supérieur du Ⴠ est très court; toutefois le bas du Ⴠ et le Ⴥ se dégagent déjà des dimensions approximatives d'un carré, pour s'allonger en forme de rectangle, dont les côtés verticaux sont sensiblement plus hauts que le côté horizontal.

Les cercles du Ⴥ et du Ⴣ sont très développés au détriment de la longueur de la hampe.

En partant de ces données, et en tenant compte de l'analogie avec les textes sabéens, l'évolution paléographique des caractères suit à peu près les processus que voici: Ⴠ, Ⴥ,

---

[1] Toutes les inscriptions ḥaḍramoutiques connues avant 1936 sont publiées dans RES, t. v–vii (1929–38). Les inscriptions relevées par H. St. J. B. Philby au cours de son voyage en Ḥaḍramout en 1936, ont été publiées par G. Ryckmans, dans *Le Muséon*, l (1937), pp. 245–51 (Philby, 1–14); par A. F. L. Beeston, ibid. li (1938), pp. 311–34 (Philby, 15–76). Voir aussi H. St. J. B. Philby, *Sheba's Daughters*, Londres, Methuen, 1939: *Appendix on the inscriptions discovered by Mr. Philby*, by A. F. L. Beeston, pp. 441–54 (Philby, 77–89), avec un essai de chronologie des inscriptions de 'Uqla, qui dateraient approximativement des IIᵉ–Iᵉʳ siècles avant J.-C. (pp. 444–5).

H, ɦ, Β, (Ш), (Π), ɦ archaïques présentent une forme qui se rapproche du carré et évolue vers un rectangle plus haut que large (44; 36; 52; puis 7; 16; 17*a*; 29); les éléments supérieurs de ɦ, ɦ, ɦ sont très courts (16; 17*a*; 44; 52), et le trait médian entre les deux petites verticales supérieures de ɦ est horizontal (7; 21; 34; 52; 53); les deux médianes horizontales de H sont assez rapprochées l'une de l'autre (12; 52). Ces deux lignes restent horizontales dans toutes les inscriptions et ne tendent pas à devenir obliques. Évoluant vers le type récent, ces lettres deviennent beaucoup plus hautes que larges (4; 9; 10; 51); les éléments supérieurs de ɦ, ɦ, ɦ s'allongent au détriment des éléments inférieurs (2; 4; 9; 10; 33; 49; 50); le trait médian supérieur de ɦ devient oblique; cette transition est caractéristique dans 37.

Dans les caractères pourvus d'un cercle, ♀, ♀, ♀, ♀ (♀ n'est pas attesté), les dimensions de celui-ci, d'abord relativement considérables (7; 12; 29; 36; 44) vont en diminuant, tandis que la hampe s'allonge (4; 9; 28; 49; 50; 51; 54); le cercle de o, d'abord considérable (29; 36) va en diminuant (4; 10; 28; 40). La hampe de ♀ se prolonge jusqu'en bas dans toutes les inscriptions; l'arc de cercle inférieur fait place à trois droites qui se coupent à angle droit dans 4, l. 4; dans cette même inscription, le cercle de ♀ se maintient (l. 3) ou devient un losange (l. 2, etc.); le cercle du ♀ se maintient (l. 3) ou devient un losange (l. 11); le cercle de ♀ se maintient (l. 4) ou tend à devenir un triangle (l. 9).

La fourche de Ψ et Y archaïques est incurvée par le bas et présente à peu près les dimensions de la hampe (12; 16; 21; 29; 36; 44); elle évolue en s'allogeant (4; 9; 10); toutefois la hampe est allongée dans certaines inscriptions archaïques (7; 31). Le Ч est connu par 9, texte récent, où la fourche est petite et à angle aigu, et où la ligne médiane de la hampe est oblique.

Les dimensions du triangle de ⊳|, d'abord assez considérables (47; 53), vont en diminuant (4; 10; 51); les angles de ⟩ d'aigus (21) deviennent obtus (9; 10); il en est de même de ceux de ≷ (7; 12; 29; 36; 53: aigus), dont l'angle central devient obtus (2; 9; 10; 49) et tend à s'incurver (4; 54). La forme d'arc de cercle ne se présente pour) que dans 21 (qui présente aussi une forme de ◊ incurvé) et 41; ailleurs il forme un angle obtus (52) qui tend à s'ouvrir et parfois à s'incurver, surtout dans les textes récents (4; 9; 10).

Il n'y a qu'un exemple de ◊ incurvé (21); ailleurs le losange (4; 17*a*; 31) évolue en s'allongeant dans le sens de la hauteur (28; 33; 50), pour se prolonger finalement en deux droites (9).

On ne constate guère de modifications sensibles dans ˥, X, X̄; le crochet oblique de 1, relativement allongé dans les texte archaïques (7; 21; 52), est plus court dans les textes récents (10); il tend à ressembler à ˥ dans 4. La section médiane de ⊙ est horizontale dans 10.

En tenant compte de ces observations, on classe approximativement les inscriptions photographiées dans les groupes suivants:

groupes archaïques: 44; 36; 52; — 7; 16; 17a; 29; — 12; 21 (?); 41 (?); 47; — 11; 34; 53; — 42; — 3; 24; — 31;

transition: 37;

groupes plus récents: 2; 33; 51; — 28; 50; — 9; 54; 49; — 10 + 26; — 4.

Ce classement est contrôlé du point de vue phonétique par la différenciation des préformantes causatives verbales et des suffixes qui se présentent dans les inscriptions de Ḥureyḍa. De ce point de vue, les textes se groupent comme suit (il est tenu compte ici des inscriptions copiées):

1° Préformante en Y (pas de suffixe): 7; 14*bis* (*a*) (graffite, nom propre); 16; 17*b* (sabéen); 18; 21; 23 (graffite); 29; 36; 37, 2; 43; 44; 45.

2° Suffixe en Y (pas de préformante): 17a (⊕ʃY); 25 (nom propre: ⊕ʃY); 41 (n. pr.).

3° Préformante en Y, suffixe en Y: 43 (suff. ⊕ʃY, n. pr.).

4° Préformante en Y, suffixe en Y et en ħ: 31, 2 (préf. Y); 31,1 (suff. ⊕ʃY, n. pr.); 31, 3 (suff. ħ).

5° Suffixe en ħ (pas de préformante): 5; 33, 2–3; 47; 48.

6° Préformante en ħ (pas de suffixe): 8; 10, 2; 50; 51.

7° Préformante en ħ, suffixe en Y: néant.

8° Préformante en ħ, suffixe en ħ: 2; 9, 2–3 (préf. ħ); 9, 5,6 (suff. ħ); 28, 2 (préf. ħ); 28, 4 (suff. ħ).

9° Préformante en ħ, suffixe en ħ ou en X: 4, 3 (préf. ħ); 4, 7 (préf. ħ); 4, 4 (suff. ħ); 4, 5 (suff. ʃħ); 4, 7,9 (suff. X).

On constatera que le suffixe en Y (2°, 3°) ne se présente qu'une fois dans 17a (en dehors des noms propres, qui forment souvent des groupes à part soumis à des influences historiques et politiques qui se manifestent dans leur structure; cf. RHODOKANAKIS, *Katab. Texte*, ii, pp. 61 ss.; pp. 79 ss.).

La préformante en Y se présente seule (1°) dans des textes classés paléographiquement comme archaïques.

La préformante en Y se présente avec le suffixe en ħ (4°) dans un texte de la période archaïque (où il y a aussi un n. pr. avec suffixe en Y).

Le suffixe en ħ (5°) se présente sans préformante dans des textes archaïques (47) comme dans des textes récents (33); les nᵒˢ 5 et 48 sont connus par des copies.

La préformante en ħ se présente seule (6°) ou avec le suffixe en ħ (8°, 9°) dans des textes appartenant aux groupes récents.

Le suffixe ⵝ (9°) ne se présente que deux fois, dans 4, texte récent; il y marque une fois la préposition ∏ (l. 9: ⵝ∏), et une fois un verbe préfixé par ħ (l. 7: ⵝ∏ɣoħ).

Il résulte de ces observations que, dans les groupes archaïques le suffixe est en ħ (à part un cas en ⊙Y et tous les cas de noms propres en Y ou en ⊙ɣY); la préformante est en Y; elle évolue, dans les groupes récents, en ħ, avec le suffixe ħ; ce dernier alterne avec ⵝ dans un texte récent.

Notons que RES 2640, 1,2; 2693, 2–3, et peut-être Caton Thompson 70c (graffite de Seyûn) présentent le suffixe ɣ. Voir au sujet d'autres inscriptions ḥaḍramoutiques en Y ou en ħ, RES 4181; 4223.

Du point de vue phonétique on constate en outre l'alternance de ħ ḥaḍr. et o sab. dans 4, 9: ɤħ pour ɤo; cf. RES 2640, 2; 2687, 5; 3250, 3; Ryckmans 166 (dans *Le Muséon*, l, 1937, p. 248); l'alternance de ⵝ ḥaḍr. et ɣ sab. dans 4, 4,5 et 10, 2,3; de ⵝ ḥaḍr. et ħ sab. dans le suffixe ħ 4, 7,9, et peut-être dans ɣɣⵝɣ, n. pr. (?), 54; l'alternance de ⵉ ḥaḍr. et ⵕ sab. dans ħⵉₘɣ, 4, 4; l'alternance de ɣ ḥaḍr. et ⵝ sab. dans ɤħⵉⵕ, 9, 3–4. Les textes qui attestent ces alternances appartiennent aux groupes récents. Les références de cas analogues en ḥaḍramoutique sont indiquées plus haut, aux endroits cités; l'alternance de ɣ ḥaḍr. et ⵝ sab. se présente pour la première fois; le cas inverse est fréquent.

III. INSCRIPTIONS RELEVÉES AUX TOMBEAUX A5 ET A6[1]

Caton Thompson 55. Ḥureyḍa Tombeau A.5.X.16. Sceau ellipsoïde en calcaire rougeâtre. Au centre l'inscription, séparée par un double trait horizontal des registres supérieur et inférieur. Ceux portent chacun deux arcs de cercle qui se rejoignent et ressemblent à une mouette en plein vol.[2] Photographie, pl. xliv, 9.

ⵕ∏ɣⵀ   *Râqibum.*

Cf. le n. pr. de sanctuaire ∏ɣⵀⵉ, RNP, i, p. 373, et le n. pr. d'homme Ḍû-l-Ruqayba, Wüstenfeld, *Register*, p. 386.

Caton Thompson 56. Ḥureyḍa, Tombeau A5.XII.6. Rebord de plat.[3] Photographie, pl. xxix, 2.

∏ħɤ⊙   *Wadd-Ab.*

Formule magique fréquente, cf. RNP, ii, p. 52. Voir des rebords de plats avec inscriptions, RES 4252; 4253; 4256; 4257; Caton Thompson 57.

---

[1] The objects in this section are all at the Fitzwilliam Museum, Cambridge.

[2] Cf. p. 79.
[3] Cf. p. 80.

Caton Thompson 57. Ḥureyḍa, *Tombeau A5.VI.8.* Rebord de plat.[1] Photographie, pl. XXIX, 1. Texte contrôlé sur un moulage.

→   ←

𐩥𐩧𐩵𐩬𐩡𐩵𐩠𐩵𐩡𐩵𐩬𐩠 𐩵𐩠𐩣

Waddum Abum.—Mass-Šamsum (?).—Ḥawl Ab (?).

𐩵𐩬𐩠 𐩵𐩠𐩣, cf. Caton Thompson 56. 𐩵𐩠𐩵𐩠𐩵, cf. 𐩣𐩠𐩠𐩵, fréquent en safaïtique; cf. D.M. 477, etc. Voir aussi les dérivés de 𐩠𐩠𐩵, RNP, i, pp. 129–30; ii, p. 12. Le deuxième 𐩠, de type éthiopien, est douteux; lire 𐩵)𐩵𐩵𐩠𐩵, Mussamirum? Cf. 𐩵)𐩵𐩵, RNP, ii, pp. 128–9. 𐩬𐩠 𐩣𐩥, à lire, d'après la direction des deux premières lettres, en sens opposé à celui du reste de l'inscription; cette section est d'ailleurs isolée par deux traits de séparation, le premier à droite du 𐩥, le second à gauche du 𐩬. On pourrait voir dans 𐩬𐩠 𐩣𐩥 une formule magique du type 𐩬𐩠 𐩵𐩣, dans laquelle le premier élément serait le nom divin 𐩣𐩦𐩥 (cf. Caton Thompson 11, 2; 32) en *scriptio defectiva*. Voir RES 4579, etc., les lectures de Grimme: 𐩵) 𐩣𐩥, que nous lisons toutefois 𐩵)𐩣𐩥. L'élément 𐩣𐩥 entre également dans la composition de divers noms propres; on connaît 𐩣𐩥𐩬𐩠, épithète (RNP, ii, p. 20); 𐩭𐩵𐩦𐩣𐩥 (RNP, i, p. 229).

Caton Thompson 57bis. Ḥureyḍa, *Tombeau A5.VIII.5.* Plaquette en bronze ajouré. Brisée à gauche. Caractères archaïques.[2] Photographie, pl. XLV, 15.

·· 𐩭𐩥   *Ḥ-Ṣ-....*

Il s'agit probablement d'un nom propre. Le British Museum possède une petite plaquette en bronze ajouré (B.M. 40652, cf. RES 3925) qui porte le nom 𐩧𐩬𐩣𐩵, *Ruqaybum*. Nous ne connaissons qu'un seul nom propre en sud-ar. commençant par 𐩭𐩥, c'est 𐩵)𐩭𐩥, provenant d'un graffite du Wadi Raḥbe (Freya Stark 52 (3), cf. Ryckmans, 'Inscriptions sud-arabes', dans *Le Muséon*, lii, 1939, p. 303, n° 322). Les noms propres *Ḥṣṣ*, *Ḥṣ* et *Ḥṣt* sont connus en safaïtique; cf. RNP, i, p. 97. D'autres mots commençant par 𐩭𐩥 connus en sud-ar. sont 𐩣𐩭𐩥, 'entourer d'un fossé'; 𐩭𐩭𐩥 et 𐩵𐩭𐩥, 'part, parcelle'. Ces sens ne conviennent pas en l'espèce.

Caton Thompson 58. Ḥureyḍa, *Tombeau A6.* Amulette en argent. Voir des amulettes du même type en CIH 473 (en bois); 474 (en bronze); 475–8 (en pierre).[3] Photographie, pl. XLIV, 14.

𐩵𐩣𐩭   *Ḥilm*

𐩭𐩡𐩠𐩣   *'Awn T.*

𐩵𐩣𐩭, cf. Lyon 9;[4] RNP, i, p. 103; voir aussi 𐩣𐩵𐩵𐩣𐩭, RNP, i, p. 230. 𐩠𐩣, cf. RNP, i, p. 160. Le 𐩭 est probablement une initiale. Cf. Ryckmans 155, 7 (dans *Le Muséon*, l, 1937, p. 240). Ces mots peuvent être aussi des substantifs: خِلْم, 'ami', et عَوْن, 'secours', se rapportant à une divinité, le 𐩭 désignant le possesseur de l'amulette. Les deux noms pourraient n'en faire qu'un:

---

[1] Cf. p. 76.
[2] Cf. p. 77.
[3] Cf. p. 88.
[4] Cf. Ryckmans, dans *Revue Biblique*, 1939, p. 552.

ɧo𐩩1𐩺, *Ḫâl-Muʿîn*, 'l'oncle apporte de l'aide', où 1𐩺 serait un élément théophore; voir les n. pr. composés de 1𐩺, RNP, i, pp. 230, 262.

Caton Thompson 71. Ḥureyḍa, Tombeau A5.VIII.4. Vase à une anse en tige.[1] Photographie, pl. xxxv, 1.

𐩭𐩢𐩢○   'A<u>d</u>îdat.

Cf. 𐩳𐩢𐩢○, Caton Thompson 10, 2–3 (?); 24; 69*a* (?). On connaît d'autres vases portant sur leur paroi un n. pr., probablement celui du propriétaire. Cf. RES 4250; 4251; 4254; 4255, etc.

Caton Thompson 72. Ḥureyḍa, Tombeau A5.I.7. Vase.[2] Photographie, pl. xxxiv, 4.

|𐩭𐩠𐩳   Cent.

Est ce un numéro d'ordre? Il est moins vraisemblable de supposer qu'un chiffre aussi élevé soit en rapport avec la capacité du vase.

Caton Thompson 73. Ḥureyḍa, Tombeau A5.V.5. Vase.[3] Photographie, pl. xxxv, 5.

)𐩣○   Parfum.

Cf. RES 3610, 6. Le même mot se présente comme n. pr. d'homme en safaïtique. Cf. RNP, i, p. 162. Le substantif convient ici à la destination de l'objet; on remarquera de plus l'absence de la mimation, caractéristique des noms de matière; cf. RES 4392, etc.

Caton Thompson 74. Ḥureyḍa, Tombeau A5.III.5. Vase à parfum.[4] Photographie, pls. xxxv, 3; lv, 7.

𐩺, initiale ou marque de potier.

Caton Thompson 75. Ḥureyḍa, Tombeau A5.XII.9. Rebord de plat.[5] Photographie, pl. xxxv, 2.

†|| 𐩢 𐩺   marques?

Caton Thompson 76. Ḥureyḍa, Tombeau A5.I.16. Fragment de Vase.[6] Photographie, pl. xxxv, 4.

𐩵 de type thamoudéen? Initiale ou marque.

IV. THE INSCRIBED SHERDS FROM THE FARMSTEAD AND VICINITY

Caton Thompson 77. Ḥureyḍa, Maison A4. Tesson de poterie,[7] pls. xxxvi, 1; liv, 12.

○𐩺?   initiales ou marques.

Caton Thompson 78. Ḥureyḍa, Maison A4. Tesson de poterie,[8] pl. xxxvi, 3.

𐩬𐩠[𐩵○]   [Wadd]-Ab(?).

Cf. 56; 57; 79 (?); 81 (?). 𐩵○ pouvait être marqué sur une deuxième anse.

---

[1] Cf. p. 77.	[2] Cf. p. 72.	[3] Cf. p. 75.	[4] Cf. p. 74.
[5] Cf. p. 80.	[6] Cf. p. 72.	[7] Cf. p. 141.	[8] Cf. p. 142.

Caton Thompson 79. *Ḥureyḍa, près de Maison A4*. Tesson de poterie,[1] pl. xxxvi, 2.

[ꛛ]⊙?   *Wa[dd-Ab]*(?).

Cf. 56; 57; 78 (?); 81 (?).

Caton Thompson 80. *Ḥureyḍa, Maison A4*. Tesson de poterie,[2] pls. xxxvi, 5; li, 1.

ꛛ○(?)   marques ou initiales.

Caton Thompson 81. *Ḥureyḍa, A4.–A5*. Tesson de poterie,[3] pl. xxxvi, 4.

ꛛ[ꛛ⊙](?)   *[Wadd-A]b* (?).

Cf. 56; 57; 78 (?); 79 (?).

Caton Thompson 82. *Ḥureyḍa, A3*. Tesson de poterie,[4] pls. xxxvi, 6; li. 2.

)ꛛꛛ   marques ou nom.

Caton Thompson 83. *Gheibun, Meshed, Wadi Do'an*. Tesson de poterie,[5] pls. xxxvi, 7; li, 3.

ꛛ)ꛛ   marques ou nom.

V. GRAFFITES SUR ROCHERS RELEVÉES PRÈS DE SEYÛN ET DE SHIBAM

Caton Thompson 59. *Wadî Djethme: Seyûn*. Graffites tracés en pointillé sur une paroi de rocher. Photographie, pl. lxix, 59.

(*a*) à droite.   ...ꛛꛛ?

(*b*) au centre.   ꛛꛛꛛ)ꛛ   *Kariba'il*(?)

(*c*)   ꛛT   *zayd?*

Cf. Caton Thompson 64*a*. Le T = X se présente en thamoudien.

Caton Thompson 60. *Wadî Djethme: Seyûn*. Graffites en pointillé sur une paroi de rocher. Au centre, un chameau, de profil vers la gauche, en pointillé. Photographie, pl. lxix, 60.

(*a*) à gauche, en direction verticale.

ꛛꛛꛛꛛ   *'Abṣal?*

Le ꛛ comme dans Freya Stark 36 (34); cf. ꛛꛛꛛ, ꛛꛛꛛꛛ, RNP, i, p. 38.

---

[1] Cf. p. 119.   [2] Cf. p. 119.   [3] Cf. p. 139.   [4] Cf. p. 130.   [5] Cf. p. 119.

(*b*) au centre, en direction verticale.

◊↑ⱶ Ψ⟩ℨ   *Šarḥ Sayf*(?)

Ψ⟩ℨ, cf. RNP, ii, p. 98. ◊↑ⱶ, cf. RNP, ii, p. 130. Le ⱶ est certain; ce n'est pas un ⱶ; le trait supérieur rejoint le bas de la patte du chameau. Le ◊, arrondi, est douteux.

(*c*) A droite du précédent, sous le chameau. Dextérogyre.

→ ⱶΓ↑(?)   *Nagiy*(?)

Cf. Χ↑⅂ⱶ, RNP, i, p. 135. Le ⱶ de type thamoudéen.

Caton Thompson 61. Wadî Djethme: Seyûn. Graffites en pointillé sur une paroi de rocher. Photographie, pl. LXIX, 61.

(*a*)   ◖◊Χ↑   *Yaśiʿum.*

Équivalent ḥaḍramoutique de ℨ◦↑↑, cf. RES 4569; voir aussi ◦ΧↂΠⱶ, RES 2687, 1; ↑ⱶ◦Χ↑Υ, RES 2687, 2, 3; pour l'alternance de Χ et ℨ, cf. Caton Thompson 4, 5, etc.

(*b*) Sous le précédent.   ◖ⱶ◖Ψ   *Ḥimmânum?*

Cf. Caton Thompson 69*b* (?); voir aussi ⱶℨΨ, RNP, i, p. 95.

Caton Thompson 62. Wadî Djethme: Seyûn. Graffites sur une paroi de rocher. Photographie, pl. LXIX, 62.

(*a*)   → ⱶΠ◦ꞵ(?)   *Abʿamm*(?)
Le ⱶ et le ◦ douteux.

(*b*) Sous le précédent.   → ꞵΣⱶ(?)   *Mušiḥḥ*(?)
Cf. Ψℨ, ΨℨΧ, RNP, i, p. 207. Le Ψ douteux.

(*c*) Sous le précédent.   → ℨꞵ   *Šamm.*
Cf. RNP, ii, p. 128.

Caton Thompson 63. Wadî Djethme: Seyûn. Graffites sur une paroi de rocher. Photographie, pl. LXIX, 63.

(*a*) Dans un cartouche.

ℨℨΥⱶ 1   *Nihmum*
ℨ)Π◦ℨ 2   *Maʿbarum*
Χ   3   *Z.*

ℨℨΥⱶ, cf. RNP, ii, p. 92; voir aussi Freya Stark 59 (33–4) *d*: ℨΥⱶ. ℨ)Π◦ℨ, épithète? Cf. le n. pr.)Π◦↑, RNP, i, p. 156 (safaïtique).

(*b*) Plus bas, à droite du précédent.

$$ΨႰᏐΥ \quad 1 \quad Hasnaḥ$$
$$Υ1Ϡ \quad 2 \quad Yaliḥ.$$

L. 1. Voir le subst. ΨႰ⋔, 'bonheur, bon augure', Freya Stark 58 (23*b*).

L. 2. Cf. ar. وَلِ, impft. يَلِ, 'être dans le trouble'; épithète?

Caton Thompson 64. *A 2 km. à l'ouest de Shibam.* Graffites, sur une paroi de rocher. Photographie, pl. LXIX, 64.

(*a*) A gauche. ⊓ႰᎻႰ *'Ad'ab.*

Cf. ⊓ႰᎻ et ses dérivés, RNP, ii, p. 46. Le Ꮋ est douteux.

En-dessous, deux caractères peu distincts.

$$TϷ(?) \quad Zayd (?).$$

Cf. Caton Thompson 59*c*.

Plus bas, un *wasm*; une croix surmontant un ⋔ éthiopien.

(*b*) A droite du précédent.

$$1 \quad ᏐꟿᏐ⋔(?) \quad Namilum (?).$$
$$⊓$$

ᏐꟿᏐ⋔, le ꟿ ressemble au ⋔ safaïtique (et thamoudéen) barré au milieu par une ligne oblique. Cf. Freya Stark 58 (2) *b*, 1, 2. Cf. ar. نَمِل, 'vif, ardent'; نَمْل, 'fourmi'. Si la ligne oblique était une simple éraflure de la pierre, la première lettre serait un ⋔ (cf. RES 4283, 4285), et on lirait ᏐꟿᏐ⋔, '*Amîlum*, cf. Freya Stark 55 (16 = 17) *h.*

A gauche un 1 surmontant un ⊓, les deux premières lettres d'un n. pr.? Cf. RYCKMANS, dans *Revue Biblique*, 1939, p. 249.

Caton Thompson 65. *Wadî Djethme: Seyûn.* Graffites mêlés à des dessins d'hommes et d'animaux, sur une paroi de rocher. Photographie, pl. LXIX, 65.

(*a*) A gauche d'un chameau monté et sous un personnage, de face, tenant une arme de la main droite.

$$ᏐꟿⵔX \quad Il\ est\ en\ rut\ (?).$$

Cf. ar. وحم, V, 'être en rut, en chaleur'.

(*b*) Sous le précédent, à droite d'un animal de profil vers la gauche et tournant la tête en arrière. Dextérogyre.

$$→ Ψ฿ \quad Ḥamm.$$

Cf. RNP, ii, p. 60; RYCKMANS 270 (*Le Muséon*, lii, 1939, p. 97).

(*c*) Sous l'animal décrit en *b*, et sous un âne (?) monté.

⟨ꜣꜣ⟩ꜣ   *Marmat̲.*

Voir le n. pr. thamoud. ꜣꜧꜣ⟩ (racine ꜣꜣ⟩), RNP, i, p. 201 ; ar. رمث, 'être en disordre'.

Caton Thompson 66. A 2 km. à l'ouest de Shibam. Graffites sur une paroi de rocher. Photographie, pl. LXIX, 66.

Ⱶⲫo   *'Awd̲um?*

β

Le Ⱶ ressemble au Ⱶ thamoudéen : tête de flèche en direction de bas en haut. Cf. Ⱶⲫo, RNP, ii, p. 105.

Caton Thompson 67. Wadî Djethme: Seyûn. Graffites sur une paroi de rocher. Photographie, pl. LXIX, 67.

(*a*) en pointillé.

Ⱶ ꜣꜣѰ Ⴟ		1	*Ḥamš*
ꜧ⟩ꜣ		2	*Murrân*
ꜣꜧꜧꜣ		3	*Mâsikum.*

L. 1. Le Ⴟ et le Ⱶ aux deux extrémités sont indépendants. ꜣꜣѰ ; cf. ce n. pr. et ꜣꜣѰꜧ, RNP, i, p. 95.

L. 2. Cf. RNP, i, p. 133 ; RES 3566, 31, etc.

L. 3. Cf. RNP, i, p. 129.

(*b*) Sous le ꜣ initial de la l. 3 du précédent, en oblique boustrophédon.

→ ꜧᒥᒥβ 1   *Kalbum*

ⲫꜣꜧᒥႿ ← 2   *Zû-Ġasamû(?)*

L. 2. Ⴟ pour Ⱶ ? Cf. Freya Stark 60 (15), 10, etc. ⲫꜣꜧᒥ, cf. ꜣꜧᒥ, RNP, ii, p. 114. Lecture douteuse ; le ᒥ 'à lunettes'? Cf. RES 4206.

(*c*) En bas, à gauche d'une crevasse du rocher, en direction de haut en bas.

ꜧoⲫ◊   *Far'ân.*

Cf. RNP, ii, p. 116. Les deux hampes du ꜧ sont très rapprochées l'une de l'autre, et débordent de la ligature centrale ; cf. Freya Stark 60 (15).

(*d*) A gauche du précédent.

ⲫѰꜧ   *'Aḫû.*

On connaît le n. pr. de lieu ꜩѰꜧ, RNP, i, p. 322.

Caton Thompson 68. A 2 km. à l'ouest de Shibam. Graffite sur une paroi de rocher.

Ѱ   ?

Caton Thompson 69. A 2 km. à l'ouest de Shibam. Graffites en pointillé sur une paroi de rocher. Photographie, pl. LXIX, 69.

(*a*) Dans un cartouche.

             ⟨𐩩⟩ 1   *Gazîzum*(?)

             ⟨𐩲⟩ 2   ʿ*Alayhum.*

L. 1. ⟨𐩢⟩, cf. ⟨𐩢⟩, RNP, i, p. 59; ar. جزّ, 'tondu'. Le ⟨𐩬⟩ est douteux; lire ⟨𐩢⟩? Cf. RNP, ii, p. 105.

L. 2. Cf. RNP, ii, p. 106 (safaït.); voir aussi ⟨𐩲⟩, RNP, i, p. 164.

(*b*) Dans un cartouche.

             ⟨𐩢⟩ 1   Ḥ*abbânum*(?)

             ⟨𐩡⟩ 2   *Lab'ân.*

L. 1. Cf. RNP, i, p. 87; lire peut-être ⟨𐩢⟩? Cf. Caton Thompson 61*b*.

L. 2. Cf. RES 4561; le ⟨𐩠⟩ de type éthiopien.

Caton Thompson 70. Wadî Djethme: Seyûn. Graffites en pointillé sur une paroi de rocher. Photographie, pl. LXIX, 70.

(*a*) Dans un cartouche, en haut, à gauche.

             ⟨𐩺⟩   *Yašbum.*

Cf. RNP, ii, p. 75.

(*b*) A droite du précédent, dans un cartouche.

                ⟨𐩲𐩺·⟩

(*c*) Sous le précédent.

              … 𐩨 … 1

            ⟨𐩲𐩺𐩨·𐩠⟩ 2

      ·⟨𐩨𐩮𐩬⟩ ⟨𐩠𐩲𐩺𐩥𐩵𐩠⟩ 3

            ⟨𐩮·𐩵𐩬⟩   4

L. 3. ⟨𐩠𐩲𐩺⟩ est un nom de ville, et aussi un nom d'édifice; cf. RNP, i, p. 357. ⟨𐩨𐩮𐩬⟩, 'sa maison'? Cf. le suffixe ḥaḍramoutique 𐩨, RES 2640, 1, etc.

No. 9

No. 54

Nos. 17*a*
and 17*b*

No. 49

No. 1

Inscriptions *in situ*

Inscriptions 2, 3, 4, 9 (with enlarged detail)
(Scale below no. 1, 10 cm.)

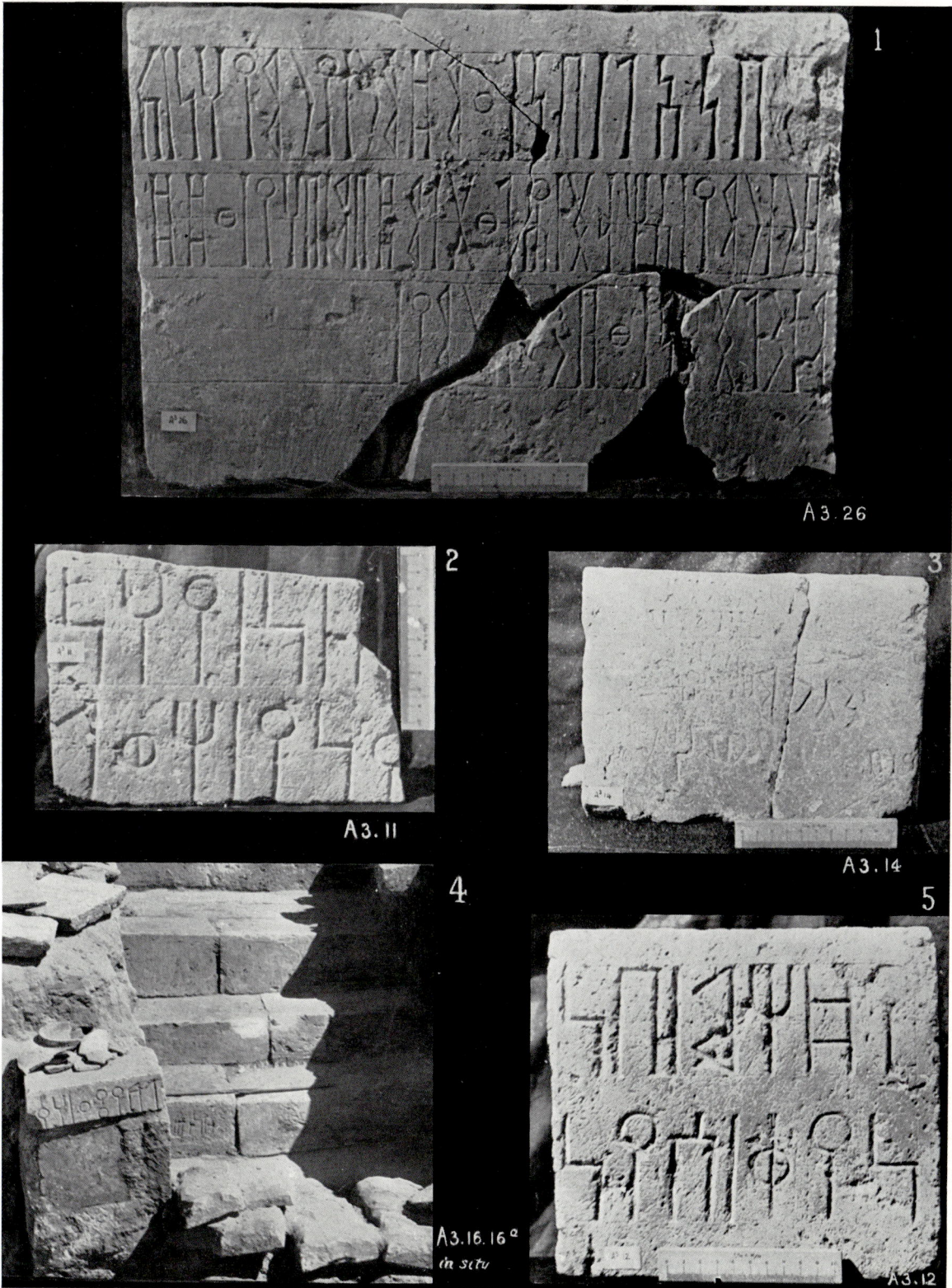

A3.26

A3.11

A3.14

A3.16.16ᵃ
in situ

A3.12

Inscriptions 11, 12, 14, 16, 16a (*in situ*), 26
(Scale 10 cm.)

Inscriptions 21, 23, 24, 27 f., 28, 36

(Scale 10 cm.)

Inscriptions 29, 31, 33, 34, 37
(Scale 10 cm.)

Inscriptions 38, 41, 42, 44, 46, 47
(Scale 10 cm.)

Inscriptions 49, 50, 51, 52, 53, 54
(Scale 10 cm.)

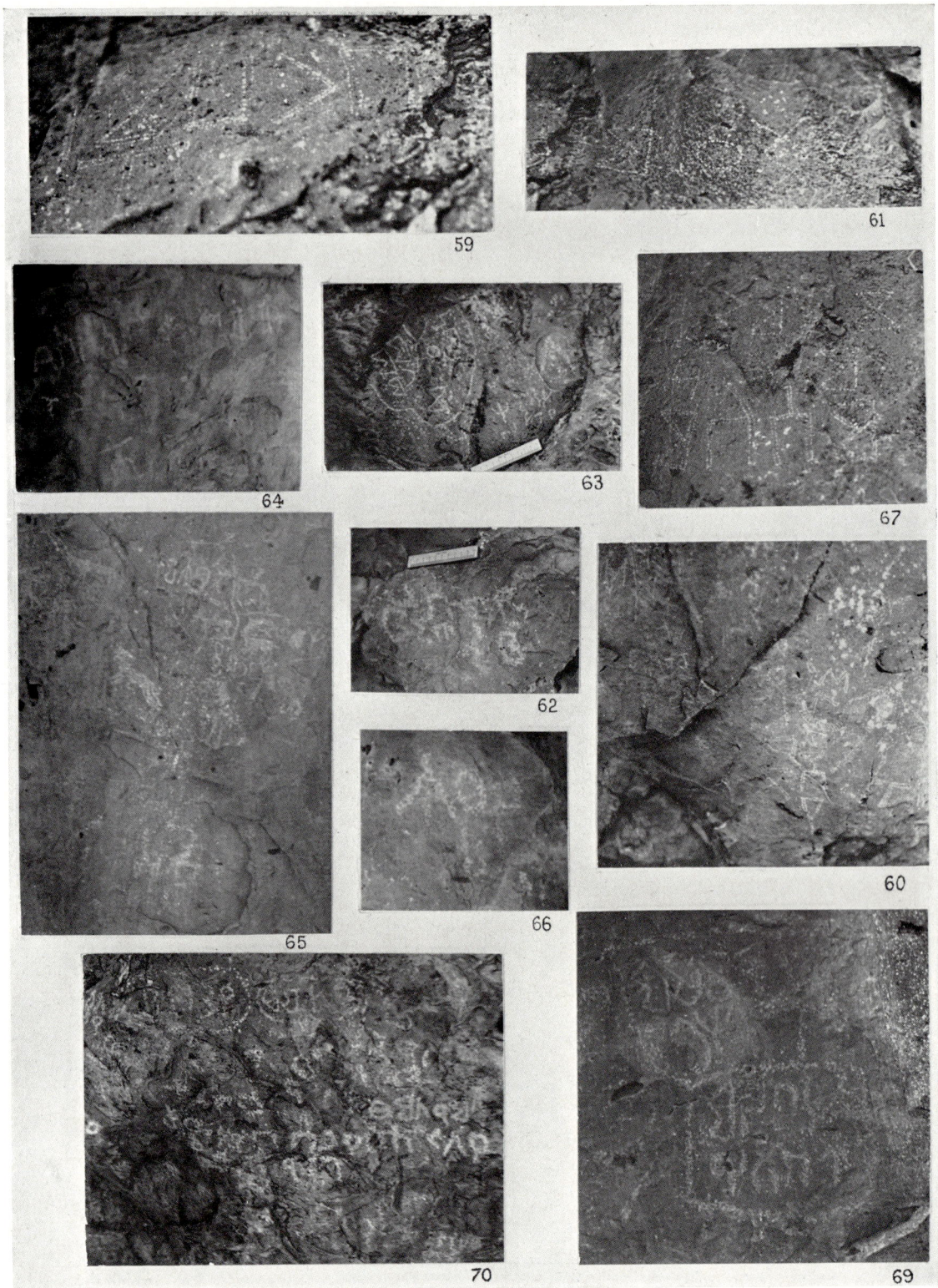

Graffiti. Nos. 59–63, 65, 67, 70, from Wadi Djethme, Seiyun. Nos. 64, 66, 69, from near Shibam

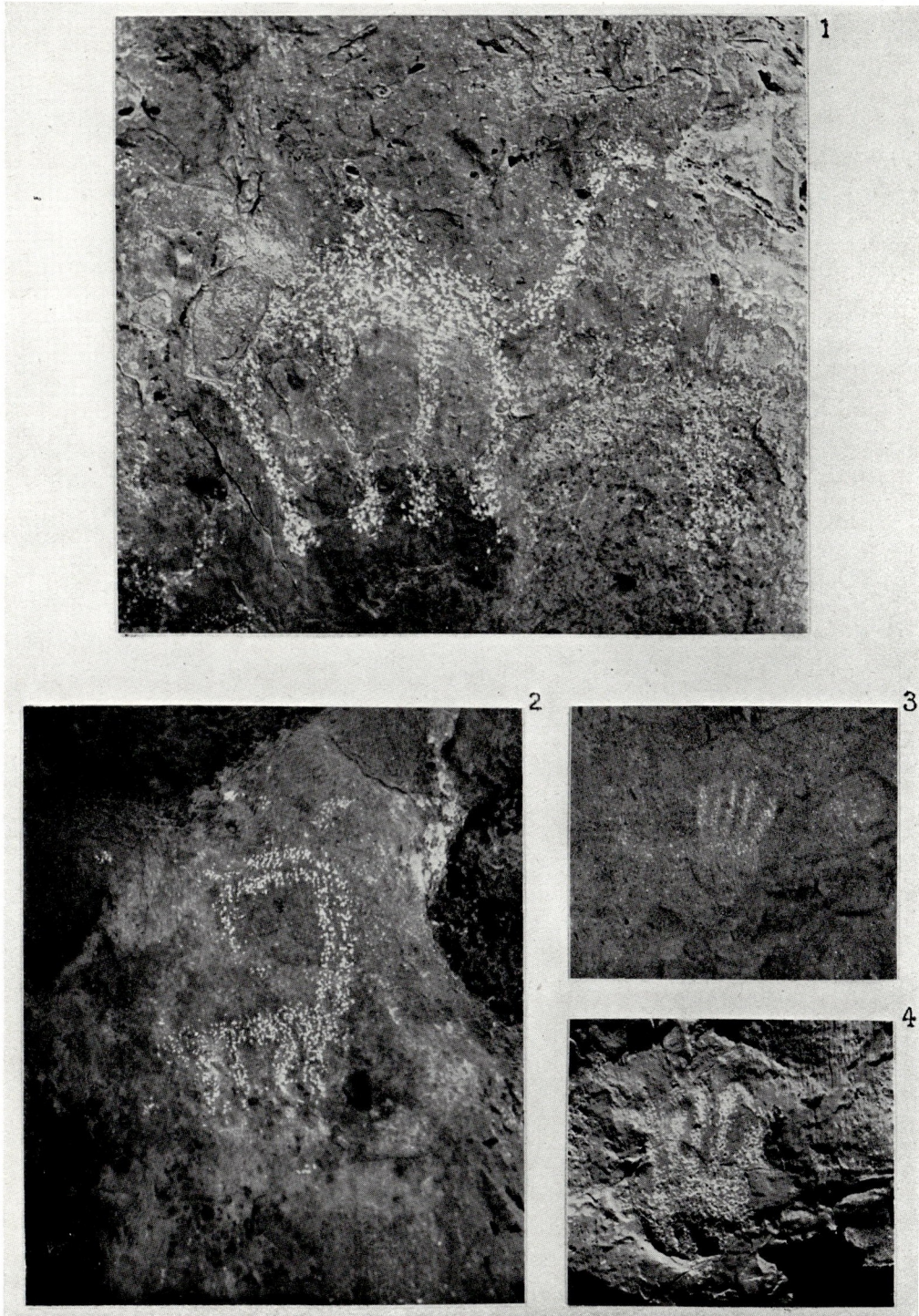

Pecked engravings. 1, 2. From Wadi Djethme, Seiyun. 3–4. From near Shibam

MODERN BIBLIOGRAPHY

BECK, H. C. 'Classification and Nomenclature of Beads and Pendants', *Archaeologia*, vol. lxxxii.
—— 'A Note on Certain Agate Beads', *Antiquaries Journal*, vol. x, No. 2.
Berytus, vol. i, 1934, pp. 12–18, 'The Essential Characteristics of Parthian and Sasanian Glyptic Art', by Nielson C. Debevoise.
British Museum Quarterly, vol. xi, 1936–7, pp. 153–6, 'A Bronze Head from the Yemen', by R. C. Hinks; 'Bronze Lion's Head from Najran, South Arabia', by Sidney Smith.
CATON THOMPSON, G. *Asia*, May, 1939, 'A Temple in the Hadhramaut'.
—— and GARDNER, E. W. *Geographical Journal*, Jan. 1939, 'Climate, Irrigation and Early Man in the Hadhramaut'.
—— *The Desert Fayum.* 1934.
Corpus Inscriptionum Semiticarum, pars 4, fasc. 1.
DELAPORTE, L. J. *Catalogue des Cylindres Orientaux de la Bibliothèque Nationale.* 1910.
FORSDYKE, J. *A Catalogue of Greek and Etruscan Vases in the British Museum.* 1925.
FRANKFORT, H. *Cylinder Seals.* 1939.
GHIRSHMAN, R. *Fouilles de Sialkh I.* 1938.
GLUECK, NELSON. *Asia*, Sept. 1939, 'Gateway to Arabia: Ezion-Geber'.
—— *Asia*, Oct. 1938, 'Solomon's Seaport: Ezion-Geber'.
HERZFELD, E. *Archaeological History of Iran.* 1935.
HILL, G. F. *Catalogue of Greek Coins of Arabia, Mesopotamia, Persia.* 1932.
HITTI, P. K. *History of the Arabs.* 1937.
HOGARTH, D. G. *A History of Arabia.* 1922.
HORSFIELD, G. and A. *The Quarterly of the Department of Antiquities in Palestine*, vols. ii, iii, No. 3, vol. ix, Nos. 2, 3, 4, 'Sela Petra, the Rock, of Edom and Nabatene'.
INGRAMS, W. H. *Report on the Social, Economic and Political Conditions of the Hadhramaut* (Colonial Office). 1937.
—— *Geographical Journal*, April 1935, 'House building in the Hadhramaut'.
—— *Ibid.*, Dec. 1936, 'A Journey to the Sei'ar Country and through the Wadi Maseila'.
—— *Ibid.*, Oct. 1938, 'The Hadhramaut: Present and Future'.
—— *Journal R. Central Asian Soc.*, July 1936, 'Unexplored Regions of the Hadhramaut'.
—— *Ibid.*, Oct. 1938, 'Peace in the Hadhramaut'.
IONIDES, M. G. *Geographical Journal*, Oct. 1938, 'Two Ancient Irrigation Canals in Northern 'Iraq'.
LEGRAIN, L. *American Journal of Archaeology*, vol. xxxviii, 3, 1934, 'In the Land of the Queen of Sheba'.
LITTLE, O. H. *Geology and Geography of Mukalla.* 1925.
MACALISTER, R. A. S. *The Excavations of Gezer.* 1912.
MACKAY, E. *Bahrein.* 1929.
MALLOWAN, M. E. L. *Iraq*, vol. iii, pt. i, 1936, 'The Excavations at Tall Chagar Bazar'.
MYERS, O. H. *The Cemeteries of Armant I.* 1937.
NIELSEN, DITLEF. *Handbuch der Altarabischen Altertumskunde*, Band i. 1937.
—— *Journal Palestine Oriental Society*, vol. vii, fasc. 4, 'The Site of the Biblical Mount Sinai'.
OSTEN, H. VON DER. *Ancient Oriental Seals in the Collection of Mrs. Agnes Brett.* 1936.
—— *The Ancient Seals from the Near East in the Metropolitan Museum.*

PHILBY, H. ST. J. *The Land of Sheba.* 1939.

POPE, A. UPHAM. *A Survey of Persian Art.* 1938.

RATHJENS, C., and WISSMANN, H. VON. *Südarabien Reise*, Band 2. 1932.

RYCKMANS, G. *Le Muséon*, tomes xl (1927), xlv (1932), xlviii (1935), l (1937), lii (1939).

—— *Revue biblique*, April 1939.

—— *Les Noms propres sud-sémitiques*, i–iii. 1934–5.

SCHMIDT, E. F. *Excavations of Tepe Hissar.*

SELIGMAN, C. G., and BECK, H. C. *Bulletin XII, Museum of Far Eastern Antiquities, Stockholm,* 'Far Eastern Glass and some Western Origins'.

STARK, F. *The Southern Gates of Arabia.* 1936.

—— *Seen in the Hadhramaut.* 1938.

—— *A Winter in Arabia.* 1940.

—— *Geographical Journal*, Feb. 1936, 'Two Months in the Hadhramaut'.

—— *Ibid.*, Jan. 1939, 'An Exploration in the Hadhramaut and Journey to the Coast'.

—— *Journal R. Asiatic Soc.*, July 1939, 'Some Pre-islamic Inscriptions on the Frankincense Route in Southern Arabia'.

STEIN, A. *Geographical Journal*, Feb. 1934, 'Archaeological Reconnaissances in Southern Persia'.

—— *Iraq*, vol. iii, pt. 2, 1936, 'An Archaeological Tour in Ancient Persis'.

THOMAS, BERTRAM. *The Arabs.* 1937.

—— *Arabia Felix.* 1932.

—— *Geographical Journal*, Jan. 1931, 'A Journey into Rubʿ al Khali'.

—— *Proc. British Academy*, vol. xxiii, 'Four Strange Tongues from South Arabia. The Hadara Group'.

VAN DER MEULEN and C. VON WISSMANN. *Hadramaut.* 1932.

WARNER, W. H. LEE. *Geographical Journal*, March 1931, 'Notes on the Hadhramaut'.

CORRIGENDUM

Owing to the renumbering of the pages of the Introduction (xi-xv) after the compilation of the Index, figures in roman numerals in the following Indexes should be reduced by four.

INDEX OF PROPER AND PLACE NAMES

GENERAL INDEX

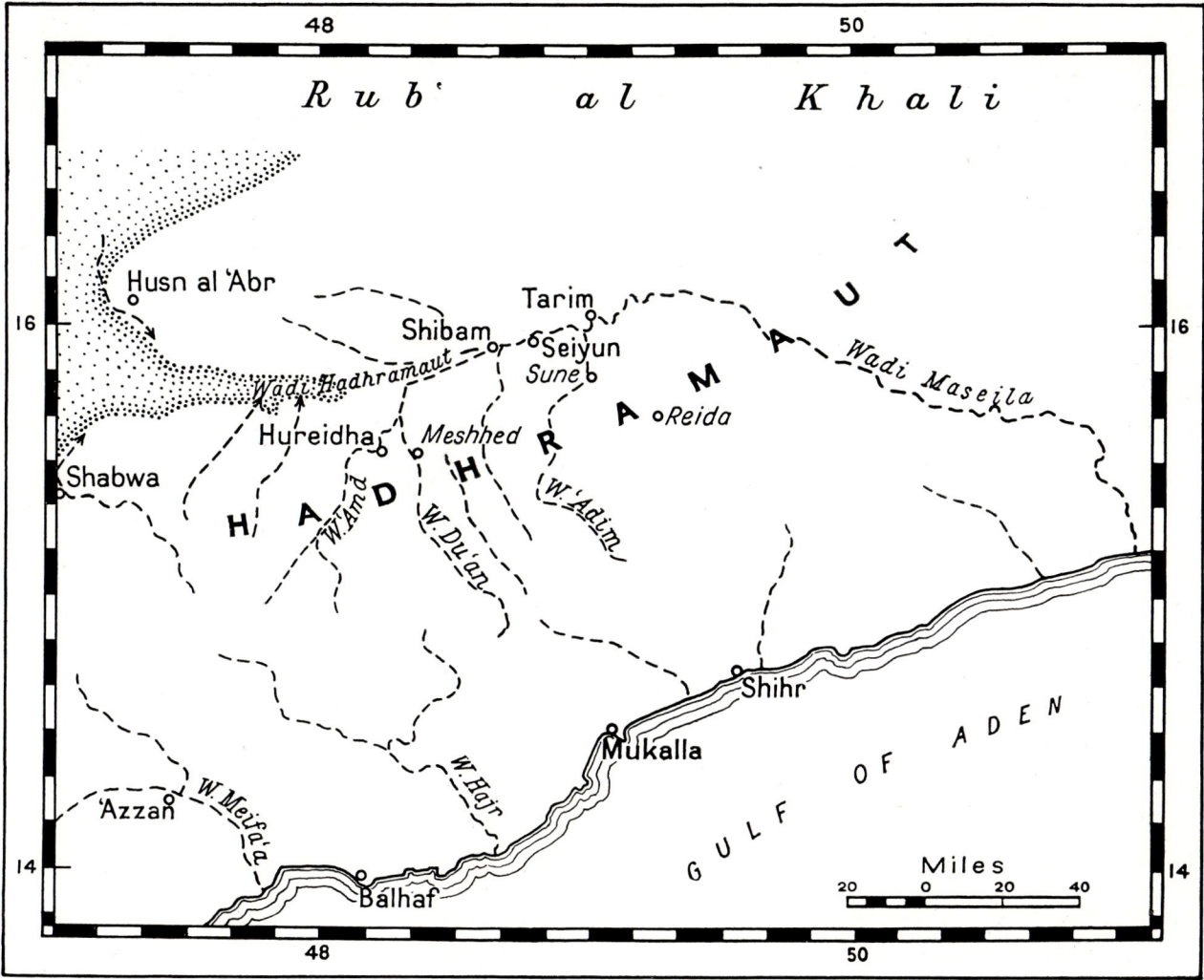

Ru b' a l Khali

Husn al 'Abr

Shibam
Tarim
Seiyun
Wadi Hadhramaut
Sune
Hureidha
Meshhed
Reida

W. 'Amd
W. Du'an
W. 'Adim

Shabwa

H A D H R A M A U T

Wadi Maseila

Shihr

W. Hajr

Mukalla

GULF OF ADEN

'Azzan
W. Meifa'a

Balhaf

Miles
20 0 20 40

The Hadhramaut, showing the wadis and towns referred to in the text

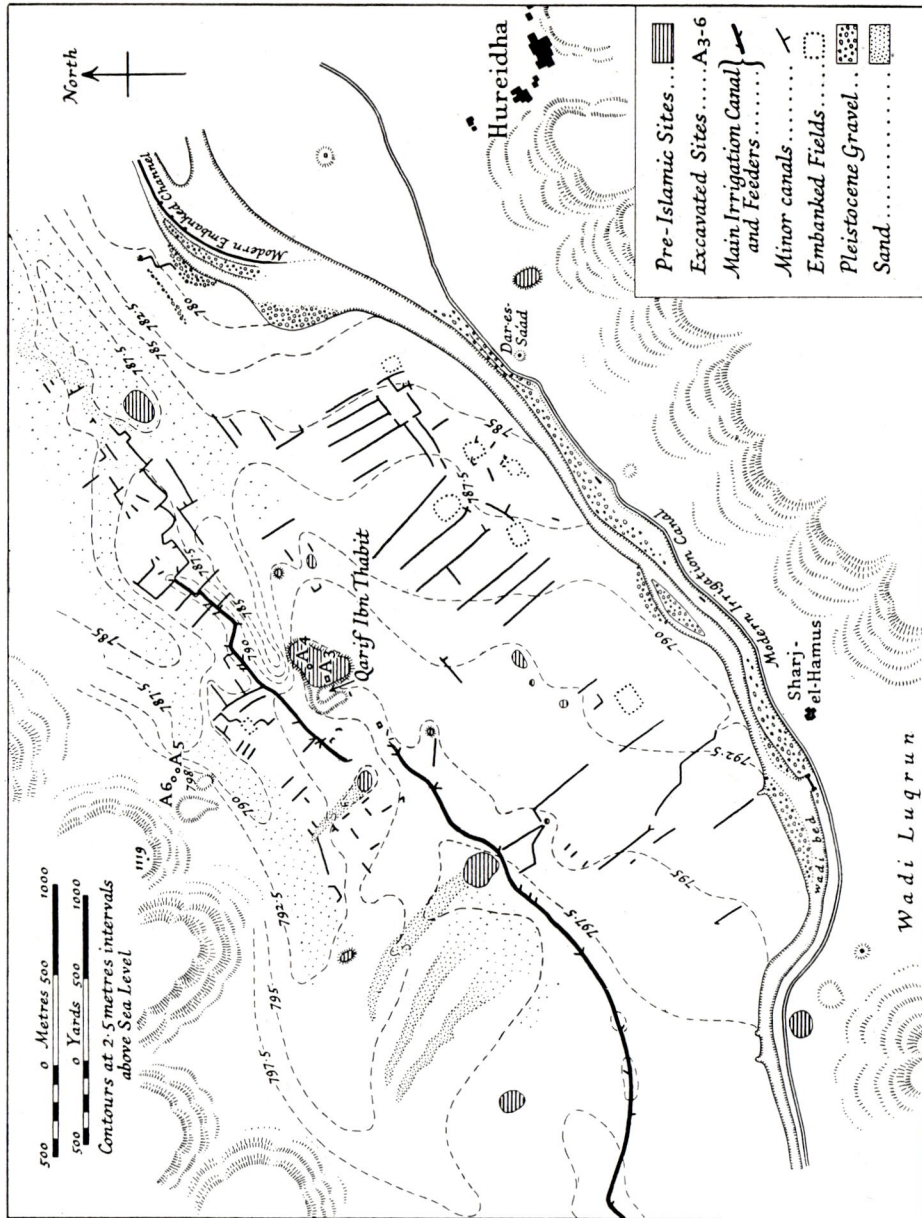

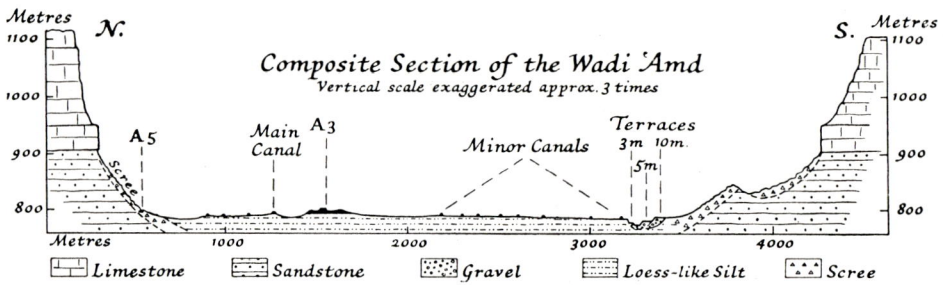

Sketch-map of ancient irrigation system near Hureidha with excavated sites and cross-section of the Wadi ʿAmd

PHASE 'A' WALLS
PHASE 'B' WALLS
PHASE 'C' WALLS
STUCCO PARTITIONS
PAVING STONES
VERTICAL STONES
INSCRIPTIONS IN SITU

Scale of Metres

Heights in Metres above Sea level

Final state, with extramural post-'C' buildings

LONGITUDINAL CROSS-SECTIONS OF MOON TEMPLE

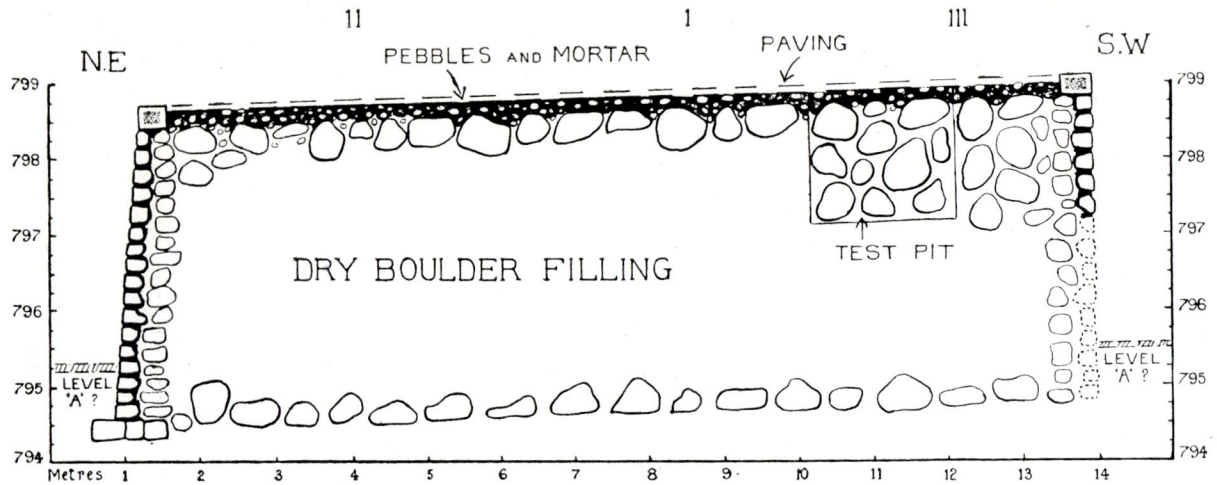

1. Phase 'A'

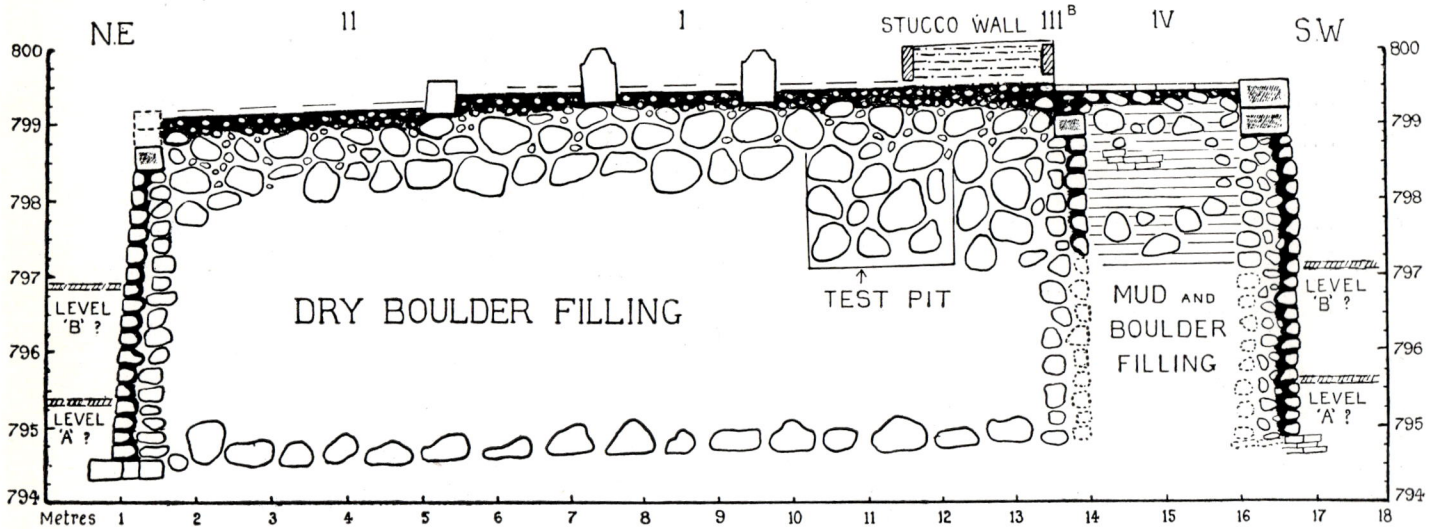

2. Phase 'B'

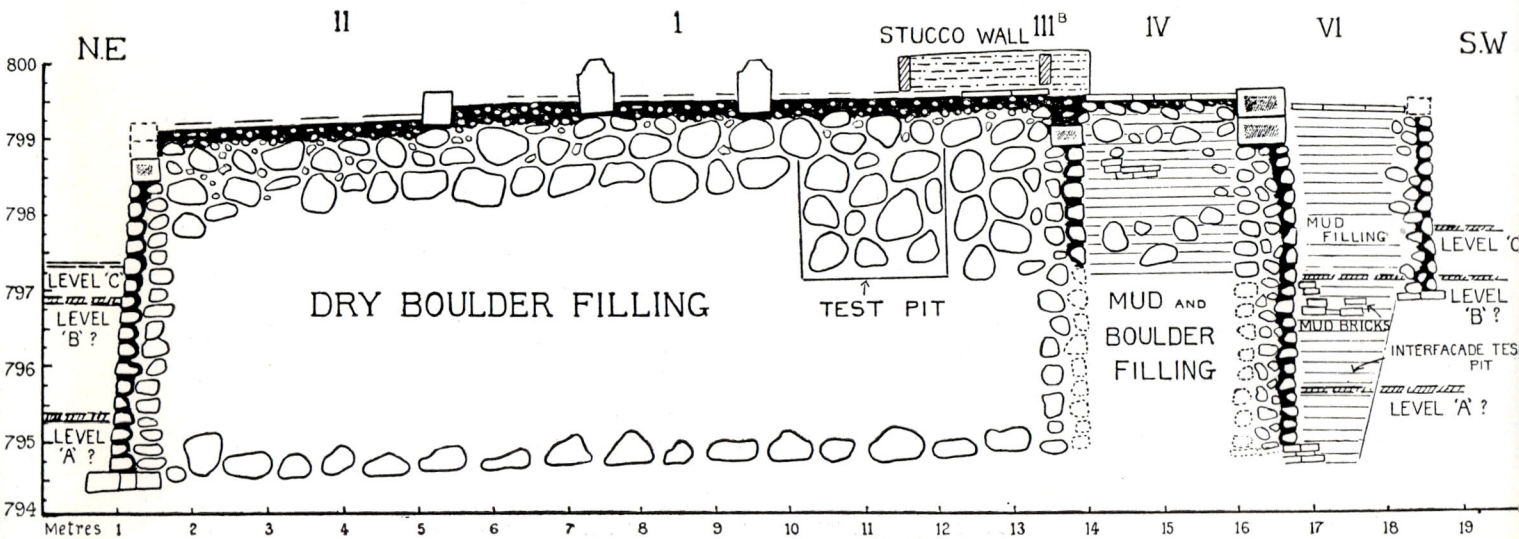

3. Phase 'C'

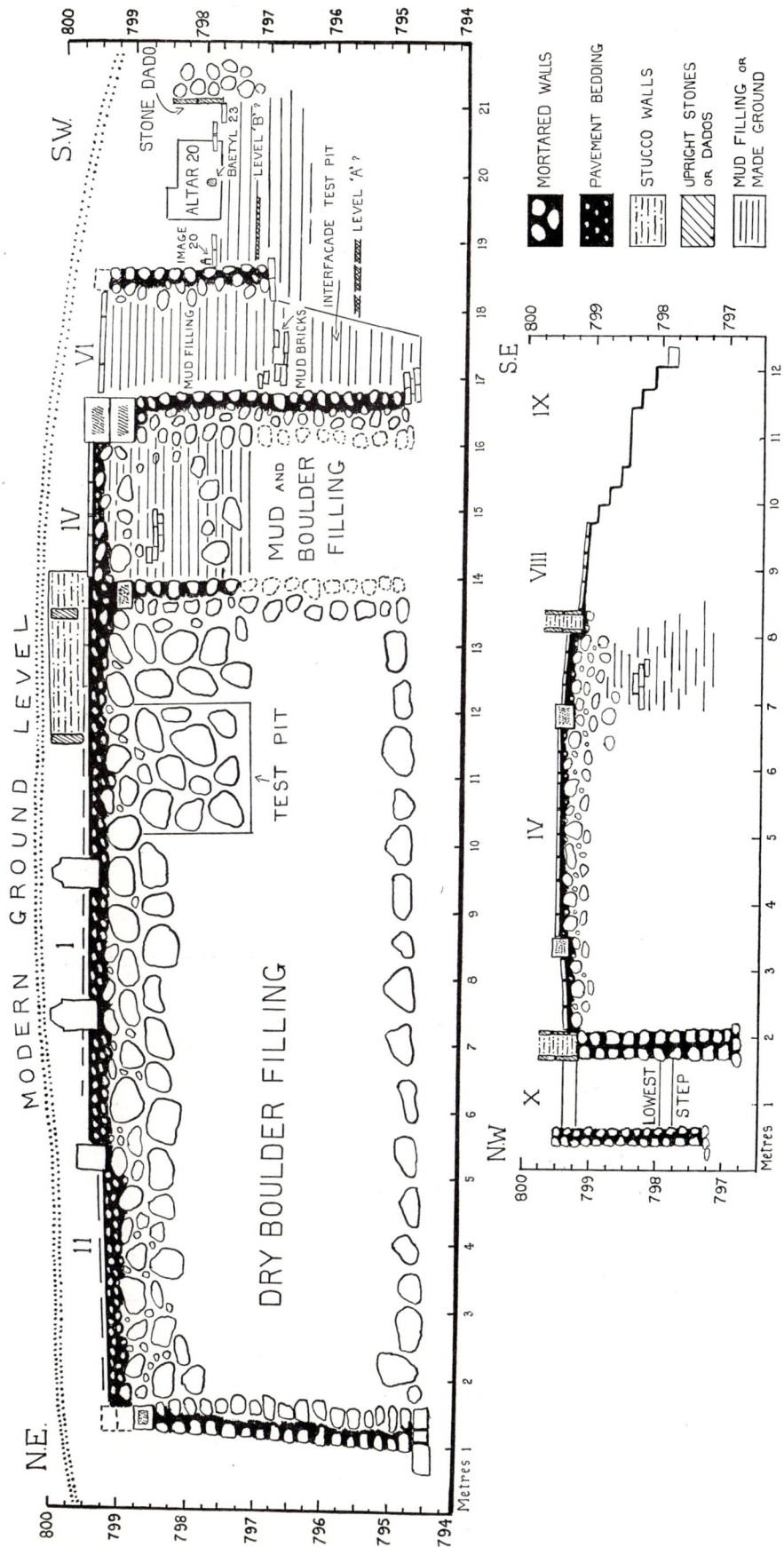

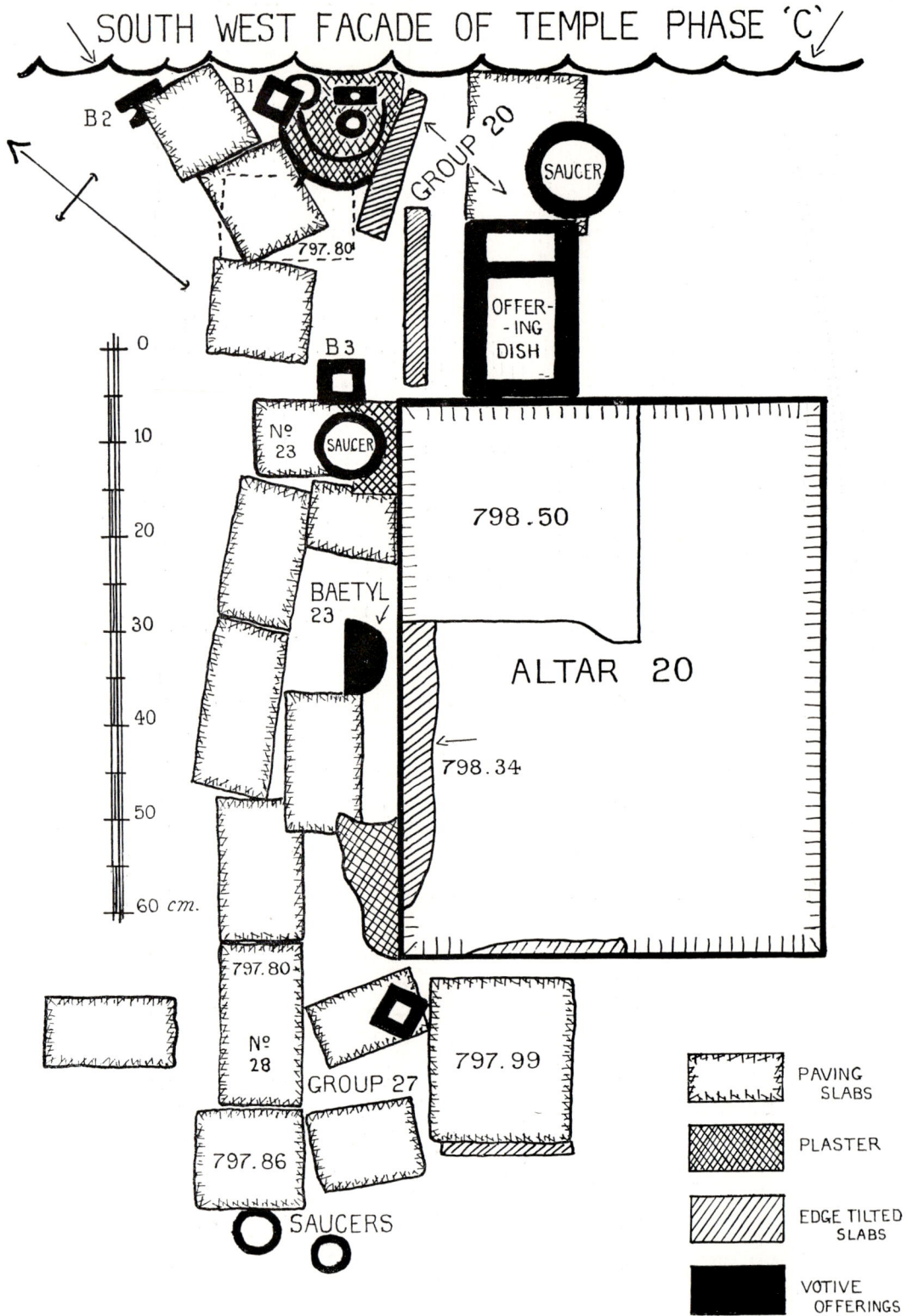

SOUTH WEST FACADE OF TEMPLE PHASE 'C'

B2
B1
GROUP 20
SAUCER
797.80
OFFER-ING DISH

B3
No 23
SAUCER
798.50
ALTAR 20
BAETYL 23
798.34

797.80
No 28
GROUP 27
797.99
797.86
SAUCERS

0
10
20
30
40
50
60 cm.

PAVING SLABS

PLASTER

EDGE TILTED SLABS

VOTIVE OFFERINGS

Detailed plan of altar 20 and votive groups around

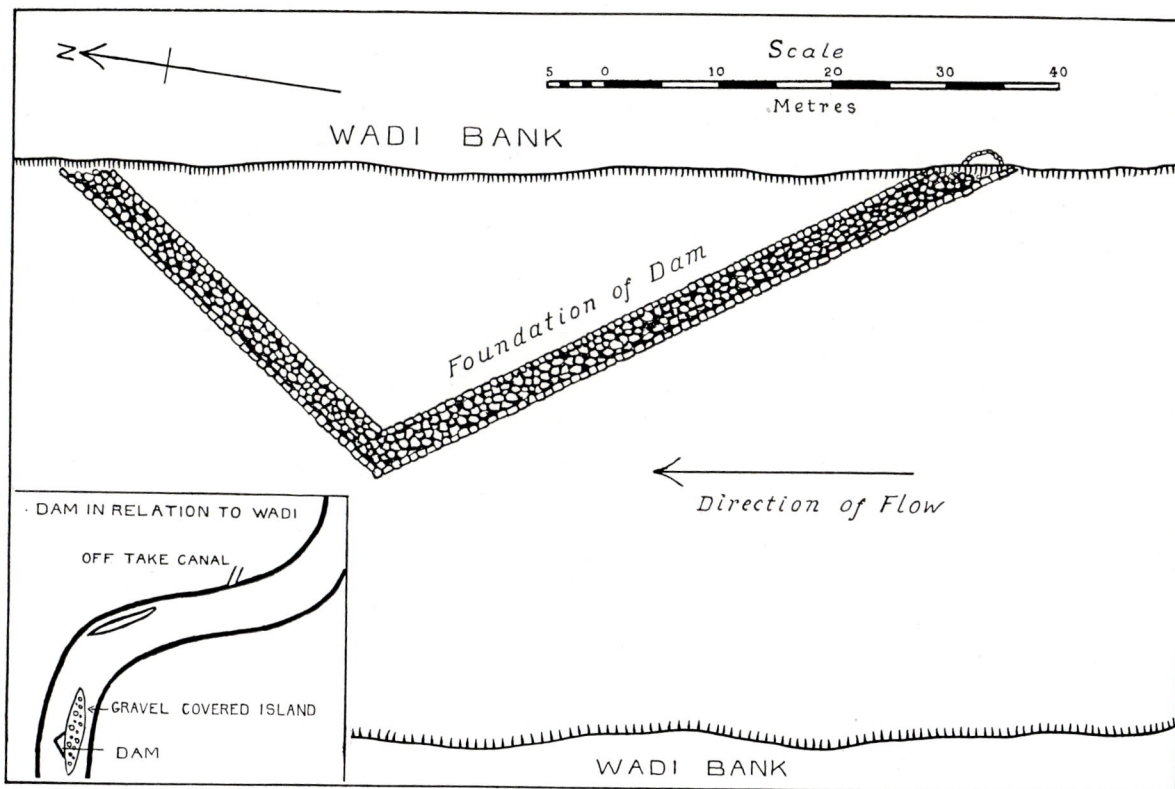

Plan of irrigation dam above Hureidha

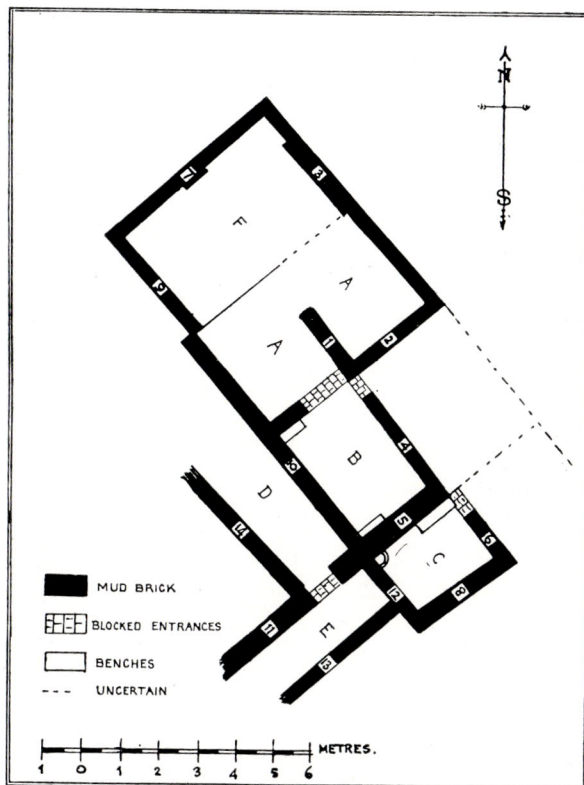

Plan of farmstead, A4

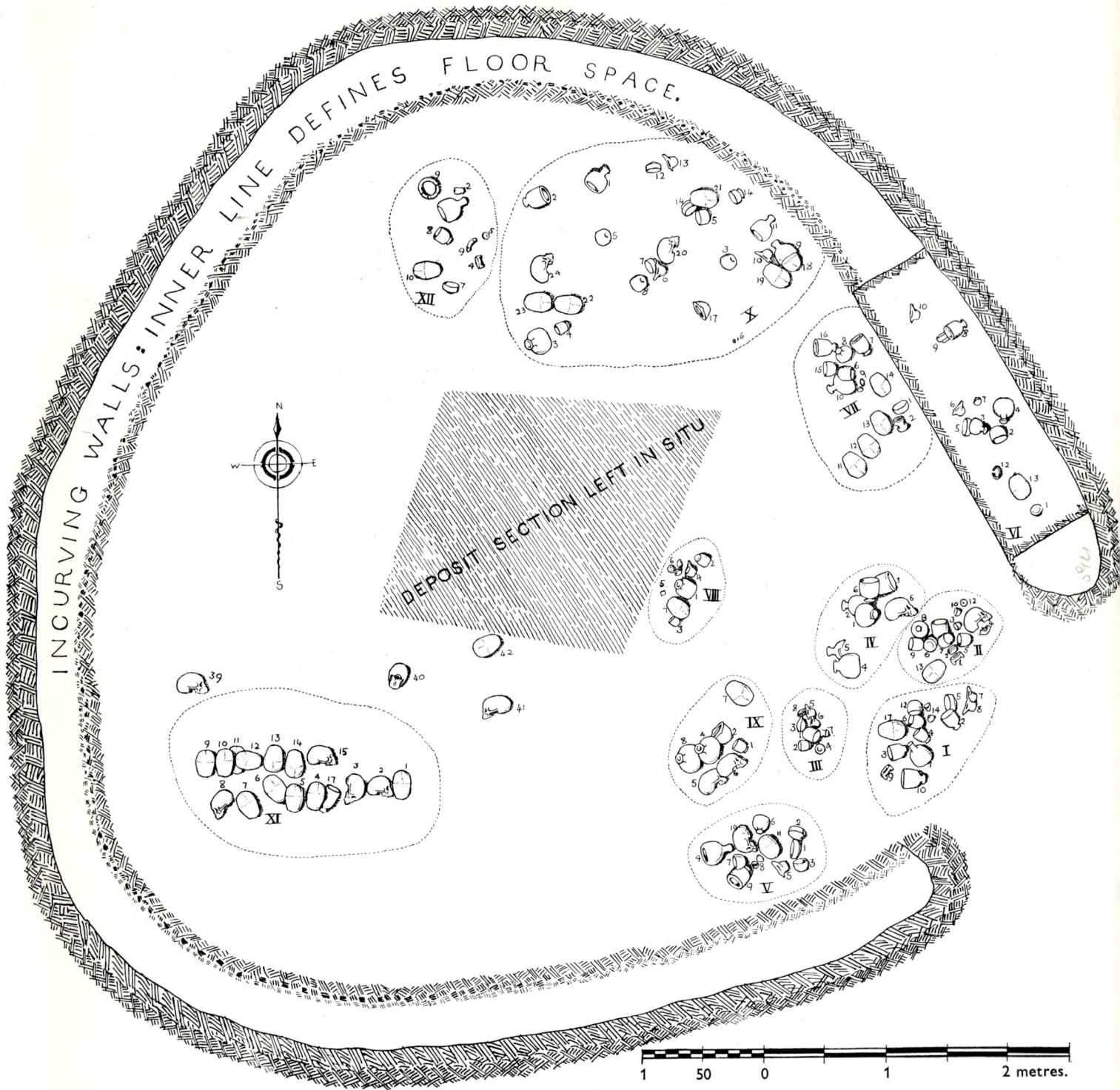

PLAN OF CAVE-TOMB, A5